Selected Works of
MAO TSE-TUNG

毛澤東

Selected Works of

MAO TSE-TUNG

Abridged by

Bruno Shaw

Harper Colophon Books
Harper & Row, Publishers
New York, Evanston, and London

There is no absurdity so palpable but that it may be firmly planted in the human head if you only begin to inculcate it before the age of five, by constantly repeating it with an air of great solemnity.
—Arthur Schopenhauer,
Studies in Pessimism

Peoples and governments never have learned anything from history, or acted on principles deduced from it.
—Georg Wilhelm Friedrich Hegel,
Introduction, Philosophy of History

SELECTED WORKS OF MAO TSE-TUNG. Copyright © 1970 by Bruno Shaw.

All rights reserved. Printed in the United States of America. No part of this book may be used or reproduced in any manner whatsoever without written permission except in the case of brief quotations embodied in critical articles and reviews. For information address Harper & Row, Publishers, Inc., 49 East 33rd Street, New York, N.Y. 10016. Published simultaneously in Canada by Fitzhenry & Whiteside Limited, Toronto.

First HARPER COLOPHON edition published 1970 by Harper & Row, Publishers, Inc. Abridgment of *Selected Works of Mao Tse-tung* published by People's Publishing House, Peking, April, 1960.

LIBRARY OF CONGRESS CATALOG CARD NUMBER: 78–112953.

Contents

Publication Note

This work is an abridgment of the English-language edition of the *Selected Works of Mao Tse-tung*, first edition, August 1965, printed in The People's Republic of China. The introductory publication note of this edition carries the following explanation: "This edition of the *Selected Works of Mao Tse-tung* includes important articles he wrote in the different periods of the Chinese revolution. . . . The present edition includes a number of important writings not included in the earlier editions. The author has read all the articles, made certain verbal changes and, in isolated cases, revised the text."

A careful reading of these English-language volumes published in Peking reveals that they were translated from the original Chinese by at least several, and possibly many, persons. Some obviously received their English-language education in the United Kingdom, and some in the United States. This shows up in the Western figures of speech that are substituted for the Chinese, which, if directly translated into English, would have little meaning.

I have used American forms of spelling where they differ from the British. Words such as "labour" and "defence" in the Peking volumes, will be found spelled "labor" and "defense" in this abridgment. For the sake of consistency, similar changes have been made in the spelling of other words.

It may be of interest to note that a distinction is made by Mao Tse-tung, and therefore by his translators, between Chinese Communists who wax overenthusiastic in their application of his tactics or strategy, or who lay too much stress on cooperation with labor and too little stress on the need of the peasants, and those who criticize or disagree with him and overstress the need of cooperation with the Kuomintang. The former commit "Left" deviations, and the latter

Right deviations—without the quotation marks. This is to show that although leftists may sometimes carry things too far, they are still good Communists, whereas the Rightists are merely rightists and outside the pale, at least temporarily, of true Communism. This practice is adhered to throughout *Selected Works;* for example, in the chapter "A Circular on the Situation" in Volume IV.

A word about the principles and method that I have tried to follow in doing this abridgment. My purpose in embarking upon it was to present a readable and yet complete abstract of Mao Tse-tung's overwhelmingly wordy four-volume *Selected Works,* the guide to the Chinese Communist world revolution now and for the future. I sought to accomplish this by abstracting every chapter, every sub-chapter, and every subsection of every subchapter of the original work, omitting only redundancies and repetitions in them which I believed were not essential for an understanding of Mao's motivations, his reasoning, and his genius as a political and military strategist. Some of his repeated statements and admonitions, where I believed them to be necessary in the context in which he delivered them, I left intact.

I omitted also many of the minute details of battles the Communist troops fought during the Civil War, which, in the original volumes were described in page after page, because the place names would be largely if not entirely unknown to any but those who participated in them, or who lived in the areas, and the officers who directed them were very largely minor characters.

I hope this abridgment will be useful as a text to be read with interest by those who have had no personal acquaintance with China and as a reference work in which can be found all the pertinent documentation of *Selected Works* that may be sought by students and teachers of Asian affairs.

BRUNO SHAW

Foreword

The world should have known from Hitler's own book, *Mein Kampf,* published in 1925, precisely the nature and the scope of the bloodbath planned for it, wrote William L. Shirer in his *Rise and Fall of the Third Reich.* "For whatever other accusations can be made against Adolf Hitler," added Shirer,

no one can accuse him of not putting down in writing exactly the kind of Germany he intended to make if he ever came to power and the kind of world he meant to create by armed German conquest. The blueprint of the Third Reich and, what is more, of the barbaric triumphant years between 1939 and 1945 is set down in all its appalling crudity at great length and in detail between the covers of this revealing book.

In 1917, as World War I neared its end, Lenin postulated the need for shattering the governments of all non-Communist states. In his *The State and the Revolution,* he said:

The teaching of Marx and Engels regarding the inevitability of violent revolution refers to the capitalist State. It cannot be replaced by the proletarian State [the dictatorship of the proletariat] through mere "withering away," but, in accordance with the general rule, can only be brought about by a violent revolution. The substitution of a proletarian for the capitalist State is impossible without a violent revolution.

Stalin, in his *Problems of Leninism* (1934), set the Leninist policy keystone firmly into the world Communist arch. Lenin, he said, made it clear that

international imperialism, with all the might of its capital and its highly organized military technique could under no circumstances, under no

ix

possible conditions, live side by side with the Soviet republic. A conflict is inevitable. This is the greatest difficulty of the Russian Revolution, its greatest historical problem: the necessity to solve international problems, the necessity to call forth the world revolution.

On July 25, 1927, Japan's Premier, Baron Giichi Tanaka, presented to his Emperor a plan for the conquest of Asia and the island nations of the South Pacific. His detailed program, the Tanaka Memorial, which became known to the world soon after he presented it to the Emperor, and which Japan began to put into effect with the bombing of Pearl Harbor on December 7, 1941, was ignored by all its intended victims. Said Tanaka:

In future if we want to control China, we must first crush the United States just as in the past we had to fight in the Russo-Japanese War. But in order to conquer China we must first conquer Manchuria and Mongolia. In order to conquer the world, we must first conquer China.

If we succeed in conquering China the rest of the Asiatic countries and the South Sea countries will fear us and surrender to us. Then the world will realize that Eastern Asia is ours and will not dare to violate our rights.

In the present decade, Communist China's rulers claim the right of apostolic succession to Lenin as true disciples of Marxism-Leninism, and they are embarked on a crusade to bring communism to all the people of the world by means of violence, subversion, and terror. Mao Tse-tung has declared, and the Chinese Communist Party has affirmed, that "China's revolution is part of the world revolution"; and that "the heroes of the colonies and the semicolonies have to stand either on the imperialist front and play a role in the world counterrevolution, or on the anti-imperialist front and play a role in the world revolution. They must choose either one of the two. There is not a third road."

Here, in this abridgment of Mao Tse-tung's *Selected Works*, is the Chinese Communist leader's program for remodeling man and his environment in two successive stages: first, by remolding the minds of China's 700 million people until they become instruments for the execution of his master plan; second, by employing this tremendous force in a crusade to remold the minds and lives of all mankind.

BRUNO SHAW

Introduction

Mao Tse-tung was born December 26, 1893, in Shaoshan, Hsiang-tan County, Hunan Province. His father was a landowning peasant, his mother a devout Buddhist. He studied *Confucius' Analects and Four Classics* in a village private school. He attended the Hunan Provincial First Normal School, in Changsha, from which he graduated in 1918. He then worked as an assistant in the Peking University library. In 1921 he was one of the twelve founders of the Chinese Communist Party in Shanghai. Thereafter, he organized a peasant movement in his home province of Hunan, followed by a "Chinese Soviet Republic" in Kiangsi Province. Harassed by Nationalist Government forces, he embarked upon what has since become known as the "Long March," taking his peasant army and propaganda establishment over vast distances and surviving incredible hardships, from central Kiangsi Province to Yenan, Shensi Province, in northwest China. There he established the political and military headquarters of the Communist Party of China, whose armies, in 1949, defeated those of the Nationalist Government. The Communist People's Republic of China renamed the capital city Peking, from Peiping, and named Mao Tse-tung Chairman of the Communist Party of China, and also Chief of State. He relinquished the latter post in 1959. His fourth wife, who has become an active political propagandist, is Chiang Ching, a former actress. She has borne him two daughters.

Mao Tse-tung may well be remembered not only as the father of his country, the People's Republic of China, but as the mother and grandmother and midwife as well. His exhortations, declarations, and criticisms in *Selected Works* range from dissertations on the proper method of settling disputes between husband and wife, through every conceivable aspect of economics, sociology, education, politics, dietetics, art, literature, and culture, to the ultimate details of how to conduct protracted warfare against the entire non-Communist world. His "thoughts" have become an integral part of Chinese Communist dogma, and for mainland Chinese youth they have supplanted Confucius's *Analects* as a guide for proper thought and conduct.

In those chapters of *Selected Works* in which Mao Tse-tung discusses the need of the Chinese people for agricultural and economic reforms, he invokes the name of the late Dr. Sun Yat Sen, the founder of the Chinese revolution which began in Wuchang, Hupeh, in 1911, who is revered by Communists and non-Communists alike. Mao's reiterated assertions of Chinese Communist Party adherence to Dr. Sun's Three People's Principles gained for him the devoted following of tens of millions of the landless Chinese peasants who constituted 90 per cent of all the people in China.

In expressing his allegiance to Dr. Sun Yat Sen's Three People's Principles, however, Mao takes occasion wherever it seems useful for him to do so to qualify their meaning to accord with Communist Party doctrine. For example, in his lecture on "The Tasks of the Chinese Communist Party," *Selected Works,* Mao asks rhetorically: "Does the Communist Party agree with the Three People's Principles? Our answer is: Yes." But then he adds, "the Chinese Communist Party has its own political and economic program . . . of socialism and communism, which is different from the Three People's Principles."

How very different this program is, is seen in Dr. Sun Yat Sen's clear rejection of communism for China: "Marx's assumption that class struggle is a cause of social progress puts effect before cause. Because of this confusion in source, Marx's theory has not been borne out and has sometimes been directly contradicted by subsequent facts in social history." Therefore, says Dr. Sun in his *Three People's Principles,* "in working out our Principle of Livelihood, we cannot use or apply in China the methods of Marx, although we have the deepest respect for his teaching."

In the third of his *Three People's Principles,* the Principle of Livelihood, Dr. Sun stresses:

The great aim of the Principle of Livelihood in our Three Principles is communism—a share in property by all. But the communism which we propose is a communism of the future, not of the present. This communism of the future is a very just proposal, and those who have had property in the past will not suffer by it. It is a very different thing from what is called in the West "nationalization of property," confiscation for the government's use of private property which the people already possess. When landowners clearly understand the principle involved in our plan for equalization of landownership, they will not be apprehensive. Our plan provides that land now fixed in value shall still be privately owned. If the land problem can be solved, one half of the problem of livelihood will be solved.

Dr. Sun Yat Sen advocated *Min-sheng*—the sharing of national resources and production by all the people. But he denounced as wholly unacceptable Communist proposals for "nationalization of property" or "confiscation of property."

"Later," said Dr. Sun, "when the *Min-sheng* principle is fully realized and the problems of the farmer are all solved, each tiller of the soil will possess his own fields—that is to be the final fruit of our efforts."

Far from being the "final fruit" of Mao Tse-tung's efforts, however, the possession of his own fields by the tiller of the soil was to be only the "first stage," the "new-democratic" stage, of the "people's revolution." The "second stage" called for abolition of private ownership of all land and taking away from the tiller the land for which he had pledged his allegiance to the Communist Party of China.

In the section The Three People's Principles, Old and New, of "On New Democracy," in Volume II, *Selected Works,* Mao Tse-tung makes a distinction between the *Three People's Principles* of Dr. Sun Yat Sen as set down in print and as "reinterpreted by Dr. Sun Yat Sen in the Manifesto of the First National Congress of the Kuomintang." It is a fact, however, that no such "reinterpretation" was ever made by Dr. Sun in that manifesto or elsewhere, and that this reinterpretation was made by Mao Tse-tung himself in accordance with rules long since established by Communist lexicographers, which provide that only that which is of benefit to the Communist cause can be considered to be truth, whether or not it bears any relation to fact. From then on, Mao continues to explain Chinese Communist Party adherence to Dr. Sun Yat Sen's Three People's Principles on the basis of the "reinterpretation" he had devised for this purpose.

The design of the flag of the People's Republic of China is a historic reminder of promises made by the Communist Party of China in its early days of coexistence, but hardly cooperation, with the Kuomintang, the political party of the Nationalist Government. It is solid red with a large yellow star in the upper left; in a semicircle below it are four smaller yellow stars. The large star denotes Communist Party leadership. The four smaller stars symbolize the equal partnership of Workers, Farmers, Petty Bourgeoisie, and National Capitalists. The Petty Bourgeoisie and the National Capitalists have long since been liquidated—physically as well as economically.

BRUNO SHAW

Volume I

The First and Second Revolutionary Civil War Periods

Volume I   Contents

I

The First Revolutionary Civil War Period

Analysis of the Classes in Chinese Society

March 1926

Who are our enemies? Who are our friends? This is a question of the first importance for the revolution. The basic reason why all previous revolutionary struggles in China achieved so little was their failure to unite with real friends in order to attack real enemies. . . . To distinguish real friends from real enemies, we must make a general analysis of the economic status of the various classes in Chinese society and of their respective attitudes toward the revolution.

What is the condition of each of the classes in Chinese society?

The landlord class and the comprador class.[1] In economically backward and semicolonial China the landlord class and the comprador class are wholly appendages of the international bourgeoisie, depending upon imperialism for their survival and growth. These classes represent the most backward and most reactionary relations of production in China and hinder the development of her productive forces. Their existence is utterly incompatible with the aims of the Chinese revolution. . . .

1. A comprador was the senior Chinese employee in a foreign establishment, who acted as credit manager, cashier, and intermediary between the foreign management and the Chinese with whom the company did business.

The middle bourgeoisie. This class represents the capitalist relations of production in China in town and country. The middle bourgeoisie, by which is meant chiefly the national bourgeoisie, is inconsistent in its attitude toward the Chinese revolution: its members feel the need for revolution and favor the revolutionary movement against imperialism and the warlords when they are smarting under the blows of foreign capital and the oppression of the warlords, but they become suspicious of the revolution when they sense that, with the militant participation of the proletariat at home and the active support of the international proletariat abroad, the revolution is threatening the hope of their class to attain the status of a big bourgeoisie. . . .

This class is against interpreting the Kuomintang's Principle of the People's Livelihood according to the theory of class struggle, and it opposes the Kuomintang's alliance with Russia and the admission of Communists and left-wingers. But its attempt to establish a state under the rule of the national bourgeoisie is quite impracticable because the present world situation is such that the two major forces, revolution and counterrevolution, are locked in a final struggle. Each has hoisted a huge banner: one is the red banner of revolution held aloft by the Third International as the rallying point for all the oppressed classes of the world; the other is the white banner of counterrevolution held aloft by the League of Nations as the rallying point for all the counterrevolutionaries of the world. The intermediate classes are bound to disintegrate quickly, some sections turning left to join the revolution, others turning right to join the counterrevolution; there is no room for them to remain "independent." Therefore the idea cherished by China's middle bourgeoisie of an "independent" revolution in which it would play the primary role is a mere illusion.

The petty bourgeoisie. Included in this category are the owner-peasants, the master handicraftsmen, the lower levels of the intellectuals—students, primary and secondary school teachers, lower government functionaries, office clerks, small lawyers—and the small traders. . . . Although all strata of this class have the same petty-bourgeois economic status, they fall into three different sections. The first section consists of those who have some surplus money or grain, that is, those who, by manual or mental labor, earn more each year than they consume for their own support. . . . This section is a minority among the petty bourgeois and constitutes its right wing.

The second section consists of those who in the main are economically self-supporting. They want to get rich, but Marshal Chao[2] never lets them. . . . This section is very numerous, making up about one-half of the petty bourgeoisie.

The third section consists of those whose standard of living is falling. Many in this section, who originally belonged to better-off families, are undergoing a gradual change from a position of being barely able to manage to one of living in more and more reduced circumstances. . . . Such people are quite important for the revolutionary movement; they form a mass of no small proportions and are the left wing of the petty bourgeoisie. . . .

The semiproletariat. What is here called the semiproletariat consists of five categories: (1) the overwhelming majority of the semiowner-peasants,[3] (2) the poor peasants, (3) the small handicraftsmen, (4) the shop assistants, and (5) the pedlars. . . .

The proletariat. The modern industrial proletariat numbers about 2 million. It is not large because China is economically backward. These 2 million industrial workers are mainly employed in five industries—railways, mining, maritime transport, textiles and ship-building—and a great number are enslaved in enterprises owned by foreign capitalists. Though not very numerous, the industrial proletariat represents China's new productive forces, is the most progressive class in modern China, and has become the leading force in the revolutionary movement. . . .

Apart from all these, there is the fairly large lumpen-proletariat, made up of peasants who have lost their land and handicraftsmen who cannot get work. They lead the most precarious existence of all. In every part of the country they have their secret societies, which were originally their mutual-aid organizations for political and economic struggle. . . .

One of China's difficult problems is how to handle these people. Brave fighters are apt to be destructive, they can become a revolutionary force if given proper guidance. . . .

2. Marshal Chao is Chao Kung-ming, God of Wealth in Chinese folklore.
3. By "semiowner-peasants" Mao Tse-tung means peasants who worked partly on their own land and partly on land rented from others.

Our closest friends are the entire semiproletariat and petty bourgeoisie. As for the vacillating middle bourgeoisie, their right wing may become our enemy and their left wing may become our friend—but we must be constantly on our guard and not let them create confusion within our ranks.

This article was written by Mao Tse-tung to combat two deviations then to be found in the Chinese Communist Party. According to Mao, exponents of the first deviation were concerned only with cooperation with the Kuomintang and forgot about the peasants; this was "right" opportunism. The exponents of the second deviation were concerned only with the labor movement, and likewise forgot about the peasants; this was "left" opportunism. Both were aware that their own strength was inadequate, but neither of them knew where to seek reinforcements or where to obtain allies on a mass scale. Mao Tse-tung pointed out that the peasantry was the staunchest and numerically the largest ally of the Chinese proletariat, and thus solved the problem of who was the chief ally in the Chinese Communist revolution.

Report on an Investigation of the Peasant Movement in Hunan

March 1927

THE IMPORTANCE OF THE PEASANT PROBLEM

. . . The present upsurge of the peasant movement is a colossal event. In a very short time, in China's central, southern and northern provinces, several hundred million peasants will rise like a mighty storm, like a hurricane, a force so swift and violent that no power, however great, will be able to hold it back. They will smash all the trammels that bind them and rush forward along the road to liberation. They will sweep all the imperialists, warlords, corrupt officials, local tyrants and evil gentry into their graves. Every revolutionary party and every revolutionary comrade will be put to the test, to be accepted or rejected as they decide. There are three alternatives. To march at their head and lead them? To trail behind them, gesticulating and criticizing? Or to stand in their way and oppose them? Every Chinese is free to choose, but events will force you to make the choice quickly.

GET ORGANIZED!

The development of the peasant movement in Hunan[1] may be divided roughly into two periods. . . . The first, from January to September of last year, was one of organization. In this period . . . the membership of the peasant associations did not exceed 300,000 to 400,000, and the masses directly under their leadership numbered little more than 1 million. . . .

The second period, from last October to January of this year, was one of revolutionary action. The membership of the associations jumped to 2 million and the masses directly under their leadership increased to 10 million. . . .

DOWN WITH THE LOCAL TYRANTS AND EVIL GENTRY! ALL POWER TO THE PEASANT ASSOCIATIONS!

The main targets of attack by the peasants are the local tyrants, the evil gentry and the lawless landlords. . . . As a result, the privileges which the feudal landlords enjoyed for thousands of years are being shattered to pieces. With the collapse of the power of the landlords, the peasant associations have now become the sole organs of authority. . . .

Even such trifles as a quarrel between husband and wife are brought to the peasant association. Nothing can be settled unless someone from the peasant association is present. Quite literally, "Whatever it says, goes." . . .

In the face of the peasant associations' power and pressure, the top

1. Hunan Province in 1926–27 was the center of Communist organization of peasants in China, and a massive slaughter of landlords took place at that time.

local tyrants and evil gentry have fled to Shanghai, those of the second rank to Hankow, those of the third to Changsha, and those of the fourth to the country towns, while the fifth rank and the still lesser fry surrender to the peasant associations in the villages. . . .

"It's Terrible!" or "It's Fine!"

The peasants' revolt disturbed the gentry's sweet dreams. . . . From the middle social strata upward to the Kuomintang right-wingers, there was not a single person who did not sum up the whole business in the phrase, "It's terrible!" . . .

In a few months the peasants have accomplished what Dr. Sun Yat Sen wanted, but failed, to accomplish in the forty years he devoted to the national revolution. This is a marvelous feat never before achieved, not only in forty but in thousands of years. It's fine. It is not "terrible" at all. . . . What the peasants are doing is absolutely right; what they are doing is fine! . . .

The Question of "Going Too Far"

Then there is another section of the people who say, "Yes, peasant associations are necessary, but they are going rather too far." This is the opinion of the middle-of-the-roaders. But what is the actual situation? True, the peasants are in a sense "unruly" in the country-side. Supreme in authority, the peasant association allows the land-lord no say and sweeps away his prestige. This amounts to striking the landlord down to the dust and keeping him there. . . .

People swarm into the houses of local tyrants and evil gentry who are against the peasant association, slaughter their pigs and consume their grain. . . . Doing whatever they like and turning everything upside down, they have created a kind of terror in the countryside. This is what some people call "going too far," or "exceeding the proper limits in righting a wrong." Such talk may seem plausible, but in fact it is wrong.

First, the local tyrants, evil gentry and lawless landlords have themselves driven the peasants to this. For ages they have used their power to tyrannize over the peasants and trample them underfoot; that is why the peasants have reacted so strongly. . . .

Secondly, a revolution is not a dinner party, or writing an essay, or painting a picture, or doing embroidery; it cannot be so refined, so leisurely and gentle, so temperate, kind, courteous, restrained and magnanimous. A revolution is an insurrection, an act of violence by which one class overthrows another. A rural revolution is a revolution by which the peasantry overthrows the power of the feudal landlord class. . . .

To put it bluntly, it is necessary to create terror for a while in every rural area, otherwise it would be impossible to suppress the activities of the counterrevolutionaries in the countryside or overthrow the authority of the gentry. . . .

The "Movement of the Riffraff"

The right wing of the Kuomintang says, "The peasant movement is a movement of the riffraff, of the lazy peasants." . . . The gentry say, "It is all right to set up peasant associations, but the people now running them are no good. They ought to be replaced." . . . In short, all those whom the gentry had despised, those whom they had trodden into the dirt, people with no right to speak, have now audaciously lifted up their heads and taken power into their hands. . . . They are issuing orders and are running everything. Those who used to rank lowest now rank above everybody else; and so this is called "turning things upside down."

Vanguards of the Revolution

. . . The peasants have done an important job for the national revolution. . . . But has this been performed by all the peasants? No. There are three kinds of peasants, the rich, the middle, and the poor peasants . . . who have different views about the revolution. . . .

Thus an official of the township peasant association (generally one of the "riffraff" type) would walk into the house of a rich peasant, register in hand, and say: "Will you please join the peasant association?" How would the rich peasant answer? A tolerably well-behaved one would say: "I never heard of such a thing before, yet I've managed to live all right. I advise you to give it up." A really vicious rich peasant would say: "Peasant association! Nonsense! Association for getting your head chopped off! Don't get people into trouble." . . .

How about the middle peasants? . . . They think, ". . . Can the Three People's Principles prevail?" Their conclusion is, "Afraid not!" They imagine it all depends on the will of Heaven and think, "A peasant association? Who knows if Heaven wills it or not?" . . . It is essential for the peasant associations to get the middle peasants to join and to do a good deal more explanatory work among them. . . .

The poor peasants have always been the main force in the bitter fight in the countryside. They have fought militantly through the two periods of underground work and of open activity. They are the most responsive to Communist Party leadership. . . . "We joined the peasant association long ago," they say to the rich peasants, "why are you still hesitating?" The rich peasants answer mockingly, "What is there to keep you from joining? You people have neither a tile over your heads nor a speck of land under your feet!" . . . What, indeed, is there to keep them from joining the associations? . . .

Without the poor peasants there would be no revolution. To deny their role is to deny the revolution. . . .

FOURTEEN GREAT ACHIEVEMENTS

Most critics of the peasant associations allege that they have done a great many bad things. . . . The peasants have done a great many things, and in order to answer people's criticism we must closely examine all their activities. . . . The peasants under the leadership of the peasant associations have the following fourteen great achievements to their credit.

1. Organizing the Peasants into Peasant Associations

This is the first great achievement of the peasants. . . . Roughly speaking, the counties in central Hunan, with Changsha as the center, are the most advanced, those in southern Hunan come second, and western Hunan is only just beginning to organize. According to the figures compiled by the provincial peasant association last November, organizations with a total membership of 1,367,727 have been set up in thirty-seven of the province's seventy-five counties. . . .

2. Hitting the Landlords Politically

Once the peasants have their organization, the first thing they do is to smash the political prestige and power of the landlord class. . . .

Checking the accounts. More often than not the local tyrants and evil gentry have helped themselves to public money passing through their hands, and their books are not in order. Now the peasants are using the checking of accounts as an occasion to bring down a great many of the local tyrants and evil gentry. . . .

Imposing fines. The peasants work out fines for such offenses as irregularities revealed by the checking of accounts. . . . A man who has been fined by the peasants completely loses face.

Levying contributions. The unscrupulous rich landlords are made to contribute for poor relief, for the organization of co-operatives or peasant credit societies, or for other purposes. . . .

Minor protests. When someone harms a peasant association and the offense is a minor one . . . he is usually let off after writing a pledge to "cease and desist."

Major demonstrations. A big crowd is rallied to demonstrate against a local tyrant or one of the evil gentry who is an enemy of the association. The demonstrators eat at the offender's house, slaughtering his pigs and consuming his grain as a matter of course. . . .

"Crowning" the landlords and parading them through the villages. This sort of thing is very common. A tall paper hat is stuck on the head of one of the local tyrants or evil gentry, bearing the words "Local tyrant So-and-so." He is led by a rope, brass gongs are beaten and flags are waved to attract people's attention. This form of punishment makes the local tyrants and evil gentry tremble. Anyone who has once been crowned with a tall paper hat loses face altogether and can never again hold up his head. . . .

Locking up the landlords in the county jail. This is a heavier punishment than wearing the tall paper hat. A local tyrant or one of the evil gentry is arrested and sent to the county jail; he is locked up and the county magistrate has to try him and punish him. . . .

"Banishment." The peasants have no desire to banish the most notorious criminals among the local tyrants and evil gentry, but would rather arrest or execute them. Afraid of being arrested or executed, they run away . . . and this amounts to banishment. . . .

Execution. This is confined to the worst local tyrants and evil gentry and is carried out by the peasants jointly with other sections of the people. . . . The execution of one big landlord reverberates through a whole county and is very effective in eradicating the remaining evils of feudalism. . . . The head of the defense corps in the town of Hsinkang was personally responsible for killing almost 1,000 poverty-stricken peasants, which he euphemistically described as "executing bandits." . . . Such was the cruelty in former days of the White terror in the countryside, and now that the peasants have risen and shot a few and created just a little terror in suppressing the counterrevolutionaries, is there any reason for saying they should not do so?

3. Hitting the Landlords Economically

Prohibition on sending grain out of the area, forcing up grain prices, and hoarding and cornering. . . . Since last October, the poor peasants have prevented the outflow of the grain of the landlords and rich peasants and have banned the forcing up of grain prices and hoarding and cornering. . . .

Prohibition on increasing rents and deposits, agitation for reduced rents and deposits. Last July and August, when the peasant associations were still weak, the landlords, following their long-established practice of maximum exploitation, served notice one after another on their tenants that rents would be increased. But by October, when the peasant associations had grown considerably in strength and had all come out against the raising of rents and deposits, the landlords dared not breathe another word on the subject. . . .

Prohibition on cancelling tenancies. In July and August of last year there were still many instances of landlords cancelling tenancies and reletting the land. But after October nobody dared cancel a tenancy. Today, the cancelling of tenancies and the reletting of land are quite out of the question. . . .

Reduction of interest. Interest has been generally reduced . . . and wherever the peasant associations are powerful, rural moneylending has virtually disappeared; the landlords fear the money will be "communized." . . . Not only is the interest on . . . old loans reduced, but the creditor is actually forbidden to press for repayment of the principal. . . .

4. Overthrowing the Feudal Rule of the Local Tyrants and Evil Gentry—Smashing the TU and TUAN

The old organs of political power in the *tu* and *tuan* (i.e., the district and the township), and especially at the *tu* level, just below the county level, used to be almost exclusively in the hands of the local tyrants and evil gentry. . . . The evil gentry who ran these organs were virtual monarchs of the countryside. . . . As a consequence of the present revolt in the countryside the authority of the landlord class has generally been struck down, and the organs of rural administration dominated by the local tyrants and evil gentry have naturally collapsed in its wake. . . .

5. Overthrowing the Armed Forces of the Landlords and Establishing Those of the Peasants

The armed forces of the landlord class were smaller in central Hunan than in the western and southern parts of the province. . . . Taking over these old armed forces is one way in which the peasants are building up their own armed forces. A new way is through the setting up of spear corps under the peasant associations. The spears have pointed, double-edged blades mounted on long shafts. . . . The revolutionary authorities in Hunan should see to it that such a corps is built up on a really extensive scale among the more than 20 million peasants in the seventy-five counties of the province; that every peasant, whether young or in his prime, possesses a spear; and that no restrictions are imposed as though a spear were something dreadful. . . .

6. Overthrowing the Political Power of the County Magistrate and His Bailiffs

. . . County government cannot be clean until the peasants rise up. . . . In a county where the peasants have risen there is clean government, whoever the magistrate. . . . In counties where the peasant power was very strong, the word of the peasant association worked miracles. If it demanded the arrest of a local tyrant in the morning, the magistrate dared not delay till noon; if it demanded arrest by noon, he dared not delay till the afternoon. . . .

In the past the villagers were afraid of the townspeople, but now the townspeople are afraid of the villagers. In particular, the vicious curs kept by the county government—the police, the armed guards and the bailiffs—are afraid to go to the villages; or if they do so, they no longer dare to practice their extortions. They tremble at the sight of the peasants' spears.

7. Overthrowing the Clan Authority of the Ancestral Temples and Clan Elders, the Religious Authority of Town and Village Gods, and the Masculine Authority of Husbands

A man in China is usually subjected to the domination of three systems of authority: (1) the state system (political authority) . . . ; (2) the clan system (clan authority) . . . ; and (3) the supernatural system (religious authority). . . . As for women, in addition to being dominated by these three systems of authority, they are also dominated by the men (the authority of the husband). These four authorities . . . are the four thick ropes binding the Chinese people. . . . The old rule barring women and poor people from banquets in the ancestral temples has also been broken. The women of Paikuo in Hengshan County gathered in force and swarmed into their ancestral temple, firmly planted their backsides on the seats and joined in the eating and drinking, while the venerable clan bigwigs had willy-nilly to let them do as they pleased. . . .

. . . Our present task is to lead the peasants to put their greatest efforts into the political struggle, so that the landlords' authority is entirely overthrown. . . . As for the clan system, superstition, and inequality between men and women, their abolition will follow as a natural consequence of victory in the political and economic struggles. . . .

While I was in the countryside, I did some propaganda against superstition among the peasants. I said:

"If you believe in the Eight Characters,[2] you hope for good luck; if you believe in geomancy,[3] you hope to benefit from the location of your ancestral graves. This year within the space of a few months the local tyrants, evil gentry and corrupt officials have all toppled from their pedestals—is it possible . . . their ancestral graves have ceased to exert a beneficial influence? The local tyrants and evil gentry jeer at your peasant association and say . . . : 'You can't even go to pass water without bumping into a committeeman.' . . . And the gods? Worship them by all means. But if you had only Lord Kuan[4] and the Goddess of Mercy and no peasant association, could you have overthrown the local tyrants and evil gentry? The gods and goddesses are indeed miserable objects. You have worshipped them for centuries, and they have not overthrown a single one of the local tyrants or evil gentry for you! Now you want to have your rent reduced. Let me ask, how will you go about it? Will you believe in the gods or in the peasant association?"

My words made the peasants roar with laughter.

8. Spreading Political Propaganda

Even if ten thousand schools of law and political science had been opened, could they have brought as much political education as the peasant associations have done in so short a time? I don't think they could. "Down with imperialism!" "Down with the warlords!" "Down with the corrupt officials!" . . . These political slogans have . . . penetrated into their minds and are on their lips. . . .

Some of the peasants can also recite Dr. Sun Yat Sen's Testament. They pick out the terms "freedom," "equality," "the Three People's Principles" and "unequal treaties," and apply them, if rather crudely, in their daily life. . . . When a policeman strikes or swears at a peasant selling vegetables, the peasant immediately answers back by

2. The "Eight Characters" was a method of fortunetelling in China based on the examination of the two cyclic characters for the year, month, day, and hour of a person's birth.

3. Mao Tse-tung is referring to the superstition that the location of one's ancestors' graves influences one's fortune. The geomancers claimed to be able to tell whether a particular site and its surroundings were auspicious, guided in part by the mystic *feng* (wind) and *shui* (water).

4. Lord Kuan (Kuan Yu, A.D. 160–219), a warrior in the epoch of the Three Kingdoms, was widely worshipped by the Chinese as the God of Loyalty and War.

invoking the Three People's Principles and that shuts the policeman up. . . .

The spread of political propaganda throughout the rural areas is entirely an achievement of the Communist Party and the peasant associations. . . . From now on, care should be taken to use every opportunity gradually to enrich the content and clarify the meaning of those simple slogans.

9. Peasant Bans and Prohibitions

When the peasant associations, under Communist Party leadership, establish their authority in the countryside, the peasants begin to prohibit or restrict the things they dislike. Gaming, gambling and opium-smoking are the three things that are most strictly forbidden.

Gaming. Where the peasant association is powerful, mahjong, dominoes and card games are completely banned. . . .

Gambling. . . . This abuse, too, has been swept away in places where the peasant association is powerful.

Opium-smoking. The prohibition is extremely strict. . . . In Liling County one of the evil gentry who did not surrender his pipes was arrested and paraded through the villages. . . .

The flower drum. Vulgar performances are forbidden in many places.

Sedan chairs. . . . In many counties . . . there have been cases of smashing of sedan chairs. . . . But peasant associations . . . say, "If you smash the chairs, you only save the rich money and lose the carriers their jobs." Seeing the point, the peasants worked out a new tactic . . . to increase the fares charged by the chair-carriers so as to penalize the rich.

Distilling and sugar-making. The use of grain for distilling spirits and making sugar is everywhere prohibited. . . .

Pigs. The number of pigs a family can keep is limited, for pigs consume grain.

Chickens and ducks. . . . In many places the raising of chickens and ducks is prohibited; ducks not only consume grain but also ruin the rice plants and so are worse than chickens.

Feasts. Sumptuous feasts are generally forbidden. . . .

Oxen. Oxen are a treasured possession of the peasants. "Slaughter an ox in this life and you will be an ox in the next" has become almost a religious tenet; oxen must never be killed. . . .

10. Eliminating Banditry

In my opinion, no ruler in any dynasty from Yu,[5] Tang, Wen and Wu down to the Ching Emperors and the Presidents of the Republic has ever shown as much prowess in eliminating banditry as have the peasant associations today.
. . . The reasons are: First, the members of the peasant associations are spread out over the hills and dales, spear or cudgel in hand. . . . Second, since the rise of the peasant movement the price of grain has dropped . . . and the problem of food has become less serious. . . . Third, members of secret societies . . . can now openly and legally vent their grievances. . . . Fourth, the armies are recruiting large numbers and many of the "unruly" have joined up. . . .

11. Abolishing Exorbitant Levies

As the country is not yet unified and the authority of the imperialists and warlords has not been overthrown, there is as yet no way of removing . . . the burden of expenditure for the revolutionary army. However, the exorbitant levies imposed on the peasants . . . have been abolished or reduced with the rise of the peasant movement. . . .

12. The Movement for Education

In China education has always been the exclusive preserve of the landlords, and the peasants have had no access to it. . . . In China 90 percent of the people have had no education, and of these the overwhelming majority are peasants. . . .

5. Emperor Yu is recorded as the eighth ruler of China. He is held to have dealt successfully with draining off the waters of a great flood and is credited with founding the first dynasty, the Hsia, to which are ascribed the doubtful dates of 2205–1705 B.C.

Now the peasants are enthusiastically establishing evening classes, which they call "peasant schools." . . . Before long, tens of thousands of schools will have sprung up in the villages throughout the province. . . .

13. The Co-operative Movement

The peasants really need co-operatives, and especially consumers' marketing and credit co-operatives. When they buy goods, the merchants exploit them; when they sell their farm produce, the merchants cheat them; . . . when they borrow money or rice, they are fleeced by the usurers; and they are eager to find a solution to these three problems. . . . A major problem is the absence of detailed, standard rules of organization. . . . Given proper guidance, the co-operative movement can spread everywhere along with the growth of the peasant associations.

14. Building Roads and Repairing Embankments

This, too, is one of the achievements of the peasant associations. Before there were peasant associations the roads in the countryside were terrible. . . .

The same is true of the embankments. The ruthless landlords . . . would never spend even a few coppers on embankment repairs; they would leave the ponds to dry up and the tenant-peasants to starve, caring about nothing but the rent. Now that there are peasant associations, the landlords can be bluntly ordered to repair the embankments. . . .

Curiously enough, it is reported from Nanchang[6] that Chiang Kai-shek, Chang Ching-chiang,[7] and other such gentlemen do not altogether approve of the activities of the Hunan peasants. This opinion is shared by Liu Yueh-chih and other right-wing leaders in

6. When Nanchang (Kiangsi) was captured by the Northern Expeditionary Army in November 1926 under General Chiang Kai-shek, the Communist-dominated forces in Hankow (Hupeh), under the guidance of the Soviet Union's Michael Borodin, declared Hankow the capital of "liberated" China. A fierce battle broke out between Chiang's forces inside the walls of Nanchang and those of the Communist faction on the outside; the Communists were defeated after several days of bitter fighting. Mao denounced this as a "counter-revolutionary plot against Wuhan" (the tri-city area on the banks of the Yangtze River, of which Hankow was the principal commercial city).

7. Chang Ching-chiang was a member of Chiang Kai-shek's planning staff.

Hunan, all of whom say, "They have simply gone Red." But where would the national revolution be without this bit of Red? To talk about "arousing the masses of the people" day in and day out and then to be scared to death when the masses do rise—what difference is there between this and Lord Sheh's[8] love of dragons?

This article was written as a reply to criticisms both inside and outside the Communist Party then being levelled at the peasants. Mao Tse-tung spent thirty-two days in Hunan Province making an investigation and wrote this report in order to answer these criticisms.

8. As told by Liu Hsiang (77 B.C.) in his *Hsin Hsu*, Lord Shen was so fond of dragons that he adorned his whole palace with drawings and carvings of them. But when a real dragon heard of his infatuation and paid him a visit, he was frightened out of his wits.

II

The Second Revolutionary Civil War
Period

Why Is It That Red Political Power
Can Exist in China?

October 3, 1928

THE INTERNAL POLITICAL SITUATION

. . . The bourgeois-democratic revolution which started in
Kwangtung Province had gone only halfway when the comprador
and landlord classes usurped the leadership and immediately shifted
it onto the road to counterrevolution; throughout the country the
workers, the peasants, the other sections of the common people, and
even the bourgeoisie,[1] have remained under counterrevolutionary
rule and obtained not the slightest particle of political or economic
emancipation. . . .

The contradictions and struggles among the cliques of warlords in
China reflect the contradictions and struggles among the imperialist

---

1. By the term "bourgeoisie," Mao Tse-tung means "the national bourgeoisie." He explains his distinction between this class and the big comprador
bourgeoisie in "On Tactics Against Japanese Imperialism" (December 1935),
and "The Chinese Revolution and the Chinese Communist Party" (December
1939).

powers. Hence, as long as China is divided among the imperialist powers, the various cliques of warlords cannot under any circumstances come to terms, and whatever compromises they may reach will only be temporary. A temporary compromise today engenders a bigger war tomorrow. . . .

According to the directives of the Communist International and the Central Committee of our Party, the content of China's democratic revolution consists in overthrowing the rule of imperialism and its warlord tools in China so as to complete the national revolution. . . . Such a revolutionary movement has been growing day by day since the Tsinan Massacre[2] in May 1928.

REASONS FOR THE EMERGENCE AND SURVIVAL OF RED POLITICAL POWER IN CHINA[3]

The long-term survival inside a country of one or more small areas under Red political power completely encircled by a White regime is a phenomenon that has never occurred anywhere else in the world. There are special reasons for this unusual phenomenon. . . .

First, it cannot occur in any imperialist country or in any colony under direct imperialist rule,[4] but can only occur in China which is economically backward, and which is semicolonial and under indirect imperialist rule. . . .

2. In 1928, Chiang Kai-shek attempted to attack Chang Tso-lin, the Japanese puppet ruler of Manchuria. Japanese troops cut the railway line to the north, preventing Chiang's advance, and on May 3, as an object lesson against attempted rebellion, the Japanese shot a number of unoffending Chinese in Tsinan.

3. The organizational form of China's Red political power was similar to that of Soviet political power. In its early stages, however, Mao Tse-tung described its nature as "a people's democratic dictatorship of the anti-imperialist, anti-feudal, new-democratic revolution led by the proletariat," which differed from the proletarian dictatorship of the Soviet Union.

4. In later years, Mao Tse-tung's views on this altered diametrically. During World War II the Communists in the Asian and Pacific Island countries waged their overt battle against the Japanese, reserving their revolutionary activities until that had been won. At the end of World War II, Mao found that it was possible for Communist units elsewhere to maintain their revolutionary bases within non-Communist areas, and to fight small and big battles against their governments, and he changed his views accordingly.

Second, the regions where China's Red political power has first emerged and has been able to last for a long time . . . have been Hunan, Kwangtung, Hupeh and Kiangsi, where the masses of workers, peasants and soldiers rose in great numbers in the course of the bourgeois-democratic revolution of 1926 and 1927. . . .

Third, whether it is possible for the people's political power in small areas to last depends on whether the nationwide revolutionary situation continues to develop. If it does, then the small Red areas will undoubtedly last for a long time, and will, moreover, inevitably become one of the many forces for winning nationwide political power. . . .

Fourth, the existence of a regular Red Army of adequate strength is a necessary condition for the existence of Red political power. . . . Therefore, even when the masses of workers and peasants are active, it is definitely impossible to create an independent regime . . . unless we have regular forces of adequate strength. . . .

Fifth, another important condition in addition to the above is required for the prolonged existence and development of Red political power: namely, that the Communist Party organization should be strong and its policy correct.

THE INDEPENDENT REGIME IN THE HUNAN-KIANGSI BORDER AREA AND THE AUGUST DEFEAT

Splits and wars among the warlords weaken the power of the White regime. Thus opportunities are provided for the rise of Red political power in small areas. . . . We were able to win a number of victories in the four months from April to July . . . although the enemy was several times stronger than us. . . .

The sole reason for the August defeat was that, failing to realize that the period was one of temporary stability for the ruling classes, some comrades adopted a strategy suited to a period of political splits within the ruling classes and divided our forces for an adventurous advance . . . an exceedingly grave mistake. The situation arising from this defeat was salvaged as a result of the corrective measures taken by the Special Committee and the Army Committee of the Party after September.

The Role of the Independent Regime of the Hunan-Kiangsi Border Area in Hunan, Hupeh and Kiangsi

The significance of the armed independent regime of workers and peasants in the Hunan-Kiangsi border area . . . is definitely not confined to the few counties in the border area; . . . this regime will play an immense role in the process of the seizure of political power in Hunan, Hupeh and Kiangsi through the insurrection of the workers and peasants in these three provinces.

Economic Problems

The shortage of necessities and cash has become a very big problem for the army and the people inside the White encirclement. Because of the tight enemy blockade, necessities such as salt, cloth and medicines have been very scarce . . . which has upset, sometimes to an acute degree, the lives of the masses of the workers, peasants and petty bourgeoisie,[5] as well as of the soldiers of the Red Army. . . . The soldiers are undernourished, many are ill, and the wounded in the hospitals are worse off. . . . An adequate solution of these economic problems undoubtedly merits the attention of every Party member.

The Problem of Military Bases

The Party in the border area has another task, namely, the consolidation of the military bases at Five Wells[6] and Chiulung. . . . Both are important . . . not only for the border area at present, but also for insurrections in Hunan, Hupeh and Kiangsi in the future. . . .

5. By "petty bourgeoisie," Mao Tse-tung means handicraftsmen, small merchants, professional people, and petty-bourgeois intellectuals. They are mostly in the cities, but there are many in the countryside as well.
6. Five Wells designates a group of villages—Big Well, Small Well, Upper Well, Middle Well, and Lower Well—in the Chingkang Mountains.

The way to consolidate these bases is, first . . . to construct adequate defenses, second, to store sufficient grain and, third, to set up comparatively good Red Army hospitals. The Party in the border area must strive to perform these three tasks effectively.

This article was part of the resolution—originally entitled "The Political Problems and the Tasks of the Border Area Party Organization"— which was drafted by Mao Tse-tung for the Second Party Congress of the Hunan-Kiangsi border area.

The Struggle in the Chingkang Mountains
November 25, 1928

THE INDEPENDENT REGIME IN THE HUNAN-KIANGSI BORDER AREA AND THE AUGUST DEFEAT

[The first section of "The Struggle in the Chingkang Mountains" is an almost word for word repetition of Mao's October 3 statement captioned "Why Is It That Red Political Power Can Exist in China?" and is therefore not repeated here. Continuing from that point:]

Military Questions

Since the struggle in the border area is exclusively military, both the Party and the masses have to be placed on a war footing. How to deal with the enemy, how to fight, has become the central problem of our daily life. An independent regime must be an armed one. . . .

The Red Army consists partly of workers and peasants and partly of lumpen-proletarians. . . . The majority of men in the Red Army come from the mercenary armies, but their character changes once they are in the Red Army. . . . They feel they are fighting for themselves and for the people and not for somebody else. So far the

Red Army has no system of regular pay, but issues grain, money for cooking oil, salt, firewood and vegetables, and a little pocket money. Land has been allotted to all Red Army officers and men who are natives of the border area, but it is rather difficult to allot land to those from other parts of the country. . . .

Ordinarily a soldier needs six months' or a year's training before he can fight, but our soldiers, recruited only yesterday, have to fight today with practically no training. . . .

Apart from the role played by the Party, the reason why the Red Army has been able to carry on in spite of such poor material conditions and frequent engagements is its practice of democracy. The officers do not beat the men; officers and men receive equal treatment; soldiers are free to hold meetings and to speak out; trivial formalities have been done away with; the accounts are open for all to inspect. . . . The very soldiers who had no courage in the White Army yesterday are very brave in the Red Army today; such is the effect of democracy. . . . In China the army needs democracy as much as the people do. Democracy in our army is an important weapon for undermining the feudal mercenary army. . . .

The most effective method in propaganda directed at the enemy forces is to release captured soldiers and give the wounded medical treatment. Whenever soldiers, platoon leaders, or company battalion commanders of the enemy forces are captured, we immediately conduct propaganda among them; they are divided into those wishing to stay and those wishing to leave, and the latter are given travelling expenses and set free. This immediately knocks the bottom out of the enemy's slander that "the Communist bandits kill everyone on sight." . . . In addition, we do as much written propaganda as possible, for instance, painting slogans. Wherever we go, we cover the walls with them. . . .

Land Question

The land situation in the border areas. Roughly speaking, more than 60 per cent of the land belonged to the landlords and less than 40 per cent to the peasants. In the Kiangsi sector . . . about 80 per cent of the land belonged to the landlords.

The question of the intermediate class. Given this land situation it is possible to win the support of the majority for the confiscation and redistribution of all the land.[1] The rural population is roughly divided into three classes, the class of the big and middle landlords, the intermediate class of small landlords and rich peasants, and the class of middle and poor peasants. . . . Consequently, in the Red area the big and middle landlord class and the intermediate class are both being attacked. . . . In the early days of the revolution, the intermediate class . . . exploited their traditional social position and clan authority to intimidate the poor peasants for the purpose of delaying the distribution of the land. When no further delay was possible, they concealed their actual holdings, or retained the good land and gave up the poor land. . . .

The defection of the intermediate class under the White terror. Having been under attack during the revolutionary upsurge, the intermediate class deserted to the enemy as soon as the White terror struck. . . .[2] It was only after we had conducted propaganda to the effect that "peasants who have defected will not be killed" and . . . "are welcome to come back to reap their crops" that some of them slowly came back. . . .

The pressure of daily life as a cause of the defection of the intermediate class. The Red and the White areas are now facing each other like two countries at war. Owing to the tight enemy blockade and to our mishandling of the petty bourgeoisie, trade between the two areas has almost ceased; necessities such as salt, cloth and medicines are scarce and costly. . . . Poor peasants are more able to bear such hardships, but the intermediate class will go over to the big landlord class when it can bear them no longer. Unless the splits and wars within the landlord class and among the warlords in China

1. Confiscation and redistribution of all the land was a provision in the Land Law promulgated in the Hunan-Kiangsi border area in 1928. This resulted in adverse reaction from many whom the Communists wished to recruit or hold in their ranks, so in April 1929 the law was changed to read "confiscate the public land and the land of the landlord class."
2. Because of their number and their economic importance at this time, Mao Tse-tung soon found that premature crackdowns on the intermediate class created antagonisms among this still useful group. To correct this, a proclamation was issued by the Fourth Red Army stating that "merchants in the towns who have gradually built up some property are to be left alone so long as they obey the authorities."

continue, and unless a nationwide revolutionary situation develops, the small independent Red regimes will come under great economic pressure and it is doubtful if they will be able to last. . . .

The criterion for land distribution. The township is taken as the unit for land distribution. . . . All the inhabitants, men and women, old and young, formerly received equal shares. A change has now been made in accordance with the Central Committee's plan, whereby labor power is taken as the criterion, so that a person with labor power is allotted twice as much land as one without.[3]

The question of concessions to the owner-peasants. . . . Among the owner-peasants, the rich peasants have requested that productive capacity should be taken as the criterion . . . that those with more manpower and capital (such as farm implements) should be allotted more land. . . . But this question deserves further discussion, and a report will be submitted when conclusions are reached.

The land tax. In Ningkang the tax rate is 20 per cent of the crop. . . . It is inadvisable to make any change now as collection is already under way, but the rate will be reduced next year. . . . There are sections . . . where the peasants are so poverty-stricken that any taxation is inadvisable. We have to rely on expropriating the local tyrants in the White areas to cover the expenses of the government and the Red Guards. . . .

Questions of Political Power

People's political power has been established everywhere at the county, district and township levels, but more in name than in reality. The executive committees of the township, district or even county governments were invariably elected at some kind of mass meeting. But mass meetings called on the spur of the moment can neither discuss questions nor help in training masses politically, and, what is more, they are only too apt to be manipulated by intellectuals or careerists. . . .

Democratic centralism can be widely and effectively practiced in mass organization only when its efficacy is demonstrated in revolu-

3. Labor power was soon found not to be a desirable criterion for land distribution, and in the Red areas land was redistributed equally on a per capita basis.

tionary struggle and the masses understand that it is the best means of mobilizing their forces and is of the utmost help to their struggle. . . . In the Red Army, conferences of soldiers' representatives are now being established on a permanent basis and at all levels so as to correct the mistake of having only soldiers' committees and not conferences. . . .

The Party enjoys immense prestige and authority among the masses, the government much less. . . . From now on the Party must carry out its task of giving leadership to the government. . . . The Party's policies and the measures it recommends must be carried out through the government organizations.

Questions of Party Organization

The struggle against opportunism. . . . In the last twelve months manifestations of opportunism continued to be widespread. . . . On the approach of the enemy, either reckless battle or precipitate flight would be proposed. . . . This opportunist ideology has been gradually corrected through prolonged inner-Party struggle and through lessons learned from actual events. . . .

Localism. . . . In the Party organization in the villages, it often happens that a branch meeting virtually becomes a clan meeting, since branches consist of members bearing the same family name and living close together. In these circumstances it is very hard indeed to build a "militant Bolshevik Party." Such members do not quite understand when they are told that the Communists draw no sharp line of demarcation between one nation and another, or between one province and another. . . . It takes White . . . suppression campaigns . . . to make the people share a common lot in struggle. . . . Localism is declining as a result of many such lessons.

The question of the native inhabitants and the settlers. There is another peculiar feature in the border counties, namely, the rift between the native inhabitants and the settlers . . . whose forefathers came from the north several hundred years ago. . . .

After the August defeat in the border area, the native landlords returned . . . bringing with them the reactionary troops and spreading the rumor that the settlers were going to massacre the native inhabitants. Most of the native peasants defected, put on white ribbons and guided the White troops in burning down houses and searching the hills. And when the Red Army routed the White troops in October . . . the native peasants fled and their property in turn was seized by the settler peasants. This situation, reflected in the Party, often leads to senseless conflicts. . . . Inside the Party, education must be intensified to ensure unity between these two sections of the membership.

The defection of the careerists. . . . In June many careerists took advantage of the Party's open recruitment of members and sneaked into the Party. . . . As soon as the White terror struck, the careerists defected and acted as guides for the counterrevolutionaries in rounding up our comrades. . . . After September the Party carried out a drastic house cleaning, and . . . underground organizations have been built up to prepare the Party for carrying on its activities when the reactionaries come. At the same time, we have been making every effort to penetrate into the White areas and operate inside the enemy camp. . . .

The leading bodies of the Party. . . . On May 20 the first Party congress of the border area was held at Maoping in Ningkang County, and it elected twenty-three people as members of the First Special Committee, with Mao Tse-tung as secretary. . . .

In October, after the Red Army's return to Ningkang, the Second Party Congress . . . elected the following nineteen people as members of the Second Special Committee: Tan Chen-lin, Chu Teh, Chen Yi, Lung Chao-ching, Chu Chang-chieh, Liu Tien-chien, Yuan Pan-chu, Tan Szu-tsung, Tan Ping, Li Chueh-fei, Sung Yi-yueh, Yuan Wen-tsai, Wang Tse-nung, Chen Cheng-jen, Mao Tse-tung, Wan Hsi-hsien, Wang Tso, Yang Kai-ming and Ho Ting-ying. A standing committee of five was formed, with Tan Chen-lin (a worker) as secretary and Chen Cheng-jen (an intellectual) as deputy secretary. . . .

The Sixth Party Congress of the Red Army was held on November 14 and it elected an Army Committee of twenty-three members, five of them forming a standing committee with Chu Teh as secretary. Both the Border Area Special Committee and the Army Committee are subordinate to the Front Committee. The Front Committee was reorganized on November 6, with the following five members designated by the Central Committee: Mao Tse-tung, Chu, Teh, the secretary of the local Party headquarters (Tan Chen-lin), a worker comrade (Sung Chiao-sheng), and a peasant comrade (Mao Ko-wen), with Mao Tse-tung as secretary. . . .

The proportion of workers and poor peasants should . . . be increased in the leading organs of the Party at all levels.

The Question of the Character of the Revolution

We fully agree with the Communist International's resolution on China. There is no doubt that China is still at the stage of the bourgeois-democratic revolution. The program for a thorough democratic revolution in China consists in, externally, the overthrow of imperialism so as to achieve complete national liberation, and, internally, the elimination of the power and influence of the comprador class in the cities, the completion of the agrarian revolution in order to abolish feudal relations in the villages, and the overthrow of the government of the warlords. We must go through such a democratic revolution before we can lay a real foundation for the transition to socialism. . . .

A special characteristic of the revolution in China, a country with a predominantly agricultural economy, is the use of military action to develop insurrection. We recommend that the Central Committee should devote great effort to military work.

The Question of the Location of Our Independent Regime

The area stretching from northern Kwangtung along the Hunan-Kiangsi border into southern Hupeh lies entirely within the Lohsiao mountain range. We have traversed the whole range, and a comparison of its different sections shows that the middle section, with Ningking as its center, is the most suitable for our armed independent regime. . . .

The middle section has the following advantages: (1) a mass base, which we have been cultivating for more than a year; (2) a fairly good basis for the Party organizations; (3) local armed forces which have been built up for more than a year and are well experienced in struggle—a rare achievement—and which, coupled with the Fourth Red Army, will prove indestructible in the face of any enemy force; (4) an excellent military base, the Chingkang Mountains, and bases for our local armed forces in all the counties; and (5) the influence this can exert on the two provinces and on the lower valleys of their rivers. . . .

. . . The fact that the Red Flag has never been lowered in the border area shows at once the strength of the Communist Party and the bankruptcy of the ruling classes, and this is of nationwide political significance. Therefore, we hold, as we have always held, that it is absolutely necessary and correct to build up and expand Red political power in the middle section of the Lohsiao mountain range.

This report was submitted by Mao Tse-tung to the Central Committee of the Chinese Communist Party.

On Correcting Mistaken Ideas in the Party

December 1929

There are various nonproletarian ideas in the Communist Party organization in the Fourth Red Army which greatly hinder the application of the Party's correct line. . . . In accordance with the spirit of the September letter of the Central Committee, this congress hereby points out the manifestations of various nonproletarian ideas in the Party organization in the Fourth Army, their sources, and the methods of correcting them, and calls upon all comrades to eliminate them thoroughly.

ON THE PURELY MILITARY VIEWPOINT

The purely military viewpoint is very highly developed among a number of comrades in the Red Army. It manifests itself as follows:

1. These comrades regard military affairs and politics as opposed to each other and refuse to recognize that military affairs are only one means of accomplishing political tasks. . . .

2. They think that the task of the Red Army, like that of the White Army, is merely to fight. They do not understand that the

Chinese Red Army is an armed body for carrying out the political tasks of the revolution. . . .

3. Hence, organizationally, these comrades subordinate the departments of the Red Army doing political work to those doing military work, and put forward the slogan: "Let Army Headquarters handle outside matters." . . .

4. . . . In propaganda work they overlook the importance of propaganda teams. . . . They neglect the organizing of soldiers' committees in the army and the organizing of the local workers and peasants. . . .

5. They become conceited when a battle is won and dispirited when a battle is lost.

6. They think only of the Fourth Army and do not realize that it is an important task of the Red Army to arm the local masses. This is cliquism in a magnified form.

7. . . . A few comrades in the Fourth Army believe that no other revolutionary forces exist . . . are addicted to conserving strength and avoiding action. This is . . . opportunism.

8. Some . . . suffer from the malady of revolutionary impetuosity . . . and will not do detailed work among the masses . . . and want only to do big things. This is a remnant of putschism.[1]

The sources of the purely military viewpoint are:

1. A low political level . . . failure to recognize the role of political leadership in the army.

2. The mentality of mercenaries . . . prisoners captured in past battles who have joined the Red Army.

3. . . . Overconfidence in military strength, and absence of confidence in the strength of the masses of the people.

4. The Party's failure actively to attend to and discuss military work. . . .

The methods of correction are as follows:

1. Raise the political level in the Party by means of education. . . . Eliminate the remnants of opportunism and putschism and break down the selfish departmentalism of the Fourth Army.

1. After the defeat of the revolution of 1927, a "Left" putschist tendency arose in the Communist Party. The putschist comrades refused to organize an orderly retreat and attempted to stage a series of local uprisings throughout the country, which had no prospect of success.

2. Intensify the political training of officers and men and especially the education of ex-prisoners. . . . Let local governments select workers and peasants experienced in struggle to join the Red Army. . . .

3. Arouse the local Party organizations to criticize the Party organizations in the Red Army. . . .

4. The Party must actively attend to and discuss military work. . . .

5. Draw up Red Army rules and regulations which clearly define its tasks, the relationship between its military and its political apparatus, the relationship between the Red Army and the masses of the people. . . .

On Ultra-Democracy

Since the Fourth Army of the Red Army accepted the directives of the Central Committee, there has been a decrease in manifestations of ultra-democracy . . . and no one any longer . . . demands: "Let the lower levels discuss all problems first, and then let the higher levels decide." Actually, however . . . ultra-democracy is still deep-rooted in the minds of many comrades. Witness the . . . reluctance to carry out Party decisions.

The methods of correction are as follows:

1. In the sphere of theory, destroy the roots of ultra-democracy. . . . The source of ultra-democracy consists in the petty bourgeoisie's individualistic aversion to discipline. . . . These ideas are utterly incompatible with the fighting tasks of the proletariat.

2. In the sphere of organization, ensure democracy under central-ized guidance . . . on the following lines:

The leading bodies of the Party must give a correct line of guidance and find solutions when problems arise, in order to establish themselves as centers of leadership. . . .

All decisions of any importance made by the Party's higher bodies must be promptly transmitted to the lower bodies and the Party rank and file. . . .

The lower bodies of the Party and the Party rank and file must discuss the higher bodies' directives in detail in order to understand their meaning thoroughly and decide on the methods of carrying them out.

On the Disregard of Organizational Discipline

Disregard of organizational discipline in the Party organization in the Fourth Army manifests itself as follows:

Failure of the minority to submit to the majority. For example, when a minority finds its motion voted down, it does not sincerely carry out the Party decisions. . . .

One requirement of Party discipline is that the minority should submit to the majority. It must support the decision passed by the majority. . . .

Inner-Party criticism is a weapon for strengthening the Party organization and increasing its fighting capacity. . . . It should not be used as a means of personal attack.

Many Party members make their criticisms not inside, but outside, the Party. . . . The method of correction is to educate Party members so that they understand the importance of Party organization and make their criticisms of Party committees or comrades at Party meetings.

On Absolute Equalitarianism

Absolute equalitarianism became quite serious in the Red Army at one time. Here are some examples. On the matter of allowances to wounded soldiers, there were objections to differentiating between light and serious cases, and a demand for equal allowances for all. When officers rode on horseback, it was regarded not as something necessary for performing their duties but as a sign of inequality. . . . It even went so far that when there were two wounded men and only one stretcher, neither could be carried away because each refused to yield priority to the other. . . .

We should point out that, before the abolition of capitalism, absolute equalitarianism is a mere illusion of peasants and small proprietors, and that even under socialism there can be no absolute equality, for material things will then be distributed on the principle of "from each according to his ability, to each according to his work" as well as on that of meeting the needs of the work. . . .

But absolute equalitarianism beyond reason must be opposed because it is not required by the struggle; on the contrary, it hinders the struggle.

ON SUBJECTIVISM

Subjectivism exists to a serious degree among some Party members, causing great harm to the analysis of the political situation and the guidance of the work . . . and results inevitably either in opportunism or in putschism. . . .

The main method of correction is to educate Party members so that a political and scientific spirit pervades their thinking and their Party life. To this end we must teach Party members to apply the Marxist-Leninist method in analyzing a political situation and appraising the class forces, instead of making a subjective analysis and appraisal; . . . help comrades to understand that without investigation of actual conditions they will fall into the pit of fantasy and putschism; . . . and guard against subjectivism, arbitrariness and vulgarization of criticism.

ON INDIVIDUALISM

The tendency toward individualism in the Red Army Party organization manifests itself as follows:

1. Retaliation. Some comrades, after being criticized inside the Party by a soldier comrade, look for opportunities to retaliate outside the Party. . . . One way is to beat or abuse the comrade. . . .

2. "Small group" mentality. Some comrades consider only the interests of their own small group and ignore the general interest. . . . Further effort is needed to overcome this.

3. The "employee" mentality. Some comrades do not understand that the Party and the Red Army, of which they are members, are both instruments for carrying out the tasks of the revolution; they do not realize that they themselves are makers of the revolution, but think that their responsibility is merely to their individual superiors. . . . This passive mentality of an "employee" is a manifestation of individualism. . . .

4. Pleasure seeking. In the Red Army there are also quite a few people whose individualism finds expression in pleasure seeking. They always hope that their unit will march into big cities. . . . The last thing they want is to work in the Red areas where life is hard.

5. Passivity. Some comrades become passive and stop working whenever anything goes against their wishes. . . .

6. The desire to leave the army. The number of people who ask for transfers from the Red Army to local work is on the increase. . . .

The method of correction is primarily to strengthen education so as to rectify individualism ideologically. Next . . . to make assignments and enforce discipline in a proper way. In addition, ways must be found to improve the material life of the Red Army . . . with rest and rehabilitation; and explain that individualism is a reflection within the Party of petty-bourgeois and bourgeois ideas.

ON THE IDEOLOGY OF ROVING REBEL BANDS

The political ideology of roving rebel bands has emerged in the Red Army because the proportion of vagabond elements is large and because there are great masses of vagabonds in China, especially in the southern provinces. . . . Some people . . . want to go to the big cities to eat and drink to their hearts' content. These manifestations . . . seriously hamper the Red Army in performing its proper tasks . . . and their eradication is an important objective. It must be understood that the ways of roving rebels of the Huang Chao[2] or Li Chuang[3] type are not permissible under present-day conditions.

2. Huang Chao was the leader of the peasant revolts toward the end of the Tang Dynasty. In A.D. 875 he led armed peasants against the imperial forces and styled himself the "Heaven-Storming General." He captured the imperial capital of Changan (now Sian in Shensi) and was crowned Emperor Chi. Internal dissensions and Tang-allied attacks compelled Huang to abandon the capital, however, and he committed suicide.

3. Li Chuang, short for Li Tzu-cheng the King Chuang (the Dare-All King), was the leader of a peasant revolt in Shensi which led to the overthrow of the Ming Dynasty, in 1628. He captured imperial Peking in 1644, and the last Ming Emperor committed suicide. Li's slogan was: "Support King Chuang and pay no grain taxes." He was eventually defeated by Wu San-kuei, a traitorous general of the Ming Dynasty.

The methods of correction are as follows:

1. Intensify education, criticize incorrect ideas, and eradicate the ideology of roving rebel bands.
2. Intensify education among the basic sections of the Red Army and among recently recruited captives to counter the vagabond outlook.
3. Draw active workers and peasants experienced in struggle into the ranks of the Red Army so as to change its composition.
4. Create new units of the Red Army from among the masses of militant workers and peasants.

On the Remnants of Putschism

The Party organization in the Red Army has already waged struggles against putschism, but not yet to a sufficient extent. . . . Their manifestations are: (1) Blind action regardless of subjective and objective conditions; (2) inadequate and irresolute application of the Party's policies for the cities; (3) slack military discipline, especially in moments of defeat; (4) acts of house-burning by some units; (5) the practices of shooting deserters and of inflicting corporal punishment, both of which smack of putschism. . . .

The methods of correction are as follows:

1. Eradicate putschism ideologically.
2. Correct putschist behavior through rules, regulations and policies.

This article was a resolution drawn up by Mao Tse-tung for the Ninth Party Congress of the Fourth Army of the Red Army. The resolution summed up the experience in the two years since the defeat of the Red Army in 1927, which encouraged the Red Army to build itself entirely on a Marxist-Leninist basis.

A Single Spark Can Start a Prairie Fire

January 5, 1930

Some comrades in our Party still do not know how to appraise the current situation correctly and how to settle the attendant question of what action to take. Though they believe that a revolutionary high tide is inevitable, they do not believe it to be imminent. . . .

They seem to think that, since the revolutionary high tide is remote, it will be labor lost to attempt to establish political power by hard work. . . . Their theory that we must first win over the masses on a countrywide scale and in all regions and then establish political power does not accord with the actual state of the Chinese revolution. This theory derives mainly from the failure to understand clearly that China is a semicolonial country for which many imperialist powers are contending. . . .

. . . In judging the political situation in China it is necessary to understand the following:

1. Although the subjective[1] forces of the revolution in China are now weak, so also are all organizations (organs of political power, armed forces, political parties, etc.) of the reactionary ruling classes, resting as they do on the backward and fragile social and economic structure of China. . . .

2. The subjective forces of the revolution have indeed been greatly weakened since the defeat of the revolution in 1927. The remaining forces are very small and those comrades who judge by appearances alone naturally feel pessimistic. But if we judge by essentials, it is quite another story. Here we can apply the old Chinese saying, "A single spark can start a prairie fire." In other words, our forces, although small at present, will grow very rapidly. . . . When we look at a thing, we must examine its essence and treat its appearance merely as an usher at the threshold, and once we cross the threshold, we must grasp the essence of the thing; this is the only reliable and scientific method of analysis.

3. Similarly, in appraising the counterrevolutionary forces, we

1. The "subjective" forces of the revolution mean the organized forces of the revolution.

must never look merely at their appearance, but should examine their essence. . . .

4. . . . There are famine and banditry everywhere and the peasant masses and the urban poor can hardly keep alive. . . . The reactionary government . . . endlessly expands its armies . . . schools have no money . . . graduates have no hope of employment. . . . All China is littered with dry faggots which will soon be aflame. The saying, "A single spark can start a prairie fire," is an apt description of how the current situation will develop. We need only look at the strikes by the workers, the uprisings by the peasants, the mutinies of soldiers and the strikes of students which are developing in many places to see that it cannot be long before a "spark" kindles "a prairie fire."

The gist of the above was already contained in the letter from the Front Committee to the Central Committee on April 5, 1929, which reads in part:

. . . Passivity among comrades in the Party will quickly disappear as the counterrevolutionary tide gradually ebbs. The masses will certainly come over to us. The Kuomintang's policy of massacre only serves to "drive the fish into deep waters,"[2] as the saying goes, and reformism no longer has any mass appeal. It is certain that the masses will soon shed their illusions about the Kuomintang. In the emerging situation, no other party will be able to compete with the Communist Party in winning over the masses. . . .

When I say that there will soon be a high tide of revolution in China, I am emphatically not speaking of something which in the words of some people "is possibly coming," something illusory, unattainable and devoid of significance for action. It is like a ship far out at sea whose mast-head can already be seen from the shore; it is like the morning sun in the east whose shimmering rays are visible from a high mountain top; it is like a child about to be born moving restlessly in its mother's womb.

This was a letter written by Mao Tse-tung in criticism of certain pessimistic views then existing in the Chinese Communist Party.

2. The quotation is from Mencius, who compared a tyrant who drove his people into seeking a benevolent ruler to the otter which "drives the fish into deep waters."

Pay Attention to Economic Work

August 20, 1933

The growing intensity of the revolutionary war makes it imperative for us to mobilize the masses in order to launch an immediate campaign on the economic front and undertake all possible and necessary tasks of economic construction. . . .

Some comrades have thought it impossible to spare time for economic construction because the revolutionary war keeps people busy enough, and they have condemned anyone arguing for it as a "Right deviationist." In their opinion economic construction is impossible in the midst of a revolutionary war and is possible only in the peaceful, tranquil conditions prevailing after final victory. Comrades, such views are wrong. Whoever holds them fails to realize that without building up the economy it is impossible to secure the material prerequisites for the revolutionary war, and the people will become exhausted in the course of a long war. . . .

Our objective is not only to expand production but also to sell our products at fair prices to the White areas and then purchase salt and cloth cheaply for distribution among our people, so as to break the enemy's blockade and check the merchants' exploitation. . . .

It will be impossible to get a rapid campaign going on the economic front without a correct style of leadership and correct methods of work. . . . For these reasons I want to direct our comrades' attention to the following.

Firstly, mobilize the masses. . . . Supervise and check up on such items of work as the sale of bonds, the formation of co-operatives, the regulation of food supplies, promotion of . . . trade. . . .

Secondly, we must not be bureaucratic in our methods of mobilizing the masses. . . . We must reject commandism; what we need is energetic propaganda to convince the masses. . . .

Thirdly, large numbers of cadres are needed to extend the campaign of economic construction. This is not a matter of scores or hundreds of people, but of thousands and tens of thousands whom we must organize, train and send to the economic construction front. . . .

Fourthly, economic construction today is inseparable not only from the general task of the war but from other tasks as well. Only if there is a thorough check-up on land distribution[1] will it be possible to abolish feudal and semifeudal ownership of land completely, enhance the peasants' enthusiasm for production and swiftly draw the peasant masses into economic construction. Only if the labor laws are resolutely enforced will it be possible to better the life of the workers, bring them speedily into active participation in economic construction and strengthen their leadership of the peasants. Only if there is correct leadership in the elections and in the exposure campaigns[2] which accompany the check-up on land distribution will it be possible to strengthen our government bodies so that they can give more vigorous leadership in the revolutionary war and in all our work, including economic work. . . .

This speech was delivered at the economic construction conference of seventeen counties in southern Kiangsi in August 1933.

How to Differentiate the Classes in the Rural Areas
October 1933

THE LANDLORD

A landlord is a person who owns land, does not engage in labor himself, or does so only to a very small extent, and lives by exploiting the peasants. . . .

Warlords, officials, local tyrants and evil gentry are political repre-

1. The Communist campaign to enlist active support of the vast peasant population was based on promises of "land to the tiller," a promise which the Communist leaders knew would encourage the nonlandowners to revolt against the landowners, but which the peasants were not told would at a later stage deprive them, too, of the land "distributed" to them.
2. "Exposure campaigns" were exhortations to the people to "expose" misdeeds by the functionaries of the Communist government.

sentatives and exceptionally ruthless members of the landlord class.
. . .[1]

Usurers are persons who rely on exploitation by usury as their main source of income, and shall be put in the same category as landlords.

THE RICH PEASANT

The rich peasant as a rule owns land. But some rich peasants own only part of their land and rent the remainder. Others have no land of their own at all and rent all their land. The rich peasant generally has rather more and better instruments of production and more liquid capital than the average and engages in labor himself, but always relies on exploitation for part or even the major part of his income. . . .

THE MIDDLE PEASANT

Many middle peasants own land. Some own only part of their land and rent the rest. Others own no land of their own at all and rent all their land. All of them have a fair number of farm implements. A middle peasant derives his income wholly or mainly from his own labor. . . .

THE POOR PEASANT

Among the poor peasants some own part of their land and have a few odd farm implements, others own no land at all but only a few odd farm implements. As a rule, poor peasants have to rent the land they work on and are subjected to exploitation, having to pay land rent and interest on loans and to hire themselves out to some extent. . . .

1. There were various forms of public land in China's rural areas—land owned by the township or district government, by the ancestral temple of a clan, by a Buddhist or Taoist temple, a Catholic church or a mosque; or land the income from which was used for public welfare purposes such as famine relief, or the building and maintenance of bridges and roads, or for educational purposes. These lands and the incomes derived from them were administered by their local governments.

THE WORKER

The worker (including the farm laborer) as a rule owns no land or farm implements, though some do own a very small amount of land and very few farm implements. Workers make their living wholly or mainly by selling their labor power.

Mao Tse-tung wrote this document in October 1933 to rectify the deviations that had occurred in the work of land reform and to provide a solution for the land problem. It was adopted by the Workers' and Peasants' Democratic Central Government of that time as establishing the criteria for determining class status in the rural areas.

Our Economic Policy

January 23, 1934

. . . The imperialists and the Kuomintang are bent on wrecking the Red areas, the work of economic construction now in progress there, and the welfare of millions of workers and peasants who have achieved liberation.[1] For this purpose, they have pursued a ruthless policy of economic blockade, in addition to organizing forces for military campaigns of "encirclement and suppression." . . . We have not only smashed one campaign after another, but have also been doing all the essential work of economic construction within our power. . . .

The focus of our economic construction is to increase agricultural and industrial production, expand our trade with the outside, and develop the co-operatives. . . .

The women are taking part in production in great numbers. None

1. Mutual-aid groups and plowing teams were organized among the peasants in the Red areas after the "distribution" of land, in order to facilitate production. After the state confiscated the land from the poor peasants to whom it had been "distributed," the mutual aid became forced communal labor on state-owned land.

of this could have happened in the Kuomintang days. With the land in the hands of the landlords, the peasants then were neither willing to improve it nor possessed the means to do so. Only since we have distributed the land to the peasants and encouraged and rewarded production has their labor enthusiasm blossomed forth and great success in production been achieved. . . .

Our economy is made up of three sectors: state enterprise, co-operative enterprise, and private enterprise.

At present, state enterprise is limited to what is possible and essential. State-operated industry and commerce have begun to grow and they have boundless prospects.

As regards the private sector of the economy, we shall not hamper it, indeed we shall promote and encourage it, so long as it does not transgress the legal limits set by the government. For the development of private enterprise is essential to the interests of the state and the people at the present stage. . . .

Co-operative enterprise is growing rapidly. There are altogether 1,423 co-operatives of various kinds, with a total capital of over 300,000 *yuan*, according to the September 1933 figures for seventeen counties in Kiangsi and Fukien. Consumers' co-operatives and grain co-operatives head the list, with the producers' co-operatives coming next, and credit co-operatives have just started functioning. . . .

At a time when the country is plunged in economic disaster, when hundreds of millions of people are suffering the terrible hardships of hunger and cold, the people's government in our areas is staunchly pressing ahead with economic construction. . . . Only by defeating imperialism and the Kuomintang and by undertaking planned, organized economic construction can we deliver the people of the whole of China from unprecedented disaster.

This report was given by Mao Tse-tung at the Second National Congress of Workers' and Peasants' Representatives held in Juichin, Kiangsi Province, in January 1934.

Be Concerned with the Well-Being of the Masses, Pay Attention to Methods of Work

January 27, 1934

There are two questions which comrades have failed to stress during the discussion and which, I feel, should be dealt with.

The first concerns the well-being of the masses.

Our central task at present is to mobilize the broad masses to take part in the revolutionary war, overthrow imperialism and the Kuomintang by means of such war, spread the revolution throughout the country, and drive imperialism out of China. . . .

I earnestly suggest to this congress that we pay close attention to the well-being of the masses, from the problems of land and labor to those of fuel, rice, cooking oil and salt. The women want to learn plowing and harrowing. Whom can we get to teach them? The children want to go to school. Have we set up primary schools? The wooden bridge over there is too narrow and people may fall off. Should we not repair it? Many people suffer from boils and other ailments. What are we going to do about it? All such problems concerning the well-being of the masses should be placed on our agenda. . . .

If we do so, the masses will surely support us and regard the revolution as their most glorious banner, as their very life. In the event of a Kuomintang attack on the Red areas they will fight the Kuomintang to the death. There can be no doubt about this. . . .

The Kuomintang is now pursuing a policy of blockhouse warfare,[1] feverishly constructing its "tortoise shells" as though they were iron bastions. . . . The czar of Russia was one of the world's most ferocious rulers, yet when the proletariat and the peasantry rose in revolution, was there anything left of him? No, nothing. His bastions of iron? They all crumbled. . . .

1. The building of blockhouses around the Red areas was a military tactic of the Nationalist Government in its campaign against Communist revolution in Kiangsi Province.

What is a true bastion of iron? It is the masses, the millions upon millions of people who genuinely and sincerely support the revolution. . . . Rallying millions upon millions of people round the revolutionary government and expanding our revolutionary war, we shall wipe out all counterrevolution and take over the whole of China.

The second question concerns our methods of work.

We are the leaders and organizers of the revolutionary war as well as the leaders and organizers of the life of the masses. . . . Unless the problem of method is solved, talk about the task is useless. Unless we pay attention to giving leadership to the work of expanding the Red Army and devote particular care to our methods, we will never succeed even though we recite the phrase "Expand the Red Army" a thousand times. Nor can we accomplish our tasks in any other field, for instance, in checking up on land distribution, or in economic construction, or culture and education, or our work in the new areas and the outlying districts, if all we do is set the tasks without attending to the methods of carrying them out, without combatting bureaucratic methods of work and adopting practical and concrete ones, and without discarding commandist methods and adopting the method of patient persuasion. . . .

This was part of the concluding speech made by Mao Tse-tung at the Second National Congress of Workers' and Peasants' Representatives held in Juichin, Kiangsi Province, in January 1934.

On Tactics Against Japanese Imperialism
December 27, 1935

THE CHARACTERISTICS OF THE PRESENT POLITICAL SITUATION

Comrades! A great change has now taken place in the political situation. Our Party has defined its tasks in the light of this changed situation.

What is the present situation?

Its main characteristic is that Japanese imperialism wants to turn China into a colony.

As we all know, for nearly a hundred years China has been a semicolonial country jointly dominated by several imperialist powers. Owing to the Chinese people's struggle against imperialism and to conflicts among the imperialist powers, China has been able to retain a semiindependent status. For a time World War I gave Japanese imperialism the opportunity of dominating China exclusively. But the treaty surrendering China to Japan, the Twenty-one Demands[1] signed by Yuan Shih-kai,[2] the archtraitor of that time, was inevitably rendered null and void as a result of the Chinese people's fight against Japanese imperialism and of the intervention of other imperialist powers. In 1922 at the Washington Nine Power Conference[3] called by the United States, a treaty was signed which once again placed China under the joint domination of several imperialist powers. But before long the situation changed again. The Incident of September 18, 1931,[4] began the present stage of Japan's colonization

1. The Twenty-one Demands on President Yuan Shih-kai's government were presented by Japan on January 18, 1915. They were made up of five main groups, the first four of which were agreed to and implemented: transfer to Japan of the territory and rights Germany had acquired in Shantung; rights to lease and own land in Manchuria and Mongolia; to reorganize the Chinese steel industry as a Sino-Japanese enterprise; not to lease or cede any coastal islands to any third power. The fifth, never implemented, was for Japan to control China's political, financial, military and police affairs.

2. Yuan Shih-kai, a northern warlord at the time of the overthrow of the Ching Dynasty, declared himself China's first President. Sun Yat Sen, who sparked the revolution, stood aside in order to avoid civil war which would have been inevitable had he made a strong bid for the post.

3. The Nine Power Conference was held in Washington, D.C., on February 6, 1922. A nine power treaty was signed by the United States, Great Britain, France, Italy, Japan, Belgium, The Netherlands, Portugal, and China. The eight powers other than China were committed by the treaty to withdraw their armed forces from China as soon as China could "assure the protection of the lives and property of foreigners." The treaty also pledged the powers to respect China's territorial integrity. After Japan invaded Manchuria in 1932, enthroned puppet Emperor Kang Teh (Mr. Henry Pu Yi), and renamed Manchuria "Manchukuo," H. R. Ekins of the United Press in his book *China Fights for Her Life* charged angrily, "China lifted her bloody head and gazed upon a world that had betrayed her."

4. On September 18, 1931, the Japanese Kwantung Army launched an assault upon the three provinces of Manchuria, as the result of which they later changed the name of the peninsula from Manchuria to Manchukuo, making it a colonial appendage of Japan. This became known as the "September 18 Incident."

of China. As Japanese aggression was temporarily limited to the four northeastern provinces, some people felt that the Japanese imperialists would probably advance no farther. Today things are different. The Japanese imperialists have already shown their intention of penetrating south of the Great Wall and occupying all China. . . . Japanese aggression was temporarily limited to the four northeastern provinces, some people felt that the Japanese imperialists would probably advance no farther. Today things are different. The Japanese imperialists have already shown their intention of penetrating south of the Great Wall and occupying all China. . . .

This faces all classes and political groups in China with the question of what to do. Resist? Surrender? Or vacillate between the two?

Now let us see how the different classes in China answer this question.

The workers and the peasants are all demanding resistance. The revolution of 1924–27, the agrarian revolution from 1927 to the present day, and the anti-Japanese tide since the Incident of September 18, 1931, have all proved that the working class and peasantry are the most resolute forces in the Chinese revolution. . . .

But how do the national bourgeoisie, the comprador and landlord classes, and the Kuomintang face up to this question? . . . Their chieftain is Chiang Kai-shek. This camp of traitors are deadly enemies of the Chinese people. Japanese imperialism could not have become so blatant in its aggression were it not for this pack of traitors. They are the running dogs of imperialism. . . . In the new situation in which China is threatened, they may change their attitude. . . . On the one hand they dislike imperialism, and on the other they fear thorough revolution, and so they vacillate between the two. This explains why they took part in the revolution of 1924–27 and why, in the end, they went over to Chiang Kai-shek's side. In what respect does the present period differ from 1927 when Chiang Kai-shek betrayed the revolution? China was then still a semicolony, but now she is on the way to becoming a colony. . . .

In making a general analysis of the attitude of the Chinese landlord class and the bourgeoisie in times of great upheaval, we should also point to another aspect, namely, that even the landlord and comprador camp is not completely united. The reason is that China is a semicolonial country for which many imperialist powers are contending. When the struggle is directed against Japanese imperialism, then the running dogs of the United States or Britain, obeying the varying tones of their masters' commands, may engage in veiled or even open strife with the Japanese imperialists and their running dogs. . . .

But such fights, such rifts, such contradictions are of use to the revolutionary people. We must turn to good account all such fights, rifts and contradictions in the enemy camp and turn them against our present main enemy. . . .

Now let us discuss the situation in the camp of China's national revolution.

First, the Red Army. For almost a year and a half the three main contingents of the Chinese Red Army have carried out great shifts of position . . . abandoned their old positions and moved to new regions. These great shifts have turned the old areas into guerrilla zones. . . . From this aspect of the overall situation, the enemy has won a temporary and partial victory, while we have suffered a temporary and partial defeat. . . . Some people say that the Central Red Army has failed. Is that correct? No. For it is not a statement of fact. In approaching a problem a Marxist should see the whole as well as the parts. A frog in a well says, "The sky is no bigger than the mouth of the well." That is untrue. . . .

In one respect the enemy won a victory (i.e., in occupying our original positions), but in another respect he has failed (i.e., failed to execute his plan of "encirclement and suppression" and of "pursuit and suppression"). That is the only appropriate formulation, for we have completed the Long March.

Speaking of the Long March, one may ask, "What is its significance?" We answer that the Long March is the first of its kind in the annals of history, that it is a manifesto, a propaganda force, a seeding machine. Since Pan Ku[5] divided the heavens from the earth and the Three Sovereigns and Five Emperors reigned, has history ever witnessed a Long March such as ours? . . .

We were encircled and pursued, obstructed and intercepted by a huge force of several hundred thousand men; yet by using our two legs we swept across a distance of more than 20,000 *li*[6] through the length and breadth of eleven provinces. . . . The Long March is

5. Pan Ku, according to Chinese mythology, was the creator of the world and the first ruler of mankind. The Three Sovereigns and Five Emperors were legendary rulers in ancient China.
6. A *li* is approximately one-third of a mile.

also a propaganda force. It has announced to some 200 million people in eleven provinces that the road of the Red Army is their only road to liberation. Without the Long March, how could the broad masses have learned so quickly about the existence of the great truth which the Red Army embodies? . . . In the eleven provinces it has sown many seeds which will sprout, leaf, blossom, and bear fruit, and will yield a harvest in the future. Without the Communist Party, a Long March of this kind would have been inconceivable. The Chinese Communist Party, its leadership, its cadres and its members fear no difficulties or hardships. Whoever questions our ability to lead the revolutionary war will fall into the morass of opportunism. . . .

THE NATIONAL UNITED FRONT

Having surveyed the situation with regard to both the counterrevolution and the revolution, we shall find it easy to define the Party's tactical tasks. . . .

We say that the present situation is one in which a new high tide in the national revolution is imminent and in which China is on the eve of a great new nationwide revolution; . . . this is a fact, and it represents one aspect of the matter. But we must also say that imperialism is still a force to be earnestly reckoned with, that the unevenness in the development of the revolutionary forces is a serious weakness, and that to defeat our enemies we must be prepared to fight a protracted war. . . .

The present situation demands that we boldly discard all closeddoorism, form a broad united front and guard against adventurism. We must not plunge into decisive battles until the time is ripe and unless we have the necessary strength. . . .

United front tactics . . . requires the recruiting of large forces for the purpose of surrounding and annihilating the enemy. Closed-door tactics . . . means fighting singlehanded in desperate combat against a formidable enemy.

The advocates of united front tactics say . . . a proper estimate must be made of the changes in alignment of the revolutionary and counterrevolutionary forces in China. . . . Without a proper estimate . . . we shall be unable . . . to use the united front as a means of organizing and rallying millions of people and all the armies that are potentially friendly to the revolution.

The advocates of closed-door tactics say . . . the forces of the revolution must be straight, absolutely straight; nothing is correct except what is literally recorded in Holy Writ; . . . not an inch must be conceded to the rich peasants; the yellow trade unions must be fought tooth and nail; . . . intellectuals are three-day revolutionaries whom it is dangerous to recruit. It follows therefore that closed-doorism is the sole wonder-working magic, while the united front is an opportunist tactic.

Comrades, which is right, the united front or closed-doorism? Which indeed is approved by Marxism-Leninism? I answer without the slightest hesitation—the united front and not closed-doorism. . . . We definitely want no closed-doorism; what we want is the revolutionary national united front, which will spell death to the Japanese imperialists and the traitors and collaborators.

THE PEOPLE'S REPUBLIC

If our government has hitherto been based on the alliance of the workers, the peasants and the urban petty bourgeoisie, from now on it must be so transformed as to include also the members of all other classes who are willing to take part in the national revolution. . . .

The revolution failed in 1927 chiefly because, with the opportunist line then prevailing in the Communist Party, no effort was made to expand our own ranks (the workers' and peasants' movement and the armed forces led by the Communist Party), and exclusive reliance was placed on a temporary ally, the Kuomintang. The result was that when imperialism ordered its lackeys, the landlord and comprador classes, to spread their numerous tentacles and draw over first Chiang Kai-shek and then Wang Ching-wei, the revolution suffered defeat. . . .

Today things are quite different. Now we have a strong Communist Party and a strong Red Army, and we also have the base areas of the Red Army. . . . However, we must be very vigilant because the Japanese imperialists and Chiang Kai-shek will undoubtedly resort to every possible form of intimidation and bribery. . . . Two basic forces are now locked in struggle, and in the nature of things all the forces in between will have to line up on one side or the other. The Japanese imperialists' policy of subjugating China and Chiang Kai-shek's policy of betraying China will inevitably drive many people over to our side—either directly into joining the ranks of the Communist Party and the Red Army or into forming a united front with us. . . .

Why change the "workers' and peasants' republic" into a "people's republic"? Our government represents not only the workers and peasants but the whole nation. . . .

There is, of course, a clash of interests between the working class and the national bourgeoisie. We shall not be able to extend the national revolution successfully unless the working class, the vanguard of the national revolution, is accorded political and economic rights and is enabled to direct its strength against imperialism and its running dogs, the traitors.

However, if the national bourgeoisie joins the anti-imperialist united front, the working class and the national bourgeoisie will have interests in common. In the period of the bourgeois-democratic revolution, the people's republic will not expropriate private property other than imperialist and feudal private property, and so far from confiscating the national bourgeoisie's industrial and commercial enterprises, it will encourage their development. We shall protect every national capitalist who does not support the imperialists or the Chinese traitors.

It is perfectly obvious that the Chinese revolution at the present stage is still a bourgeois-democratic and not a proletarian socialist revolution in nature. Only the counterrevolutionary Trotskyites talk such nonsense as that China has already completed her bourgeois-democratic revolution and that any further revolution can only be socialist. . . .

The change in the revolution will come later. In the future the democratic revolution will inevitably be transformed into a socialist revolution. As to when the transition will take place, that will depend on the presence of the necessary conditions, and it may take quite a long time. . . .

International Support

Finally, a word is necessary about the relation between the Chinese and the world revolution.

There is an old adage, "In the Spring and Autumn Era there were no righteous wars." . . .[7]

All wars anywhere in the world in which the people rise up to fight their oppressors are just struggles. The February and October Revolutions in Russia were just wars. The revolutions of the people in various European countries after World War I were just struggles. In China, the Anti-Opium War,[8] the War of the Taiping Heavenly Kingdom,[9] the Yi Ho Tuan War,[10] the Revolutionary War of 1911,[11] the Northern Expedition of 1926–27, the Agrarian Revolutionary War from 1927 to the present, and the present resistance to

7. This quotation is from Mencius. Mencius made the remark because, in the period known as the Spring and Autumn Era (722–481 B.C.) the feudal princes of China incessantly fought one another for power.

8. One of the most deplorable of the many eighteenth- and nineteenth-century assaults upon peoples unable to defend themselves, by so-called civilized Western nations, was the Opium War, in 1840–42, in which Britain, by force of arms, introduced opium from the Near East into China (until then it had been entirely unknown there), with great profit to the British opium merchants and dreadful consequences to the Chinese people.

9. The Taiping Rebellion, an abortive war that devastated several provinces of China, was organized and led by Hung Hsiu-chuan, a schoolteacher who had failed in the civil service examinations, and who then, through his own interpretation of Protestant missionary teachings, believed he was called by God to wean the Chinese people from worship of idols. With the help of a British officer, Major Charles George Gordon, nicknamed "Chinese Gordon," the Manchu Government quashed the rebellion in 1864. It cost millions of lives, to no useful purpose.

10. The Yi Ho Tuan (Righteous Harmony Fists) War, in 1900, known to the West as the Boxer Rebellion, had as its slogan "Protect the country, destroy the foreigner." It erupted as an attempt by Chinese in Peking and the surrounding areas to rebel against foreign aggression and encroachment upon China. The Boxers murdered scores of foreign Protestant and Catholic missionaries and thousands of Chinese Christians. In retaliation, a mixed force of Western Powers invaded Peking on August 14, and, without declaration of war, destroyed the Boxer forces, looted the capital city, and levied war indemnities on the government of the Dowager Empress who had hoped, without herself becoming involved, that the foreigners would be driven out of China.

11. The forerunner of the 1926–27 revolution was prematurely set in motion in 1911, under the leadership of Dr. Sun Yat Sen, but it was inadequately organized and led. On October 10, 1911, the imperial troops in Wuchang mutinied, and the rebellion spread to several neighboring provinces. General Yuan Shih-kai, who had been removed from command of the Manchu Government's troops for offenses against the late Emperor a decade previously, was recalled to command the government's northern armies, and in November he was made Premier. On February 12, 1912, the boy-Emperor (the six-year-old nephew of the childless late Emperor Kwang Hsu) was made to abdicate

Japan and punitive actions against traitors—these are all just wars.
. . . All just wars support each other, while all unjust wars should
be turned into just wars—this is the Leninist line.

Our war against Japan needs the support of the people of the
whole world and, above all, the support of the people of the Soviet
Union, which they will certainly give us because they and we are
bound together in a common cause. . . .

**This report was given by Mao Tse-tung at the conference of Party
activists held at Wayaopao, northern Shensi, after the meeting of the
Political Bureau of the Central Committee in December 1935. This
meeting criticized the view in the Party that the Chinese national
bourgeoisie could not be an ally of the workers and peasants in the
fight against Japan.**

Problems of Strategy
in China's Revolutionary War

December 1936

CHAPTER I: HOW TO STUDY WAR

The Laws of War Are Developmental

The laws of war are a problem which anyone directing a war must
study and solve.

The laws of revolutionary war are a problem which anyone directing
a revolutionary war must study and solve. . . .

War is the highest form of struggle for resolving contradictions,
when they have developed to a certain stage, between classes, nations,
states, or political groups, and it has existed ever since the emergence
of private property and of classes. . . .

---

the throne, and Yuan Shih-kai assumed full powers to organize a republican
government. In order to prevent civil war between north and south, Sun Yat
Sen, who had set up a provisional government in Nanking, resigned, and
Yuan Shih-kai was acknowledged to be the Republic's first President. His first
act was to transfer the seat of the Republic of China from Nanking to Peking.

Revolutionary war, whether a revolutionary class war or a revolutionary national war, has its own specific circumstances and nature, in addition to the circumstances and nature of war in general. . . .

China's revolutionary war, whether civil war or national war, is waged in the specific environment of China and so has its own specific circumstances and nature, distinguishing it both from war in general and from revolutionary war in general. . . .

Some people hold a wrong view, which we refuted long ago. They say that it is enough merely to study the laws of war in general, merely to follow the military manuals published by the reactionary military academies in China. . . . If we . . . apply them without . . . change we shall be "cutting the feet to fit the shoes". . . and shall be defeated. . . .

Others hold a second wrong view. . . . They say it is enough merely to study the experience of revolutionary war in Russia . . . and the military manuals published by Soviet military organizations. This would also be "cutting the feet to fit the shoes." . . . They fail to see that while we should set special store by the war experience of the Soviet Union . . . under the guidance of Lenin and Stalin, we should . . . cherish the experience of China's revolutionary war, because there are many factors that are specific to the Chinese revolution and the Chinese Red Army.

Still others hold a third wrong view . . . that the most valuable experience is that of the Northern Expedition of 1926–27, and that we must . . . imitate the Northern Expedition in driving straight ahead to seize the big cities. . . . Because the circumstances of our present war are different, we should take from the Northern Expedition only what still applies today, and work out something of our own in the light of present conditions. . . .

The Aim of War Is to Eliminate War

War, this monster of mutual slaughter among men, will be finally eliminated by the progress of human society, and in the not too distant future too. . . . History knows only two kinds of war, just and unjust. We support just wars and oppose unjust wars. All counterrevolutionary wars are unjust, all revolutionary wars are just. . . .

A war waged by the majority of mankind and of the Chinese

people is beyond doubt a just war, a most lofty and glorious undertaking for the salvation of mankind and China, and a bridge to a new era in world history. When human society advances to the point where classes and states are eliminated, there will be no more wars, counterrevolutionary or revolutionary, unjust or just; that will be the era of perpetual peace for mankind. Our study of the laws of revolutionary war springs from the desire to eliminate all wars; herein lies the distinction between us Communists and all the exploiting classes.

Strategy Is the Study of the Laws of a War Situation as a Whole

Wherever there is war, there is a war situation as a whole. The war situation as a whole may cover the entire world, may cover an entire country, or may cover an independent guerrilla zone or an independent major operational front. . . . The task of the science of strategy is to study those laws for directing a war that govern a war situation as a whole. The task of the science of campaigns and the science of tactics is to study those laws for directing a war that govern a partial situation. . . .

The problems of strategy include the following:

Giving proper consideration to the relation between the enemy and ourselves. Giving proper consideration to the relationship between various campaigns or between various operational areas. Giving proper consideration to those parts which have a bearing on (are decisive for) the situation as a whole. Giving proper consideration to the special features contained in the general situation. Giving proper consideration to the relation between the front and the rear. Giving proper consideration to the distinction between fighting and resting, between concentration and dispersion, between attack and defense, between advance and retreat, between concealment and exposure, between the main attack and supplementary attacks, between assault and containing action, between centralized command and decentralized command, between protracted war and war of quick decision, between positional war and mobile war, between our own forces and friendly forces, between one military arm and another, between higher and lower levels, between cadres and the rank and file, between old and new soldiers, between Red areas and White areas, between old Red areas and new ones, between the central district and the borders of a given base area, between the warm season and the cold season, between victory and defeat, between large and small troop formations, between the regular army and the guerrilla forces, between destroying the enemy and winning over the masses, between expanding the Red Army and consolidating it, between military work and political work, between past and present tasks, between present and future tasks, between tasks arising from one set of circumstances and tasks arising from another, between fixed fronts and fluid fronts, between civil war and national war, between one historical stage and another, etc., etc.

None of these problems of strategy is visible to the eye, and yet, if we think hard, we can comprehend, grasp and master them all, and solve them. Our task in studying the problems of strategy is to attain this goal.

The Important Thing Is to Be Good at Learning

. . . To learn is no easy matter and to apply what one has learned is even harder. Many people appear impressive when discoursing on military science in classrooms or in books, but when it comes to actual fighting, some win battles and others lose them. . . .

In real life, we cannot ask for "ever-victorious generals," who are few and far between in history. What we can ask for is generals who are brave and sagacious and who normally win their battles in the course of a war, generals who combine wisdom with courage. To become both wise and courageous one must acquire a method, a method to be employed in learning as well as in applying what has been learned. . . .

All military laws and military theories which are in the nature of principles are the experience of past wars summed up by people in former days or in our own times. We should seriously study these lessons, paid for in blood, which are a heritage of past wars. That is one point. But there is another. We should put these conclusions to the test of our own experience, assimilating what is useful, rejecting what is useless, and adding specifically our own. The latter is very important, for otherwise we cannot direct a war.

Reading is learning . . . but our chief method is to learn warfare through warfare. A person who has had no opportunity to go to school can also learn warfare—he can learn through fighting in war. . . .

CHAPTER II: THE CHINESE COMMUNIST PARTY
AND CHINA'S REVOLUTIONARY WAR

China's revolutionary war, which began in 1924, has passed through two stages, the first from 1924 to 1927, and the second from 1927 to 1936; the stage of national revolutionary war against Japan will now commence. In all three of its stages this revolutionary war has been, is and will be fought under the leadership of the Chinese proletariat and its Party, the Chinese Communist Party. . . .

In this era, any revolutionary war will definitely end in defeat if it lacks, or runs counter to, the leadership of the proletariat and the Communist Party. . . .

This revolutionary war is led by the Communist Party alone, which has established absolute leadership over it. This absolute leadership is the most important condition enabling the revolutionary war to be carried through firmly to the end. Without it, it is inconceivable that the revolutionary war could have been carried on with such perseverance. . . .

The Chinese Communist Party has led and continues to lead the stirring, magnificent and victorious revolutionary war. This war is not only the banner of China's liberation, but has international revolutionary significance as well. The eyes of the revolutionary people the world over are upon us. In the new stage, the stage of the anti-Japanese national revolutionary war, we shall lead the Chinese revolution to its completion and exert a profound influence on the revolution in the East and in the whole world. . . .

CHAPTER III: CHARACTERISTICS OF
CHINA'S REVOLUTIONARY WAR

The Importance of the Subject

People who do not know that China's revolutionary war has its own characteristics have equated the war waged by the Red Army against the Kuomintang forces with the civil war in the Soviet Union. The experience of the civil war in the Soviet Union directed by Lenin and Stalin has a worldwide significance. All Communist parties, including the Chinese Communist Party, regard this experience and its theoretical summing up by Lenin and Stalin as their guide. But this does not mean that we should apply it mechanically to our own conditions. In many of its aspects China's revolutionary war has characteristics distinguishing it from the civil war in the Soviet Union. This point has been fully borne out in our ten years of war.

Our enemy has made similar mistakes. He did not recognize that fighting against the Red Army required a different strategy and different tactics from those used in fighting other forces. He took us lightly and stuck to his old methods. . . . That was how Chiang Kai-shek's Officers' Training Corps at Lushan came into being and how the new reactionary military principles applied in the fifth campaign of "encirclement and suppression" were evolved.

But when the enemy changed his military principles to suit operations against the Red Army, there appeared in our ranks a group of people who reverted to the "old ways." . . . This group of people called themselves "Marxist-Leninists," but actually they had not learned an iota of Marxism-Leninism. Lenin said that the most essential thing in Marxism, the living soul of Marxism, is the concrete analysis of concrete conditions.[1] That was precisely the point these comrades of ours forgot. . . .

Without an understanding of the characteristics of China's revolutionary war, it is impossible to direct it and lead it to victory.

What Are the Characteristics of China's Revolutionary War?

What are the characteristics of China's revolutionary war? I think there are four principal ones.

The first is that China is a vast, semicolonial country which is unevenly developed politically and economically and which has gone through the revolution of 1924–27. . . .

The second characteristic is that our enemy is big and powerful. . . .

1. See V. I. Lenin, "Communism," in which Lenin, criticizing the Hungarian Communist Bela Kun, said that he "gives up the most essential thing in Marxism, the living soul of Marxism, the concrete analysis of concrete conditions."—From *Collected Works* (Russ. ed., Moscow, 1950), Vol. XXXI, p. 143.

The third characteristic is that the Red Army is small and weak. . . .

The fourth characteristic is Communist Party leadership and the agrarian revolution . . . which has the support of the peasantry.

Our Strategy and Tactics Ensuing from These Characteristics

Thus the four principal characteristics . . . determine the line for guiding China's revolutionary war. . . . It is possible for the Chinese Red Army to grow and defeat its enemy. . . . It is impossible for the Chinese Red Army to grow very rapidly or defeat its enemy quickly. . . . In other words, the war will be protracted and may even be lost if it is mishandled. . . .

It is clear that we must correctly settle all the following matters of principle:

Determine our strategic orientation correctly, oppose adventurism when on the offensive, oppose conservatism when on the defensive, and oppose flightism when shifting from one place to another.

Oppose guerrillaism in the Red Army, while recognizing the guerrilla character of its operations.

Oppose protracted campaigns and a strategy of quick decision, and uphold the strategy of protracted war and campaigns of quick decision.

Oppose fixed battle lines and positional warfare, and favor fluid battle lines and mobile warfare.

Oppose fighting merely to rout the enemy, and uphold fighting to annihilate the enemy.

Oppose the strategy of striking with two "fists" in two directions at the same time, and uphold the strategy of striking with one "fist" in one direction at one time.

Oppose the principle of maintaining one large rear area, and uphold the principle of small rear areas.

Oppose an absolutely centralized command, and favor a relatively centralized command.

Oppose the purely military viewpoint and the ways of roving rebels, and recognize that the Red Army is a propagandist and organizer of the Chinese revolution.

Oppose bandit ways, and uphold strict political discipline.

Oppose warlord ways, and favor both democracy within proper limits and an authoritative discipline in the army.

Oppose an incorrect, sectarian policy on cadres, and uphold the correct policy on cadres.

Oppose the policy of isolation, and affirm the policy of winning over all possible allies.

Oppose keeping the Red Army at its old stage, and strive to develop it to a new stage. . . .

CHAPTER IV: "ENCIRCLEMENT AND SUPPRESSION" AND COUNTERCAMPAIGNS AGAINST IT —THE MAIN PATTERN OF CHINA'S CIVIL WAR

In the ten years since our guerrilla war began, every independent Red guerrilla unit, every Red Army unit or every revolutionary base area has been regularly subjected by the enemy to "encirclement and suppression." The enemy looks upon the Red Army as a monster and seeks to capture it the moment it shows itself. He is forever pursuing the Red Army and forever trying to encircle it. For ten years this pattern of warfare has not changed, and unless the civil war gives place to a national war, the pattern will remain the same till the day the enemy becomes the weaker contestant and the Red Army the stronger.

The Red Army's operations take the form of countercampaigns against "encirclement and suppression." For us victory means chiefly victory in combatting "encirclement and suppression," that is, strategic victory and victories in campaigns. The fight against each "encirclement and suppression" campaign constitutes a countercampaign, which usually comprises several or even scores of battles, big and small. Until an "encirclement and suppression" campaign has been basically smashed, one cannot speak of strategic victory or of victory in the countercampaign as a whole, even though many battles may have been won. The history of the Red Army's decade of war is a history of countercampaigns against "encirclement and suppression." . . .

The only entirely correct proposition is that a revolution or a revolutionary war is an offensive but also involves defense and retreat. To defend in order to attack, to retreat in order to advance, to move against the flanks in order to move against the front, and to take a roundabout route in order to get onto the direct route—this is inevitable in the process of development of many phenomena, especially military movements. . . .

When will the pattern of repeated "encirclement and suppression" campaigns come to an end? In my opinion, if the civil war is prolonged, this repetition will cease when a fundamental change takes place in the balance of forces. It will cease when the Red Army has become stronger than the enemy and when he will be resorting to countercampaigns but political and military conditions will not allow him to attain the same position as that of the Red Army in its countercampaigns. It can be definitely asserted that by then the pattern of repeated "encirclement and suppression" campaigns will have largely, if not completely, come to an end.

Chapter V: The Strategic Defensive

Under this heading I would like to discuss the following problems: (1) active and passive defense; (2) preparations for combatting "encirclement and suppression" campaigns; (3) strategic retreat; (4) strategic counteroffensive; (5) starting the counteroffensive; (6) concentration of troops; (7) mobile warfare; (8) war of quick decision; and (9) war of annihilation.

Active and Passive Defense

. . . Active defense is also known as offensive defense, or defense through decisive engagements. Passive defense is also known as purely defensive defense or pure defense. Passive defense is actually a spurious kind of defense, and the only real defense is active defense, defense for the purpose of counterattacking and taking the offensive. As far as I know, there is no military manual of value nor any sensible military expert, ancient or modern, Chinese or foreign, that does not oppose passive defense, whether in strategy or tactics. Only a complete fool or a madman would cherish passive defense as a talisman. However, there are people in this world who do such things. That is an error in war, a manifestation of conservatism in military matters, which we must resolutely oppose. . . .

When Marx said that once an armed uprising is started there must not be a moment's pause in the attack,[2] he meant that the masses, having taken the enemy unawares in an insurrection, must give the reactionary rulers no chance to retain or recover their political power, must seize this moment to beat the nation's reactionary ruling forces when they are unprepared, and must not rest content with the victories already won, underestimate the enemy, slacken their attacks or hesitate to press forward, and so let slip the opportunity of destroying the enemy, bringing failure to the revolution. This is correct. It does not mean, however, that when we are already locked in battle with an enemy who enjoys superiority, we revolutionaries should not adopt defensive measures even when we are hard-pressed. Only a prize idiot would think that way. . . .

In our civil war, when the strength of the Red Army surpasses that of the enemy, we shall, in general, no longer need the strategic defensive. Our policy then will be the strategic offensive alone. This change will depend on an overall change in the balance of forces. By that time the only remaining defensive measures will be of a partial character.

Preparations for Combatting "Encirclement and Suppression" Campaigns

Unless we have made necessary and sufficient preparations against a planned enemy "encirclement and suppression" campaign, we shall certainly be forced into a passive position. To accept battle in haste is to fight without being sure of victory. Therefore, when the enemy is preparing an "encirclement and suppression" campaign, it is absolutely necessary for us to prepare our countercampaign. To be opposed to such preparations, as some people in our ranks were at one time, is childish and ridiculous.

There is a difficult problem here over which controversy may easily arise. When should we conclude our offensive and switch to the phase of preparing our countercampaign against "encirclement and suppression"? . . . Sometimes the enemy will start his offensive just as our new offensive is beginning, thus putting us in a difficult position.

Generally speaking . . . on the question of timing the preparations, it is preferable to start them too early rather than too late. For the former involves smaller losses and has the advantage that pre-

2. See letter from Karl Marx to L. Kugelmann on the Paris Commune.

paredness averts peril and puts us in a fundamentally invincible position.

The essential problems during the preparatory phase are the preparations for the withdrawal of the Red Army, political mobilization, recruitment, arrangements for finance and provisions, and the handling of politically alien elements. . . .

The extent of success in a struggle against "encirclement and suppression" is closely related to the degree to which the tasks of the preparatory phase have been fulfilled. Relaxation of preparatory work which is due to underestimation of the enemy and panic which is due to being terrified of the enemy's attacks are harmful tendencies, and both should be resolutely opposed. What we need is an enthusiastic but calm state of mind and intense but orderly work.

Strategic Retreat

. . . We all know that when two boxers fight, the clever boxer usually gives a little ground at first, while the foolish one rushes in furiously and uses up all his resources at the very start, and in the end he is often beaten by the man who has given ground.

In the novel *Shui Hu Chuan*,[3] the drillmaster Hung, challenging Lin Chung to fight on Chai Chin's estate, shouts, "Come on! Come on! Come on!" In the end it is the retreating Lin Chung who spots Hung's weak point and floors him with one blow.

During the Spring and Autumn Era, when the states of Lu and Chi[4] were at war, Duke Chuang of Lu wanted to attack before the Chi troops had tired themselves out, but Tsai Kuei prevented him. When instead he adopted the tactic of "The enemy tires, we attack," he defeated the Chi army. This is a classic example from China's military history of a weak force defeating a strong force. Here is the account given by the historian Tsochiu Ming:[5]

3. *Shui Hu Chuan (Heroes of the Marshes)* is a celebrated Chinese novel describing a peasant war. The novel is attributed to Shih Nai-an, who lived around the end of the Yuan Dynasty and the beginning of the Ming Dynasty (fourteenth century). Lin Chung and Chai Chin are both heroes in the novel. Hung is the drillmaster on Chai Chin's estate.

4. Lu and Chi were feudal states in the Spring and Autumn Era (722–481 B.C.). Chi was a big state in the central part of the present Shantung Province, and Lu a smaller one in the southern part. Duke Chuang reigned over Lu from 693 to 662 B.C.

5. Tsochiu Ming was the author of *Tso Chuan*, a classical chronicle of the Chou Dynasty. The passage quoted is from the section in *Tso Chuan* entitled "The Tenth Year of Duke Chuang" (684 B.C.).

In the spring the Chi troops invaded us. The Duke was about to fight. Tsao Kuei requested an audience. His neighbors said, "This is the business of meat-eating officials, why meddle with it?" Tsao replied, "Meat-eaters are fools, they cannot plan ahead." So he saw the Duke. And he asked, "What will you rely on when you fight?" The Duke answered, "I never dare to keep all my food and clothing for my own enjoyment, but always share them with others." Tsao said, "Such paltry charity cannot reach all. The people will not follow you." The Duke said, "I never offer to the gods less sacrificial beasts, jade or silk than are due to them. I keep good faith." Tsai said, "Such paltry faith wins no trust. The gods will not bless you." The Duke said, "Though unable personally to attend to the details of all trials, big and small, I always demand the facts." Tsai said, "That shows your devotion to your people. You can give battle. When you do so, I beg to follow you." The Duke and he rode in the same chariot. The battle was joined at Changshao. When the Duke was about to sound the drum for the attack, Tsao said, "Not yet." When the men of Chi had drummed thrice, Tsao said, "Now we can drum." The army of Chi was routed. The Duke wanted to pursue. Again Tsao said, "Not yet." He got down from the chariot to examine the enemy's wheeltracks, then mounted the armrest of the chariot to look afar. He said, "Now we can pursue!" So began the pursuit of the Chi troops. After the victory the Duke asked Tsao why he had given such advice. Tsao replied, "A battle depends upon courage. At the first drum courage is aroused, at the second it flags, and with the third it runs out. When the enemy's courage ran out, ours was still high and so we won. It is difficult to fathom the moves of a great state, and I feared an ambush. But when I examined the enemy's wheeltracks and found them crisscrossing and looked afar and saw his banners drooping, I advised pursuit."

. . . Our war began in the autumn of 1927, and we then had no experience at all. . . . By May 1928, however, basic principles of guerrilla warfare, simple in nature and suitable to the conditions of the time, had already been evolved, that is, the sixteen-character formula: "The enemy advances, we retreat; the enemy camps, we harass; the enemy tires, we attack; the enemy retreats, we pursue." . . .

To prepare for a counteroffensive we must select or create conditions favorable to ourselves, but unfavorable to the enemy, so as to bring about a change in the balance of forces, before we go on to the stage of counteroffensive.

In the light of our past experience, during the stage of retreat we should in general secure at least two of the following conditions before we can consider the situation as being favorable to us and unfavorable to the enemy and before we can go over to the counter-offensive. These conditions are:

(1) The population actively supports the Red Army. (2) The terrain is favorable for operations. (3) All the main forces of the Red Army are concentrated. (4) The enemy's weak spots have been discovered. (5) The enemy has been reduced to a tired and demoralized state. (6) The enemy has been induced to make mistakes.

. . . A strategic retreat is a planned strategic step taken by an inferior force for the purpose of conserving its strength and biding its time to defeat the enemy, when it finds itself confronted with a superior force whose offensive it is unable to smash quickly. . . .

Strategic retreat is aimed solely at switching over to the counter-offensive and is merely the first stage of the strategic defensive. The decisive link in the entire strategy is whether victory can be won in the stage of the counteroffensive which follows.

Strategic Counteroffensive

To defeat the offensive of an enemy who enjoys absolute superiority we rely on the situation created during the stage of our strategic retreat, a situation which is favorable to ourselves, unfavorable to the enemy and different from that at the beginning of his offensive. It takes many elements to make up such a situation. . . .

However, the presence of these conditions and of a situation favorable to ourselves and unfavorable to the enemy does not mean that we have already defeated him. Such conditions and such a situation provide the possibility for our victory and his defeat . . . but only a decisive battle can settle the question as to which army is the victor and which the vanquished. This is the sole task in the stage of strategic counteroffensive. The counteroffensive is a long process, the most fascinating, the most dynamic, and also the final stage of a defensive campaign. . . .

Starting the Counteroffensive

The problem of starting a counteroffensive is the problem of the "initial battle" or "prelude." . . .

Our army's experience in . . . five countercampaigns against "encirclement and suppression" proves that the first battle in the counteroffensive is of the greatest importance for the Red Army, which is on the defensive, if it is to smash a large and powerful enemy "suppression" force. Victory or defeat in the first battle has a tremendous effect upon the entire situation. Hence we arrive at the following conclusions:

First, the first battle must be won. We should strike only when positively certain that the enemy's situation, the terrain and popular support are all in our favor and not in his. Otherwise we should rather fall back and carefully bide our time. There will always be opportunities; we should not rashly accept battle. . . .

Second, the plan for the first battle must be the prelude to, and an organic part of, the plan for the whole campaign. . . . Although the result may not—and, in fact, definitely will not—turn out exactly as we expect, we must think everything out carefully and realistically in the light of the general situation on both sides. Without a grasp of the situation as a whole, it is impossible to make any really good move on the chessboard.

Third, one must also consider what will happen in the next strategic stage of the war. Whoever directs strategy will not be doing his duty if he occupies himself only with the counteroffensive and neglects the measures to be taken after it succeeds, or in case it fails. . . .

These are the three principles we must never forget when we begin a counteroffensive, that is, when we fight the first battle.

Concentration of Troops

The concentration of troops seems easy but is quite hard in practice. Everybody knows that the best way is to use a large force to defeat a small one, and yet many people fail to do so and on the contrary often divide their forces up. The reason is that such military leaders have no head for strategy and are confused by complicated circumstances; hence, they are at the mercy of these circumstances, lose their initiative and have recourse to passive response. . . .

Concentration of troops, mobile warfare, war of quick decision and war of annihilation are all necessary conditions for the full achievement of this aim. And of these, concentration of troops is the first and most essential.

This concentration is necessary for the purpose of reversing the situation between the enemy and ourselves. First, its purpose is to reverse the situation as regards advance and retreat . . . in which we advance and he retreats.

Second, its purpose is to reverse the situation with regard to attack and defense. . . .

Third, its purpose is to reverse the situation with regard to interior and exterior lines . . . so that we can put the enemy who is in a strong position strategically into a weak position in campaigns and battles. . . .

The Red Army can stand greater hardships than the White Army. We use the few to defeat the many—this we say to the rulers of China as a whole. We use the many to defeat the few—this we say to each separate enemy force on the battlefield. That is no longer a secret, and in general the enemy is now well acquainted with our way. However, he can neither prevent our victories nor avoid his own losses, because he does not know when and where we shall act. This we keep secret. The Red Army generally operates by surprise attacks.

Mobile Warfare

Mobile warfare or positional warfare? Our answer is mobile warfare. So long as we lack a large army or reserves of ammunition, and so long as there is only a single Red Army force to do the fighting in each base area, positional warfare is generally useless to us. For us, positional warfare is generally inapplicable in attack as well as in defense.

One of the outstanding characteristics of the Red Army's operations, which follows from the fact that the enemy is powerful while the Red Army is deficient in technical equipment, is the absence of fixed battle lines. . . .

"Fight when you can win, move away when you can't win"—this is the popular way of describing our mobile warfare today. There is no military expert anywhere in the world who approves of fighting and never moving, though few people do as much moving as we do. . . .

Mobile warfare is primary, but we do not reject positional warfare where it is possible and necessary. It should be admitted that positional warfare should be employed for the tenacious defense of particular key points in a containing action during the strategic defensive, and when, during the strategic offensive, we encounter an enemy force that is isolated and cut off from help. We have had considerable experience in defeating the enemy by such positional warfare; we have cracked open many enemy cities, blockhouses and forts and broken through fairly well-fortified enemy field positions. . . .

The waging of mobile warfare involves many problems, such as reconnaissance, judgment, decision, combat disposition, command, concealment, concentration, advance, deployment, attack, pursuit, surprise attack, positional attack, positional defense, encounter action, retreat, night fighting, special operations, evading the strong and attacking the weak, besieging the enemy in order to strike at his reinforcements, feint attack, defense against aircraft, operating amongst several enemy forces, by-passing operations, consecutive operations, operating without a rear, the need for rest and building up energy. . . .

War of Quick Decision

A strategically protracted war and campaigns or battles of quick decision are two aspects of the same thing, two principles which should receive equal and simultaneous emphasis in civil wars and which are also applicable in anti-imperialist wars.

Because the reactionary forces are very strong, revolutionary forces grow only gradually, and this fact determines the protracted nature of our war. Here impatience is harmful and advocacy of "quick decision" is incorrect. To wage a revolutionary war for ten years as we have done might be surprising in other countries, but for us it is like the opening sections in an "eight-legged essay"[6]—the "presentation,

6. The "eight-legged essay" was the prescribed form of essay in the imperial competitive examinations in feudal China from the fifteenth to the nineteenth century. Structurally the main body had eight parts—presentation, amplification, preliminary exposition, initial argument, inceptive paragraphs, middle paragraphs, rear paragraphs, and concluding paragraphs; and the fifth to eighth parts each had to have two "legs" (i.e., two antithetical paragraphs), hence the name. Mao Tse-tung uses the development of the theme in this kind of essay as a metaphor to illustrate the development of the revolution through its various stages; he employs the term "eight-legged essay" to ridicule dogmatism.

amplification, and preliminary exposition of the theme"—and many exciting parts are yet to follow. . . .

The reverse is true of campaigns and battles—here the principle is not protractedness but quick decision. Quick decision is sought in campaigns and battles, and this is true at all times and in all countries. In a war as a whole, too, quick decision is sought at all times and in all countries, and a long-drawn-out war is considered harmful. China's war, however, must be handled with the greatest patience and treated as a protracted war. . . .

A quick decision cannot be achieved simply by wanting it, but requires many specific conditions. The main requirements are: adequate preparations, seizing the opportune moment, concentration of superior forces, encircling and outflanking tactics, favorable terrain, and striking at the enemy when he is on the move, or when he is stationary but has not yet consolidated his positions. Unless these requirements are satisfied, it is impossible to achieve quick decision in a campaign or battle. . . .

War of Annihilation

It is inappropriate to advocate a "contest of attrition" for the Chinese Red Army today. A "contest of treasures" not between Dragon Kings but between a Dragon King and a beggar would be rather ludicrous. For the Red Army which gets almost all its supplies from the enemy, war of annihilation is the basic policy. Only by annihilating the enemy's effective strength can we smash his "encirclement and suppression" campaigns and expand our revolutionary base areas. Inflicting casualties is a means of annihilating the enemy, otherwise there would be no sense to it. We incur losses ourselves by inflicting casualties on the enemy, but we replenish ourselves by annihilating his units, thereby not only making good our losses but adding to the strength of our army. A battle in which the enemy is routed is not basically decisive in a contest with a foe of great strength. A battle of annihilation, on the other hand, produces a great and immediate impact on any enemy. Injuring all of a man's ten fingers is not as effective as chopping off one, and routing ten enemy divisions is not as effective as annihilating one of them. . . .

Mao Tse-tung wrote this work to sum up the experience of the Second Revolutionary Civil War and used it for his lectures at the Red Army College in northern Shensi. Only five chapters were completed. The chapters on the strategic offensive, political work and other problems were left undone because of his involvement in the Sian Incident. This work, a result of a major inner-Party controversy on military questions during the Second Revolutionary Civil War, gives expression to one line in military affairs as against another. The enlarged meeting of the Political Bureau of the Central Committee held at Tsunyi in January 1935 settled the controversy about the military line and reaffirmed Mao Tse-tung's views.

A Statement on Chiang Kai-shek's Statement

December 28, 1936

In Sian, Chiang Kai-shek accepted the demand for resistance to Japan put forward by Generals Chang Hsueh-liang and Yang Hu-cheng and the people of the northwest and, as an initial step, he has ordered his civil war troops to withdraw from the provinces of Shensi and Kansu. This marks the beginning of Chiang's reversal of his wrong policy in the past decade. . . .[1]

On December 26 Chiang Kai-shek issued a statement[2] in Loyang,

1. On December 12, 1936, General Chiang Kai-shek arrived in Sian, Shensi Province, to confer with his military commanders in that area—General Yang Hu-cheng, Pacification Commissioner of Shensi Province, and General Chang Hsueh-liang, Vice-Commander-in-Chief of the Northwestern Bandit Suppression Forces. While Chiang was in the house provided for him, the commanders' soldiers opened fire upon his bodyguards. It was late at night, and although Chiang succeeded in escaping from the building without being detected, he was badly injured when he fell into a 30-foot ditch, where he was found and taken into custody by a search party. His captors were motivated by the belief that if Chiang could be persuaded to pledge all-out war against Japan, it would unite the nation in resistance. On Christmas Day they agreed to release him upon his promise to place their demands before the Nationalist Government in Nanking and his agreement to abide by its decision. The entire affair has since become known as the Sian Incident.

2. An annotation at this point in the Peking edition of *Selected Works* says that Chiang Kai-shek "was forced to accept the terms of unity with the Com-

the so-called Admonition to Chang Hsueh-liang and Yang Hu-cheng, which is so ambiguous and evasive as to be an interesting specimen among China's political documents. . . . The statement of December 26 cannot meet the demands of the Chinese masses.

However, it does contain one praiseworthy passage, in which Chiang asserts that "Promises must be kept and action must be resolute." This means that, although he did not sign the terms set forth by Chang and Yang in Sian, he is willing to accept such demands as are beneficial to the state and the nation and will not break his word on the grounds that he did not sign. We shall see whether, after he has withdrawn his troops, Chiang will act in good faith and carry out the terms he has accepted. The terms are: (1) to reorganize the Kuomintang and the National Government, expel the pro-Japanese group and admit anti-Japanese elements; (2) to release the patriotic leaders in Shanghai and all other political prisoners, and guarantee the freedoms and rights of the people; (3) to end the policy of "suppressing the Communists" and enter into an alliance with the Red Army to resist Japan; (4) to convene a national salvation conference, representing all parties, groups, sections of the population and armies, to decide on the policy of resisting Japan and saving the nation; (5) to enter into co-operation with countries sympathetic to China's resistance to Japan; and (6) to adopt other specific ways and means to save the nation. . . .[3]

Chiang should remember that he owes his safe departure from

---

munist Party and resistance to Japan, and was then set free to return to Nanking." The terms Chiang accepted were not as broad as this might indicate, but were limited to those outlined in note 1 above. Before leaving Sian, Chiang received Generals Yang and Chang, who had asked him for an audience, and charged them with having acted treasonably. He had no fear of death, he told them, and he declared that he would make no promise nor sign any paper under duress. "I consider life or death a small matter compared with the upholding of moral principles," he said, and added, "I have said more than once that if I should make any promise to you or sign anything while at Sian, it would amount to the destruction of the nation."

3. The terms of the demands upon Chiang Kai-shek comprised eight points, not six as stated by Mao Tse-tung, and they were worded quite differently from the way in which Mao has stated them. They were: (1) Reorganize the Nanking Government so that members of other parties and cliques might come in and help save the nation; (2) stop all civil wars; (3) release immediately the patriotic leaders who had been arrested in Shanghai; (4) pardon all political offenders; (5) guarantee the people's liberty of assembly; (6) give a free hand to the people to carry out patriotic movement; (7) carry out the Leader's (Sun Yat Sen's) will faithfully; (8) call a National Salvation Conference immediately.

Sian to the mediation of the Communist Party, as well as to the efforts of Generals Chang and Yang, the leaders in the Sian Incident. Throughout the incident, the Communist Party stood for a peaceful settlement and made every effort to that end, acting solely in the interests of national survival. . . .

Chiang was set free upon his acceptance of the Sian terms. From now on the question is whether he will carry out to the letter his pledge that "Promises must be kept and action must be resolute," and strictly fulfill all the terms for saving the nation. . . . If he wavers on the issue of resisting Japan or delays in fulfilling his pledge, then the nationwide revolutionary tide will sweep him away. . . .

As early as August 25, the Communist Party promised support to Chiang and the Kuomintang in its letter to the Kuomintang.[4] The people throughout the country have known for fifteen years that the Communist Party observes the maxim "Promises must be kept and action must be resolute." They undoubtedly have more confidence in the words and deeds of the Communist Party than in those of any other party or group in China.

The Tasks of the Chinese Communist Party in the Period of Resistance to Japan

May 3, 1937

THE PRESENT STAGE OF DEVELOPMENT OF CHINA'S EXTERNAL AND INTERNAL CONTRADICTIONS

. . . China has long been in the grip of two basic contradictions, the contradiction between China and imperialism and the contradiction between feudalism and the masses of the people. In 1927 the bourgeoisie, represented by the Kuomintang, betrayed the revolution

4. In its lengthy letter of August 25, 1936, which runs to many thousands of words, the Communist Party of China made this interesting demand which, of course, is totally contrary to its ultimate objective: "What the whole nation demands is centralization and unification for fighting Japan and saving the nation. . . . The people demand a democratic republican government which will serve their interests. . . . The Chinese Communist Party and the Chinese Red Army hereby solemnly declare: we stand for the setting up of a unified democratic republic for the whole country and the convening of a parliament elected by universal suffrage."

and sold China's national interests to imperialism, thus creating a situation in which the state power of the workers and peasants stood in sharp antagonism to that of the Kuomintang, and, of necessity, the task of the national and democratic revolution devolved upon the Chinese Communist Party alone.

Since the Incident of September 18, 1931, and especially since the Northern China Incident of 1935, the following changes have taken place in these contradictions:

The contradiction between China and imperialism in general has given way to the particularly salient and sharp contradiction between China and Japanese imperialism. Japanese imperialism is carrying out a policy of total conquest of China. Consequently, the contradictions between China and certain other imperialist powers have been relegated to a secondary position, while the rift between these powers and Japan has been widened. Consequently also, the Chinese Communist Party and the Chinese people are faced with the task of linking China's anti-Japanese national united front with the world peace front. This means that China should not only unite with the Soviet Union, which has been the consistently good friend of the Chinese people, but as far as possible should work for the joint opposition to Japanese imperialism with those imperialist countries which, at the present time, are willing to maintain peace and are against new wars of aggression. The aim of our united front must be resistance to Japan, and not simultaneous opposition to all the imperialist powers.

The contradiction between China and Japan has changed internal class relations within China and Japan and has confronted the bourgeoisie and even the warlords with the question of survival, so that they and their political parties have been undergoing a gradual change in their political attitude. This has placed the task of establishing an anti-Japanese national united front before the Chinese Communist Party and the Chinese people. Our united front should include the bourgeoisie and all who agree to the defense of the motherland; it should represent national solidarity against the foreign foe. This task not only must, but can be fulfilled. . . .

THE STRUGGLE FOR DEMOCRACY AND FREEDOM

Japanese imperialism is now intensifying in preparation for the invasion of China south of the Great Wall. In concert with the intensified preparations of Hitler and Mussolini for predatory war in the West, Japan is exerting every ounce of energy in the East in order to prepare the ground, according to a definite plan, for the subjugation of China at a single stroke. . . .

China must at once start democratic changes in the two following respects. First, in the matter of the political system, the reactionary Kuomintang dictatorship of one party and one class must be changed into a democratic government based on the co-operation of all parties and all classes. In this respect, a start should be made by changing the undemocratic procedures for electing and convening the national assembly, and by holding democratic elections to the assembly and ensuring freedom in the conduct of its meetings, after which it will be necessary to go on to framing and adopting a truly democratic constitution, convening a truly democratic parliament, and electing a genuinely democratic government that will carry out genuinely democratic policies. Only thus can internal peace be truly consolidated, internal armed hostilities ended and internal unity strengthened, enabling the whole nation to unite and resist the foreign foe. . . .

Our enemies—the Japanese imperialists, the Chinese traitors, the pro-Japanese elements and the Trotskyites—have been doing their utmost to wreck every move for peace and unity, democracy and freedom in China and for resistance to Japan. . . .

From now on, in the struggle for democracy and freedom, we must not only exert ourselves in propaganda, agitation and criticism directed toward the Kuomintang diehards and the backward sections of the people, but must also fully expose and firmly combat the intrigues of the Japanese imperialists and of the pro-Japanese elements and Trotskyites who serve as their running dogs in the invasion of China. . . .

For the sake of internal peace, democracy and armed resistance, and for the sake of establishing the anti-Japanese national united front, the Chinese Communist Party has made the following four pledges in its telegram to the Third Plenary Session of the Central Executive Committee of the Kuomintang:

1. the Communist-led government in the Shensi-Kansu-Ningsia revolutionary base area will be renamed the Government of the Special Region of the Republic of China, and the Red Army will be redesignated as part of the National Revolutionary Army, and they

will come under the direction of the Central Government in Nanking and its Military Council respectively;

2. a thoroughly democratic system will be applied in the areas under the Government of the Special Region;

3. the policy of overthrowing the Kuomintang by armed force will be discontinued; and

4. the confiscation of the land of the landlords will be discontinued.

These pledges are necessary as well as permissible. For only thus can we transform the state of antagonism between the two different regimes within the country and achieve unity for common action against the enemy, in line with the changes in the relative political importance of China's external and internal contradictions. . . . To describe this as capitulation by the Communist Party is nothing but Ah Q-ism[1] or malicious slander.

Does the Communist Party agree with the Three People's Principles? Our answer is, Yes we do.[2] The Three People's Principles have undergone changes in the course of their history. The revolutionary Three People's Principles of Dr. Sun Yat Sen won the people's confidence and became the banner of the victorious revolution of 1924–27 because they were resolutely applied as a result of his co-operation with the Communist Party. In 1927, however, the

1. Ah Q is the leading character in *The True Story of Ah Q*, a famous novel by the great Chinese writer Lu Hsun. Ah Q typifies all those who compensate themselves for their failures and setbacks in real life by regarding them as moral or spiritual victories.

2. Sun Yat Sen, in his *Three People's Principles*, declared himself unequivocally against communism for China; and particularly against confiscation of land as a means of solving China's agrarian problem. But because Dr. Sun was revered throughout China as a revolutionary and reformer, the Chinese Communist strategy was to make use of his name and his program by means of customary double-talk, as witness this paragraph in explanation of Mao Tse-tung's categorical answer "Yes, we do," to the question "Does the Communist Party agree with the Three People's Principles?" The annotator of the Peking issue says: "In the stage of China's bourgeois-democratic revolution, the Communists agreed with the basic points of Sun Yat Sen's program and co-operated with him, which did not mean that they agreed with the bourgeois and petty-bourgeois world outlook or ideological system of which he was the exponent. As the vanguard of the Chinese proletariat, the Chinese Communists had an entirely different world outlook or ideological system and theoretical approach to the national and other problems from those of Sun Yat Sen."

Kuomintang turned on the Communist Party[3] (the Party purge and the anti-Communist war) and pursued an opposite policy, bringing the revolution down in defeat and endangering the nation; consequently the people lost confidence in the Three People's Principles. . . .

The Chinese Communist Party has its own political and economic program. Its maximum program is socialism and communism, which is different from the Three People's Principles. . . .

Was our past slogan of a workers' and peasants' democratic republic wrong? No, it was not. . . . Our policy, including the confiscation of the land of the landlords and the enforcement of the eight-hour working day, never went beyond the bounds of capitalist private ownership; our policy was not to put socialism into practice then. What will be the composition of the new democratic republic? It will consist of the proletariat, the peasantry, the urban petty bourgeoisie, the bourgeoisie, and all those in the country who agree with the national and democratic revolution. . . .

The first question to be settled is whether China's land will be owned by the Japanese or the Chinese. Since the solution of the land problem of the peasants is predicated on the defense of China, it is absolutely necessary for us to turn from the method of forcible confiscation to appropriate new methods. It was correct to put forward the slogan of a workers' and peasants' democratic republic in the past, and it is correct to drop it today. . . .

OUR RESPONSIBILITY TO LEAD

It is a law confirmed by Chinese history that the Chinese bourgeoisie, which may participate in fighting imperialism and feudalism

3. After an abortive attempt by the Communists to take over the Kuomintang by force, in 1924, the national political party became an alliance which included the Communists, in an attempt to consolidate all revolutionary forces under one banner. In 1927, however, the Communists staged a bloodbath of middle-class farmers and landowners in the province of Hunan, and set up a national political government in Hankow, Hupeh, under the guidance of the Soviet strategist, Michael Borodin. This came to an end in March 1927, when Chiang Kai-shek denounced it from his military headquarters in Nanking. The Chinese Communist leaders and their Russian advisers fled overland to Moscow, and the head of their conglomerate military forces, General Tang Sen-chi, looted the Bank of China branch in Hankow of 200,000 *taels* in silver and fled aboard a Japanese ship to sanctuary for several years in Japan.

in certain historical circumstances, vacillates and turns traitor in others, because of its economic and political flabbiness. Thus it is history's verdict that China's bourgeois-democratic revolt against imperialism and feudalism is a task that can be completed, not under the leadership of the bourgeoisie, but only under that of the proletariat. . . .

How does the proletariat give political leadership through its party to all the revolutionary classes in the country? First, by putting forward basic political slogans that accord with the course of historical development, and by putting forward slogans of action for each stage of development and each major turn of events in order to translate these political slogans into reality: . . . such slogans as "An anti-Japanese National United Front," "A Unified Democratic Republic." "End the Civil War," "Fight for Democracy." . . .

Second, the proletariat, and especially its vanguard the Communist Party, should set an example through its boundless enthusiasm and loyalty in achieving the specific objectives when the whole country goes into action for them. . . .

Third, the Communist Party should establish proper relations with its allies and develop and consolidate its alliance with them, while adhering to the principle of never relinquishing its defined political objectives. . . .[4]

Fourth, it should expand the ranks of the Communist Party and maintain its ideological unity and strict discipline. . . .

It is by doing all these things that the Communist Party . . . will win complete victory and not be disrupted by the vacillations of our allies.

Mao Tse-tung delivered this report at the National Conference of the Chinese Communist Party, held in Yenan in May 1937.

---

4. It should be borne in mind, as is stated here, that the unchanging Communist objective is total ownership by the State of all resources and all means of production and distribution—Marxism-Leninism to the nth degree.

Win the Masses in Their Millions for the Anti-Japanese National United Front

May 7, 1937

THE QUESTION OF PEACE

. . . For nearly two years our Party has fought for internal peace. After the Third Plenary Session of the Kuomintang Central Executive Committee, we declared that peace had been attained, that the stage of "fighting for peace" was over, and that the new task was to "consolidate the peace." . . .

There is no doubt that the Japanese imperialists and the pro-Japanese group are still endeavoring to prolong civil war in China. That is precisely why peace is not yet consolidated. Such being the case, we have come to the conclusion that, instead of reverting to the old slogans of "End the Civil War" and "Fight for Peace," we should take a step forward and adopt the new slogan of "Fight for Democracy," for this is the only way to consolidate internal peace and bring the war of resistance against Japan into being. . . .

THE QUESTION OF DEMOCRACY

. . . In the new stage, democracy is the most essential thing for resistance to Japan, and to work for democracy is to work for resistance to Japan. Resistance and democracy are interdependent, just as are resistance and internal peace, democracy and internal peace. Democracy is the guarantee of resistance, while resistance can provide favorable conditions for developing the movement for democracy. . . .

If there were a revolution in Japan and she really withdrew from China, it would help the Chinese revolution and would be just what we want, marking the beginning of the collapse of the world front of aggression. . . . But . . . this is not what is happening; Sato's diplomatic moves are preparations for a major war, and a major war confronts us. . . .

Why do we place so much emphasis on a national assembly? Because it is something which can affect every aspect of life, because it is the bridge from reactionary dictatorship to democracy, because it is connected with national defense, and because it is a legal institution. . . .

The Question of the Future of the Revolution

. . . We are exponents of the theory of the transition of the revolution[1] and we are for the transition of the democratic revolution in the direction of socialism. The democratic revolution will develop through several stages, all under the slogan of a democratic republic. The change from the predominance of the bourgeoisie to that of the proletariat is a long process of struggle for leadership in which success depends on the work of the Communist Party in raising the level of political consciousness and organization both of the proletariat and of the peasantry and urban petty bourgeoisie. . . .

We are exponents of the theory of the transition of the revolution, and not of the Trotskyite theory of "permanent revolution."[2] We are for the attainment of socialism by going through all the necessary stages of the democratic republic. . . . To reject the participation of the bourgeoisie on the ground that it can only be temporary . . . is a Trotskyite approach, with which we cannot agree. Today such an alliance is in fact a necessary bridge on the way to socialism.

The Question of Cadres

A great revolution requires a great party and many first-rate cadres to guide it. In China, with a population of 450 million, it is impossible to carry through our great revolution, which is unprecedented in history, if the leadership consists of a small, narrow group and if the Party leaders and cadres are petty-minded, shortsighted and incompetent. . . .

Our Party organizations must be extended all over the country and

1. Peking annotation: See Karl Marx and Frederick Engels, *Manifesto of the Communist Party*, Part IV; V. I. Lenin, *Two Tactics of Social Democracy in the Democratic Revolution*, Part XII and Part XIII; *History of the Communist Party of the Soviet Union* (Bolsheviks), *Short Course*, Chap. 3, Sec. 3.

2. Peking annotation: See J. V. Stalin, "The Foundations of Leninism," Part III; "The October Revolution and the Tactics of the Russian Communists," Part II; "Concerning Questions of Leninism," Part III.

we must purposefully train tens of thousands of cadres and leaders . . . versed in Marxism-Leninism, politically farsighted, competent in work, full of the spirit of self-sacrifice, capable of tackling problems on their own, steadfast in the midst of difficulties and loyal and devoted in serving the nation, the class and the Party. . . .

Our revolution depends on cadres. As Stalin said, "Cadres decide everything."[3]

The Question of Democracy Within the Party

To attain this aim, inner-Party democracy is essential. If we are to make the Party strong, we must practice democratic centralism to stimulate the initiative of the whole membership . . . train new cadres in great numbers, eliminate the remnants of sectarianism, and unite the whole Party as solidly as steel.

Unity in the Conference and in the Whole Party

After explanation, the dissenting views on political issues voiced at this conference have given way to agreement, and the earlier difference between the line of the Central Committee and the line of retreat adopted under the leadership of certain comrades has also been settled; this shows that our Party is very solidly united. . . .

Win the Masses in Their Millions for the Anti-Japanese National United Front

The aim of our correct political policy and of our solid unity is to win the masses in their millions for the anti-Japanese national united front. The broad masses of the proletariat, the peasantry and the urban petty bourgeoisie need our work of propaganda, agitation and

3. J. V. Stalin, "Address Delivered in the Kremlin Palace to the Graduates from the Red Army Academies" in May 1935, in which he said: ". . . of all the valuable capital the world possesses, the most valuable and most decisive is people, cadres. It must be realized that under our present conditions, 'Cadres decide everything.' "

organization. Further efforts on our part are also needed to establish an alliance with those sections of the bourgeoisie which are opposed to Japan. . . . This requires unrelenting and strenuous, painstaking and patient effort. Without such effort, we shall achieve nothing. . . .

This was the concluding speech made by Mao Tse-tung at the National Conference of the Chinese Communist Party, held in Yenan in May 1937.

On Practice

July 1937

ON THE RELATION BETWEEN KNOWLEDGE AND PRACTICE, BETWEEN KNOWING AND DOING

Before Marx, materialism examined the problem of knowledge apart from the social nature of man and apart from his historical development, and was therefore incapable of understanding the dependence of knowledge on social practice, that is, the dependence of knowledge on production and the class struggle.

Above all, Marxists regard man's activity in production as the most fundamental practical activity, the determinant of all his other activities. Man's knowledge depends mainly on his activity in material production, through which he comes gradually to understand the phenomena, the properties and the laws of nature, and the relations between himself and nature; and through his activity in production he also gradually comes to understand, in varying degrees, certain relations that exist between man and man. None of this knowledge can be acquired apart from activity in production. In a classless society every person, as a member of society, joins in common effort with the other members, enters into definite relations of production with them and engages in production to meet man's material needs. . . .

Man's social practice is not confined to activity in production, but takes many other forms—class struggle, political life, scientific and artistic pursuits; in short, as a social being, man participates in all spheres of the practical life of society. . . .

Marxists hold that man's social practice alone is the criterion of the truth of his knowledge of the external world. What actually happens is that man's knowledge is verified only when he achieves the antici- pated results in the process of social practice (material production, class struggle or scientific experiment). If a man wants to succeed in his work, that is, to achieve the anticipated results, he must bring his ideas into correspondence with the laws of the objective external world; if they do not correspond, he will fail in his practice. . . .

. . . Lenin said, "Practice is higher than (theoretical) knowledge, for it has not only the dignity of universality, but also of immediate actuality."[1] The Marxist philosophy of dialectical materialism has two outstanding characteristics. One is its class nature; it openly avows that dialectical materialism is in the service of the proletariat. The other is its practicality; it emphasizes the dependence of theory on practice . . . emphasizes that theory is based on practice and in turn serves practice. Only social practice can be the criterion of truth. The standpoint of practice is the primary and basic standpoint in the dialectical-materialist theory of knowledge. . . .[2]

As social practice continues, things that give rise to man's sense perceptions and impressions in the course of his practice are repeated many times; then a sudden change (leap) takes place in the brain in the process of cognition, and concepts are formed. Concepts are no longer the phenomena, the separate aspects and the external relations of things; they grasp the essence, the totality and the internal rela- tions of things. Between concepts and sense perceptions there is not only a quantitative but also a qualitative difference. Proceeding further, by means of judgment and inference one is able to draw logical conclusions. The expression in San Kuo Yen Yi,[3] "Knit the brows and a stratagem comes to mind," or in everyday language, "Let

1. V. I. Lenin, "Conspectus of Hegel's *The Science of Logic*," *Collected Works* (Russ. ed., Moscow, 1958), Vol. XXXVIII, p. 205.

2. Karl Marx, "Theses on Feuerbach," Karl Marx and Frederick Engels, *Selected Works*, in two volumes (Eng. ed., FLPH, Moscow, 1958), Vol. II, p. 403; and V. I. Lenin, *Materialism and Empiric-Criticism* (Eng. ed., FLPH, Moscow, 1952), pp. 136–142.

3. *San Kuo Yen Yi (Tales of the Three Kingdoms)* is a Chinese historical novel by Lo Kuan-chung (late fourteenth and early fifteenth century).

me think it over," refers to man's use of concepts in the brain to form judgments and inferences. This is the second stage of cognition. . . . This stage of conception, judgment and inference is the more important stage in the entire process of knowing a thing; it is the stage of rational knowledge. . . .

Marxist philosophy holds that the most important problem does not lie in understanding the laws of the objective world and thus being able to explain it, but in applying the knowledge of these laws actively to change the world. From the Marxist viewpoint, theory is important, and its importance is fully expressed in Lenin's statement, "Without revolutionary theory there can be no revolutionary movement."[4] But Marxism emphasizes the importance of theory precisely and only because it can guide action. If we have a correct theory but merely prate about it, pigeonhole it and do not put it into practice, then that theory, however good, is of no significance. . . .

In the present epoch of the development of society, the responsibility of correctly knowing and changing the world has been placed by history upon the shoulders of the proletariat and its party. This process, the practice of changing the world, which is determined in accordance with scientific knowledge, has already reached a historic moment in the world and in China, a great moment unprecedented in human history, that is, the moment for completely banishing darkness from the world and from China and for changing the world into a world of light such as never previously existed.

The struggle of the proletariat and the revolutionary people to change the world comprises the fulfillment of the following tasks: to change the objective world and, at the same time, their own subjective world—to change their cognitive ability and change the relations between the subjective and the objective world. Such a change has already come about in one part of the globe, the Soviet Union. There the people are pushing forward this process of change. The people of China and the rest of the world either are going through, or will go through, such a process. And the objective world which is to be changed also includes all the opponents of change, who, in order to be changed, must go through a stage of compulsion before they can enter the stage of voluntary, conscious change. The epoch of

4. V. I. Lenin, "What Is To Be Done?" *Collected Works* (Eng. ed., FLPH, Moscow, 1961), Vol. V, p. 369.

world communism will be reached when all mankind voluntarily and consciously changes itself and the world. . . .

"On Practice" was written by Mao to give his views on the subjectivist errors of dogmatism and empiricism in the Chinese Communist Party, and especially the error of dogmatism, from the standpoint of the Marxist theory of knowledge. It was entitled "On Practice" because its stress was on exposing the dogmatist kind of subjectivism, which be-littles practice. The ideas contained in this essay were presented by Mao Tse-tung in a lecture at the Anti-Japanese Military and Political College in Yenan.

On Contradiction

August 1937

The law of contradiction in things, that is, the law of the unity of opposites, is the basic law of materialist dialectics. Lenin said, "Dialectics in the proper sense is the study of contradiction *in the very essence of objects.*"[1] Lenin often called this law the essence of dialectics; he also called it the kernel of dialectics.[2]

In studying this law, therefore, we cannot but touch upon a variety of questions, upon a number of philosophical problems. If we can become clear on all these problems, we shall arrive at a fundamental understanding of materialist dialectics. The problems are: the two world outlooks, the universality of contradiction, the particularity of contradiction, the principal contradiction and the principal aspect of a contradiction, the identity and struggle of the aspects of a contradiction, and the place of antagonism in contradiction. . . .

1. V. I. Lenin, "Conspectus of Hegel's *Lectures on the History of Philosophy,*" *Collected Works,* Vol. XXXVIII, p. 249.
2. V. I. Lenin's essay, "On the Question of Dialectics," *Collected Works* (Russ. ed., Moscow, 1958), Vol. XXXVIII, p. 357: "The splitting in two of a single whole and the cognition of its contradictory parts is the *essence* of dialectics."

The Two World Outlooks

Throughout the history of human knowledge, there have been two conceptions concerning the law of development of the universe, the metaphysical conception and the dialectical conception, which form two opposing world outlooks. Lenin said:

The two basic (or two possible? or two historically observable?) conceptions of development (evolution) are: development as decrease and increase, as repetition, *and* development as a unity of opposites (the division of a unity into mutually exclusive opposites and their reciprocal relation).

Here Lenin was referring to these two different world outlooks.

In China another name for metaphysics is *hsuan-hsueh*. For a long period in history, whether in China or in Europe, this way of thinking which is part and parcel of the idealist world outlook occupied a dominant position in human thought. . . .

In China, there was the metaphysical thinking exemplified in the saying: "Heaven changeth not, likewise the Tao changeth not,"[3] and it was supported by the decadent feudal ruling classes for a long time. Mechanical materialism and vulgar evolutionism, which were imported from Europe in the last hundred years, are supported by the bourgeoisie. . . .

The dialectical world outlook emerged in ancient times both in China and in Europe. Ancient dialectics, however, had a somewhat spontaneous and naïve character; in the social and historical conditions then prevailing, it was not yet able to form a theoretical system, hence it could not fully explain the world and was supplanted by metaphysics. The famous German philosopher Hegel, who lived in the late eighteenth and early nineteenth centuries, made most important contributions to dialectics, but his dialectics was idealist. It was not until Marx and Engels, the great protagonists of the proletarian movement, had synthesized the positive achievements in the history of human knowledge and, in particular, critically absorbed the rational elements of Hegelian dialectics and created the great theory

3. A saying of Tung Chung-shu (179–104 B.C.), a well-known exponent of Confucianism in the Han Dynasty.

of dialectical and historical materialism that an unprecedented revolution occurred in the history of human knowledge. This theory was further developed by Lenin and Stalin. As soon as it spread to China, it wrought tremendous changes in the world of Chinese thought.

This dialectical world outlook teaches us primarily how to observe and analyze the movement of opposites in different things and, on the basis of such analysis, to indicate the methods for resolving contradictions. It is therefore most important for us to understand the law of contradictions in things in a concrete way.

The Universality of Contradiction

For convenience of exposition, I shall deal first with the universality of contradiction and then proceed to the particularity of contradiction. The reason is that the universality of contradiction can be explained more briefly, for it has been widely recognized ever since the materialist-dialectical world outlook was discovered and materialist dialectics applied with outstanding success to analyzing many aspects of human history and natural history and to changing many aspects of society and nature (as in the Soviet Union) by the great creators and continuers of Marxism—Marx, Engels, Lenin and Stalin; whereas the peculiarity of contradiction is still not clearly understood by many comrades, and especially by the dogmatists. . . .

Engels said, "Motion itself is a contradiction."[4] Lenin defined the law of the unity of opposites as "the recognition (discovery) of the contradictory, *mutually exclusive*, opposite tendencies in *all* phenomena and processes of nature (*including* mind and society)."[5]

Are these ideas correct? Yes, they are. The interdependence of the contradictory aspects present in all things and the struggle between these aspects determine the life of all things and push their development forward. There is nothing that does not contain contradiction; without contradiction nothing would exist. . . .

Lenin illustrated the universality of contradiction as follows:

In mathematics: $+$ and $-$. Differential and integral.
In mechanics: action and reaction.

4. Frederick Engels, "Dialectics, Quantity and Quality," *Anti-Dühring* (Eng. ed., FLPH, Moscow, 1959), p. 166.
5. V. I. Lenin, "On the Question of Dialectics," Vol. XXXVIII, pp. 357–358.

In physics: positive and negative electricity.
In chemistry: the combination and dissociation of atoms.
In social science: the class struggle.[6]

. . . As Lenin pointed out, Marx in his *Capital* gave a model analysis of this movement of opposites which runs through the process of development of things from beginning to end. This is the method that must be employed in studying the development of all things. Lenin, too, employed this method correctly and adhered to it in all his writings. . . .

Chinese Communists must learn this method; only then will they be able correctly to analyze the history and the present state of the Chinese revolution and infer its future.

THE PARTICULARITY OF CONTRADICTION

Contradiction is present in the process of development of all things; it permeates the process of development of each thing from beginning to end. This is the universality and absoluteness of contradiction which we have discussed above. Now let us discuss the particularity and relativity of contradiction. . . .

For example, positive and negative numbers in mathematics; action and reaction in mechanics; positive and negative electricity in physics; dissociation and combination in chemistry; forces of production and relations of production, classes and class struggle in social science; offense and defense in military science; idealism and materialism, the metaphysical outlook and the dialectical outlook, in philosophy; and so on—all these are the objects of study of different branches of science precisely because each branch has its own particular contradiction and particular essence. . . .

As regards the sequence in the movement of man's knowledge, there is always a gradual growth from the knowledge of individual and particular things to the knowledge of things in general. Only after man knows the particular essence of many different things can he proceed to generalization and know the common essence of things. When a man attains the knowledge of this common essence, he uses it as a guide and proceeds to study various concrete things which have not yet been studied, or studied thoroughly, and to discover the

6. *Ibid.*

particular essence of each; only thus is he able to supplement, enrich and develop his knowledge of their common essence and prevent such knowledge from withering or petrifying. . . .

Our dogmatists are lazybones. They refuse to undertake any pains-taking study of concrete things, they regard general truths as emerg-ing out of the void, they turn them into purely abstract unfathomable formulas, and thereby completely deny and reverse the normal sequence by which man comes to know truth. Nor do they under-stand the interconnection of the two processes in cognition—from the particular to the general and then from the general to the particular. They understand nothing of the Marxist theory of knowledge. . . .

Qualitatively different contradictions can only be resolved by qualitatively different methods. For instance, the contradiction be-tween the proletariat and the bourgeoisie is resolved by the method of socialist revolution; the contradiction between the great masses of the people and the feudal system is resolved by the method of democratic revolution; the contradiction between the colonies and imperialism is resolved by the method of national revolutionary war; the contradic-tion between the working class and the peasant class in socialist society is resolved by the method of collectivization and mechaniza-tion in agriculture; contradiction within the Communist Party is resolved by the method of criticism and self-criticism; the contradic-tion between society and nature is resolved by the method of develop-ing the productive forces. . . . The principle of using different methods to resolve different contradictions is one which Marxist-Leninists must strictly observe. . . .

In studying a problem, we must shun subjectivity, one-sidedness and superficiality. . . . When Sun Wu Tzu said in discussing military science, "Know the enemy and know yourself, and you can fight a hundred battles with no danger of defeat,"[7] he was referring to the two sides in a battle. Wei Cheng[8] of the Tang Dynasty also understood the error of one-sidedness when he said "Listen to both sides and you will be enlightened, heed only one side and you will be benighted." But our comrades often look at problems one-sidedly, and

7. Sun Wu Tzu, or Sun Wu, was a famous Chinese military scientist in the fifth century B.C. who wrote *Sun Tzu*, a treatise on war containing thirteen chapters. This quotation is from Chapter 3, "The Strategy of Attack."

8. Wei Cheng (A.D. 580–643) was a statesman and historian of the Tang Dynasty.

so they often run into snags. In the novel *Shui Hu Chuan*, Sung Chiang thrice attacked Chu Village. Twice he was defeated because he was ignorant of the local conditions and used the wrong method. Later he changed his method; first he investigated the situation, and he familiarized himself with the maze of roads, then he broke up the alliance between the Li, Hu and Chu Villages and sent his men in disguise into the enemy camp to lie in wait, using a stratagem similar to that of the Trojan Horse in the foreign story. And on the third occasion he won. There are many examples of materialist dialectics in *Shui Hu Chuan*, of which the episode of the three attacks on Chu Village is one of the best.

Lenin said:

. . . in order really to know an object we must embrace, study, all its sides, all connections and "mediations." We shall never achieve this completely, but the demand for all-sidedness is a safeguard against mistakes and rigidity.[9]

. . . When Stalin explained the historical roots of Leninism in his famous work, *The Foundations of Leninism*, he analyzed the international situation in which Leninism arose, analyzed those contradictions of capitalism which reached their culmination under imperialism, and showed how these contradictions made proletarian revolution a matter for immediate action and created favorable conditions for a direct onslaught on capitalism. What is more, he analyzed the reasons why Russia became the cradle of Leninism, why czarist Russia became the focus of all the contradictions of imperialism, and why it was possible for the Russian proletariat to become the vanguard of the international revolutionary proletariat. Thus, Stalin analyzed the universality of contradiction in imperialism, showing why Leninism is the Marxism of the era of imperialism and proletarian revolution, and at the same time analyzed the particularity of czarist Russian imperialism within this general contradiction, showing why Russia became the birthplace of the theory and tactics of proletarian revolution and how the universality of contradiction is contained in this particularity. Stalin's analysis provides us with a

9. V. I. Lenin: "Once Again on the Trade Unions, the Present Situation and the Mistakes of Trotsky and Bukharin," *Selected Works* (Eng. ed., International Publishers, New York, 1943), Vol. IX, p. 66.

model for understanding the particularity and the universality of contradictions and their interconnection. . . .

THE PRINCIPAL CONTRADICTION AND THE PRINCIPAL ASPECT OF A CONTRADICTION

There are still two points in the problem of the particularity of contradiction which must be singled out for analysis, namely, the principal contradiction and the principal aspect of a contradiction. . . .

In a semicolonial country such as China, the relationship between the principal contradiction and the nonprincipal contradictions presents a complicated picture.

When imperialism launches a war of aggression against such a country, all its various classes, except for some traitors, can temporarily unite in a national war against imperialism. At such a time, the contradiction between imperialism and the country concerned becomes the principal contradiction, while all the contradictions among the various classes within the country (including what was the principal contradiction, between the feudal system and the great masses of the people) are temporarily relegated to a secondary and subordinate position. So it was in China in the Opium War of 1840, the Sino-Japanese War of 1894 and the Yi Ho Tuan War of 1900, and so it is now in the present Sino-Japanese War. . . .

THE IDENTITY AND STRUGGLE OF THE ASPECTS OF A CONTRADICTION

When we understand the universality and the particularity of contradiction, we must proceed to study the problem of the identity and struggle of the aspects of a contradiction.

Identity, unity, coincidence, interpenetration, interpermeation, interdependence (or mutual dependence for existence), interconnection or mutual co-operation—all these different terms mean the same thing and refer to the following two points: first, the existence of each of the two aspects of a contradiction in the process of the development of a thing presupposes the existence of the other aspect, and both aspects co-exist in a single entity; second, in given conditions, each of the two contradictory aspects transforms itself into its opposite. This is the meaning of identity.

Lenin said:

> *Dialectics* is the teaching which shows how *opposites* can be and how they happen to be (how they become) *identical*—under what conditions they are identical, transforming themselves into one another—why the human mind should take these opposites not as dead, rigid, but as living, conditional, mobile, transforming themselves into one another.[10]

What does this passage mean? The contradictory aspects in every process exclude each other, struggle with each other and are in opposition to each other. Without exception, they are contained in the process of development of all things and in all human thought. A simple process contains only a single pair of opposites, while a complex process contains more. And in turn, the pairs of opposites are in contradiction to one another. That is how all things in the objective world and all human thought are constituted and how they are set in motion. . . .

Our agrarian revolution has been a process in which the landlord class owning the land is transformed into a class that has lost its land, while the peasants who once lost their land are transformed into small holders who have acquired land; and it will be such a process once again. In given conditions, having and not having, acquiring and losing, are interconnected; there is identity of the two sides. Under socialism, private peasant ownership is transformed into the public ownership of socialist agriculture; this has already taken place in the Soviet Union, as it will take place everywhere else. There is a bridge leading from private property to public property, which in philosophy is called identity, or transformation into each other, or interpenetration. . . .

In speaking of the identity of opposites in given conditions, what we are referring to is real and concrete opposites and the real and concrete transformations of opposites into one another. There are innumerable transformations in mythology, for instance, Kua Fu's race with the sun in *Shan Hai Ching*,[11] Yi's shooting down of nine

10. V. I. Lenin: "Conspectus of Hegel's *The Science of Logic*," *Collected Works*, Vol. XXXVIII, pp. 97–98.

11. *Shan Hai Ching* (*Book of Mountains and Seas*) was written in the Era of the Warring States (403–221 B.C.). In one of its fables Kua Fu, a superman, pursued and overtook the sun. But he died of thirst, whereupon his staff was transformed into the forest of Teng.

suns in *Huai Nan Tzu,*[12] the Monkey King's seventy-two metamor-
phoses in *Hsi Yu Chi,*[13] the numerous episodes of ghosts and foxes
metamorphosed into human beings in the *Strange Tales of Liao
Chai,*[14] etc. But these legendary transformations of opposites are not
concrete changes reflecting concrete contradictions. They are naïve,
imaginary, subjectively conceived transformations conjured up in
men's minds by innumerable real and complex transformations of
opposites into one another. Marx said, "All mythology masters and
dominates and shapes the forces of nature in and through the
imagination; hence it disappears as soon as man gains mastery over
the forces of nature." . . .[15] That is to say, in myths or nursery tales
the aspects constituting a contradiction have only an imaginary identity, not a concrete identity. The scientific reflection of the identity in
real transformation is Marxist dialectics.

Why can an egg but not a stone be transformed into a chicken?
Why is there identity between war and peace and none between war
and a stone? Why can human beings give birth only to human beings
and not to anything else? The sole reason is that the identity of
opposites exists only in necessary given conditions. Without these
necessary given conditions there can be no identity whatsoever. . . .

Such is the problem of identity. What then is struggle? And what
is the relation between identity and struggle?

Lenin said:

The unity (coincidence, identity, equal action) of opposites is condi-
tional temporary, transitory, relative. The struggle of mutually exclusive
opposites is absolute, just as development and motion are absolute.[16]

12. Yi is one of the legendary heroes of ancient China, famous for his
archery. According to a legend in *Huai Nan Tzu,* compiled in the second
century B.C., there were ten suns in the sky in the days of Emperor Yao. To
put an end to the damage to vegetation caused by these scorching suns, Emperor Yao ordered Yi to shoot nine of them down.

13. *Hsi Yu Chi (Pilgrimage to the West)* is a sixteenth-century novel, the
hero of which is the monkey king Sun Wu-kung. He could miraculously
change at will into seventy-two different shapes, such as a bird, a tree, and a
stone.

14. *The Strange Tales of Liao Chai,* written by Pu Sung-ling in the
seventeenth century, is a well-known collection of 431 tales, mostly about
ghosts and fox spirits.

15. Karl Marx: "Introduction to the Critique of Political Economy," *A
Contribution to the Critique of Political Economy.*

16. V. I. Lenin: "On the Question of Dialectics."

What does this passage mean? All processes have a beginning and an end, all processes transform themselves into their opposites. The constancy of all processes is relative, but the mutability manifested in the transformation of one process into another is absolute. . . .

We Chinese often say, "Things that oppose each other also complement each other."[17] That is, things opposed to each other have identity. This saying is dialectical and contrary to metaphysics. "Oppose each other" refers to the mutual exclusion or the struggle of two contradictory aspects. "Complement each other" means that in given conditions the two contradictory aspects unite and achieve identity. Yet struggle is inherent in identity and without struggle there can be no identity.

In identity there is struggle, in particularity there is universality, and in individuality there is generality. To quote Lenin, ". . . there *is* an absolute *in* the relative."[18]

THE PLACE OF ANTAGONISM IN CONTRADICTION

The question of the struggle of opposites includes the question of what is antagonism. Our answer is that antagonism is one form, but not the only form, of the struggle of opposites. . . .

Before it explodes, a bomb is a single entity in which opposites co-exist in given conditions. The explosion takes place only when a new condition, ignition, is present. An analogous situation arises in all those natural phenomena which finally assume the form of open conflict to resolve old contradictions and produce new things.

It is highly important to grasp this fact. It enables us to understand that revolutions and revolutionary wars are inevitable in class society and that without them, it is impossible to accomplish any leap in social development and to overthrow the reactionary ruling classes and therefore impossible for the people to win political power. Communists must expose the deceitful propaganda of the reactionaries, such as the assertion that social revolution is unnecessary and impossible. They must firmly uphold the Marxist-Leninist theory of

17. The saying: "Things that oppose each other also complement each other," first appeared in the *History of the Earlier Han Dynasty* by Pan Ku, a celebrated historian in the first century A.D.
18. V. I. Lenin: "On the Question of Dialectics."

social revolution and enable the people to understand that social revolution is not only necessary but also entirely practicable, and that the whole history of mankind and the triumph of the Soviet Union have confirmed this scientific truth. . . .

The history of the Communist Party of the Soviet Union shows us that the contradictions between the correct thinking of Lenin and Stalin and the fallacious thinking of Trotsky, Bukharin and others did not at first manifest themselves in an antagonistic form, but that later they did develop into antagonism. There are similar cases in the history of the Chinese Communist Party. . . . But in a socialist country and in our revolutionary base areas, this antagonistic contradiction has changed into one that is nonantagonistic; and when Communist society is reached it will be abolished.

Lenin said: "Antagonism and contradiction are not at all one and the same. Under socialism, the first will disappear, the second will remain."[19] That is to say, antagonism is one form, but not the only form, of the struggle of opposites; the formula of antagonism cannot be arbitrarily applied everywhere.

Conclusion

We may now say a few words to sum up. The law of contradiction in things, that is, the law of the unity of opposites, is the fundamental law of nature and of society and therefore also the fundamental law of thought. It stands opposed to the metaphysical world outlook. It represents a great revolution in the history of human knowledge. According to dialectical materialism, contradiction is present in all processes of objectively existing things and of subjective thought and permeates all these processes from beginning to end; this is the universality and absoluteness of contradiction. Each contradiction and each of its aspects have their respective characteristics; this is the particularity and relativity of contradiction. In given conditions, opposites possess identity, and consequently can co-exist in a single entity and can transform themselves into each other; this again is the particularity and relativity of contradiction. But the struggle of opposites is ceaseless, it goes on both when the opposites are co-

19. V. I. Lenin, "Remarks on N. I. Bukharin's *Economics of the Transitional Period*," *Selected Works* (Russ. ed., Moscow-Leningrad, 1931), Vol. XI, p. 357.

existing and when they are transforming themselves into each other, and becomes especially conspicuous when they are transforming themselves into one another; this again is the universality and absoluteness of contradiction. In studying the particularity and relativity of contradiction, we must give attention to the distinction between the principal contradiction and the nonprincipal contradictions and to the distinction between the principal aspect and the nonprincipal aspect of a contradiction; in studying the universality of contradiction and the struggle of opposites in contradiction, we must give attention to the distinction between the different forms of struggle. Otherwise we shall make mistakes. If, through study, we achieve a real understanding of the essentials explained above, we shall be able to demolish dogmatist ideas which are contrary to the basic principles of Marxism-Leninism and detrimental to our revolutionary cause; and our comrades with practical experience will be able to organize their experience into principles and avoid repeating empiricist errors. These are a few simple conclusions from our study of the law of contradiction.

This essay on philosophy was written by Mao Tse-tung after his essay "On Practice" and with the same object of overcoming what Mao Tse-tung considered to be the serious error of dogmatist thinking to be found in the Chinese Communist Party at the time. Originally delivered as a series of lectures at the Anti-Japanese Military and Political College in Yenan, it was revised by the author for inclusion in his *Selected Works*.

Volume II

The Period of the War
of Resistance Against Japan, I

Volume II   Contents

104   Selected Works of Mao Tse-tung

Policies, Measures and Perspectives
for Resisting the Japanese Invasion

July 23, 1937

TWO POLICIES

On July 8, the day after the Lukouchiao Incident,[1] the Central Committee of the Communist Party of China issued a Manifesto to the whole nation calling for a war of resistance. The Manifesto reads in part:

Fellow countrymen! Peiping and Tientsin are in peril! Northern China is in peril! The Chinese nation is in peril! A war of resistance by the whole nation is the only way out. We demand immediate and resolute resistance to the invading Japanese armies and immediate preparations to meet all emergencies. From top to bottom the whole nation must at once abandon any idea of being able to live in submissive peace with the Japanese aggressors. . . . We call upon the poeple of the whole country to throw all their strength behind the sacred war of self-defense against Japan. . . . Let the people of the whole country . . . unite and build up the national united front as our solid Great Wall of resistance to Japanese aggression! Let the Kuomintang and the Communist Party

1. On July 7, 1939, Japanese troops stationed at Lukouchiao (Marco Polo Bridge) some 10 kilometers southwest of Peking opened fire on Chinese troops on the other side of the bridge on the trumped-up charge that the Chinese soldiers were interfering with Japanese troop maneuvers.

closely co-operate and resist the new attacks of the Japanese aggressors! Drive the Japanese aggressors out of China!

This is a declaration of policy.

On July 17, Mr. Chiang Kai-shek made a statement at Lushan. Setting out as it did a policy of preparing for a war of resistance . . . the statement listed four conditions for the settlement of the Lukouchiao Incident: (1) Any settlement must not infringe China's sovereignty and territorial integrity; (2) there must be no unlawful change in the administrative structure of Hopei and Chahar Provinces; (3) there must be no dismissal and replacement, at the demand of others, of local officials appointed by the Central Government; (4) the 29th Army must not be confined to the area in which it is now stationed.

The concluding remarks of the statement read:

Concerning the Lukouchiao Incident, the government has decided on a policy and a stand to which it will always adhere. We realize that when the whole nation goes to war, sacrifices to the bitter end will be called for, and we should not cherish the faintest hope of an easy way out. Once war breaks out, every person, young or old, in the north or in the south, must take up the responsibility of resisting Japan and defending our homeland.

This, too, is a declaration of policy.

Here we have two historic political declarations on the Lukouchiao Incident, one by the Communist Party and the other by the Kuomintang. They have this point in common: both stand for a resolute war of resistance and oppose compromise and concessions. . . .

Let all the armed forces in the country, including the Red Army, support Mr. Chiang Kai-shek's declaration, oppose compromise and concessions and conduct resolute armed resistance! . . .

Two Sets of Measures

To achieve its purpose the policy of resolute armed resistance calls for a whole set of measures. . . . The principal ones are the following:

1. *Mobilize all the armed forces of the whole country*. Mobilize our standing armed forces of well over 2 million men, including the land, sea and air forces, the Central Army, the local troops and the Red

Army. . . . Establish the principle that guerrilla warfare should carry the responsibility for one aspect of the strategic task. . . .

2. *Mobilize the whole people.* Lift the ban on patriotic movements, release political prisoners, annul the "Emergency Decree for Dealing with Actions Endangering the Republic"[2] and the "Press Censorship Regulations," grant legal status to existing patriotic organizations . . .

3. *Reform the government apparatus.* Bring representatives of all political parties and groups and public leaders into the government for joint management of the affairs of the state and weed out the hidden pro-Japanese elements and traitors in the government. . . .

4. *Adopt an anti-Japanese foreign policy.* Accord the Japanese imperialists no advantages or facilities, but on the contrary confiscate their property, repudiate their loans, weed out their lackeys and expel their spies. Immediately conclude a military and political alliance with the Soviet Union . . . enlist the sympathy of Britain, the United States and France for our resistance to Japan. . . .

5. *Proclaim a program for improving the livelihood of the people and immediately begin to put it into effect.* Start with the following minimum points: Abolish exorbitant taxes and miscellaneous levies, reduce land rent, restrict usury, increase the workers' pay, improve the livelihood of the soldiers and junior officers, improve the livelihood of office workers, and provide relief for victims of natural calamities.

6. *Institute education for national defense.* . . . Newspapers, books and magazines, films, plays, literature and art should all serve national defense. Traitorous propaganda must be prohibited.

7. *Adopt financial and economic policies for resisting Japan.* Financial policy should be based on the principle that those with money should contribute money . . . and economic policy should be based on the principle of boycotting Japanese goods and promoting home products.

2. The Republic of China had promulgated this decree on January 31, 1931, as an emergency defense measure against Chinese Communist violence and rebellion.

8. *Unite the entire Chinese people . . . and build up the national united front. . . .* The key is close co-operation between the Kuomintang and the Communist Party. Let . . . the whole people unite on the basis of such co-operation between the two parties.

Whoever is sincere about the policy of resolute armed resistance must put this set of measures into practice. . . . There is another set of measures which is contrary to this set in every respect.

Measures stem from policy. If the policy is one of nonresistance, all measures will reflect nonresistance; we have been taught this lesson over the last six years. If the policy is one of resolute armed resistance, then it is imperative to apply the appropriate measures—the Eight-Point Program.

Two Perspectives

. . . Pursue the first policy and adopt the first set of measures, and the perspective will definitely be the expulsion of Japanese imperialism and the attainment of China's liberation. . . .

Pursue the second . . . and the perspective will definitely be the occupation of China by the Japanese imperialists.

Conclusion

It is imperative to carry out the first policy, to adopt the first set of measures and to strive for the first perspective.

It is imperative to oppose the second policy . . . and to avert the second perspective.

For the Mobilization of All the Nation's Forces for Victory in the War of Resistance

August 25, 1937

A. The Lukouchiao Incident of July 7 marked the beginning of the Japanese imperialist all-out invasion of China south of the Great Wall. . . . The initial changes in the Kuomintang's policy with the Sian Incident and the Third Plenary Session of its Central Executive Committee as their starting point, Mr. Chiang Kai-shek's Lushan statement of July 17 on the question of resistance to Japan, and many of his measures of national defense, all deserve commendation.

B. But on the other hand, even after the Lukouchiao Incident of July 7, the Kuomintang authorities are continuing to pursue the wrong policy they have pursued ever since the September 18 Incident, making compromises and concessions, suppressing the zeal of the patriotic troops and clamping down on the patriotic people's national salvation movement. . . . If, at this critical juncture of life or death for our nation, the Kuomintang continues in the same old groove and does not quickly change its policy, it will bring disaster to the War of Resistance. . . . Such a war requires a complete and drastic change in Kuomintang policy and the joint efforts of the whole nation . . . in the spirit of the revolutionary Three People's Principles and the Three Great Policies[1] drawn up personally by Dr. Sun Yat Sen during the first period of Kuomintang-Communist co-operation.

C. In all earnestness the Chinese Communist Party proposes to the Kuomintang, to the people of the whole country, to all political parties and groups, to people in all walks of life and to all the armed forces a Ten-Point National Salvation Program for the purpose of completely defeating the Japanese aggressors. . . . The ten points are as follows:

1. Overthrow Japanese imperialism. . . .
2. Mobilize the military strength of the whole nation. . . .
3. Mobilize the people of the whole country. . . .
4. Reform the government apparatus. . . .
5. Adopt an anti-Japanese foreign policy. . . .
6. Adopt wartime financial and economic policies. . . .

1. The annotation by Chinese Communist editors in the *Selected Works* published in Peking makes this statement: "In the Manifesto adopted by the Kuomintang at its First National Congress in 1924 Sun Yat Sen restated the Three People's Principles. . . . Thus the Three People's Principles were transformed into the new Three People's Principles characterized by the Three Great Policies, that is, alliance with Russia, co-operation with the Communist Party" . . .

These statements are not true. No such transformation was ever made by Dr. Sun in the Kuomintang Manifesto. Neither Russia nor the Communist Party were even so much as mentioned in the Manifesto, and he flatly rejected Communism in his Three People's Principles.

7. Improve the people's livelihood. . . .

8. Adopt an anti-Japanese educational policy.

9. Weed out traitors and pro-Japanese elements and consolidate the rear.

10. Achieve national unity against Japan. . . .

D. It is imperative to discard the policy of resistance by government alone and to enforce the policy of total resistance by the whole nation. The government must unite with the people, fully restore the revolutionary spirit of Dr. Sun Yat Sen, put the above Ten-Point Program into effect and strive for victory.

This was an outline for propaganda and agitation written by Mao Tse-tung in August 1937 for the propaganda organs of the Central Committee of the Chinese Communist Party.

Combat Liberalism
September 7, 1937

We stand for active ideological struggle because it is the weapon for ensuring unity within the Party and the revolutionary organizations in the interest of our fight. Every Communist and revolutionary should take up this weapon.

But liberalism rejects ideological struggle and stands for unprincipled peace, thus giving rise to a decadent, philistine attitude. . . .

Liberalism manifests itself in various ways. To let things slide for the sake of peace and friendship when a person has clearly gone wrong. . . . To indulge in irresponsible criticism. . . . To let things drift if they do not affect one personally. . . . Not to obey orders but to give pride of place to one's own opinions. . . . To indulge in personal attacks, pick quarrels, vent personal spite or seek revenge. . . . To hear incorrect views without rebutting them and even to hear counterrevolutionary remarks without reporting them. . . . To be among the masses and fail to conduct propaganda and agitation. . . . To see someone harming the interests of the masses and yet not feel indignant. . . . To be aware of one's own mistakes and yet make no attempt to correct them.

Liberalism is extremely harmful in a revolutionary collective. It is a corrosive which eats away unity, undermines cohesion, causes apathy and creates dissension.

People who are liberals look upon the principles of Marxism as abstract dogma. They approve of Marxism but are not prepared to practice it or to practice it in full; they are not prepared to replace their liberalism by Marxism. . . .

Liberalism is a manifestation of opportunism and conflicts fundamentally with Marxism. . . . We must use Marxism, which is positive in spirit, to overcome liberalism, which is negative.

All loyal, honest, active and upright Communists must unite to oppose the liberal tendencies shown by certain people among us, and set them on the right path. This is one of the tasks on our ideological front.

Urgent Tasks Following the Establishment of Kuomintang-Communist Cooperation

September 29, 1937

As far back as 1933, the Chinese Communist Party issued a declaration stating that it was ready to conclude an agreement for resisting Japan with any section of the Kuomintang Army on three conditions, namely, that attacks on the Red Army be stopped, that democratic freedoms be granted to the people and that the people be armed. This declaration was made because after the September 18 Incident in 1931, resistance to the Japanese imperialist invasion became the primary task of the Chinese people. But we did not succeed in our objective.

On February 10 this year, the Central Committee of the Chinese Communist Party sent a telegram to the Third Plenary Session of the Kuomintang Central Executive Committee on the eve of its meeting, making comprehensive proposals for concrete cooperation between the two parties. . . . Since then the two parties have moved a step closer to each other in their negotiations. . . .

Now the newly formed united front between the two parties has ushered in a new period in the Chinese revolution. There are still people who do not understand the historical role of the united front and its great future and regard it as a mere temporary makeshift devised under the pressure of circumstances; nevertheless, through this united front, the wheel of history will propel the Chinese revolution forward to a completely new stage. . . .

Whether China can extricate herself from the national and social crisis which is now so grave depends on how this united front will develop. There is already fresh evidence that the prospects are favorable. First, as soon as the policy of the united front was put forward by the Chinese Communist Party, it won the approval of the people everywhere. . . . Second, immediately after the Sian Incident was settled peacefully and the two parties ended the civil war, all political parties and groups, people in all walks of life and all armed forces in the country achieved unprecedented unity. . . . Third, and most striking of all, is the fact that the nationwide War of Resistance has started. . . . Fourth, there is the effect abroad. The proposal for the anti-Japanese united front put forward by the Chinese Communist Party has won the support of the workers and peasants and Communist parties all over the world. . . .

Should the Anti-Japanese National United Front be confined to the Kuomintang and the Communist Party? No, it should be a united front of the whole nation, with the two parties forming only a part of it. . . . And the only way to save it is to put Dr. Sun Yat Sen's Testament into practice, to "arouse the masses of the people."

The present anti-Japanese united front still lacks a political program to replace the Kuomintang's policy of autocratic rule, a program accepted by both parties and formally promulgated. . . . What should the common program be? It should be the Three People's Principles of Dr. Sun Yat Sen and the Ten-Point Program for Resisting Japan and Saving the Nation proposed by the Communist Party on August 25 this year.

In its declaration announcing Kuomintang-Communist cooperation, the Chinese Communist Party stated that "the Three People's Principles of Dr. Sun Yat Sen being what China needs today, our Party is ready to fight for their complete realization." Some people find it strange that the Communist Party should be ready to put the Three People's Principles of the Kuomintang into practice. . . . These people think that communism and the Three People's Principles are incompatible. This is a purely formal approach. Communism will be put into practice at a future stage of the development of the revolution; at the present stage the Communists harbor no illusions about being able to realize it but will carry out the national and democratic revolution as required by history. . . .

The agrarian revolution put into effect the principle of "land to the tiller," which is precisely what Dr. Sun Yat Sen proposed. We have now discontinued it for the sake of uniting greater numbers of people against Japanese imperialism, but that does not mean China does not need to solve her land problem. . . . The question now is not whether it is the Communist Party which believes in or carries out the revolutionary Three People's Principles, but whether it is the Kuomintang which does so. . . .

It is impossible to put this program into practice throughout the country without the consent of the Kuomintang, because the Kuomintang today is still the biggest Party in China and the Party in power. . . . In his statement of September 23, Mr. Chiang Kai-shek declared:

I hold that we who stand for the revolution should put aside personal grudges and prejudices and devote ourselves to the realization of the Three People's Principles. At this critical juncture of life and death, we should all the more let bygones be bygones and together with the whole nation make a completely fresh start, and work strenuously for unity in order to preserve the very life and existence of our country.

This is most true. The urgent task at present is to strive for the realization of the Three People's Principles, to discard personal and factional prejudices, to change the old set of practices, to carry out a revolutionary program in line with the Three People's Principles immediately and to make a completely fresh start together with the whole nation. . . . But there must be instruments for carrying out the Three People's Principles and the Ten-Point Program, and this raises the question of reforming the government and the army. . . .

The fate of our nation is at stake—let the Kuomintang and the Communist Party unite closely! Let all our fellow countrymen who refuse to become slaves unite closely on the basis of Kuomintang-Communist unity! The urgent task in the Chinese revolution today is to make all the reforms necessary to overcome all difficulties. When this task is accomplished, we can surely defeat Japanese imperialism. If we try hard, our future will be bright.

Interview with the British Journalist James Bertram[1]

October 25, 1937

THE COMMUNIST PARTY OF CHINA AND THE WAR OF RESISTANCE

JAMES BERTRAM: What specific pronouncements has the Chinese Communist Party made before and since the outbreak of the Sino-Japanese War?

MAO TSE-TUNG: Before the war broke out, the Chinese Communist Party warned the whole nation time and again that war with Japan was inevitable, and that all the Japanese imperialists' talk of a "peaceful settlement" and all the fine phrases of the Japanese diplomats were only so much camouflage to screen their preparations for war. . . .

Soon afterward we announced the Ten-Point Program for Resisting Japan and Saving the Nation, in which we set out the policies that the Chinese Government ought to adopt in the War of Resistance. . . . In the present period our basic slogan is "Total resistance by the whole nation."

THE WAR SITUATION AND ITS LESSONS

QUESTION: As you see it, what are the results of the war up to the present?

ANSWER: There are two main aspects. On the one hand, by capturing our cities, seizing our territory, raping, plundering, burning and massacring, the Japanese imperialists have irrevocably brought the Chinese people face to face with the danger of national subjugation. . . .

1. James Bertram is the author of *First Act in China—The Story of the Sian Mutiny,* and of *Unconquered,* his journal of a year's adventures in China, which included six months' experience with the Communist Eighth Route Army in the northern hills. He is a Rhodes Scholar from New Zealand, who went from Oxford to the Far East in 1937.

QUESTION: What do you think are Japan's objectives, and how far have they been achieved?

ANSWER: Japan's plan is to occupy northern China and Shanghai as the first step and then to occupy other regions of China. . . .

QUESTION: In your opinion, has China scored any achievement in the War of Resistance? If there are any lessons to be drawn, what are they?

ANSWER: . . . They are to be seen in the following: (1) Never since imperialist aggression began against China has there been anything comparable to the present War of Resistance Against Japan. . . . (2) The war has changed a disunited country into a relatively united one. . . . (3) The war has the sympathy of world public opinion. . . . (4) The war has inflicted heavy losses on the Japanese aggressors. . . . (5) We have learned some lessons from the war. They have been paid for in territory and blood.

As for the lessons, they are likewise great ones. . . . As in the past, the broad masses are restrained by the government from taking part, and so the war is not yet of a mass character. . . . Therefore, although the present armed resistance is a revolutionary one, its revolutionary character is incomplete because it is not yet a mass war. . . . Most of the political prisoners have not yet been released, and the ban on political parties has not been completely lifted. . . . We can never win by fighting this way. For the attainment of victory, policies radically different from the present ones are necessary in both the political and the military fields. These are the lessons we have learned.

QUESTION: What, then, are the political and military prerequisites?

ANSWER: On the political side, first, the present government must be transformed into a united front government in which the representatives play their part. . . . Secondly, the people must be granted freedom of speech, freedom of the press, and freedom of assembly and association and the right to take up arms. . . . Thirdly, the people's livelihood must be improved through such measures as the abolition of exorbitant taxes and miscellaneous levies, the reduction of rent and interest. . . . Fourthly, there should be a positive foreign policy. Fifthly, cultural and educational policy should be changed. Sixthly, traitors must be suppressed. . . . All these political and military prerequisites are listed in our published Ten-Point

Program. They all conform to the spirit of Dr. Sun Yat Sen's Three People's Principles, his Three Great Policies and his Testament. The war can be won only when they are carried into effect.

QUESTION: What is the Communist Party doing to carry out this program?

ANSWER: We take it as our task tirelessly to explain the situation and to unite with the Kuomintang and all other patriotic parties and groups in the effort to expand and consolidate the Anti-Japanese National United Front, mobilize all forces and achieve victory in the War of Resistance. . . . We agree to accept Dr. Sun's revolutionary Three People's Principles, Three Great Policies[2] and Testament as the common program of the united front of all political parties and all social classes. But so far this program has not been accepted by all the parties, and above all the Kuomintang has not agreed to the proclamation of such an overall program. . . . It is the duty of the Communist Party to raise its voice and tirelessly and persuasively explain all this to the Kuomintang and the whole nation so that the genuinely revolutionary Three People's Principles, the Three Great Policies and Dr. Sun Yat Sen's Testament are fully and thoroughly applied throughout the country, and the Anti-Japanese National United Front is broadened and consolidated.

THE EIGHTH ROUTE ARMY IN THE WAR OF RESISTANCE

QUESTION: Please tell me about the Eighth Route Army in which so many people are interested—for instance, about its strategy and tactics, its political work, and so on.

ANSWER: . . . First, about its field of operations. Strategically, the Eighth Route Army is centering them on Shansi. . . . The Japanese troops in Shansi are being strategically encircled by the Eighth Route Army and other Chinese troops. We may say with certainty that the Japanese troops will meet with the most stubborn resistance in northern China. . . .

Next about strategy and tactics. We are doing what the other Chinese troops have not done, that is, operating chiefly on the

2. The "Three Great Policies" is an invention of Mao Tse-tung's. It includes an "alliance" with the Soviet Union, which was never advocated by Sun Yat Sen.

enemy's flanks and rear. This way of fighting is vastly different from purely frontal defense. . . . The first essential in war is to preserve oneself and to destroy the enemy, and for this purpose it is necessary to wage guerrilla and mobile warfare independently and with the initiative in our hands and to avoid all passive and inflexible tactics. If a vast number of troops wage mobile warfare with the Eighth Route Army, assisting them by guerrilla warfare, our victory will be certain.

Next about political work. Another highly significant and distinctive feature of the Eighth Route Army is its political work, which is guided by three basic principles. First, the principle of unity between officers and men. . . . Second, the principle of unity between the army and the people. . . . Third, the principle of disintegrating the enemy troops and giving lenient treatment to prisoners of war. . . .

QUESTION: In your opinion, can these good points of the Eighth Route Army also be acquired by the other Chinese armies?

ANSWER: Certainly they can. In 1924–27 the spirit of the Kuomintang troops was broadly similar to that of the Eighth Route Army today. The Communist Party and the Kuomintang were then cooperating in organizing armed forces of a new type. . . . These forces later grew into an army corps and still more troops came under its influence; only then did the Northern Expedition take place. . . .

QUESTION: Japanese army discipline being what it is, will not your policy of giving lenient treatment to prisoners of war prove ineffective? For instance, the Japanese command may kill the prisoners when you release them and the Japanese Army as a whole will not understand the meaning of your policy.

ANSWER: That is impossible. The more they kill, the more sympathy will be aroused for the Chinese forces among the Japanese soldiers. Such facts cannot be concealed from the rank and file. . . .

CAPITULATIONISM IN THE WAR OF RESISTANCE

QUESTION: I understand that while carrying on the war, Japan is spreading peace rumors in Shanghai. What are her real objectives?

ANSWER: After succeeding in certain of their plans, the Japanese imperialists will once again put up a smoke screen of peace in order to attain three objectives. They are: (1) To consolidate the positions already captured for use as a strategic springboard for further offensives; (2) to split China's anti-Japanese front; and (3) to break up the international front of support for China. . . .

QUESTION: As you see it, what could this danger lead to?

ANSWER: There can be only two courses of development: either the Chinese people will overcome capitulationism, or capitulationism will prevail, with the result that the anti-Japanese front will be split and China will be plunged into disorder.

QUESTION: Which of the two is more likely?

ANSWER: . . . I am sure that the capitulationists cannot win mass support and that the masses will overcome capitulationism, persevere in the war and achieve victory.

QUESTION: May I ask how capitulationism can be overcome?

ANSWER: Both by words . . . and by deeds. . . . We must show the masses of the people the victorious prospects of the war and help them to understand that our defeats and difficulties are temporary and that, as long as we keep on fighting in spite of all setbacks, the final victory will be ours. . . .

DEMOCRACY AND THE WAR OF RESISTANCE

QUESTION: What is the meaning of "democracy" as put forward by the Communist Party in its program? Does it not conflict with a "wartime government?"

ANSWER: Not at all. The Communist Party put forward the slogan of a "democratic republic" as early as August 1926. Politically and organizationally this slogan signifies: (1) The state and government must not belong to a single class but must be based on the alliance of all the anti-Japanese classes to the exclusion of traitors and collaborators . . . ; (2) the organizational form of such a government will be democratic centralism . . . with the two seeming opposites of democracy and centralization united in a definite form; (3) the government will grant the people all the necessary political freedoms, especially the freedom to organize and train and arm themselves in self-defense. . . .

QUESTION: Is not "democratic centralism" a self-contradictory term?

ANSWER: We must look not only at the term but at the reality.

There is no impassable gulf between democracy and centralism. . . .
On the one hand, the government we want must be truly representative of the popular will. . . . On the other hand, the centralization and administrative power is also necessary, and once the policy measures demanded by the people are transmitted to their own elected government through their representative body, the government will carry them out. . . .

QUESTION: This does not correspond to a war cabinet, does it?

ANSWER: It does not correspond to some of the war cabinets of the past.

QUESTION: Have there ever been any war cabinets of this kind?

ANSWER: Yes. Systems of government in wartime may generally be divided into two kinds, as determined by the nature of the war—one kind is democratic centralism and the other absolute centralism. All wars in history may be divided into two kinds according to their nature: just wars and unjust wars. For instance, the Great War in Europe some twenty years ago was an unjust, imperialist war. The governments of the imperialist countries forced the people to fight for the interests of imperialism and thus went against the people's interests. . . . China's war of national liberation has the full approval of the people and cannot be won without their participation; therefore democratic centralism becomes a necessity. . . .

QUESTION: Then what steps are you prepared to take for this system of government to be instituted?

ANSWER: The key question is co-operation between the Kuomintang and the Communist Party.

QUESTION: Why?

ANSWER: For the last fifteen years, the relationship between the Kuomintang and the Communist Party has been the decisive political factor in China. . . . The split between the two parties in 1927 resulted in the unfortunate situation of the last decade. . . . Through our ceaseless efforts, the establishment of cooperation has at last been announced, but the point is that both sides must accept a common program and act upon it. An essential part of such a program is the setting up of a new system of government.

QUESTION: How can the new system be set up through the co-operation of the two parties?

ANSWER: . . . We propose that a provisional national assembly be convened to meet the present emergency. Delegates to this assembly should be chosen in due proportion from the various anti-Japanese political parties, anti-Japanese armies and anti-Japanese popular and business organizations, as Dr. Sun Yat Sen suggested in 1924. This assembly should function as the supreme organ of state authority to decide on the policies for saving the nation, adopt a constitutional program and elect the government. . . . We are exchanging views with the Kuomintang about this proposal and hope to obtain its agreement.

QUESTION: Has not the National Government announced that the national assembly has been called off?

ANSWER: It was right to call it off. What has been called off is the national assembly which . . . according to the Kuomintang's stipulations . . . would not have had the slightest power . . . and was entirely in conflict with the popular will. . . . The provisional assembly we are proposing is radically different from the one that has been called off. The convening of this provisional national assembly will undoubtedly impart a new spirit to the whole country and provide the essential prerequisite for reconstructing the government apparatus and the army and for mobilizing the entire people. On this hinges the favorable turn in the War of Resistance.

The Situation and Tasks in the Anti-Japanese War After the Fall of Shanghai and Taiyuan

November 12, 1937

THE PRESENT SITUATION IS ONE OF TRANSITION FROM A WAR OF PARTIAL RESISTANCE TO A WAR OF TOTAL RESISTANCE

1. We support any kind of war of resistance, even though partial, against the invasion of Japanese imperialism. . . .

2. However, a war of partial resistance by the government alone without the mass participation of the people will certainly fail. . . . For it is not a national revolutionary war in the full sense, not a people's war.

3. We stand for a national revolutionary war in the full sense, a war in which the entire people are mobilized. . . .

4. Although the war of partial resistance advocated by the Kuomintang also constitutes a national war . . . it can never successfully defend the motherland.

5. Herein lies the difference in principle between the stand of the Communist Party and the present stand of the Kuomintang with respect to resistance. . . .

6. In a national revolutionary war in the full sense . . . it is essential to put into effect the Ten-Point Program for Resisting Japan and Saving the Nation proposed by the Communist Party. . . .

7. The situation after the fall of Shanghai and Taiyuan is as follows:

(a) . . . the Japanese aggressors have broken through the Kuomintang's battle lines and are advancing on Nanking and the Yangtze Valley. . . .

(b) In their own imperialist interests, the governments of Britain, the United States and France have indicated that they will help China, but so far there has been . . . no practical aid whatsoever.

(c) The German and Italian Fascists are doing everything to assist Japanese imperialism.

(d) The Kuomintang is still unwilling to make any fundamental change in its one-party dictatorship. . . .

This is one side of the picture. The other side is seen in the following:

(a) The political influence of the Communist Party and the Eighth Route Army is spreading fast and far. . . .

(b) The mass movement has developed a step further.

(c) The national bourgeoisie is leaning toward the left.

(d) Forces favoring reforms are growing within the Kuomintang.

(e) The movement to oppose Japan and aid China is spreading among the people of the world.

(f) The Soviet Union is preparing to give practical assistance to China.

8. Therefore, the present situation is one of transition from partial to total resistance. . . .

CAPITULATION MUST BE COMBATTED
BOTH INSIDE THE PARTY
AND THROUGHOUT THE COUNTRY

In 1927 Chen Tu-hsiu's capitulationism led to the failure of the revolution. No member of our Party should ever forget this historical lesson written in blood.

With regard to the Party's line of an Anti-Japanese National United Front, the main danger inside the Party before the Lukouchiao Incident was "Left" opportunism, that is, closed-doorism, the reason being chiefly that the Kuomintang had not yet begun to resist Japan.

Since the Lukouchiao Incident the main danger inside the Party is no longer "Left" closed-doorism but Right opportunism, that is, capitulationism, the reason being chiefly that the Kuomintang has begun to resist Japan. . . .

In relation to the current specific political task this question means: Is the Kuomintang to be raised to the level of the Ten-Point Program for Resisting Japan and Saving the Nation, to the level of the total resistance advocated by the Communist Party? Or is the Communist Party to sink to the level of the Kuomintang dictatorship of the landlords and bourgeoisie, to the level of partial resistance? . . .

We must sharply pose the question of who is to lead and must resolutely combat capitulationism in view of the grave situation described above. . . .

In the Country as a Whole, Oppose
National Capitulationism

. . . The left wing of the Anti-Japanese United Front is composed of Communist-led masses, which include the proletariat, the peasantry and the urban petty bourgeoisie. Our task is to do our utmost to extend and consolidate this wing . . . for turning partial resistance into total resistance and for overthrowing Japanese imperialism.

The intermediate section of the Anti-Japanese National United Front is composed of the national bourgeoisie and the upper stratum of the petty bourgeoisie. . . . Our task is to help the intermediate section to move forward and change its stand.

The right wing of the Anti-Japanese National United Front consists of the big landlords and big bourgeoisie, and it is the nerve center of national capitulationism. It is inevitable that these people should tend toward capitulationism, for they fear both the destruction of their property in the war and the rise of the masses. . . . Our task is to combat national capitulationism resolutely and, in the course of this struggle, to expand and consolidate the left wing and help the intermediate section to move forward and change its stand.

The Relation Between Class Capitulationism and National Capitulationism

Class capitulationism is actually the reserve force of national capitulationism . . . ; it is a vile tendency that lends support to the camp of the right wing and leads to defeat in the war. We must fight this tendency inside the Communist Party . . . in order to achieve the liberation of the Chinese nation and the emancipation of the toiling masses.

This was the outline for a report made by Mao Tse-tung in Yenan at a meeting of Party activists.

Proclamation by the Government of the Shensi-Kansu-Ningsia Border Region[1] and the Rear Headquarters of the Eighth Route Army

May 15, 1938

Be it hereby proclaimed: Ever since the Lukouchiao Incident, all our patriotic countrymen have been firmly waging the War of Resistance. . . . Nobody will be allowed to neglect his duty and nothing will be allowed to undermine the cause of national salvation.

1. The Shensi-Kansu-Ningsia Border Region was the Communist base area which was built up after 1931 through guerrilla war in northern Shensi. It included twenty-three counties along the common borders of the three provinces.

However, recent investigations in the Border Region have disclosed that, disregarding public interest, some persons are using various means to force the peasants to return land and houses that have been distributed to them, to compel debtors to pay back old cancelled loans,[2] to coerce the people into changing the democratic system . . .

Accordingly, we hereby unequivocally proclaim:

(1) The Government . . . forbids any unauthorized change in the distribution of land or houses and in the cancellation of debts. . . . (2) the Government will protect the activities of all the military, political, economic, cultural and mass organizations . . . and stop all intrigues and disruptive activities against them . . . ; (3) but to guard against impostors and keep out traitors, we prohibit any person, whatever his activities, from entering and staying in the Border Region unless he secures permission and written authorization from the Government . . . ; (4) it is right and proper for the people to report any person who tries to sabotage, engage in disruption, stir up sedition. . . .

These four regulations must be observed by all members of the armed forces and all civilians throughout the Border Region. . . . This proclamation is hereby issued with the full force of the law.

This proclamation was written by Mao Tse-tung for the government of the Shensi-Kansu-Ningsia Border Region and the Rear Headquarters of the Eighth Route Army to combat what the Chinese Communist Party charged was a disruptive plot by the Kuomintang.

2. By 1936 most places in the Border Region had confiscated the land of the landlords and distributed it among the peasants, and had cancelled the old debts of the peasants.

Problems of Strategy in Guerrilla War Against Japan

May 1938

Chapter I: Why Raise the Question of Strategy in Guerrilla War?

In the War of Resistance Against Japan, regular warfare is primary and guerrilla warfare supplementary. . . . Why then raise the question of strategy?

If China were a small country in which the role of guerrilla warfare was only to render direct support over short distance to the campaigns of the regular army, there would, of course, be only tactical problems but no strategic ones. On the other hand, if China were a country as strong as the Soviet Union and the invading enemy could either be quickly expelled . . . or could not occupy extensive areas, then again guerrilla warfare would . . . involve only tactical but not strategic problems.

The question of strategy in guerrilla war does arise, however, in the case of China, which is neither small nor like the Soviet Union, but which is both a large and a weak country. . . . It is in these circumstances that vast areas have come under enemy occupation and that the war has become a protracted one. . . . The protracted nature of the war and its attendant ruthlessness have made it imperative for guerrilla warfare to undertake many unusual tasks; hence such problems as those of the base areas, the development of guerrilla warfare into mobile warfare, and so on. For all these reasons, China's guerrilla warfare against Japan has broken out of the bounds of tactics to knock at the gates of strategy, and it demands examination from the viewpoint of strategy. . . .

Chapter II: The Basic Principle of War Is to Preserve Oneself and Destroy the Enemy

All the guiding principles of military operations grow out of the one basic principle: to strive to the utmost to preserve one's own strength and destroy that of the enemy. In a revolutionary war, this principle is directly linked with basic political principles. . . . In terms of military action this principle means the use of armed force to defend our motherland and to drive out the Japanese invaders. . . . Every war exacts a price, sometimes an extremely high one. Is this not in contradiction with "preserving oneself"? In fact, there is no contradiction at all . . . for such sacrifice is essential not only for destroying the enemy but also for preserving oneself. . . .

CHAPTER III: SIX SPECIFIC PROBLEMS OF STRATEGY IN GUERRILLA WAR AGAINST JAPAN

Now let us see what policies or principles have to be adopted in guerrilla operations against Japan before we can attain the object of preserving ourselves and destroying the enemy. . . .

The main principles are as follows: (1) The use of initiative, flexibility and planning in conducting offensives . . . battles of quick decision within protracted war . . . ; (2) co-ordination with regular warfare; (3) the establishment of base areas; (4) the strategic defensive and the strategic offensive; (5) the development of guerrilla warfare into mobile warfare; and (6) correct relationship of command. . . .

CHAPTER IV: INITIATIVE, FLEXIBILITY AND PLANNING IN CONDUCTING OFFENSIVES WITHIN THE DEFENSIVE, BATTLES OF QUICK DECISION WITHIN PROTRACTED WAR, AND EXTERIOR-LINE OPERATIONS WITHIN INTERIOR-LINE OPERATIONS

Here the subject may be dealt with under four headings: (1) The relationship between the defensive and the offensive, between protractedness and quick decision, and between the interior and exterior lines; (2) the initiative in all operations; (3) flexible employment of forces; and (4) planning in all operations.

To start with the first. If we take the War of Resistance as a whole, the fact that Japan is a strong country and is attacking while China is a weak country and is defending herself makes our war strategically a defensive and protracted war. . . . It is possible and necessary to use tactical offensives within the strategic defensive, to fight campaigns and battles of quick decision within a strategically protracted war and to fight campaigns and battles on exterior lines within strategically interior lines. Such is the strategy to be adopted in the War of Resistance as a whole. It holds true both for regular and for guerrilla warfare. . . .

Now let us discuss initiative, flexibility and planning in guerrilla warfare. What is the initiative in guerrilla warfare? In any war, the opponents contend for the initiative, whether on a battlefield, in a battle area, in a war zone or in the whole war, for the initiative means freedom of action for an army. Any army which, losing the initiative, is forced into a passive position and ceases to have freedom of action, faces the danger of defeat or extermination. . . . The question of the initiative is even more vital in guerrilla warfare. For most guerrilla units operate in very difficult circumstances, fighting without a rear, with their own weak forces facing the enemy's strong forces. . . . The initiative is not an innate attribute of genius, but is something an intelligent leader attains through open-minded study and correct appraisal of the objective conditions and through correct military and political dispositions. It follows that the initiative is not ready-made but is something that requires conscious effort. . . .

Next, let us deal with flexibility. Flexibility is a concrete expression of the initiative. The flexible employment of forces is more essential in guerrilla warfare than in regular warfare. A guerrilla commander must understand that the flexible employment of his forces is the most important means of changing the situation as between the enemy and ourselves and of gaining the initiative. The nature of guerrilla warfare is such that guerrilla forces must be employed flexibly in accordance with the task in hand and with such circumstances as the state of the enemy, the terrain and the local population; and the chief ways of employing the forces are dispersal, concentration and shifting of position. . . . But a commander proves himself wise not just by recognition of the importance of employing his forces flexibly but by skill in dispersing, concentrating or shifting them in good time according to the specific circumstances. . . . Prudent consideration of the circumstances is essential to prevent flexibility from turning into impulsive action.

Lastly, we come to planning. Without planning, victories in guerrilla warfare are impossible. Any idea that guerrilla warfare can be conducted in haphazard fashion indicates either a flippant attitude or ignorance of guerrilla warfare. The operations in a guerrilla zone as a whole, or those of a guerrilla unit or formation, must be preceded by as thorough planning as possible, by preparation in advance for every action. Grasping the situation, setting the tasks, disposing the forces, giving military and political training, securing supplies, putting the equipment in good order, making proper use of people's help, etc.—all these are part of the work of the guerrilla commanders. . . . True, guerrilla conditions do not allow as high a degree of planning as do those of regular warfare. . . . But it is necessary to plan as thoroughly as the objective conditions permit, for it should be understood that fighting the enemy is no joke.

Chapter V: Co-ordination with Regular Warfare

The second problem of strategy in guerrilla warfare is its co-ordination with regular warfare. It is a matter of clarifying the relation between guerrilla and regular warfare on the operational level, in the light of the nature of actual guerrilla operations. . . . Take the case of the guerrilla warfare in the three northeastern provinces. . . . Every enemy soldier the guerrillas kill there, every bullet they make the enemy expend, every enemy soldier they stop from advancing south of the Great Wall, can be reckoned a contribution to the total strength of the resistance. . . .

In addition, guerrilla warfare performs the function of co-ordination with regular warfare in campaigns. . . . If each guerrilla zone or unit goes it alone without giving any attention to co-ordinating with the campaigns of the regular forces, its role in strategic co-ordination will lose a great deal of its significance. . . .

Finally, co-ordination with the regular forces in battles, in actual fighting on the battlefield, is the task of all guerrilla units in the vicinity of an interior-line battlefield. . . . In such cases a guerrilla unit has to perform whatever task it is assigned by the commander of the regular forces. . . . To sit by idly, neither moving nor fighting, or to move about without fighting, would be an intolerable attitude for a guerrilla unit.

Chapter VI: The Establishment of Base Areas

The third problem of strategy in anti-Japanese guerrilla warfare is the establishment of base areas, which is important and essential because of the protracted nature and ruthlessness of the war. . . . With ruthlessness thus added to protractedness, it will be impossible to sustain guerrilla warfare behind the enemy lines without base areas. . . .

Without such strategic bases, there will be nothing to depend on in carrying out any of our strategic tasks or achieving the aim of the war. It is characteristic of guerrilla warfare behind the enemy lines that it is fought without a rear, for the guerrilla forces are severed from the country's general rear. But guerrilla warfare could not last long or grow without base areas. The base areas, indeed, are its rear. . . .

1. The Types of Base Areas

Base areas in anti-Japanese guerrilla warfare are mainly of three types, those in the mountains, those on the plains and those in the river-lake-estuary regions. . . .

Of course, the plains are less suitable than the mountains, but it is by no means impossible to develop guerrilla warfare or establish any base areas there. Indeed, the widespread guerrilla warfare in the plains of Hopei and of northern and northwestern Shantung proves that it is possible to develop guerrilla warfare in the plains. . . .

2. Guerrilla Zones and Base Areas

In guerrilla warfare behind the enemy lines, there is a difference between guerrilla zones and base areas. Areas which are surrounded by the enemy but whose central parts are not occupied or have been recovered, like some counties in the Wutai mountain region . . . are ready-made bases for the convenient use of guerrilla units. . . . Thus the transformation of a guerrilla zone into a base area is an arduous creative process, and its accomplishment depends on the extent to which the enemy is destroyed and the masses are aroused. . . .

As for the big cities, the railway stops and the areas in the plains which are strongly garrisoned by the enemy, guerrilla warfare can only extend to the fringes and not right into these places which have relatively stable puppet regimes. . . .

Mistakes in our leadership or strong enemy pressure may cause a reversal of the state of affairs described above. . . . Such changes are possible, and they deserve special vigilance on the part of guerrilla commanders.

3. Conditions for Establishing Base Areas

The fundamental conditions for establishing a base area are that there should be anti-Japanese armed forces, that these armed forces should be employed to inflict defeats on the enemy and that they should arouse the people to action. . . . If there is no armed force or if the armed force is weak, nothing can be done. This constitutes the first condition.

The second indispensable condition for establishing a base area is that the armed forces should be used in co-ordination with the people to defeat the enemy. . . .

The third indispensable condition for establishing a base area is the use of all our strength, including our armed forces, to arouse the masses for struggle against Japan. . . .

A base area for guerrilla war can be truly established only with the gradual fulfillment of the three basic conditions, that is, only after the anti-Japanese armed forces are built up, the enemy has suffered defeats and the people are aroused.

4. The Consolidation and Expansion of Base Areas

In order to confine the enemy invaders to a few strongholds, that is, to the big cities and along the main communication lines, the guerrillas must do all they can to extend guerrilla warfare from their base areas as widely as possible and hem in all the enemy's strongholds, thus threatening his existence and shaking his morale while expanding the base areas.

Given a protracted war, the problem of consolidating and expanding base areas constantly arises for every guerrilla unit.

5. Forms in Which We and the Enemy Encircle One Another

Taking the War of Resistance as a whole, there is no doubt that we are strategically encircled by the enemy, because he is on the strategic offensive and is operating on exterior lines while we are on the strategic defensive and are operating on interior lines. This is the first form of enemy encirclement. We on our part encircle each of the enemy columns advancing on us along separate routes. . . . This is the first form of our encirclement of the enemy. Next, if we consider the guerrilla bases in the enemy's rear, each area taken singly is surrounded by the enemy on all sides. . . . This is the second form of enemy encirclement. However, if one considers all the guerrilla base areas together and in their relation to the battle fronts of the regular forces, one can see that we in turn surround a great many enemy forces. . . . This is the second form of our encirclement of the enemy. Thus there are two forms of encirclement by the enemy forces and two forms of encirclement by our own— rather like a game of *weichi*.[1]

Chapter VII: The Strategic Defensive and the Strategic Offensive in Guerrilla War

The fourth problem of strategy in guerrilla war concerns the strategic defensive and the strategic offensive. This is the problem of how the policy of offensive warfare, which we mentioned in our discussion of the first problem, is to be carried out in practice, when we are on the defensive and when we are on the offensive in our guerrilla warfare against Japan. . . .

1. The Strategic Defensive in Guerrilla War

To wipe out the guerrillas and their base areas, the enemy frequently resorts to converging attacks. . . . When the enemy

1. *Weichi* is an old Chinese game in which the two players try to encircle each other's pieces on the board. When a player's pieces are encircled, they are counted as "dead" (captured). But if there is a sufficient number of blank spaces among the encircled pieces, then the latter are still "alive" (not captured).

launches a converging attack in several columns, the guerrilla policy
should be to smash it by counterattack. It can be easily smashed if
each advancing enemy column consists of only one unit, whether big
or small, has no follow-up units and is unable to station troops along
the route of advance, construct blockhouses or build motor roads.
. . . The enemy, though strong, will be weakened by repeated surprise attacks and will often withdraw when he is halfway; the guerrilla units can then make more surprise attacks during the pursuit
and weaken him still further. . . .

Should the enemy stay put in our base area, we may reverse the
tactics, namely, leave some of our forces in the base area to invest the
enemy, while employing the main force to attack the region whence
he has come and to step up our activities there, in order to induce
him to withdraw and attack our main force; this is the tactic of
"Relieving the state of Chao by besieging the State of Wei."[2]

When the enemy retreats, he often burns down the houses in the
cities and towns he has occupied and razes the villages along his
route, with the purpose of destroying the guerrilla base areas; but in
so doing he deprives himself of shelter and food in his next offensive,
and the damage recoils upon his own head. This is a concrete illustra-
tion of what we mean by one and the same thing having two contradictory aspects. . . . Since we have had the experience of being able
to maintain guerrilla warfare during the civil war, there is not the
slightest doubt of our greater capacity to do so in a national war. . . .

2. The Strategic Offensive in Guerrilla War

After we have smashed an enemy offensive and before the enemy
starts a new offensive, he is on the strategic defensive and we are on
the strategic offensive.

At such times our operational policy is not to attack enemy forces

2. In 353 B.C., the state of Wei laid siege to Hantan the capital of the
state of Chao. The King of the state of Chi, an ally of Chao, ordered his
generals Tien Chi and Sun Pin to aid Chao with their troops. Knowing that
the crack forces of Wei had entered Chao and left their own territory weakly
garrisoned, General Sun Pin attacked the state of Wei, whose troops withdrew
to defend their own country. Taking advantage of their exhaustion, the troops
of Chi engaged and routed them at Kueiling (northeast of the present Hotse
County in Shantung). The siege of Hantan, capital of Chao, was thus lifted.
Since then Chinese strategists have referred to similar tactics as "Relieving the
state of Chao by besieging the state of Wei."

which are entrenched in defensive positions and which we are not sure of defeating, but systematically to destroy or drive out the small enemy units and puppet forces in certain areas, which our guerrilla units are strong enough to deal with. . . .

CHAPTER VIII: THE DEVELOPMENT OF GUERRILLA WARFARE INTO MOBILE WARFARE

To transform guerrilla units waging guerrilla warfare into regular forces waging mobile warfare, two conditions are necessary—an increase in numbers and an improvement in quality. Apart from directly mobilizing the people to join the forces, increased numbers can be attained by amalgamating small units, while better quality depends on steeling the fighters and improving their weapons in the course of the war.

In amalgamating small units, we must, on the one hand, guard against localism, whereby attention is concentrated exclusively on local interests and centralization is impeded, and, on the other, guard against the purely military approach, whereby local interests are brushed aside. . . .

To raise the quality of the guerrilla units it is imperative to raise their political and organizational level and improve their equipment, military technique, tactics and discipline, so that they gradually pattern themselves on the regular forces and shed their guerrilla ways. . . . To accomplish all these tasks requires a prolonged effort, and it cannot be done overnight; but that is the direction in which we must develop.

CHAPTER IX: THE RELATIONSHIP OF COMMAND

The last problem of strategy in guerrilla war against Japan concerns the relationship of command. A correct solution of this problem is one of the prerequisites for the unhampered development of guerrilla warfare.

Since guerrilla units are a lower level of armed organization characterized by dispersed operations, the methods of command in guerrilla warfare do not allow as high a degree of centralization as in

regular warfare. . . . However, guerrilla warfare cannot be successfully developed without some centralized command. When extensive
regular warfare and extensive guerrilla warfare are going on at the
same time, their operations must be properly co-ordinated. . . .

Hence, as opposed both to absolute centralization and to absolute
decentralization, the principle of command in guerrilla war should be
centralized strategic command and decentralized command in campaigns and battles. . . .

Absence of centralization where it is needed means negligence by
the higher levels or usurpation of authority by the lower levels,
neither of which can be tolerated in the relationship between higher
and lower levels, especially in the military sphere. If decentralization
is not affected where it should be, that means monopolization of
power by the higher levels and lack of initiative on the part of the
lower levels, neither of which can be tolerated in the relationship
between higher and lower levels, especially in the command of guerrilla warfare. The above principles constitute the only correct policy
for solving the problem of the relationship of command.

**This proclamation was written by Mao Tse-tung for the government of
the Shensi-Kansu-Ningsia border region and the Rear Headquarters of
the Eighth Route Army. Its purpose, said Mao Tse-tung, was to "counter
disruptive activities by the Chiang Kai-shek clique."**

On Protracted War

May 1938

A Statement of the Problem

It will soon be July 7, the first anniversary of the Great War of
Resistance Against Japan. Rallying in unity, persevering in resistance
and persevering in the united front, the forces of the whole nation
have been valiantly fighting the enemy for almost a year. . . .

But what actually will be the course of the war? Can we win? Can
we win quickly? Many people are talking about a protracted war, but
why is it a protracted war? How to carry on a protracted war? Many

people are talking about final victory, but why will final victory be ours? How shall we strive for final victory? . . . Defeatist exponents of the theory of national subjugation have come forward to tell people that China will be subjugated. . . . On the other hand, some impetuous friends have come forward to tell people that China will win very quickly without having to exert any great effort. . . . However, most people have not yet grasped what we have been saying. . . . Now things are better; the experience of ten months of war has been quite sufficient to explode the utterly baseless theory of national subjugation and to dissuade our impetuous friends from their theory of quick victory. . . .

A serious study of protracted war is necessary in order to enable every Communist to play a better and greater part in the War of Resistance. . . .

During these ten months of war all kinds of views which are indicative of impetuosity have also appeared. . . . At the outset of the war many people were groundlessly optimistic, underestimating Japan . . . they disagreed with the Eighth Route Army's strategy. . . . After the Taierhchuang[1] victory, some people maintained that the . . . policy of protracted war should be changed. They said such things as, "This campaign marks the last desperate struggle of the enemy."

The question now is: Will China be subjugated? The answer is, No, she will not be subjugated, but will win final victory. Can China win quickly? The answer is, No, she cannot win quickly, and the War of Resistance will be a protracted war.

As early as two years ago, we broadly indicated the main arguments on these questions. On July 16, 1936, five months before the Sian Incident and twelve months before the Lukouchiao Incident, in an interview with the American correspondent, Mr. Edgar Snow,[2] I

1. Taierhchuang is a town in southern Shantung where the Chinese Army fought a battle in March 1938, and won its first victory in positional warfare against the Japanese. By pitting 400,000 men against Japan's attacking 70,000 to 80,000, the Chinese defeated the Japanese decisively.

2. Edgar Snow, a native of Missouri, went to the Far East in the mid-1920's, when he was twenty-two. In Shanghai he was associate editor of J. B. Powell's *China Weekly Review*. Later he worked successively for the Chicago *Tribune*, New York *Sun*, New York *Herald Tribune*, and London *Daily Herald*, and during World War II he reported wartime events from Europe and Asia for the *Saturday Evening Post*. He is the author of ten books, including *Red Star Over China*, *The Other Side of the River*.

made a general estimate of the situation. . . . The following excerpts may serve as a reminder:

QUESTION: Under what conditions do you think China can defeat and destroy the forces of Japan?

ANSWER: Three conditions are required: first, the establishment of an anti-Japanese united front in China; second, the formation of an international anti-Japanese united front; third, the rise of the revolutionary movement of the people in Japan and the Japanese colonies.

QUESTION: How long do you think such a war would last?

ANSWER: . . . If China's anti-Japanese united front is greatly expanded and effectively organized horizontally and vertically, if the necessary help is given to China by those governments and peoples which recognize the Japanese imperialist menace to their own interests and if revolution comes quickly in Japan, the war will speedily be brought to an end and China will speedily win victory. If these conditions are not realized quickly, the war will be prolonged. . . .

QUESTION: What is your opinion of the probable course of development of such a war, politically and militarily?

ANSWER: Japan's continental policy is already fixed, and those who think they can halt the Japanese advance by making compromises . . . are indulging in mere fantasy. Moreover, Japan wants to occupy the Philippines, Siam, Indochina, the Malay Peninsula and the Dutch East Indies. . . .

QUESTION: If the war drags on . . . would the Communist Party agree to the negotiation of a peace with Japan and recognize her rule in northeastern China?

ANSWER: No. Like the people of the whole country, the Chinese Communist Party will not allow Japan to retain an inch of Chinese territory.

QUESTION: What, in your opinion, should be the main strategy and tactics to be followed in this "war of liberation"?

ANSWER: Our strategy should be to employ our main forces to operate over an extended and fluid front. . . . This means large-scale mobile warfare, and not positional warfare depending exclusively on defense works with deep trenches, high fortresses and successive rows of defensive positions. . . .

Besides employing trained armies to carry on mobile warfare, we must organize great numbers of guerrilla units among the peasants. . . . The Chinese peasants have very great latent power; properly organized and directed, they can keep the Japanese Army busy twenty-four hours a day and worry it to death. . . .

In the course of the war, China will be able to capture many Japanese soldiers and seize many weapons and munitions with which to arm herself; at the same time China will win foreign aid to reinforce the equipment of her troops gradually. . . . The combination of all these and other factors will enable us to make the final and decisive attacks on the fortifications and bases in the Japanese-occupied areas and drive the Japanese forces of aggression out of China.
. . .

THE BASIS OF THE PROBLEM

Why is the War of Resistance Against Japan a protracted war? Why will the final victory be China's? . . .

The Japanese side. First, Japan is a powerful imperialist country, which ranks first in the East in military, economic and political-organizational power, and is one of the five or six foremost imperialist countries in the world. . . . Secondly, however, the imperialist character of Japan's social economy determines the imperialist character of her war, a war that is retrogressive and barbarous. . . . The reactionary and barbarous character of Japan's war constitutes the primary reason for her inevitable defeat. Thirdly, Japan's war is conducted on the basis of her great military, economic and political-organizational power, but at the same time it rests on an inadequate natural endowment . . . and she cannot stand a long war. . . .

The Chinese side. First, we are a semicolonial and semifeudal country. The Opium War,[3] the Taiping Revolution,[4] the Reform

3. In the later part of the eighteenth century, Britain began exporting increasing quantities of opium to China, importation of which had been prohibited by the Chinese Government. By 1839 the traffic had become so large that Peking sent a special commissioner, Lin Tse-hsu, to Canton to stamp it out. British armed forces subdued the Chinese attempt to assert its sovereign right to prohibit the importation of opium, and the end result was the Treaty of Nanking, which provided for the payment of indemnities and the cession of Hong Kong to Britain, and stipulated that Shanghai, Foochow, Amoy, Ningpo and Canton were to be opened to British trade.

4. See note 9, p. 57.

Movement of 1898,[5] the Revolution of 1911,[6] and the Northern Expedition[7]—the revolutionary or reform movements which aimed at extricating China from her semicolonial and semifeudal state—all met with serious setbacks, and China remains a semicolonial and semifeudal country . . . a weak country and manifestly inferior to the enemy in military, economic and political-organizational power. . . . Secondly, however, China's liberation movement, with its cumulative development over the last hundred years, is now different from that of any previous period. . . . By contrast with Japanese imperialism, which is declining, China is a country rising like the morning sun. . . . China is a very big country with vast territory, rich resources, a large population and plenty of soldiers, and is capable of sustaining a long war. Fourthly and lastly, there is broad international support for China stemming from the progressive and just character of her war, which is again exactly the reverse of the meager support for Japan's unjust cause. . . .

REFUTATION OF THE THEORY OF NATIONAL SUBJUGATION

The theorists of national subjugation, who see nothing but the contrast between the enemy's strength and our weakness, used to say, "Resistance will mean subjugation," and now they are saying, "The

5. The Reform Movement of 1898 was a short-lived attempt by a budding liberal movement to gain civil reforms under the Empress Dowager Tzu Hsi. It failed, and its leader, Tan Szu-tung, was beheaded.

6. China's revolution began in Wuchang, Hupeh, on October 10, 1911 (celebrated as the Double Ten anniversary), with a revolt of government troops against the Manchu regime. Yuan Shih-kai, retired commander of the Manchu Government's armies, was called back into service to defend the dynasty. In January 1912, the provisional government of the Republic of China was set up in Nanking, with Sun Yat Sen as provisional President. The following month the Manchu "boy-Emperor" was made to abdicate the throne. A deal between the defending and the revolutionary forces resulted in Sun Yat Sen's resigning the presidency and allowing Yuan Shi-kai to be named President in his stead, ending the last imperial Chinese dynasty.

7. The Northern Expedition was a war against the warlords of the northern provinces, a joint Kuomintang-Communist venture, under the command of General Chiang Kai-shek. When its armies reached Hankow, Hupeh, on the Yangtze River in the autumn of 1926, the Communists, under the leadership of Michael Borodin, set up a government entirely dominated by the Communist Party. This resulted in a split between the Kuomintang and Communist Party forces, and eventually to war between the two factions.

continuance of the war spells subjugation." . . . They can adduce historical instances, such as the destruction of the Sung Dynasty by the Yuan and the destruction of the Ming Dynasty by the Ching, to prove that a small but strong country can vanquish a large but weak one. . . .

What then are the grounds we should advance? . . . The China of today cannot be compared with the China of any other historical period. She is a semicolony and a semifeudal society, and she is consequently considered a weak country. But at the same time, China is historically in her era of progress; this is the primary reason for her ability to defeat Japan. . . .

In the existing international situation, China is not isolated in the war, and this fact too is without precedent in history. In the past, China's wars, and India's too, were wars fought in isolation. . . .

The existence of the Soviet Union is a particularly vital factor in present-day international politics, and the Soviet Union will certainly support China with the greatest enthusiasm;[8] there was nothing like this twenty years ago. . . .

If the subjugationists quote the history of the failure of liberation movements in modern China to prove their assertions first that "resistance will mean subjugation," and then that "the continuance of the war spells subjugation," here again our answer is, "Times are different." . . . These are favorable conditions such as never existed before in any period of our history, and that is why the War of Resistance Against Japan, unlike the liberation movements of the past, will not end in failure.

COMPROMISE OR RESISTANCE?
CORRUPTION OR PROGRESS?

. . . The question of compromise has its social roots, and as long as these roots exist the question is bound to arise. But compromise will not avail. To prove the point, again we need only look for substantiation to Japan, China, and the international situation. First

8. The Soviet Union gave China no support whatever, until seven years later, after Japan had been defeated by two atom bomb attacks, the first on August 6, 1945, on Hiroshima, and the second on August 9, 1945, on Nagasaki. The same day (August 9), the Soviet Union, in compliance with the Yalta Conference agreement signed in February 1945 launched an attack against the Japanese Army in Manchuria.

take Japan. At the very beginning of the War of Resistance, we estimated that the time would come when an atmosphere conducive to compromise would arise, in other words, that after occupying northern China, Kiangsu and Chekiang, Japan would probably resort to the scheme of inducing China to capitulate. . . . Had China capitulated, every Chinese would have become a slave without a country. . . .

Second, let us take China. There are three factors contributing to China's perseverance in the War of Resistance. In the first place, the Communist Party, which is the reliable force leading the people to resist Japan. Next, the Kuomintang, which depends on Britain and the United States and hence will not capitulate to Japan unless they tell it to. Finally, the other political parties and groups, most of which oppose compromise and support the War of Resistance. . . .

Third, take the international aspect. Except for Japan's allies and certain elements in the upper strata of other capitalist countries, the whole world is in favor of resistance, and not of compromise by China.

. . . Hence we may conclude that the danger of compromise exists but can be overcome. . . .

. . . Every just, revolutionary war is endowed with tremendous power, which can transform many things or clear the way for their transformation. The Sino-Japanese War will transform both China and Japan. . . the old Japan will surely be transformed into a new Japan and the old China into a new China. . . . To say that Japan can also be transformed is to say that the war of aggression by her rulers will end in defeat and may lead to a revolution by the Japanese people. The day of triumph of the Japanese people's revolution will be the day Japan is transformed. All this is closely linked with China's War of Resistance and is a prospect we should take into account.

The Theory of National Subjugation Is Wrong and the Theory of Quick Victory Is Likewise Wrong

. . . The subjugationists stress the contradiction between strength and weakness and puff it up until it becomes the basis of their whole argument on the question, neglecting all the other contradictions.
. . .

The exponents of quick victory are likewise wrong. . . . They presumptuously take the balance of forces at one time and place for the whole situation, as in the old saying, "A leaf before the eye shuts out Mount Tai." In a word, they lack the courage to admit that the enemy is strong while we are weak. . . . These friends have their hearts in the right place, and they, too, are patriots. But while "the gentlemen's aspirations are indeed lofty," their views are wrong, and to act according to them would certainly be to run into a brick wall. . . .

Not that we would not like a quick victory; everybody would be in favor of driving the "devils" out overnight. But we point out that, in the absence of certain definite conditions, quick victory is something that exists only in one's mind and not in objective reality, and that it is a mere illusion, a false theory . . . and we reject the theory of quick victory, which is just idle talk and an effort to get things on the cheap.

Why a Protracted War?

Let us now examine the problem of protracted war. A correct answer to the question "Why a protracted war?" can be arrived at only on the basis of all the fundamental contrasts between China and Japan.

. . . During a certain stage of the war, to a certain degree the enemy will be victorious and we shall suffer defeat. But why is it that at this stage the enemy's victories and our defeats are definitely restricted in degree and cannot be transcended by complete victory or complete defeat? The reason is that, first, from the very beginning the enemy's strength and our weakness have been relative and not absolute; and that, second, our efforts in persevering in the War of Resistance and in the united front have further accentuated this relativeness. . . . On both sides, strength and weakness, superiority and inferiority, have never been absolute. . . . Therefore, in this stage the enemy's victory and our defeat are definitely restricted in degree, and hence the war becomes protracted.

The Three Stages of the Protracted War

Since the Sino-Japanese War is a protracted one and final victory will belong to China, it can reasonably be assumed that this protracted war will pass through three stages. The first stage covers the period of the enemy's strategic offensive and our strategic defensive. The second stage will be the period of the enemy's strategic consolidation and our preparation for the counteroffensive. The third stage will be the period of our strategic counteroffensive and the enemy's strategic retreat. . . .

The first stage has not yet ended. The enemy's design is to occupy Canton, Wuhan and Lanchow and link up these three points. To accomplish this aim the enemy will have to use at least fifty divisions, or about one and a half million men, spend from one and a half to two years, and expend more than 10,000 million *yen*. In penetrating so deeply, he will encounter immense difficulties, with consequences disastrous beyond imagination. . . .

In the second stage, the enemy will attempt to safeguard the occupied areas and to make them his own by the fraudulent method of setting up puppet governments, while plundering the Chinese people to the limit; but again he will be confronted with stubborn guerrilla warfare. . . . The fighting in the second stage will be ruthless, and the country will suffer serious devastation. But the guerrilla warfare will be successful, and if it is well conducted the enemy may be able to retain only about one-third of his occupied territory, with the remaining two-thirds in our hands, and this will constitute a great defeat for the enemy and a great victory for China. . . .

The third stage will be the stage of the counteroffensive to recover our lost territories. Their recovery will depend mainly upon the strength which China has built up in the preceding stage. But China's strength alone will not be sufficient, and we shall also have to rely on the support of international forces and on the changes that will take place inside Japan. . . . Ultimately the enemy will lose and we will win, but we shall have a hard stretch of road to travel.

A War of Jigsaw Pattern

We can say with certainty that the protracted War of Resistance Against Japan will write a splendid page unique in the war history of mankind. One of the special features of this war is the interlocking "jigsaw" pattern which arises from such contradictory factors as the barbarity of Japan and her shortage of troops on the one hand, and the progressiveness of China and the extensiveness of her territory on the other. . . . Its jigsaw pattern manifests itself as follows.

Interior and exterior lines. The anti-Japanese war as a whole is being fought on interior lines; but as far as the relation between the main forces and the guerrilla units is concerned, the former are on the interior lines while the latter are on the exterior lines, presenting a remarkable spectacle of pincers around the enemy. . . .

Encirclement and counterencirclement. Taking the war as a whole, there is no doubt that we are strategically encircled by the enemy because he is on the strategic offensive and operating on exterior lines while we are on the strategic defensive and operating on interior lines. . . .

But our encirclement, like the hand of Buddha, will turn into the Mountain of Five Elements lying athwart the universe, and the modern Sun Wu-kungs[9]—the facist aggressors—will finally be buried underneath it, never to rise again. Therefore, if on the international plane we can create an anti-Japanese front in the Pacific region, with China as one strategic unit, with the Soviet Union and other countries . . . as still another strategic unit, and thus form a gigantic net from which the fascist Wu-kungs can find no escape, then that will be our enemy's day of doom . . . the day of the complete overthrow of Japanese imperialism. . . .

FIGHTING FOR PERPETUAL PEACE

The protracted nature of China's anti-Japanese war is inseparably connected with the fight for perpetual peace in China and the whole world. Never has there been a historical period such as the present in which war is so close to perpetual peace. . . . This war, we can foresee, will not save capitalism, but will hasten its collapse. It will be greater in scale and more ruthless than the war of twenty years ago, all nations will inevitably be drawn in, it will drag on for a very long

9. Sun Wu-kung is the monkey king in the sixteenth-century novel *Hsi Yu Chi* (*Pilgrimage to the West*). He could cover 108,000 *li* (a *li* is about a third of a mile) by turning a somersault. Yet once in the palm of the Buddha, he could not escape from it, however many somersaults he turned. With a flick of his palm, Buddha transformed his fingers into the five-peak Mountain of Five Elements and buried Sun Wu-kung.

time, and mankind will suffer greatly. But, owing to the existence of the Soviet Union and the growing political consciousness of the people of the world, great revolutionary wars will undoubtedly emerge from this war, thus giving it the character of a struggle for perpetual peace. . . . Once man has eliminated capitalism, he will attain the era of perpetual peace, and there will be no more need for war. . . .

History shows that wars are divided into two kinds, just and unjust. All wars that are progressive are just, and all wars that impede progress are unjust. We Communists oppose all unjust wars that impede progress, but we do not oppose progressive just wars. Not only do we Communists not oppose just wars, we actively participate in them. . . .

Our war is sacred and just, it is progressive and its aim is peace. The aim is peace not just in one country but throughout the world, not just temporary but perpetual peace. . . . This is no vain hope, for the whole world is approaching this point in the course of its social and economic development, and provided that the majority of mankind work together, our goal will surely be attained in several decades.

Man's Dynamic Role in War

We have so far explained why the war is a protracted war and why the final victory will be China's, and in the main dealt with what protracted war is and what it is not. Now we shall turn to the question of what to do and what not to do. . . . Let us start with the problem of man's dynamic role. . . .

. . . Protracted war and final victory will not come about without human action. For such action to be effective there must be people who derive ideas, principles or views from the objective facts, and put forward plans, directives, policies, strategies and tactics. Ideas, etc., are subjective, while deeds or actions are the subjective translated into the objective, but both represent the dynamic role peculiar to human beings. We term this kind of dynamic role "man's conscious dynamic role," and it is a characteristic that distinguishes man from all other beings. All ideas based upon and corresponding to objective facts are correct ideas, and all deeds or actions based upon correct ideas are correct actions. . . .

It is a human characteristic to exercise a conscious dynamic role. Man strongly displays this characteristic in war. . . . In seeking victory, those who direct a war cannot overstep the limitations imposed by the objective conditions; within these limitations, however, they can and must play a dynamic role in striving for victory. . . . We do not want any of our commanders in the war to detach himself from the objective conditions and become a blundering hothead, but we decidedly want every commander to become a general who is both bold and sagacious. . . . Swimming in the ocean of war, they must not flounder but make sure of reaching the opposite shore with measured strokes. Strategy and tactics, as the laws for directing war, constitute the art of swimming in the ocean of war.

War and Politics

"War is the continuation of politics." In this sense war is politics and war itself is a political action; since ancient times there has never been a war that did not have a political character. . . . And the tendency among the anti-Japanese armed forces to belittle politics by isolating war from it and advocating the idea of war as an absolute is wrong and should be corrected.

But war has its own particular characteristics and in this sense it cannot be equated with politics in general. "War is the continuation of politics by other . . . means."[10] When politics develops to a certain stage beyond which it cannot proceed by the usual means, war breaks out to sweep the obstacles from the way. . . . But if the obstacle is not completely swept away, the war will have to continue till the aim is fully accomplished. . . . It can therefore be said that politics is war without bloodshed while war is politics with bloodshed. . . . Hence war experience is a particular kind of experience. All who take part in war must rid themselves of their customary ways and accustom themselves to war before they can win victory.

10. This definition of war, in fact made by Karl von Clausewitz (1780–1831), is attributed by Mao Tse-tung to V. I. Lenin, *Socialism and War* (Eng. ed., Moscow, 1950), p. 19.

Political Mobilization for the War of Resistance

A national revolutionary war as great as ours cannot be won without extensive and thoroughgoing political mobilization. . . . The mobilization of the common people throughout the country will create a vast sea in which to drown the enemy, create the conditions that will make up for our inferiority in arms and other things, and create the prerequisites for overcoming every difficulty in the war. . . . To wish for victory and yet neglect political mobilization is like wishing to "go south by driving the chariot north," and the result would inevitably be to forfeit victory.

What does political mobilization mean? First, it means telling the army and the people about the political aim of the war. It is necessary for every soldier and civilian to see why the war must be fought and how it concerns him. . . . By word of mouth, by leaflets and bulletins, by newspapers, books and pamphlets, through plays and films, through schools, through the mass organizations and through our cadres. . . . We must link the political mobilization for the war with developments in the war and with the life of the soldiers and the people, and make it a continuous movement. This is a matter of immense importance on which our victory in the war primarily depends.

The Object of War

Here we are not dealing with the political aim of the war; the political aim of the War of Resistance Against Japan has been defined above as "To drive out Japanese imperialism and build a new China of freedom and equality." Here we are dealing with the elementary object of war, as "politics with bloodshed," as mutual slaughter by opposing armies. The object of war is specifically "to preserve oneself and destroy the enemy." . . . It should be pointed out that destruction of the enemy is the primary object of war and self-preservation the secondary, because only by destroying the enemy in large numbers can one effectively preserve oneself. . . . In actual warfare the chief role is played by defense much of the time and by attack for the rest of the time, but if war is taken as a whole, attack remains primary. . . . Thus, no technical, tactical, or strategical principles or operations can in any way depart from the object of war, and this object pervades the whole of a war and runs through it from beginning to end. . . .

Offense Within Defense, Quick Decisions Within a Protracted War, Exterior Lines Within Interior Lines

. . . Since Japan is a strong imperialist power and we are a weak semicolonial and semifeudal country, she has adopted the policy of the strategic offensive while we are on the strategic defensive. Japan is trying to execute the strategy of a war of quick decision; we should consciously execute the strategy of protracted war. . . . However, we can make use of our two advantages, namely, our vast territory and large forces, and, instead of stubborn positional warfare, carry on flexible mobile warfare, employing several divisions against one enemy division, several tens of thousands of our men against ten thousand of his, several columns against one of his columns, and suddenly encircling and attacking a single column from the exterior lines of the battlefield. In this way, while the enemy is on exterior lines and on the offensive in strategic operations, he will be forced to fight on interior lines and on the defensive in campaigns and battles. And for us, interior lines and the defensive in strategic operations will be transformed into exterior lines and the offensive in campaigns and battles. . . . We should concentrate a big force under cover beforehand alongside the route which the enemy is sure to take, and while he is on the move, advance suddenly to encircle and attack him before he knows what is happening, and thus quickly conclude the battle. . . .

If we resolutely apply "quick-decision offensive warfare on exterior lines" on a battlefield, we shall not only change the balance of forces on that battlefield, but also gradually change the general situation. . . . After many such battles have been victoriously fought, the general situation between us and the enemy will change. . . . When that happens, these changes, together with other factors on our side and together with the changes inside the enemy camp and a favorable international situation, will turn the overall situation between us and the enemy first into one of parity and then into one of superiority for us. That will be the time for us to launch the counter-offensive and drive the enemy out of the country. . . .

INITIATIVE, FLEXIBILITY AND PLANNING

. . . Initiative is inseparable from superiority in capacity to wage war, while passivity is inseparable from inferiority in capacity to wage war. Such superiority or inferiority is the objective basis of initiative or passivity. . . . As for China, though placed in a some-what passive position strategically because of her inferior strength, she is nevertheless quantitatively superior in territory, population and troops, and also superior in the morale of her people and army and their patriotic hatred of the enemy. . . . Any passivity, however, is a disadvantage, and one must strive hard to shake it off. . . .

Yet war is in no way supernatural, but a mundane process governed by necessity. That is why Sun Wu Tzu's axiom, "Know the enemy and know yourself, and you can fight a hundred battles with no danger of defeat," remains a scientific truth. . . .

The thesis that incorrect subjective direction can change superiority and initiative into inferiority and passivity, and that correct subjective direction can effect a reverse change, becomes all the more convincing when we look at the record of defeats suffered by big and powerful armies and of victories won by small and weak armies. There are many such instances in Chinese and foreign history. Examples in China are the Battle of Chengpu between the states of Tsin and Chu,[11] the Battle of Chengkao between the states of Chu and Han,[12] the battle in which Han Hsin defeated the Chao armies,[13] the Battle of Kunyang between the states of Hsin and

11. Chengpu, in Shantung Province, was the scene of a great battle between the states of Tsin and Chu in 632 B.C. Initially the Chu troops were on top, but the Tsin troops, after retreating 90 *li*, picked the enemy's weak spots and defeated them.

12. Chengkao, in Honan Province, was the scene of battles in 203 B.C. between Liu Pang, King of Han, and Hsiang Yu, King of Chu. When almost defeated, Liu Pang waited until Hsiang Yu's troops were in midstream crossing the Szeshui River, then crushed them, and recaptured Chengkao.

13. In 204 B.C. Han Hsin, a general of the state of Han, deployed his much smaller army in pincer formation against the enemy whose troops were then destroyed.

Han,[14] the Battle of Kuantu between Yuan Shao and Tsao Tsao,[15] the Battle of Chihpi between the states of Wu and Wei,[16] the Battle of Yiling between the states of Wu and Shu,[17] the Battle of Feishui between the states of Chin and Tsin,[18] etc. Among examples to be found abroad are most of Napoleon's campaigns and the civil war in the Soviet Union after the October Revolution. In all these instances, victory was won by small forces over big and by inferior over superior forces. In every case, the weaker force, pitting local superiority and initiative against the enemy's local inferiority and passivity, first inflicted one sharp defeat on the enemy and then turned on the rest of his forces and smashed them one by one, thus transforming the overall situation into one of superiority and initiative. . . .

To have misconceptions and to be caught unawares may mean to lose superiority and initiative. Hence, deliberately creating misconceptions for the enemy and then springing surprise attacks upon him are two ways—indeed two important means—of achieving superiority and seizing the initiative. What are misconceptions? "To see every bush and tree on Mount Pakung as an enemy soldier" is an example of misconception. And "making a feint to the east but attacking in

14. Liu Hsiu, founder of the Eastern Han Dynasty, defeated the troops of Wang Mang, Emperor of the Hsin Dynasty, in A.D. 23, by taking advantage of the negligence of Wang Mang's generals, and crushed the enemy troops.
15. Kuantu was in northeast Honan Province, scene of a battle between the armies of Tsao Tsao and Yuan Shao in A.D. 200. Tsao Tsao, with a meager force, took advantage of his enemy's lack of vigilance, and in a surprise attack set his supplies on fire, throwing the enemy into confusion and then wiping out his main force.
16. In A.D. 208 Chihpi, on the south bank of the Yangtze River in Hupeh Province, was attacked by Tsao Tsao of the state of Wei. The defenders, with only 30,000 men against the attacker's 500,000, set the enemy fleet on fire and crushed his army.
17. Lu Sun, a general of the state of Wu, defeated the far stronger army of Liu Pei, ruler of Shu, at Yiling, near Ichang, Hupeh Province, in A.D. 222. He did so by avoiding battle for seven months until Liu Pei was at his wits' end, and then, taking advantage of a favorable wind, setting fire to Liu Pei's tents and routing his army.
18. In A.D. 383, Hsieh Hsuan, a general of the Eastern Tsin Dynasty, defeated Fu Chien, ruler of the state of Chin, by a simple stratagem. Their armies on opposite sides of the Feishui River in Anhwei Province, Hsieh Hsuan asked Fu Chien to move his troops back from the riverbank, so that he could bring his troops across to do battle. Fu Chien complied, but when he ordered withdrawal, his troops panicked and fled, and Hsieh Hsuan crossed the river and easily defeated those who were left.

the west" is a way of creating misconceptions among the enemy. When the mass support is sufficiently good to block the leakage of news, it is often possible by various ruses to succeed in leading the enemy into a morass of wrong judgments and actions so that he loses his superiority and the initiative. The saying "There can never be too much deception in war," means precisely this. . . .

We are not Duke Hsiang of Sung[19] and have no use for his asinine ethics. In order to achieve victory we must as far as possible make the enemy blind and deaf by sealing his eyes and ears, and drive his commanders to distraction by creating confusion in their minds. . . .

Now let us discuss flexibility. . . . We should know not only how to employ tactics but how to vary them. For flexibility of command the important task is to make changes such as from the offensive to the defensive or from the defensive to the offensive, from advance to retreat or from retreat to advance, from containment to assault or from assault to containment, from encirclement to outflanking or from outflanking to encirclement, and to make such changes properly and in good time according to the circumstances of the troops and terrain on both sides. . . .

Let us now discuss the question of planning. Because of the uncertainty peculiar to war, it is much more difficult to prosecute war according to plan than is the case with other activities. Yet, since "Preparedness ensures success and unpreparedness spells failure," there can be no victory in war without advance planning and preparations. . . . Tactical plans, such as plans for attack or defense by small formations or units, often have to be changed several times a day. . . . A strategic plan based on the overall situation of both belligerents . . . has to be changed when the war moves toward a new stage. . . .

Because of the fluidity of war, some people categorically deny that war plans or policies can be relatively stable, describing such plans or policies as "mechanical." This view is wrong. . . . But one must not deny the need for war plans or policies that are relatively stable over

19. Duke Hsiang of Sung ruled in the Spring and Autumn Era. In 638 B.C. the state of Sung fought with the powerful state of Chu. One of his officers suggested that as the Chu troops were numerically stronger, it would be well to attack them while they were crossing the river. But the Duke said, "No, a gentleman should never attack one who is unprepared." As a result, he suffered defeat and was himself wounded.

given periods; to negate this is to negate everything, including the war itself, as well as the negator himself. . . .

MOBILE WARFARE, GUERRILLA WARFARE AND POSITIONAL WARFARE

A war will take the form of mobile warfare when its content is quick-decision offensive warfare on exterior lines in campaigns and battles within the framework of the strategy of interior lines, protracted war and defense. Mobile warfare is the form in which regular armies wage quick-decision offensive campaigns and battles on exterior lines along extensive fronts and over big areas of operations. . . . Its characteristics are regular armies, superiority of forces in campaigns and battles, the offensive, and fluidity. . . . We must oppose "Only retreat, never advance," which is flightism, and at the same time oppose "Only advance, never retreat," which is desperate recklessness. . . .

We have always advocated the policy of "luring the enemy in deep," precisely because it is the most effective military policy for a weak army strategically on the defensive to employ against a strong army.

Among the forms of warfare in the anti-Japanese war mobile warfare comes first and guerrilla warfare second. . . . Guerrilla warfare does not bring as quick results or as great renown as regular warfare, but "A long road tests a horse's strength and a long task proves a man's heart," and in the course of this long and cruel war, guerrilla warfare will demonstrate its immense power. . . . The principle of the Eighth Route Army is: "Guerrilla warfare is basic, but lose no chance for mobile warfare under favorable conditions." This principle is perfectly correct; the views of its opponents are wrong. . . .

Hence, throughout the War of Resistance China will not adopt positional warfare as primary; the primary or important forms are mobile warfare and guerrilla warfare. These two forms of warfare will afford full play to the art of directing war and to the active role of man—what a piece of good fortune out of our misfortune!

WAR OF ATTRITION AND WAR OF ANNIHILATION

. . . Since there are three forms of warfare, mobile, positional and guerrilla . . . and since they differ in degrees of effectiveness, there arises the broad distinction between war of attrition and war of annihilation. . . . Unless we fight campaigns of annihilation . . . we cannot win time to improve our internal and international situation and alter our unfavorable position. Hence, campaigns of annihilation are the means of attaining the objective of strategic attrition. In this sense war of annihilation *is* war of attrition. It is chiefly by using the method of attrition through annihilation that China can wage protracted war.

But the objective of strategic attrition may also be achieved by campaigns of attrition. Generally speaking, mobile warfare performs the task of annihilation, positional warfare performs the task of attrition, and guerrilla warfare performs both simultaneously. . . .

The strength of the Japanese Army lies not only in its weapons but also in the training of its officers and men—its degree of organization, its self-confidence arising from never having been defeated, its superstitious belief in the Mikado and in supernatural beings, its arrogance, its contempt for the Chinese people and other such characteristics, all of which stem from long years of indoctrination. . . . This is the chief reason why we have taken very few prisoners although we have killed and wounded a great many enemy troops. . . . To destroy these enemy characteristics will be a long process. . . . The chief method of destroying them is to win over the Japanese soldiers politically . . . and, by treating prisoners of war leniently, lead the Japanese soldiers to see the anti-popular character of the aggression committed by the Japanese rulers. . . .

THE POSSIBILITIES OF EXPLOITING THE ENEMY'S MISTAKES

. . . In the ten months of his war of aggression the enemy has already made many mistakes in strategy and tactics. There are five major ones:

First, piecemeal reinforcement. This is due to the enemy's underestimation of China and also to his shortage of troops. The enemy has always looked down on us. . . . The conclusion the enemy came to was that the Chinese nation is a heap of loose sand. Thus, thinking that China would crumble at a single blow, he mapped out a plan of "quick decision," attempting with very small forces to send us scampering in panic. . . .

Second, absence of a main direction of attack. Before the Taierh-chuang campaign, the enemy had divided his forces more or less evenly between northern and central China and had again divided them inside each of these areas. . . .

Third, lack of strategic co-ordination. On the whole, co-ordination exists within the groups of enemy forces in northern China and in central China, but there is glaring lack of co-ordination between the two. . . .

Fourth, failure to grasp strategic opportunities. This failure was conspicuously shown in the enemy's halt after the occupation of Nanking and Taiyuan. . . .

Fifth, encirclement of large, but annihilation of small, numbers. Before the Taierhchuang campaign . . . many Chinese troops were routed but few were taken prisoner, which shows the stupidity of the enemy command.

. . . However, although much of the enemy's strategic and campaign command is incompetent, there are quite a few excellent points in his battle command, that is, in his unit and small formation tactics, and here we should learn from him.

THE QUESTION OF DECISIVE ENGAGEMENTS IN THE ANTI-JAPANESE WAR

The question of decisive engagements in the anti-Japanese war should be approached from three aspects: we should resolutely fight a decisive engagement in every campaign or battle in which we are sure of victory; we should avoid a decisive engagement in every campaign or battle in which we are not sure of victory; and we should absolutely avoid a strategically decisive engagement on which the fate of the whole nation is staked. . . .

Are we not afraid of being denounced as "nonresisters"? No, we are not. Not to fight at all but to compromise with the enemy—that is nonresistance, which should not only be denounced but must never be tolerated. We must resolutely fight the War of Resistance, but in order to avoid the enemy's deadly trap, it is absolutely necessary that we should not allow our main forces to be finished off at one blow . . . in brief, it is absolutely necessary to avoid national subjugation. . . .

Is it not self-contradictory to fight heroically first and then abandon territory? Will not our heroic fighters have shed their blood in vain? That is not at all the way questions should be posed. To eat and then to empty your bowels—is this not to eat in vain? To sleep and then to get up—is this not to sleep in vain? Can questions be posed in such a way? I would suppose not. . . . As everybody knows, although in fighting and shedding our blood in order to gain time and prepare the counteroffensive we have had to abandon some territory, in fact we have gained time, we have achieved the objective of annihilating and depleting enemy forces, we have acquired experience in fighting, we have aroused hitherto inactive people and improved our international standing. . . . We are for protracted war and final victory, we are not gamblers who risk everything on a single throw.

THE ARMY AND THE PEOPLE
ARE THE FOUNDATION OF VICTORY

Japanese imperialism will never relax in its aggression against and repression of revolutionary China; this is determined by its imperialist nature. If China did not resist, Japan would easily seize all China without firing a single shot, as she did the four northeastern provinces. . . . Now that Japan has launched war against China, so long as she does not suffer a fatal blow from Chinese resistance and still retains sufficient strength, she is bound to attack Southeast Asia or Siberia, or even both. She will do so once war breaks out in Europe; in their wishful calculations, the rulers of Japan have it worked out on a grandiose scale. Of course, it is possible that Japan will have to drop her original plan of invading Siberia and adopt a mainly defensive attitude toward the Soviet Union on account of Soviet strength and of the serious extent to which Japan herself has been weakened by her war against China. But in that case, so far from relaxing her aggression against China she will intensify it, because then the only way left to her will be to gobble up the weak. China's task of persevering in the War of Resistance, the united front and the protracted war will then become all the more weighty, and it will be all the more necessary not to slacken our efforts in the slightest. . . .

The richest source of power to wage war lies in the masses of the

munists should work in harmony with all progressives outside the Party and endeavor to unite the entire people to do away with whatever is undesirable. It must be realized that Communists form only a small section of the nation, and that there are large numbers of progressives and activists outside the Party with whom we must work. It is entirely wrong to think that we alone are good and no one else is any good. . . . In a long war and in adverse circumstances, the dynamic energy of the whole nation can be mobilized in the struggle to overcome difficulties, defeat the enemy and build a new China only if the Communists play an exemplary vanguard role, to the best of their ability, together with all the advanced elements among the friendly parties and armies among the masses.

UNITE THE WHOLE NATION AND COMBAT ENEMY AGENTS IN ITS MIDST

. . . However, there are already enemy agents playing a disruptive role within our national united front, namely, the traitors, Trotskyites and pro-Japanese elements. Communists must always be on the lookout for them, expose their criminal activities with factual evidence and warn the people not to be duped by them. . . .

EXPAND THE COMMUNIST PARTY AND PREVENT INFILTRATION BY ENEMY AGENTS

To overcome the difficulties, defeat the enemy and build a new China, the Communist Party must expand its organization and become a great mass Party by opening its doors to the masses of workers, peasants and young activists who are truly devoted to the revolution. . . . But at the same time, there must be no slackening of vigilance against infiltration by enemy agents. The Japanese imperialist secret services are ceaselessly trying to disrupt our Party and to smuggle undercover traitors, Trotskyites, pro-Japanese elements, degenerates and careerists into its ranks in the guise of activists. Not for a moment must we relax our vigilance and our strict precautions against such persons. . . . The only correct policy is: "Expand the Party boldly but do not let a single undesirable in."

MAINTAIN BOTH THE UNITED FRONT AND THE INDEPENDENCE OF THE PARTY

It is only by firmly maintaining the national united front that the difficulties can be overcome, the enemy defeated and a new China built. This is beyond all doubt. At the same time, every party and group in the united front must preserve its ideological, political and organizational independence; this holds good for the Kuomintang, the Communist Party or any other party or group. In inter-Party relations, the Principle of Democracy in the Three People's Principles permits both the union of all parties and groups and the independent existence of each. To speak of unity alone while denying independence is to abandon the Principle of Democracy, and to this neither the Communist Party nor any other Party would agree. . . . Unity against Japan requires an appropriate policy of adjustment in class relations, a policy which does not leave the laboring people without political and material safeguards but also gives consideration to the interests of the rich, thereby meeting the demands of solidarity against the enemy. It is bad for the War of Resistance to pay attention only to the one side and neglect the other.

CONSIDER THE SITUATION AS A WHOLE, THINK IN TERMS OF THE MAJORITY, AND WORK TOGETHER WITH OUR ALLIES

In leading the masses in struggle against the enemy, Communists must consider the situation as a whole, think in terms of the majority of the people and work together with their allies. They must grasp the principle of subordinating the needs of the part to the needs of the whole. . . . Wherever there are democratic parties or individuals willing to co-operate with us, the proper attitude for Communists is to talk things over with them and work together with them. . . . We have had serious shortcomings in this respect, and we must still give the matter attention.

CADRES POLICY

The Chinese Communist Party is a Party leading a great revolutionary struggle in a nation several hundred million strong, and it cannot fulfill its historic task without a large number of leading cadres who combine ability with political integrity. . . . We have the responsibility for organizing and training them and for taking good care and making proper use of them. Cadres are a decisive factor, once the political line is determined. . . .[1]

Our concern should extend to non-Party cadres as well as to Party cadres . . . and to work well with non-Party cadres, give them sincere help, have a warm, comradely attitude toward them and enlist their initiative in the great cause of resisting Japan and reconstructing the nation. . . .

We must know how to take good care of cadres. There are several ways of doing so:

First, give them guidance. . . . Second, raise their level. . . . Third, check up on their work, and help them sum up their experience, carry forward their achievements and correct their mistakes. . . . Fourth, in general, use the method of persuasion with cadres who have made mistakes, and help them correct their mistakes. . . . Fifth, help them with their difficulties. When cadres are in difficulty as a result of illness, straitened means or domestic or other troubles, we must be sure to give them as much care as possible.

This is how to take good care of cadres.

PARTY DISCIPLINE

In view of Chang Kuo-tao's serious violations of discipline, we must affirm anew the discipline of the Party, namely: (1) the individual is subordinate to the organization; (2) the minority is subordinate to the majority; (3) the lower level is subordinate to the higher

1. In his report to the Eighteenth Congress of the C.P.S.U. in March 1939, Stalin said: "After a correct political line has been worked out and tested in practice, the Party cadres become the decisive force in the leadership exercised by the Party and the state"—*Problems of Leninism* (Eng. ed., FLPH, Moscow, 1954), p. 784.

level; and (4) the entire membership is subordinate to the Central Committee. . . .

Party Democracy

Ours is a country in which small-scale production and the patriarchal system prevail, and taking the country as a whole there is as yet no democratic life; consequently, this state of affairs is reflected in our Party. This phenomenon hinders the entire Party from exercising its initiative to the full. . . . For these reasons, education in democracy must be carried on within the Party so that members can understand the meaning of democratic life, the meaning of the relationship between democracy and centralism, and the way in which democratic centralism should be put into practice. . . .

Our Party Has Consolidated Itself and Grown Strong Through the Struggle on Two Fronts

Broadly speaking, in the last seventeen years our Party has learned to use the Marxist-Leninist weapon of ideological struggle against incorrect ideas within the Party on two fronts—against Right opportunism and against "Left" opportunism. . . .

What are the lessons which have been derived from these two inner-Party struggles? They are:

1. The tendency to "left" impetuosity, which disregards both the subjective and the objective factors, is extremely harmful to a revolutionary war and, for that matter, to any revolutionary movement. . . .

2. The opportunism of Chang Kuo-tao, however, was right opportunism in the revolutionary war and was a combination of a retreatist line, warlordism and anti-Party activity. . . . Men of fine quality . . . were able to free themselves from its toils and return to the correct line of the Central Committee.

3. Striking results were achieved in the great organizational work of the ten years of the Agrarian Revolutionary War—in army building, government work, mass work and Party building. . . .

These lessons, these achievements, have furnished us with the prerequisites for uniting the whole Party, for strengthening its ideological, political and organizational unity, and for successfully waging the War of Resistance. Our Party has consolidated itself and grown strong through the struggle on the two fronts.

The Present Struggle on Two Fronts

From now on, it is of paramount importance to wage a political struggle against rightist pessimism in the War of Resistance, although it is still necessary to keep an eye on "left" impetuosity. . . .

Ideological struggle on the two fronts must suit the concrete circumstances of each case, and we must never approach a problem subjectively or permit the bad old habit of "sticking labels" on people to continue. . . .

Only by sharpening the vigilance of cadres and Party members against such behavior can we strengthen Party discipline.

Study

Generally speaking, all Communist Party members who can do so should study the theory of Marx, Engels, Lenin and Stalin, study our national history and study current movements and trends; moreover, they should help to educate members with less schooling. . . . No political Party can possibly lead a great revolutionary movement to victory unless it possesses revolutionary theory and a knowledge of history and has a profound grasp of the practical movement.

The theory of Marx, Engels, Lenin and Stalin is universally applicable. . . . It is not just a matter of understanding the general laws derived by Marx, Engels, Lenin and Stalin from their extensive study of real life and revolutionary experience, but of studying their standpoint and method in examining and solving problems. . . . Our Party's fighting capacity will be much greater . . . if there are 100 or 200 comrades with a grasp of Marxism-Leninism which is systematic and not fragmentary, genuine and not hollow.

Another of our tasks is to study our historical heritage and use the Marxist method to sum it up critically. . . . We should sum up our history from Confucius to Sun Yat Sen and take over this valuable legacy . . . but we can put Marxism into practice only when it is integrated with the specific characteristics of our country and acquires a definite national form. . . . Foreign stereotypes must be abolished, there must be less singing of empty, abstract tunes, and dogmatism must be laid to rest; these must be replaced by the fresh, lively Chinese style and spirit which the common people of China love. . . .

Whoever refuses to study these problems seriously and carefully is no Marxist. Complacency is the enemy of study. We cannot really learn anything until we rid ourselves of complacency. Our attitude toward ourselves should be "to be insatiable in learning" and toward others "to be tireless in teaching."

UNITY AND VICTORY

Unity within the Chinese Communist Party is the fundamental prerequisite for uniting the whole nation to win the War of Resistance and build a new China. Seventeen years of tempering have taught the Chinese Communist Party many ways of attaining internal unity, and ours is now a much more seasoned Party. Thus, we are able to form a powerful nucleus for the whole people in the struggle to win victory in the War of Resistance and to build a new China. Comrades, so long as we are united, we can certainly reach this goal.

This report was made by Mao Tse-tung to the Sixth Plenary Session of the Sixth Central Committee of the Chinese Communist Party. The session endorsed the line of the Political Bureau headed by Mao Tse-tung.

The Question of Independence and Initiative Within the United Front

November 5, 1938

HELP AND CONCESSIONS SHOULD BE POSITIVE, NOT NEGATIVE

All political parties and groups in the united front must help each other and make mutual concessions for the sake of long-term co-operation, but such help and concessions should be positive, not negative. . . . The people want the government to satisfy their political and economic demands . . . the factory workers demand better conditions from the owners, and at the same time work hard in the interests of resistance; for the sake of unity against foreign aggression, the landlords should reduce rent and interest, and at the same time the peasants should pay rent and interest. . . . Each side should refrain from undermining the other and from organizing secret Party branches within the other's Party, government and army. For our part we organize no secret Party branches inside the Kuomintang and its government or army, and so set the Kuomintang's mind at rest, to the advantage of the War of Resistance. The saying "Refrain from doing some things to be able to do other things,"[1] exactly meets the case. . . . Negative measures have yielded positive results. "To fall back the better to leap forward"[2]— that is Leninism. To regard concessions as something purely negative is contrary to Marxism-Leninism. . . .

THE IDENTITY BETWEEN THE NATIONAL AND THE CLASS STRUGGLE

To sustain a long war by long-term co-operation or, in other words, to subordinate the class struggle to the present national struggle against Japan—such is the fundamental principle of the united

1. A quotation from Mencius.
2. V. I. Lenin, "Conspectus of Hegel's *Lectures on the History of Philosophy*," *Collected Works* (Moscow, 1958), Vol. XXXVIII, p. 275.

front. . . . Only thus can co-operation be promoted, indeed only thus can there be any co-operation at all. . . . Thus there is identity in the united front between unity and independence and between the national struggle and the class struggle.

"Everything Through the United Front" Is Wrong

The Kuomintang is the Party in power, and so far has not allowed the united front to assume an organizational form. Comrade Liu Shao-chi has rightly said that if "everything through" were simply to mean through Chiang Kai-shek and Yen Hsi-shan, it would mean unilateral submission, and not "through the united front" at all. . . . The Kuomintang has deprived all other political parties of equal rights and is trying to compel them to take its orders. . . . Since the policy of the Kuomintang is to restrict our growth, there is no reason whatever for us to propose such a slogan, which simply binds us hand and foot. . . . In short, we must not split the united front, but neither should we allow ourselves to be bound hand and foot, and hence the slogan of "Everything Through the United Front" should not be put forward. . . . Our policy is one of independence and initiative within the united front, a policy both of unity and of independence.

This is part of Mao Tse-tung's concluding speech at the Sixth Plenary Session of the Sixth Central Committee of the Chinese Communist Party.

Problems of War and Strategy
November 6, 1938

China's Characteristics and Revolutionary War

The seizure of power by armed force, the settlement of the issue by war, is the central task and the highest form of revolution. This

Marxist-Leninist principle of revolution holds good universally, for China and for all other countries. . . .

On the issue of war, the Communist parties in the capitalist countries oppose the imperialist wars waged by their own countries; if such wars occur, the policy of these parties is to bring about the defeat of the reactionary governments of their own countries. The one war they want to fight is the civil war for which they are preparing. . . . And when the time comes to launch such an insurrection and war, the first step will be to seize the cities, and then advance into the countryside . . . this has been done by Communist parties in capitalist countries, and it has been proved correct by the October Revolution in Russia. . . .

"In China the armed revolution is fighting the armed counterrevolution. That is one of the specific features and one of the advantages of the Chinese revolution."[1] This thesis of Comrade Stalin's is perfectly correct. . . .

In most of China, Party organizational work and mass work are directly linked with armed struggle; there is not, and cannot be, any Party work or mass work that is isolated and stands by itself. . . . In a word, the whole Party must pay great attention to war, study military matters and prepare itself for fighting.

The War History of the Kuomintang

It will be useful for us to look at the history of the Kuomintang and see what attention it pays to war.

From the start, when he organized a small revolutionary group, Sun Yat Sen staged armed insurrection against the Ching Dynasty. . . .[2]

After Sun Yat Sen came Chiang Kai-shek, who brought the Kuomintang's power to its zenith. . . . He has held firmly to the vital point that whoever has an army has power and that war

1. J. V. Stalin, "The Prospects of the Revolution in China," *Works* (Engl. ed., Moscow, 1954) Vol. VIII, p. 379.
2. In 1894, Dr. Sun Yat Sen formed a small revolutionary organization in Honolulu called the Hsing Chung Hui (Society for China's Regeneration). With the support of local secret societies which flourished at the time, he staged two armed insurrections in Kwangtung Province against the Ching Government after its defeat in the Sino-Japanese War in 1895—one in Canton in 1895 and the other at Huichow in 1900.

decides everything. In this respect we ought to learn from him. In this respect both Sun Yat Sen and Chiang Kai-shek are our teachers. . . .

Communists do not fight for personal military power (they must in no circumstances do that) . . . but they must fight for military power for the Party, for military power for the people. . . . Every Communist must grasp the truth, "Political power grows out of the barrel of a gun." . . . Having guns, we can create Party organizations . . . cadres . . . schools . . . culture . . . mass movements. . . . All things grow out of the barrel of a gun. . . . Some people ridicule us as advocates of the "omnipotence of war." Yes, we are advocates of the omnipotence of revolutionary war; that is good, not bad; it is Marxist. . . . We are advocates of the abolition of war, we do not want war; but war can only be abolished through war, and in order to get rid of the gun it is necessary to take up the gun.

The War History of the Chinese Communist Party

Our Party failed to grasp the importance of engaging itself directly in preparations for war. . . . Through helping the Kuomintang in the wars in Kwangtung Province and participating in the Northern Expedition, the Party gained leadership over some armed forces. Then, having learned a bitter lesson from the failure of the revolution, the Party organized the Nanchang Uprising. . . .[3]

Today we can say with confidence that in the struggles of the past seventeen years the Chinese Communist Party has forged not only a firm Marxist political line but also a firm Marxist military line. . . . There are only three armies in the whole world which belong to the proletariat and the laboring people, the armies led by the Communist parties of the Soviet Union, of China and of Spain . . . hence our army and our military experience are all the more precious.

3. On August 1, 1927, Communist troops under the united front leadership of General Chiang Kai-shek in the Northern Expedition, staged a revolt in Nanchang, capital of Kiangsi Province. It was quickly subdued by Nationalist Government forces. Mao Tse-tung speaks of this as a "people's uprising."

Changes in the Party's Military Strategy in the Civil War and the National War

The changes in our Party's military strategy are worth studying. . . . The first of the three changes encountered great difficulties. It involved a twofold task. On the one hand, we had to combat the Right tendency of localism and guerrillaism . . . on the other hand, we also had to combat the "Left" tendency of overcentralization and adventurism which put undue stress on regularization. . . .

The second change in strategy took place in the autumn of 1937 (after the Lukouchiao Incident), at the juncture of the two different wars. We faced a new enemy, Japanese imperialism, and had as our ally our former enemy, the Kuomintang (which was still hostile to us), and the theater of war was the vast expanse of northern China. . . .

The third change, from guerrilla to regular warfare against Japan, belongs to the future development of the war, which will presumably give rise to new circumstances and new difficulties. . . .

The Strategic Role of Guerrilla Warfare Against Japan

In the anti-Japanese war as a whole, regular warfare is primary and guerrilla warfare supplementary, for only regular warfare can decide the final outcome of the war. . . .

All the same, guerrilla warfare has its important strategic place throughout the war. Without guerrilla warfare and without due attention to building guerrilla units and guerrilla armies and to studying and directing guerrilla warfare, we shall likewise be unable to defeat Japan. . . .

Given a big country, guerrilla warfare is possible; hence there was guerrilla warfare in the past too. But guerrilla warfare can be persevered in only when led by the Communist Party. That is why guerrilla warfare generally failed in the past and why it can be victorious only in modern times and only in big countries in which Communist parties have emerged, as in the Soviet Union during its civil war and in China at present. . . .

Through guerrilla warfare, we shall build up our strength and turn ourselves into a decisive element in the crushing of Japanese imperialism.

PAY GREAT ATTENTION TO THE STUDY OF MILITARY MATTERS

All the issues between two hostile armies depend on war for their solution, and China's survival or extinction depends on her victory or defeat in the present war. Hence our study of military theory, of strategy and tactics and of army political work brooks not a moment's delay. . . . The popularization of military knowledge is an urgent task for the Party and the whole country. . . . I deem it imperative that we arouse interest in the study of military theory and direct the attention of the whole membership to the study of military matters.

This article is part of Mao Tse-tung's concluding speech at the Sixth Plenary Session of the Sixth Central Committee of the Chinese Communist Party.

The May Fourth Movement

May 1939

The May Fourth Movement twenty years ago marked a new stage in China's bourgeois-democratic revolution against imperialism and feudalism. . . . Around the time of the May Fourth Movement, hundreds of thousands of students courageously took their place in the van. In these respects the May Fourth Movement went a step beyond the Revolution of 1911.

If we trace China's bourgeois-democratic revolution back to its formative period, we see that it has passed through a number of stages in its development: the Opium War, the War of the Taiping Heavenly Kingdom, the Sino-Japanese War of 1894,[1] the Reform

1. Korea had long been in an ill-defined position of vassalage to China. In 1894 Japan decided to challenge China's suzerainty over the Korean Peninsula, and on August 1 of that year landed an invasion force, invading Shantung and Manchuria, and capturing Weihaiwei and Port Arthur, the sea approaches to Peking. The Chinese sued for peace, and by the resulting Treaty

Movement of 1898,[2] the Yi Ho Tuan Movement,[3] the Revolution of 1911, the May Fourth Movement, the Northern Expedition, and the War of the Agrarian Revolution. The present War of Resistance Against Japan is yet another stage, and is the greatest, most vigorous and most dynamic stage of all. The bourgeois-democratic revolution can be considered accomplished only when the forces of foreign imperialism and domestic feudalism have basically been overthrown and an independent democratic state has been established.

The Orientation of the Youth Movement

May 4, 1939

Today is the twentieth anniversary of the May Fourth Movement, and the youth of Yenan all gathered here for this commemoration meeting. . . .

First, May 4 has now been designated as China's Youth Day,[4] and rightly so. . . . The May Fourth Movement was directed against a government of national betrayal, a government which conspired with imperialism and sold out the interests of the nation, a government which oppressed the people. . . . Just consider, long before the May Fourth Movement Dr. Sun Yat Sen was already a rebel against the government of his day; he opposed and overthrew the Chin Govern-

---

of Shimonoseki China recognized the independence of Korea, which Japan proceeded to dominate as a colonial property; the treaty also ceded to Japan the island of Taiwan, the Pescadores, the Liaotung Peninsula in Manchuria, and an indemnity of 200 million *taels*. (A *tael* is slightly more than an ounce of silver.)

2. The Reform Movement of 1898 was supported by Emperor Kuang Hsu. His army chief, Yuan Shih-kai, betrayed him and the leaders of the movement to Empress Dowager Tzu Hsi. She imprisoned the Emperor and had the leaders beheaded, and the movement collapsed.

3. The Yi Ho Tuan Movement in 1900 was what became known to the outside world as the Boxer Uprising.

4. Youth Day was officially proclaimed a national holiday by the Administrative Council of the Central People's Government in December 1949 after the establishment of the People's Republic of China on the China mainland.

ment. . . . For the government he opposed did not resist imperialism but conspired with it. . . .

. . . Secondly, what is the Chinese revolution directed against? Today we are making a bourgeois-democratic revolution, and nothing we do goes beyond its scope. By and large, we should not destroy the bourgeois system of private property for the present. . . .

Will there always be a place for capitalists in China? No, definitely not in the future. This is true not only of China, but of the whole world. In the future no country, whether it be Britain, the United States, France, Japan, Germany or Italy, will have any place for capitalists, and China will be no exception.

Thirdly, what are the lessons of the Chinese revolution? . . . It was only with Dr. Sun Yat Sen that a more or less clearly defined bourgeois-democratic revolution began. . . . Dr. Sun Yat Sen said in his Testament:

For forty years I have devoted myself to the cause of the national revolution with the aim of winning freedom and equality for China. My experiences during these forty years have firmly convinced me that to achieve this aim we must arouse the masses of the people and unite in a common struggle with those nations of the world which treat us as equals.

. . . What is the lesson of the revolution during these years? Fundamentally, it is "Arouse the masses of the people."

Fourthly, to return to the youth movement. . . . How should we judge whether a youth is a revolutionary? How can we tell? There can only be one criterion, namely, whether or not he is willing to integrate himself with the broad masses of workers and peasants and does so in practice. If he is willing to do so and actually does so, he is a revolutionary; otherwise he is a nonrevolutionary or a counterrevolutionary. . . .

Fifthly, the present War of Resistance Against Japan marks a new stage—the greatest, most dynamic and most vigorous stage—in the Chinese revolution. . . . The basic policy in this war is the Anti-Japanese National United Front, whose aim it is to overthrow Japanese imperialism and the Chinese collaborators, transform the old China into a new China, and liberate the whole nation from its semicolonial and semifeudal status. . . .

Sixthly and lastly, I want to speak about the youth movement in

Yenan. . . . Most of you attending this meeting today have come to Yenan from thousands of miles away; whether your surname is Chang or Li, whether you are a man or a woman, a worker or a peasant, you are all of one mind. . . . The youth in Yenan, besides being united among themselves, have integrated themselves with the masses of workers and peasants, and more than anything else this makes you a model for the whole country. . . . You have been learning the theory of revolution and studying the principles and methods for resisting Japan and saving the nation. . . . You must each be different from before and resolve to unite the youth and organize the people of the whole country for the overthrow of Japanese imperialism and the transformation of the old China into a new China. That is what I expect of all of you.

Mao Tse-tung wrote this article for newspapers in Yenan to commemorate the twentieth anniversary of the May Fourth Movement.

Oppose Capitulationist Activity

June 30, 1939

Ever since the Chinese nation was confronted with the Japanese aggression, the first and foremost question has been to fight or not to fight. This question aroused serious controversy in the period from the Incident of September 18, 1931, to the Lukouchiao Incident of July 7, 1937. The conclusion reached by all patriotic political parties and groups and by all our patriotic fellow countrymen was: "To fight is to survive, not to fight is to perish." The conclusion reached by all the capitulationists was: "To fight is to perish, not to fight is to survive." . . . Now the issue has been raised again, worded in a slightly different way as a question of "peace or war." Thus a controversy has arisen inside China between those who favor continuing the war and those who favor making peace. . . . The former comprises all patriotic parties and all patriots and they make up the great majority of the nation, while the latter, that is, the capitulationists, constitutes only a small wavering minority within the anti-Japanese front. . . . Many people in the peace group bank on the exertion of pressure by the big powers, not only on Japan, so that they can say to the war group: "Look! In the present international climate, we have to make peace!" and "A Pacific international conference would be to China's advantage. It would not be another Munich, but a step toward China's rejuvenation." This forms the sum total of the views . . . of the Chinese capitulationists. . . .

We Communists openly proclaim that, at all times, we stand with those who favor continuing the war and resolutely oppose those who favor making peace. We have but one desire, that is . . . put the Three People's Principles into effect, carry the War of Resistance through to the end, fight all the way to the Yalu River and recover all our lost territories.

The Reactionaries Must Be Punished

August 1, 1939

Today, the First of August, we are gathered here for a memorial meeting. Why are we holding this memorial meeting? Because the reactionaries have killed our revolutionary comrades, killed fighters against Japan. . . . Who gave the order to kill? The reactionaries . . . among the victims were Comrades Tu Cheng-ken and Lo Tze-ming, responsible comrades of the Pingkiang Liaison Office of the New Fourth Army. . . . Obviously, the killing was perpetrated by a gang of Chinese reactionaries acting on the orders of the Japanese imperialists and Wang Ching-wei. . . .

Has anyone taken action on this serious case of the murder of anti-Japanese comrades? The murder was committed at 3 P.M. on June 12, today is August 1, but in all this time have we seen anyone step forward and take action? No. . . . What is the reason? The reason is, China is not unified.

China must be unified; there can be no victory without unification. . . . The Pingkiang massacre proves it. . . . Comrades Tu Cheng-ken, Lo Tze-ming and the others who upheld unity have been punished, have been brutally murdered, whereas the scoundrels who undermine unity are allowed to go scot-free. That is not unification. . . .

At the present time certain secret measures known as "Measures for Restricting the Activities of Alien Parties" are being extensively enforced. They are reactionary to the core, helpful to Japanese imperialism and detrimental to resistance, unity and progress. . . . How can the Communist Party and all the other anti-Japanese political parties, which are united in resistance to Japan, be called "Alien Parties"? . . . Why restrict the Communist Party, which is the most resolute in resisting Japan, the most revolutionary and the most progressive? It is absolutely wrong. . . . We must oppose the "Measures for Restricting the Activities of Alien Parties," for such measures are at the very root of all kinds of criminal actions that wreck unity. . . . "Measures for Restricting the Activities of Alien Parties" must be abolished, the capitulators and reactionaries must be punished, and all revolutionary comrades, all the comrades and people resisting Japan must be protected. (*Warm applause and slogan shouting*)

This speech was delivered by Mao Tse-tung at a memorial meeting held by the people of Yenan for the Communists who had been executed at Pingkiang.·

Interview With a *New China Daily* Correspondent on the New International Situation

September 1, 1939

CORRESPONDENT: What is the significance of the Treaty of Non-Aggression Between the Soviet Union and Germany?[1]

MAO TSE-TUNG: The . . . treaty is the result of the growing socialist strength of the Soviet Union and the policy of peace persistently followed by the Soviet government. The treaty has shattered the intrigues by which the reactionary international bourgeoisie

1. The Treaty of Non-Aggression Between the Soviet Union and Germany was signed on August 23, 1939.

represented by Chamberlain and Deladier sought to instigate a Soviet-German war. . . .

QUESTION: Some people do not realize yet that the Soviet-German non-aggression treaty is the result of the breakdown of the Anglo-French-Soviet talks, but think that the Soviet-German treaty caused the breakdown. Will you please explain why the Anglo-Soviet-French talks failed?

ANSWER: The talks failed purely because the British and French governments were insincere. . . . Britain and France flatly rejected the Soviet Union's repeated proposals for a genuine front against aggression. . . . Their aim was to step forward when the belligerents had worn each other out. . . . This policy . . . reached its climax in the Munich agreement of September last year. . . . As I said in October 1938 at the Sixth Plenary Session of the Sixth Central Committee of our Party, "The inevitable result of Chamberlain's policy will be like 'lifting a rock only to drop it on one's own toes.'"

QUESTION: In your opinion, how will the present situation develop?

ANSWER: The international situation has already entered a new phase. . . . In Europe, a large-scale war is imminent between the German-Italian and the Anglo-French imperialist blocs. . . . This war is not at all a just war. The only just wars are nonpredatory wars, wars of liberation. Communists will in no circumstances support any predatory war. They will, however, bravely step forward to support every just and nonpredatory war for liberation. . . .

Beside these two big blocs, there is a third bloc in the capitalist world, headed by the United States. . . . In the name of neutrality, U.S. imperialism is temporarily refraining from joining either of the belligerents, so as to be able to come on the scene later and contend for the leadership of the capitalist world. . . .

Outside the capitalist world there is a world of light, the socialist Soviet Union. The Soviet-German treaty enables the Soviet Union to give greater help to the world movement for peace and to China in her resistance to Japan. . . .

QUESTION: In these circumstances, what are the prospects for China?

ANSWER: . . . Beyond any doubt, China must on no account miss the present opportunity or make a wrong decision but must take a firm political stand.

In other words: First, firm adherence to the stand of resistance to Japan and opposition to any moves toward compromise.

Second, firm adherence to the stand of unity and opposition to any moves toward a split. . . . All internal friction harmful to the War of Resistance must be sternly checked.

Third, firm adherence to the stand of progress and opposition to any retrogression. . . .

If all this is done, China will be able effectively to build up her strength for the counteroffensive. . . .

Interview with Three Correspondents from the Central News Agency, The *Sao Tang Pao* and the *Hsin Min Pao*[1]

September 16, 1939

CORRESPONDENT: May we ask for your views on a few questions? . . . Our written questions are divided into three groups and we would be glad if you would give us your views on each of them.

MAO TSE-TUNG: I shall deal with them according to your list. You ask if the War of Resistance has reached the stage of stalemate. I think it has—in the sense that there is a new international situation and that Japan is facing greater difficulties while China has stood firm against compromise. . . . We have stood for regeneration through our own efforts, and this has become even more important in the new international situation. The essence of such regeneration is democracy.

QUESTION: You have just said that democracy is essential to winning victory. . . . How can such a system be brought into being in the present circumstances?

ANSWER: Dr. Sun Yat Sen originally envisaged the three stages of military rule, political tutelage and constitutional government. But in

1. Then Central News Agency was the official Kuomintang news agency; the *Sao Tang Pao* was published by Kuomintang military sources; and the *Hsin Min Pao* was a privately owned general circulation newspaper.

his "Statement on My Departure for the North"[2] issued shortly
before his death, he no longer spoke of three stages, but said instead
that a national assembly must be convened immediately. . . . Opinions differ on this question. Some say that the common people are
ignorant and democratic government cannot be introduced. They are
wrong. . . . The question should be thrown open to public discussion.

In the second group on your list, you raise the question of "restricting alien parties," that is, the question of the friction in various
localities. Your concern over this matter is justified. There has been
some improvement recently, but fundamentally the situation remains
unchanged.

QUESTION: Has the Communist Party made its position on this
question clear to the Central Government?

ANSWER: We have protested.

QUESTION: In what way?

ANSWER: Our Party representative, Comrade Chou En-lai, wrote a
letter to Generalissimo Chiang Kai-shek as early as July. Then again
on August 1, people from all walks of life in Yenal sent a telegram to
the Generalissimo. . . .

QUESTION: Has there been any reply from the Central Government?

ANSWER: No. But it is said that there are also people in the
Kuomintang who disapprove of these measures. As everybody knows
. . . a political party that participates in the common fight against
Japan is a friendly party, not an "alien party." . . .

QUESTION: How about friction in northern China?

ANSWER: Chang Yin-wu and Chin Chi-jung are the two expert
friction mongers there. . . . They seldom fight the enemy but often
attack the Eighth Route Army. . . .

QUESTION: Is there any friction with the New Fourth Army?

ANSWER: Yes, there is. The incident of the Pingkiang massacre
has shocked the whole nation.

QUESTION: Some people say that the united front is important but

2. This statement was made by Dr. Sun Yat Sen on November 10, 1924,
two days before he left Canton for a conference in Peking at the invitation
of Feng Yu-hsiang, the bearded "Christian warlord," who dominated north
China at the time. General Feng was reported to have fallen from a sight-
seeing boat and drowned in the Volga River some years later, on a visit to
the Soviet Union at the invitation of Stalin.

that the Border Region Government should be abolished for the sake of unification. What do you think of this?

ANSWER: Nonsense of all sorts is being talked everywhere, the so-called abolition of the Border Region being one example. . . . Moreover, Generalissimo Chiang long ago recognized the Border Region and the Executive Yuan of the National Government officially recognized it as long ago as the winter of the twenty-sixth year of the Republic (1937). China certainly needs to be unified, but it must be unified on the basis of resistance, unity and progress. . . .

QUESTION: Since there are different interpretations of unification, is there any possibility of a split between the Kuomintang and the Communist Party?

ANSWER: If we are merely talking about possibilities, we can envisage both the possibility of unity and the possibility of a split, depending on the attitudes of the Kuomintang and the Communist Party. . . . As far as we Communists are concerned, we have long made it clear that our policy is co-operation. . . . "Persist in unity and oppose a split," "Persist in resistance and oppose capitulation," "Persist in progress and oppose retrogression"—these are the three great political slogans our Party put forward in its Manifesto of July 7 this year. In our opinion, this is the only way China can avoid subjugation and drive out the enemy. There is no other way.

The Identity of Interests Between the Soviet Union and All Mankind

September 28, 1939

With the approach of the twenty-second anniversary of the Great October Socialist Revolution, the Sino-Soviet Cultural Association has asked me for an article. . . .

Some people say that the Soviet Union does not want the world to remain at peace because the outbreak of a world war is to its advantage, and that the present war was precipitated by the Soviet Union's conclusion of a non-aggression treaty with Germany instead of a treaty of mutual assistance with Britain and France. I consider this view incorrect. . . . The Soviet Union has long devoted great energy to the cause of world peace. For instance, it has joined the League of Nations,[1] signed treaties of mutual assistance with France and Czechoslovakia[2] and tried hard to conclude security pacts with Britain and all other countries that might be willing to have peace. After Germany and Italy jointly invaded Spain . . . the Soviet Union . . . gave the Spanish Republican forces active help. . . . When Britain and France connived at Hitler's aggression and sacrificed Austria and Czechoslovakia, the Soviet Union spared no effort in exposing the sinister aims behind the Munich policy. . . . When Poland became the burning question . . . the Soviet Union negotiated with Britain and France for over four months . . . in an endeavor to conclude a treaty of mutual assistance to prevent the outbreak of war. . . . Their refusal to come to terms with the Soviet Union . . . proved that they wanted not peace but war. . . . The plan of Britain, the United States and France was to egg Germany on to attack the Soviet Union, so that they themselves, "sitting on top of the mountain to watch the tigers fight," could come down and take over after the Soviet Union and Germany had worn each other out. The Soviet-German non-aggression treaty smashed this plot. . . .

The Soviet Union is a socialist country, a country in which the Communist Party is in power, and it necessarily maintains a clear-cut twofold attitude toward wars: (1) It firmly refuses to take part in any unjust, predatory and imperialist war and maintains strict neutrality toward the belligerents. . . . (2) It actively supports just and nonpredatory wars of liberation. . . .

Trade must not be confused with participation in war or with rendering assistance. For example, the Soviet Union traded with Germany and Italy during the Spanish war, yet nobody in the world said that the Soviet Union was helping Germany and Italy in their aggression against Spain; on the contrary, people said that it was

1. The League of Nations was founded at Geneva, Switzerland, on January 10, 1920. The Soviet Union joined the League in 1934, one year after Japan withdrew from it.
2. The Treaty of Mutual Assistance Between the Union of Soviet Socialist Republics and France and that between the USSR and Czechoslovakia were concluded in 1935.

helping Spain in resisting this aggression, the reason being that the Soviet Union actually did give help to Spain. . . .

Many people in China are bewildered by the fact that Soviet troops have entered Poland.[3] The Polish question should be viewed from various angles. . . . As for the Polish Government, it was a fascist, reactionary government of the Polish landlords and bourgeoisie which ruthlessly exploited the workers and peasants and oppressed the Polish democrats . . . which ruthlessly oppressed the non-Polish minority nationalities. . . . What the Soviet Union has now done is merely to recover its lost territory, liberate the oppressed Byelorussians and Ukrainians and save them from German oppression. The news dispatches of the last few days show how warmly these minority nationalities are welcoming the Red Army with food and drink as their liberator . . . while not a single report of this kind has come in from western Poland which has been occupied by German troops. . . . This shows clearly that the Soviet Union's war is a just and nonpredatory war of liberation. . . .

The whole situation since the conclusion of the Soviet-German non-aggression treaty constitutes a great blow to Japan and a great help to China . . . and weakens the capitulators. . . . As for talk about a Japanese-Soviet non-aggression treaty . . . even if such a treaty were to be concluded, the Soviet Union would certainly not agree to anything that would restrict its freedom of action in helping China. . . . I hold this as absolutely beyond doubt.

Introducing *The Communist*

October 4, 1939

The Central Committee has long planned to publish an internal Party journal, and now at last the plan has materialized. Such a journal is necessary for building up a bolshevized Chinese Communist Party. . . .

3. On September 1, 1939, the Germans invaded Poland from the south and the Soviet Union invaded the country from the east. Within the month Poland was conquered and divided between the two. A Polish Government in exile in London was recognized by the United States, pending free elections which were never held because of total domination by the Soviet Union after World War II.

This internal Party journal is called *The Communist*. . . . Its purpose is to help build a bolshevized Chinese Communist Party which is national in scale, has a broad mass character, and is fully consolidated ideologically, politically and organizationally. The building of such a Party is imperative for the victory of the Chinese revolution and on the whole the subjective and objective conditions for it are present; indeed this great undertaking is now in progress. A special Party periodical is needed to help achieve this great task, which is beyond the capability of an ordinary Party publication, and that is why *The Communist* is now being published.

The Current Situation and the Party's Tasks

October 10, 1939

1. The outbreak of the imperialist world war is the result of the attempt of the imperialist countries to extricate themselves from a new economic and political crisis. Whether on the German side or the Anglo-French, the war is unjust, predatory and imperialist in character. The Communist parties throughout the world must firmly oppose this war and also the criminal action of the social-democratic parties in betraying the proletariat by supporting it.

2. The policy of Japanese imperialism in this new international situation is to concentrate its attacks on China in order to settle the China question, in preparation for extending its international adventures in the future.

3. The danger of capitulation, a split and retrogression within the anti-Japanese united front is still the greatest current danger, and the present anti-Communist and retrogressive actions of the big landlords and the big bourgeoisie continue to be preparatory steps to their capitulation. . . . It is still our task . . . to keep up guerrilla warfare, defeat the enemy's "mopping-up" operations, disrupt the enemy's occupation of the areas he has seized, and introduce radical political and economic changes beneficial to the masses who are resisting Japan . . . convene a national assembly truly representative of

the people's will and invested with real power, draw up and adopt a constitution, and put constitutional government into practice. Any vacillation or procrastination, any contrary policy, is absolutely wrong. . . .

This was a decision drafted by Mao Tse-tung for the Central Committee of the Communist Party of China.

Recruit Large Numbers of Intellectuals[1]
December 1, 1939

In the long and ruthless war of national liberation, in the great struggle to build a new China, the Communist Party must be good at winning intellectuals, for only in this way will it be able to organize great strength for the War of Resistance. . . . Without the participation of the intellectuals, victory in the revolution is impossible. . . .

But many of the army cadres are not yet alive to the importance of the intellectuals, they still regard them with some apprehension and are even inclined to discriminate against them or shut them out. . . . All this is due to failure to understand . . . the difference between intellectuals who serve the landlords and the bourgeoisie and those who serve the working class and the peasantry, as well as the seriousness of the situation in which the bourgeois political parties are desperately contending with us for the intellectuals and in which the Japanese imperialists are also trying in every possible way to buy over Chinese intellectuals or corrupt their minds. . . .

From now on attention should therefore be paid to the following:

All Party organizations in the war areas and all army units led by the Party should recruit large numbers of intellectuals into our army, training institutes and organs of government. . . .

1. The term "intellectuals" refers to all those who have had middle school or higher education and those with similar educational levels. They include university and middle school teachers and staff members, university and middle school students, primary school teachers, professionals, engineers and technicians.

In applying the policy of recruiting intellectuals in large numbers, we must undoubtedly take great care to prevent the infiltration of those elements sent in by the enemy and the bourgeois political parties and to keep out other disloyal elements. . . .

We should assign appropriate work to all intellectuals who are reasonably loyal and useful, and we should earnestly give them political education and guidance so that . . . they gradually overcome their weaknesses. . . .

The necessity of admitting intellectuals into our work should be brought home to those cadres, and especially to certain cadres in the main forces of our army, who are opposed to their admission. . . .

All our Party comrades must understand that a correct policy toward the intellectuals is an important prerequisite for victory in the revolution. . . . The Central Committee hopes that the Party committees at all levels and all Party comrades will give this matter their serious attention.

This was a decision drafted by Mao Tse-tung for the Central Committee of the Chinese Communist Party.

The Chinese Revolution and the Chinese Communist Party

December 1939

Chapter I: Chinese Society

The Chinese Nation

China is one of the largest countries in the world, her territory being about the size of the whole of Europe. . . . From ancient times our forefathers have labored, lived and multiplied on this vast territory. . . .

China has a population of 450 million, or almost a quarter of the world total. Over nine-tenths . . . belong to the Han nationality. There are also scores of minority nationalities, including the Mongol, Hui, Tibetan, Uighur, Miao, Yi, Chuang, Chungchia and Korean nationalities, all with long histories though at different levels of cultural development. . . .

Throughout the history of Chinese civilization . . . there have been many great thinkers, scientists, inventors, statesmen, soldiers, men of letters and artists, and we have a rich store of classical works. The compass was invented in China very long ago.[1] The art of papermaking was discovered as early as 1,800 years ago.[2] Block printing was invented 1,300 years ago,[3] and movable type 800 years ago.[4] The use of gunpowder was known to the Chinese before the Europeans.[5] Thus China has one of the oldest civilizations in the world; she has a recorded history of nearly 4,000 years. . . .

The Old Feudal Society

Although China is a great nation . . . her economic, political and cultural development was sluggish for a long time after the transition from slave to feudal society. This feudal society, beginning with the Chou and Chin Dynasties, lasted about 3,000 years. . . .

The feudal ruling class composed of landlords, the nobility and the Emperor owned most of the land, while the peasants had very little or none at all. The peasants tilled the land of the landlords . . . and had to turn over to them . . . 40, 50, 60, 70 or even 80 per cent or more of the crop. In effect the peasants were still serfs. . . . The landlord had the right to beat, abuse or even kill them at will, and they had no political rights whatsoever. . . .

The ruthless economic exploitation and political oppression of the

1. The magnetic power of the lodestone was mentioned as early as the third century B.C. by Lu Pu-wei in his *Almanac;* and at the beginning of the first century A.D., Wang Chung, materialist philosopher, observed in his *Lun Heng* that the lodestone points to the South, indicating that magnetic polarity was known by then. By the twelfth century the compass was already in use by Chinese navigators, according to works written at that time.

2. It is recorded in ancient documents that Tsai Lun, a eunuch of the Eastern Han Dynasty (A.D. 25–220) invented paper, which he had made from bark, hemp, rags and worn-out fishing nets. In A.D. 105 (the last year of the Emperor Ho Ti), Tsai Lun presented his invention to the Emperor, and subsequently this method of making paper from plant fiber gradually spread in China.

3. Block printing was invented about A.D. 600, in the Sui Dynasty.

4. Movable type was invented by Pi Sheng in the Sung Dynasty between 1041 and 1048.

5. Gunpowder was invented in China in the ninth century, and by the eleventh century it was already in use for firing cannon.

Chinese peasants forced them into numerous uprisings against land-lord rule. There were hundreds of uprisings, great and small, all of them peasant revolts or peasant revolutionary wars. . . .

However, since neither new productive forces, nor new relations of production, nor new class forces, nor any advanced political party existed in those days, the peasant uprisings and wars did not have correct leadership such as the proletariat and the Communist Party provide today; every peasant revolution failed . . . although some social progress was made after each great peasant revolutionary struggle, the feudal economic relations and political system remained basically unchanged. . . .

Present-Day Colonial, Semicolonial and Semifeudal Society

As explained above, Chinese society remained feudal for 3,000 years. But is it still completely feudal today? No, China has changed. . . .

As China's feudal society had developed a commodity economy . . . China would of herself have developed slowly into a capitalist society. . . . Penetration by foreign capitalism accelerated this process. . . .

About forty years ago . . . China's national capitalism took its first steps forward. Then about twenty years ago, during the first imperialist world war, China's national industry expanded, chiefly in textiles and flour milling, because the imperialist countries in Europe and America were preoccupied with the war and temporarily relaxed their oppression of China. . . .

However, the emergence and development of capitalism is only one aspect of the change that has taken place since the imperialist penetration of China. There is another concomitant and obstructive aspect, namely, the collusion of imperialism with the Chinese feudal forces to arrest the development of Chinese capitalism. . . .

To this end the imperialist powers have used and continue to use military, political, economic and cultural means of oppression, so that China has gradually become a semicolony and colony. . . .

The imperialist powers have forced China to sign numerous unequal treaties by which they have acquired the right to station land and sea forces and exercise consular jurisdiction in China, and they have carved up the whole country into imperialist spheres of influence. . . .

Furthermore, the imperialist powers have never slackened their efforts to poison the minds of the Chinese people. This is their policy of cultural aggression. And it is carried out through missionary work, through establishing hospitals and schools, publishing newspapers and inducing Chinese students to study abroad. Their aim is to train intellectuals who will serve their interests and to dupe the people. . . .

Under the twofold oppression of imperialism and feudalism, and especially as a result of the large-scale invasion of Japanese imperialism, the Chinese people, and particularly the peasants, have become more and more impoverished and have even been pauperized in large numbers, living in hunger and cold and without any political rights. The poverty and lack of freedom among the Chinese people are on a scale seldom found elsewhere.

Such are the characteristics of China's colonial, semicolonial and semifeudal society. . . .

Chapter II: The Chinese Revolution

The Revolutionary Movements in the Last Hundred Years

The history of China's transformation into a semicolony and colony by imperialism in collusion with Chinese feudalism is at the same time a history of struggle by the Chinese people against imperialism and its lackeys. . . . The national revolutionary struggle of the Chinese people has a history of fully 100 years counting from the Opium War of 1840, or of thirty years counting from the Revolution of 1911. It has not yet run its full course, nor has it performed its tasks with any signal success; therefore the Chinese people, and above all the Communist Party, must shoulder the responsibility of resolutely fighting on. . . .

The Targets of the Chinese Revolution

. . . Since the nature of present-day Chinese society is colonial, semicolonial and semifeudal, what are the chief targets or enemies at this stage of the Chinese revolution?

They are imperialism and feudalism, the bourgeoisie of the imperialist countries and the landlord class of our own country. . . .

Since Japan's armed invasion of China, the principal enemy of the revolution has been Japanese imperialism, together with all the Chinese traitors and reactionaries in league with it, whether they have capitulated openly or are preparing to do so. . . .

In the face of such enemies, the Chinese revolution cannot be other than protracted and ruthless. . . . In the face of such enemies, the principal means or form of the Chinese revolution must be armed struggle, not peaceful struggle. . . .

In leading the people in struggle against the enemy, the Party must adopt the tactics of advancing step by step slowly and surely, keeping to the principle of waging struggles on just grounds, to our advantage, and with restraint, and making use of such open forms of activity as are permitted by law, decree and social custom; empty clamor and reckless action can never lead to success.

The Tasks of the Revolution

Imperialism and the feudal landlord class being the chief enemies of the Chinese revolution at this stage, what are the present tasks of the revolution?

Unquestionably, the main tasks are to strike at these two enemies, to carry out a national revolution to overthrow foreign imperialist oppression and a democratic revolution to overthrow feudal landlord oppression, the primary and foremost task being the national revolution to overthrow imperialism. . . .

The Motive Forces of the Chinese Revolution

Since Chinese society is colonial, semicolonial and semifeudal, since the targets of the revolution are mainly foreign imperialist rule and domestic feudalism, and since its tasks are to overthrow these two oppressors, which of the various classes and strata in Chinese society constitute the forces capable of fighting them? This is the question of the motive forces of the Chinese revolution at the present stage. A clear understanding of this question is indispensable to a correct solution of the problem of the basic tactics of the Chinese revolution. . . .

Let us now analyze the different classes in Chinese society.

The landlord class. The landlord class forms the main social base for imperialist rule in China; it is a class which uses the feudal system to exploit and oppress the peasants, obstructs China's political, economic and cultural development and plays no progressive role whatsoever.

Therefore, the landlords, as a class, are a target and not a motive force of the revolution.

The bourgeoisie. There is a distinction between the comprador big bourgeoisie and the national bourgeoisie.

The comprador big bourgeoisie is a class which directly serves the capitalists of the imperialist countries and is nurtured by them; countless ties link it closely with the feudal forces in the countryside. Therefore, it is a target of the Chinese revolution, and never in the history of the revolution has it been a motive force. . . .

The different sections of the petty bourgeoisie other than the peasantry. The petty bourgeoisie, other than the peasantry, consists of the vast numbers of intellectuals, small tradesmen, handicraftsmen and professional people.

Their status somewhat resembles that of the middle peasants, they all suffer under the oppression of imperialism, feudalism and the big bourgeoisie, and they are being driven ever nearer to bankruptcy or destitution. . . .

Let us analyze the different sections . . .

First, the intellectuals and student youth. They do not constitute a separate class or stratum. In present-day China most of them may be placed in the petty-bourgeois category, judging by their family origin, their living conditions and their political outlook. . . .

Second, the small tradesmen. Generally they run small shops and employ few or no assistants.

Third, the handicraftsmen. They are very numerous. They possess their own means of production and hire no workers, or only one or two apprentices or helpers. . . .

Fourth, professional people. They include doctors and men of other professions. They do not exploit other people, or do so only to a slight degree. . . .

These sections of the petty bourgeoisie make up a vast multitude of people whom we must win over and whose interests we must protect. . . .

The peasantry. The peasantry constitutes approximately 80 per cent of China's total population and is the main force in her national economy today.

A sharp process of polarization is taking place among the peasantry.

First, the rich peasants. They form about 5 per cent of the rural population (or about 10 per cent together with the landlords) and constitute the rural bourgeoisie. . . . The rich peasant form of production will remain useful for a definite period. . . . Therefore we should not regard the rich peasants as belonging to the same class as the landlords and should not prematurely adopt a policy of liquidating the rich peasantry.

Second, the middle peasants. They form about 20 per cent of China's rural population. . . . They have no political rights. Some of them do not have enough land, and only a section (the well-to-do middle peasants) have some surplus land. Not only can the middle peasants join the anti-imperialist revolution . . . but they can also accept socialism. . . .

Third, the poor peasants. The poor peasants in China, together with the farm laborers, form about 70 per cent of the rural population. They are the broad peasant masses with no land or insufficient land, the semiproletariat of the countryside, the biggest motive force of the Chinese revolution. . . .

The proletariat. Among the Chinese proletariat, the modern industrial workers number from 2.5 to 3 million, the workers in small-scale industry and in handicrafts and the shop assistants in the cities total about 12 million, and in addition there are . . . other propertyless people in the cities and the countryside.

In addition to the basic qualities it shares with the proletariat everywhere . . . the Chinese proletariat has many other outstanding qualities. What are they?

First, the Chinese proletariat is more resolute and thoroughgoing in revolutionary struggle than any other class because it is subject to a threefold oppression—imperialist, bourgeois and feudal. . . .

Secondly, from the moment it appeared on the revolutionary scene, the Chinese proletariat came under the leadership of its own revolutionary Party—the Communist Party of China—and became the most politically conscious class in Chinese society.

Thirdly, because the Chinese proletariat by origin is largely made up of bankrupted peasants, it has natural ties with the peasant masses, which facilitates its forming a close alliance with them. . . .

Among all the classes in Chinese society, the peasantry is a firm ally of the working class, the urban petty bourgeoisie is a reliable ally, and the national bourgeoisie is an ally in certain periods and to a certain extent. This is one of the fundamental laws established by China's modern revolutionary history.

The vagrants. China's status as a colony and semicolony has given rise to a multitude of rural and urban unemployed. Denied proper means of making a living, many of them are forced to resort to illegitimate ones, hence the robbers, gangsters, beggars and prostitutes. . . . These people lack constructive qualities and are given to destruction rather than construction. . . . Therefore, we should know how to remold them and guard against their destructiveness.

The above is our analysis of the motive forces of the Chinese revolution.

The Character of the Chinese Revolution

We have now gained an understanding of the nature of Chinese society, namely, of the specific conditions in China. . . . We can now understand another basic issue of the revolution at the present stage, namely, the character of the Chinese revolution. . . .

Is it a bourgeois-democratic or a proletarian-socialist revolution? Obviously, it is not the latter but the former. . . .

The new-democratic revolution is part of the world proletarian-socialist revolution, for it resolutely opposes imperialism, that is, international capitalism. . . . The new-democratic revolution is vastly different from the democratic revolutions in Europe and America in that it results not in a dictatorship of the bourgeoisie but in a dictatorship of the united front of all the revolutionary classes under the leadership of the proletariat. . . .

The new-democratic revolution also differs from a socialist revolution in that it overthrows the rule of the imperialists, traitors and reactionaries in China but does not destroy any section of capitalism which is capable of contributing to the anti-imperialist, anti-feudal struggle.

The new-democratic revolution is basically in line with the revolution envisaged in the Three People's Principles as advocated by Dr. Sun Yat Sen in 1924. In the Manifesto of the First National Congress of the Kuomintang issued in that year, Dr. Sun stated:

The so-called democratic system in modern states is usually monopolized by the bourgeoisie and has become simply an instrument for oppressing the common people. On the other hand, the Kuomintang's Principle of Democracy means a democratic system shared by all the common people and not privately owned by the few.

He added:

Enterprises, such as banks, railways and airlines, whether Chinese-owned or foreign-owned, which are either monopolistic in character or too big for private management, shall be operated and administered by the state, so that private capital cannot dominate the livelihood of the people: this is the main principle of the regulation of capital.

And again in his Testament, Dr. Sun pointed out the fundamental principle for domestic and foreign policy: "We must arouse the masses of the people and unite in a common struggle with those nations of the world which treat us as equals." . . . (Here we shall not deal with the fact that, while communism and the Three People's Principles agree on the basic political program for the democratic revolution, they differ in all other respects.) . . .

The Perspectives of the Chinese Revolution

Now that the basic issues—the nature of Chinese society and the targets, tasks, motive forces and character of the Chinese revolution at the present stage—have been clarified, it is easy to see its perspectives, that is, to understand the relation between the bourgeois-democratic and the proletarian-socialist revolution, or between the present and future stages of the Chinese revolution. . . .

A certain degree of capitalist development will be an inevitable result of the victory of the democratic revolution in economically backward China. But that will be only one aspect of the outcome of the Chinese revolution and not the whole picture. The whole picture will show the development of socialist as well as capitalist factors.

What will the socialist factors be? The increasing relative importance of the proletariat and the Communist Party among the political forces in the country. . . . With the addition of a favorable international environment, these factors render it highly probable that China's bourgeois-democratic revolution will ultimately avoid a capitalist future and enjoy a socialist future.

The Twofold Task of the Chinese Revolution and the Chinese Communist Party

Summing up the foregoing sections of this chapter, we can see that the Chinese revolution taken as a whole involves a twofold task. That is to say, it embraces both the bourgeois-democratic revolution (the new-democratic revolution) and the proletarian-socialist revolution, that is, both the present and future stages of the revolution. . . .

To complete China's bourgeois-democratic revolution . . . and to transform it into a socialist revolution when all the necessary conditions are ripe—such is the sum total of the great and glorious revolutionary task of the Chinese Communist Party. . . .

It is a task at once glorious and arduous. And it cannot be accomplished without a bolshevized Chinese Communist Party which is national in scale and has a broad mass character, a Party fully consolidated ideologically, politically and organizationally. Therefore every Communist has the duty of playing an active part in building up such a Communist Party.

The Chinese Revolution and the Chinese Communist Party is a textbook which was written jointly by Mao Tse-tung and several associates in Yenan in the winter of 1939. The views on New Democracy set out by Mao Tse-tung in Chapter II were further developed in his "On New Democracy" written in January 1940.

Stalin, Friend of the Chinese People

December 30, 1939

On the twenty-first of December, Comrade Stalin will be sixty years old. We can be sure that his birthday will evoke warm and affectionate congratulations from the hearts of all revolutionary people throughout the world who know of the occasion. . . .

Living in a period of the bitterest suffering in our history, we Chinese people most urgently need help from others. The *Book of Odes* says, "A bird sings out to draw a friend's response." This aptly describes our present situation.

But who are our friends?

There are so-called friends, self-styled friends of the Chinese people, whom even some Chinese unthinkingly accept as friends. But such friends can only be classed with Li Lin-fu,[1] the Prime Minister in the Tang Dynasty who was notorious as a man with "honey on his lips and murder in his heart." They are indeed "friends" with "honey on their lips and murder in their hearts." Who are these people? They are the imperialists who profess sympathy with China.

However, there are friends of another kind, friends who have real sympathy with us and regard us as brothers. Who are they? They are the Soviet people and Stalin.

No other country has renounced its privileges in China; the Soviet Union alone has done so. . . .

Stalin is the true friend of the cause of liberation of the Chinese people. No attempt to sow dissension, no lies and calumnies, can affect the Chinese people's wholehearted love and respect for Stalin and our genuine friendship for the Soviet Union.

1. Li Lin-fu (eighth century) was a Prime Minister under Emperor Hsuan Tsung of the Tang Dynasty. Although feigning friendship, he plotted the ruin of all those who surpassed him in ability and fame or found favor in the Emperor's eyes.

In Memory of Norman Bethune[1]

December 21, 1939

Comrade Norman Bethune, a member of the Communist Party of Canada, was around fifty when he was sent by the Communist parties of Canada and the United States to China; he made light of travelling thousands of miles to help us in our War of Resistance Against Japan. He arrived in Yenan in the spring of last year, went to work in the Wutai Mountains, and to our great sorrow died a martyr at his post. . . .

Comrade Bethune's spirit, his utter devotion to others without any thought of self, was shown in his great sense of responsibility in his work and his great warmheartedness toward all comrades and the people. . . .

Comrade Bethune was a doctor, the art of healing was his profession and he was constantly perfecting his skill, which stood very high in the Eighth Route Army's medical service. . . .

Comrade Bethune and I met only once. Afterward he wrote me many letters. But I was busy, and I wrote him only one letter and do not even know if he ever received it. I am deeply grieved over his death. Now we are all commemorating him, which shows how profoundly his spirit inspires everyone.

1. Dr. Norman Bethune was a member of the Communist medical corps in 1936 in Spain during the civil war. He arrived in Yenan in the spring of 1938, contracted blood poisoning while operating on wounded soldiers there, and died in Tanghsien, Hopei, on November 12, 1939.

On New Democracy

January 1940

WHITHER CHINA?

A lively atmosphere has prevailed throughout the country ever since the War of Resistance began . . . and people no longer knit their brows in despair. Of late, however, the dust and din of compromise and anti-communism have once again filled the air. . . . The question again arises: What is to be done? Whither China? On the occasion of the publication of *Chinese Culture*,[1] it may therefore be profitable to clarify the political and cultural trends in the country. I am a layman in matters of culture. . . . Fortunately, there are many comrades in Yenan who have written at length in this field, so that my rough and ready words may serve the same purpose as the beating of the gongs before a theatrical performance. Our observations may contain a grain of truth for the nation's advanced cultural workers and may serve as a modest spur to induce them to come forward with valuable contributions of their own. . . . There is but one truth. . . . the revolutionary practice of millions of people. This, I think, can be regarded as the attitude of *Chinese Culture*.

WE WANT TO BUILD A NEW CHINA

. . . Not only do we want to change a China that is politically oppressed and economically exploited into a China that is politically free and economically prosperous; we also want to change the China which is being kept ignorant and backward under the sway of the old culture into an enlightened and progressive China. . . . Our aim in the cultural sphere is to build a new Chinese national culture.

1. *Chinese Culture* was a magazine founded in January 1940 in Yenan; the present article appeared in the first number.

CHINA'S HISTORICAL CHARACTERISTICS

We want to build a new national culture, but what kind of culture should it be?

. . . Marx says, "It is not the consciousness of men that determines their being, but, on the contrary, their social being that determines their consciousness."[2] He also says, "The philosophers have only *interpreted* the world, in various ways; the point, however, is to *change* it." . . .[3] These basic concepts must be kept in mind in our discussions of China's cultural problems. . . .

From the Chou and Chin Dynasties onwards, Chinese society was feudal, as were its politics and its economy. And the dominant culture, reflecting the politics and economy, was feudal culture. . . .

China today is colonial in the Japanese-occupied areas and basically semicolonial in the Kuomintang areas, and it is predominantly feudal or semifeudal in both. . . .

In the course of its history the Chinese revolution must go through two stages, first, the democratic revolution, and second, the socialist revolution, and by their very nature they are two different revolutionary processes. Here democracy does not belong to the old category—it is not the old democracy, but belongs to the new category—it is New Democracy. . . .

THE CHINESE REVOLUTION IS PART OF THE WORLD REVOLUTION

. . . The correct thesis that "The Chinese revolution is part of the world revolution" was put forward as early as 1924–27 during the period of China's first great revolution. It was put forward by the Chinese Communists and endorsed by all those taking part in the anti-imperialist and anti-feudal struggle of the time. However, the significance of this thesis was not fully expounded in those days, and consequently it was only vaguely understood.

2. Karl Marx, "Preface to *A Contribution to the Critique of Political Economy*," *Selected Works of Marx and Engels* (Engl. ed., Moscow, 1958), Vol. 1, p. 363.
3. Karl Marx, "Theses on Feuerbach," *Selected Works of Marx and Engels, op. cit.*, p. 405.

The "world revolution" no longer refers to the old-world revolution, for the old bourgeois-world revolution has long been a thing of the past; it refers to the new-world revolution, the socialist-world revolution. . . .

This correct thesis advanced by the Chinese Communists is based on Stalin's theory. As early as 1918, in an article commemorating the first anniversary of the October Revolution, Stalin wrote:

The great worldwide significance of the October Revolution chiefly consists in the fact that: (1) It has widened the scope of . . . emancipating . . . oppressed peoples. (2) It has opened up wide possibilities for . . . the oppressed peoples of the West and the East. . . . (3) *It has thereby created a bridge between the socialist West and the enslaved East . . . against* world imperialism. . . .

The Chinese revolution has become a very important part of the world revolution.

THE POLITICS OF NEW DEMOCRACY

In China, it is perfectly clear that whoever can lead the people in overthrowing imperialism and the forces of feudalism can win the people's confidence, because these two, and especially imperialism, are the moral enemies of the people. . . .

Therefore, the proletariat, the peasantry, the intelligentsia and the other sections of the petty bourgeoisie undoubtedly constitute the basic forces determining China's fate. . . .

The Chinese democratic republic which we desire to establish . . . will be different from the old European-American form of capitalist republic under bourgeois dictatorship, which is the old democratic form and already out of date. On the other hand, it will also be different from the socialist republic of the Soviet type under the dictatorship of the proletariat which is already flourishing in the USSR. . . .

Thus the numerous types of state system in the world can be reduced to three basic kinds according to the class character of their political power: (1) republics under the bourgeois dictatorship; (2) republics under the dictatorship of the proletariat; (3) republics under the joint dictatorship of several revolutionary classes.

The first kind comprises the old democratic states. . . . The second kind exists in the Soviet Union . . . it will be the dominant form throughout the world for a certain period. The third kind is the transitional form of state to be adopted in the revolutions of the colonial and semicolonial countries. . . .

The question under discussion here is that of the "state system." After several decades of wrangling since the last years of the Ching Dynasty, it has still not been cleared up. . . . The kind of state we need today is a dictatorship of all the revolutionary classes over the counterrevolutionaries and traitors.

The so-called "democratic system" in modern states is usually monopolized by the bourgeoisie and has become simply an instrument for oppressing the common people. On the other hand, the Kuomintang's Principle of Democracy means a democratic system shared by all the common people and not privately owned by the few.

Such was the solemn declaration made in the Manifesto of the First National Congress of the Kuomintang, held in 1924 during the period of Kuomintang-Communist co-operation. For sixteen years the Kuomintang has violated this declaration and as a result it has created the present grave national crisis. . . .

The Economy of New Democracy

If such a republic is to be established in China, it must be new-democratic not only in its politics but also in its economy.

It will own the big banks and the big industrial and commercial enterprises. . . .

The republic will take certain necessary steps to confiscate the land of the landlords and distribute it to those peasants having little or no land, carry out Dr. Sun Yat Sen's slogan of "land to the tiller," abolish feudal relations in the rural areas, and turn the land over to the private ownership of the peasants. . . . In general, socialist agriculture will not be established at this stage, though various types of co-operative enterprises developed on the basis of "land to the tiller" will contain elements of socialism.

Refutation of Bourgeois Dictatorship

More than 90 per cent of the people are in favor of a republic of this kind with its new-democratic politics and new-democratic economy; there is no alternative road.

What about the road to a capitalist society under bourgeois dictatorship? . . . In the first place international capitalism, or imperialism, will not permit the establishment in China of a capitalist society under bourgeois dictatorship.

. . . In the second place, socialism will not permit it. All the imperialist powers in the world are our enemies, and China cannot possibly gain her independence without the assistance of the land of socialism and the international proletariat. . . .

"If there is food, let everyone share it." This old Chinese saying contains much truth. Since we all share in fighting the enemy, we should all share in eating, we should all share in the work to be done, and we should all share access to education.

We Communists will never push aside anyone who is revolutionary . . . but it will not do if certain people want to push aside the Communist Party, it will not do if they want to split the united front. . . .

Refutation of "Left" Phrasemongering

If the capitalist road of bourgeois dictatorship is out of the question, then is it possible to take the socialist road of proletarian dictatorship? No, that is not possible either.

Without a doubt, the present revolution is the first step, which will develop into the second step, that of socialism, at a later date. And China will attain true happiness only when she enters the socialist era. But today is not yet the time to introduce socialism. . . .

Certain malicious propagandists, deliberately confusing these two distinct revolutionary stages, advocate the so-called theory of a single revolution in order to prove that the Three People's Principles apply to all kinds of revolutions and that communism therefore loses its *raison d'être*. Utilizing this "theory," they frantically oppose communism and the Communist Party. . . .

Having determined on their policy, they have lost no time in hiring some "metaphysics mongers" plus a few Trotskyites who, brandishing their pens like lances, are tilting in all directions and bedlam. Hence the whole bag of tricks for deceiving those who do not know what is going on in the world around them. . . .

But there are other people, apparently with no evil intentions, who are misled by the "theory of a single revolution" and the fanciful notion of "accomplishing both the political revolution and the social revolution at one stroke." . . . Their approach is likewise very harmful because it confuses the steps to be taken in the revolution and weakens the effort directed toward the current task.

REFUTATION OF THE DIEHARDS

The bourgeois diehards in their turn come forward and say: "Well, you Communists have postponed the socialist system to a later stage and have declared, 'The Three People's Principles being what China needs today, our Party is ready to fight for their complete realization.' All right then, fold up your communism for the time being." . . . In essence it is the howl of the diehards for bourgeois despotism. Out of courtesy, however, we may simply describe it as totally lacking in common sense.

Communism is at once a complete system of proletarian ideology and a new social system. It is different from any other ideology or social system, and is the most complete, progressive, revolutionary and rational system in human history. . . .

Without communism to guide it, China's democratic revolution cannot possibly succeed, let alone move on to the next stage. This is the reason why the bourgeois diehards are so loudly demanding that communism be "folded up." But it must not be "folded up," for once communism is "folded up," China will be doomed. The whole world today depends on communism for its salvation, and China is no exception. . . .

We Communists find it possible to recognize "the Three People's Principles as the political basis for the anti-Japanese united front" . . . the kind of united front Dr. Sun Yat Sen had in mind[4] when he said: "Communism is the good friend of the Three People's Principles."

4. As stressed earlier, it is true that Dr. Sun advocated friendship with the Soviet Union and with communism, as he did with every nation and political party that treated China and the Chinese people as equals. But it was his stated belief that the Chinese Communists themselves did not understand communism, and that communism was not applicable to China.

THE THREE PEOPLE'S PRINCIPLES, OLD AND NEW

The bourgeois diehards have no understanding whatsoever of historical change. . . . They do not know the difference either between communism and the Three People's Principles or between the new Three People's Principles and the old.

We Communists recognize . . . that "the Three People's Principles being what China needs today, our Party is ready to fight for their complete realization." . . . But which kind of Three People's Principles? The Three People's Principles as reinterpreted by Dr. Sun Yat Sen in the Manifesto of the First National Congress of the Kuomintang, and no other. . . .

In the first place, the revolutionary, new or genuine Three People's Principles must include alliance with Russia. . . . In the second place, the new and genuine Three People's Principles must include co-operation with the Communist Party. . . . In the third place, the revolutionary, new and genuine Three People's Principles must include the policy of assisting the peasants and workers. . . .

As for the old Three People's Principles, they were a product of the old period of the Chinese revolution. Russia was then an imperialist power, and naturally there could be no policy of alliance with her; there was then no Communist Party in existence in our country, and naturally there could be no co-operation with it; the movement of the workers and peasants had not yet revealed its full political significance and aroused people's attention, and naturally there could be no policy of alliance with them. Hence the Three People's Principles of the period before the reorganization of the Kuomintang in 1924 belonged to the old category, and they became obsolete. . . . Dr. Sun Yat Sen in his wisdom saw this point, secured the help of the Soviet Union and the Chinese Communist Party and reinterpreted the Three People's Principles so as to endow them with new characteristics suited to the times. . . .[5] As a result, a united front was formed between the Three People's Principles and communism. . . . Kuomintang-Communist co-operation was established. . . .

5. There were no "new" and "old" categories of the Three People's Principles. Mao fabricated "new characteristics" to persuade the Chinese masses that communism and Dr. Sun Yat Sen's democratic principles were interchangeable.

The Culture of New Democracy

. . . There is in China an imperialist culture which is a reflection of imperialist rule. . . . Unless it is swept away, no new culture of any kind can be built up. . . .

As for the new culture, it is the ideological reflection of the new politics and the new economy which it sets out to serve.

These new political, economic and cultural forces are all revolutionary forces which are opposed to the old politics, the old economy and the old culture. The old is composed of two parts, one being China's own semifeudal politics, economy and culture, and the other the politics, economy and culture of imperialism, with the latter heading the alliance. Both are bad and should be completely destroyed. . . .

The Historical Characteristics of China's Cultural Revolution

On the cultural or ideological front, the two periods preceding and following the May Fourth Movement form two distinct historical periods.

Before the May Fourth Movement, the struggle on China's cultural front was one between the new culture of the bourgeoisie and the old culture of the feudal class. The struggles between the modern school system and the imperial examination system, between the new learning and the old learning, and between Western learning and Chinese learning, were all of this nature. . . .

But since the May Fourth Movement things have been different. A brand-new cultural force came into being in China, that is, the Communist culture and ideology guided by the Chinese Communists, or the Communist world outlook and theory of social revolution. The May Fourth Movement occurred in 1919, and in 1921 came the founding of the Chinese Communist Party and the real beginning of China's labor movement. . . .

The new-democratic culture is the anti-imperialist and anti-feudal culture of the broad masses. . . . This culture can be led only by the culture and ideology of the proletariat, by the ideology of communism. . . .

The Four Periods

. . . The history of the united front in the cultural revolution during the last twenty years can be divided into four periods.

The first period extended from the May Fourth Movement of 1919 to the founding of the Chinese Communist Party in 1921. The May Fourth Movement was its chief landmark. . . .

In the second period, whose landmarks were the founding of the Chinese Communist Party, the May Thirtieth Movement and the Northern Expedition, the united front of the three classes formed in the May Fourth Movement was continued and expanded, the peasantry was drawn into it and a political united front of all these classes, the first instance of Kuomintang-Communist co-operation, was established. . . .

The third period was the new revolutionary period of 1927–37. . . . With the big bourgeoisie going over to the counterrevolutionary camp . . . the Chinese revolution . . . entered a new period in which the Chinese Communist Party alone gave leadership to the masses. . . .

The fourth period is that of the present anti-Japanese war. . . .

The progress achieved during the twenty years since the May Fourth Movement not only exceeds that of the preceding eighty years but virtually surpasses that achieved in the thousands of years of Chinese history. . . . The unbridled forces of darkness . . . are already in their death throes . . . and the people are gradually approaching victory. . . .

Some Wrong Ideas
About the Nature of Culture

The bourgeois diehards are as hopelessly wrong on the question of culture as on that of political power. They neither understand the historical characteristics of this new period in China, nor recognize the new-democratic culture of the masses.

. . . So far as the orientation of our national culture is concerned, Communist ideology plays the guiding role. . . . However, taken as a whole, the political, economic and cultural situation so far is new-democratic and not socialist. For the Chinese revolution in its present stage is not yet a socialist revolution for the overthrow of capitalism. . . . There are socialist elements in our politics and our economy . . . but we do not have a socialist politics and a socialist economy yet, so that there cannot be a wholly socialist national culture. . . .

Beyond all doubt, now is the time to spread Communist ideas more widely and put more energy into the study of Marxism-Leninism. . . . However, we must guide the present democratic revolution . . . we must keep the spreading of Communist ideas and propaganda about the Communist social system distinct from the practical application of the new-democratic program of action. . . . It is undoubtedly inappropriate to mix the two up. . . .

A National, Scientific and Mass Culture

New-democratic culture is national. It opposes imperialist oppression and upholds the dignity and independence of the Chinese nation. . . . As a revolutionary national culture it can never link up with any reactionary imperialist culture of whatever nation. . . .

New-democratic culture is scientific. Opposed as it is to all feudal and superstitious ideas, it stands for seeking truth from facts, for objective truth and for the unity of theory and practice. . . . A splendid old culture was created during the long period of Chinese feudal society. To study the development of this old culture, to reject its feudal dross and assimilate its democratic essence is a necessary condition for developing our new national culture and increasing our national self-confidence. . . .

New-democratic culture belongs to the broad masses and is therefore democratic. It should serve the toiling masses of workers and peasants who make up more than 90 per cent of the nation's population. . . .

Combine the politics, the economy and the culture of New Democracy, and you have the new-democratic republic, the Republic of China both in name and in reality, the new China we want to create. Behold, New China is within sight. Let us all hail her! Her masts have already risen above the horizon. Let us all cheer in welcome!

Raise both your hands. New China is ours!

Overcome the Danger of Capitulation and Strive for a Turn for the Better

January 28, 1940

Current developments confirm the correctness of the Central Committee's appraisals. The line of capitulation taken by the big landlord class and the big bourgeoisie runs sharply counter to the line of armed resistance taken by the proletariat, the peasantry, the urban petty bourgeoisie and the middle bourgeoisie, and there is a struggle between the two. . . .

In these circumstances, our Party has a twofold task. On the one hand, it must resolutely resist the military and political offensives of the capitulators and diehards. On the other, it must actively develop the united front of the political parties, the government organs, the armed forces, the civilian population and the intellectuals; it must do its utmost to win over the majority of the Kuomintang, the intermediate classes . . . the civilian population and the intellectuals. . . .

Now that Wang Ching-wei has announced his traitorous pact[1] and Chiang Kai-shek has published his message to the nation, it is beyond doubt that the agitation for peace will suffer a setback and the forces favoring resistance will grow; on the other hand, the "military and political restriction of the Communist Party" will continue . . . and the Kuomintang may stress so-called "unification against the foreign enemy" in order to attack us. . . .

A mass rally to denounce Wang Ching-wei's traitorous pact is scheduled to be held on February 1 in Yenan. Together with the people of all circles and with the anti-Japanese members of the Kuomintang, we should organize similar mass rallies in all areas in the early part or the middle of February in order to create a nation-

1. Wang Ching-wei, who was soon to become a puppet "head of state" in Nanking for the Japanese, signed a secret pact agreeing to prohibit all anti-Japanese activities, to appoint Japanese advisers and officials, and in effect to make all China as much of a colony of Japan as Manchuria had been since 1931.

wide upsurge against capitulation, against the collaborators and against "friction."

This was an inner-Party directive written by Mao Tse-tung on behalf of the Central Committee of the Chinese Communist Party.

Unite All Anti-Japanese Forces and Combat the Anti-Communist Diehards

February 1, 1940

Why are we, the people of all circles in Yenan, meeting here today? We are here to denounce the traitor Wang Ching-wei, we are here to unite all anti-Japanese forces and to combat the anti-Communist diehards. . . .

. . . The Wang Ching-wei clique and the anti-Communist diehards in the Kuomintang have been working in collusion, one from without and the other from within, and have created pandemonium.

This state of affairs has infuriated large numbers of people who think that the resistance to Japan is now finished and done for and that the members of the Kuomintang are all scoundrels who ought to be opposed. We must say that their fury is entirely justified, for how can anybody help becoming infuriated in the face of such a grave situation? But resistance to Japan is not finished and done for, nor are all Kuomintang members scoundrels. . . .

Therefore, we should show goodwill toward those Kuomintang members who are not capitulators or anti-Communist diehards but are loyal to the War of Resistance; we should unite with them, respect them and be willing to continue our long-term co-operation with them so as to put our country in order. . . .

The anti-Communist diehards within the Kuomintang emphasize unification, but their so-called unification is not genuine but a sham, not a rational but an irrational unification. . . . They howl for unification, but what they really want is to liquidate the Communist Party, the Eighth Route and New Fourth Armies and the Shensi-Kansu-Ningsia Border Region, on the pretext that China cannot be unified so long as these exist. . . . They want to turn everything over to the Kuomintang and not merely to continue but to extend their one-Party dictatorship. . . . Only people without any sense of shame dare suggest anything so shameful. . . .

This is a plot, an attempt to perpetuate autocratic rule under the guise of unification, to sell the dog meat of their one-Party dictatorship under the label of the sheep's head of unification; it is a plot of brazen-faced braggarts who are lost to all sense of shame. We are meeting here today precisely to punch holes in this paper tiger of theirs. Let us relentlessly combat these anti-Communist diehards.

Mao Tse-tung delivered this speech at a mass rally in Yenan to denounce Wang Ching-wei.

Ten Demands on the Kuomintang

February 1, 1940

This mass rally against Wang Ching-wei, held in Yenan on February 1, unanimously resolves . . . to wage the War of Resistance to the very end. . . . We hereby submit ten major points for saving the country, in the hope that the National Government, all political parties and groups, all officers and men fighting in the War of Resistance and all our fellow countrymen will accept them and act upon them.

1. Let the whole nation denounce the Wang Ching-weis. 2. Strengthen unity. 3. Put constitutional government into effect. 4. Put an end to the "friction." 5. Protect the youth. 6. Support the front. 7. Proscribe the secret service. 8. Dismiss corrupt officials. 9. Put the Testament of Dr. Sun Yat Sen into effect. 10. Put the Three People's Principles into effect.

This was an open telegram drafted by Mao Tse-tung on behalf of the Yenan mass rally denouncing Wang Ching-wei.

Introducing *The Chinese Worker*[1]

February 7, 1940

The publication of *The Chinese Worker* meets a need. Led by its own political party, the Communist Party of China . . . *The Chinese Worker* will explain the hows and whys of many issues to the workers, report the realities of the working-class struggle in the War of Resistance and sum up the experience gained. . . . The working class should welcome the help of the revolutionary intellectuals and never refuse it. . . .

I hope that the journal will be well edited and that it will publish a good deal of lively writing, carefully avoiding wooden and trite articles which are flat, insipid and unintelligible. Once started, a journal must be run conscientiously and well. . . .

With these few words I express my hopes; let them serve as an introduction to *The Chinese Worker*.

We Must Stress Unity and Progress

February 10, 1940

Resistance, unity and progress—these are the three major principles which the Communist Party put forward last July 7 on the second anniversary of the War of Resistance. . . .

For the sake of . . . resistance, it is necessary to fight against capitulation. . . . For the sake of unity, it is necessary to oppose splitting activities and internal "friction," to oppose the stabbing of the Eighth Route and New Fourth Armies in the back. . . . For the

1. *The Chinese Worker* was a monthly founded in February 1940 in Yenan and published under the auspices of the Trade Union Commission of the Central Committee of the Chinese Communist Party.

sake of progress, it is necessary to oppose retrogression and the shelving of the Three People's Principles. . . .

Without opposing all these and without unity and progress, "resistance" will be just empty talk and victory a vain hope.

This article was written by Mao Tse-tung for the New China News of Yenan on the occasion of its first anniversary.

New-Democratic Constitutional Government

February 20, 1940

It is highly significant that representatives of the people of all circles in Yenan are meeting here today to inaugurate the Association for the Promotion of Constitutional Government and that everybody has become interested in constitutionalism. . . .

Armed resistance to Japan, which we all support, is already being carried out. . . . But there is something else, namely, democracy, which is not being carried out. Both are of paramount importance to China today. . . .

What is constitutional government? It is democratic government. I agree with what our old Comrade Wu[1] has just said. What kind of democratic government do we need today? New-democratic government, the constitutional government of New Democracy. Not the old, outmoded, European-American type of so-called democracy which is bourgeois dictatorship, nor as yet the Soviet type of democracy which is the dictatorship of the proletariat.

What is new-democratic constitutional government? It is the joint dictatorship of several revolutionary classes over the traitors and reactionaries. Someone once said, "If there is food, let everyone share it." I think this can serve to illustrate New Democracy. Just as everyone should share what food there is, so there should be no monopoly of power by a single party, group or class. This idea was

1. Wu Yu-chang, who was then chairman of the Yenan Association for the Promotion of Constitutional Government.

well expressed by Dr. Sun Yat Sen in the Manifesto of the First National Congress of the Kuomintang:

The so-called democratic system in modern states is usually monopolized by the bourgeoisie and has become simply an instrument for oppressing the common people. On the other hand, the Kuomintang's Principle of Democracy means a democratic system shared by all the common people and not privately owned by the few. . . .

The purpose of our meeting today is to promote or urge the establishment of constitutional government. . . . Where does the term "urge" come from? . . . That great and venerated man, Dr. Sun Yat Sen, who said: "For forty years I have devoted myself to the cause of the national revolution. . . ." Read his Testament and you will find the following words: "Most recently I have recommended the convocation of the national assembly . . . and its realization in the shortest possible time must in particular be urged. This is my heartfelt charge to you." . . .

For years we have been hearing the words "constitutional government," but so far we have seen no trace of it. . . . As for democracy and freedom, heaven alone knows when they will give you that. China has already had a constitution. Did not Tsao Kun[2] promulgate one? But where were democracy and freedom to be found? As for Presidents, there have been a number of them. The first, Sun Yat Sen, was good, but he was edged out by Yuan Shih-kai.[3] The second was Yuan Shih-kai, the third Li Yuan-hung,[4] the fourth Feng Kuo-chang,[5] and the fifth Hsu Shih-chang,[6] indeed a great many, but were they any different from the despotic Emperors? Both the constitution and the Presidents were fakes. . . .

2. Tsao Kun was a northern warlord who, in 1923, had himself elected President of the Republic by bribing 590 members of Parliament with 5,000 silver dollars each.
3. Yuan Shih-kai proclaimed himself Emperor on December 12, 1915, but was forced to give up the title on March 22, 1916.
4. Li Yuan-hung was originally commander of a brigade in the armed forces of the Ching Dynasty. He joined in the armed forces military uprising in Wuchang in 1911, was made military governor of Hupeh Province, later becoming Vice President, and then President.
5. Feng Kuo-chang was one of Yuan Shih-kai's underlings. After Yuan's death, he became leader of the Chihli (Hopeh) group of northern warlords. In 1917 he got rid of Li Yuan-hung and became President himself.
6. Hsu Shih-chang was a northern warlord politician, who was elected President in 1918 by a Parliament controlled by Tuan Chi-jui.

Should we then lament the cause as lost? Things are so difficult that it seems hopeless. But that is not so either. There is still hope for constitutional government, and great hope at that, and China will certainly become a new-democratic state. . . . For the people throughout the country demand it . . . and the wheel of history cannot be pushed back.

Mao Tse-tung delivered this speech before the Yenan Association for the Promotion of Constitutional Government.

On the Question of Political Power in the Anti-Japanese Base Areas

March 6, 1940

This is a time when the anti-Communist diehards of the Kuomintang are doing all they can to prevent us from setting up organs of anti-Japanese democratic power in northern and central China and other places, while we on our part must set them up. . . . The political power we are establishing during the anti-Japanese war is of a united front character . . . it is the joint democratic dictatorship of several revolutionary classes over the traitors and reactionaries. . . .

The convening of the Hopei Provincial Assembly and the elections to the Hopei Administrative Council, preparations for which have just been started, will be of exceptional importance. . . .

In accordance with the united front principle concerning the organs of political power, the allocation of places should be one-third for Communists, one-third for non-Party left progressives, and one-third for the intermediate sections who are neither left nor right. . . .

Our aim in allocating one-third of the places to the intermediate sections is to win over the middle bourgeoisie and the enlightened gentry. . . .

The above figures for the allocation of places are not rigid quotas to be filled mechanically; they are in the nature of a rough proportion which every locality must apply according to its specific circumstances. . . .

The united front policy on suffrage should be that every Chinese who reaches the age of eighteen and is in favor of resistance and democracy should enjoy the right to elect and to be elected, irrespective of class, nationality, sex, creed, Party affiliation or educational level. . . .

The non-Party people who work in our organs of political power should not be required to live, talk and act like Communists, or otherwise they may feel dissatisfied or ill at ease. . . .

All regional and subregional bureaus of the Central Committee, all area Party committees and all heads of army units are hereby instructed to give a clear explanation of this directive to Party members, and ensure that it is fully carried out in the work of our organs of political power.

This inner-Party directive was written by Mao Tse-tung on behalf of the Central Committee of the Communist Party of China.

Current Problems of Tactics in the Anti-Japanese United Front

March 11, 1940

The present situation is as follows:

Japanese imperialism has been dealt a heavy blow by China's War of Resistance and is already incapable of launching any more large-scale military offensives, so that the relation of forces between the enemy and ourselves has now reached the stage of strategic stalemate. . . .

Britain and France are finding their position in the East weakened by the war in Europe, while the United States is continuing its policy of "sitting on top of the mountain and watching the tigers fight," so that an Eastern Munich Conference is out of the question for the moment.

The Soviet Union has gained new successes in its foreign policy and is maintaining its policy of giving active support to China's War of Resistance.

The pro-Japanese section of the big bourgeoisie, having completely capitulated to Japan, is ready to play the puppet. . . .

The basic condition for victory in the War of Resistance is the extension and consolidation of the anti-Japanese united front. The tactics required for this purpose are to develop the progressive forces, win over the middle forces and combat the die-hard forces. . . .

In our propaganda we should stress the following program:

(a) Carry out the Testament of Dr. Sun Yat Sen by arousing the masses for united resistance to Japan;

(b) carry out the Principle of Nationalism by firmly resisting Japanese imperialism and striving for complete national liberation and the equality of all the nationalities within China;

(c) carry out the Principle of Democracy by granting the people absolute freedom to resist Japan and save the nation, by enabling them to elect governments at all levels, and by establishing the revolutionary democratic political power of the Anti-Japanese National United Front;

(d) carry out the Principle of the People's Livelihood by abolishing exorbitant taxes and miscellaneous levies, reducing land rent and interest, enforcing the eight-hour working day, developing agriculture, industry and commerce, and improving the livelihood of the people; and

(e) carry out Chiang Kai-shek's declaration that "Every person, young or old, in the north or in the south, must take up the responsibility of resisting Japan and defending our homeland." . . .

In the stage of the bourgeois-democratic revolution, this program of the Kuomintang's is basically the same as ours, but the ideology of the Kuomintang is entirely different from that of the Communist Party. It is this common program of the democratic revolution that we should put into practice, but on no account should we follow the ideology of the Kuomintang.

Mao Tse-tung wrote this outline for the report he made at a meeting of the Chinese Communist Party's senior cadres in Yenan.

Freely Expand the Anti-Japanese Forces and Resist the Onslaughts of the Anti-Communist Diehards

May 4, 1940

In all regions behind the enemy lines and in all the war zones, stress should be laid not on particularity, but on identity; to do otherwise would be a gross error. While each region has its individual peculiarities, they are all identical in that we are confronted by the enemy and all are engaged in the War of Resistance, whether in northern, central, or southern China. . . . It follows that in all cases we can and should expand. . . . To expand means to reach out into all enemy-occupied areas and not to be bound by the Kuomintang's restrictions but to go beyond the limits allowed by the Kuomintang . . . to expand the armed forces freely and independently, set up base areas unhesitatingly . . . and build up united front organs of political power under the leadership of the Communist Party. . . .

At a time when the anti-Communist diehards in the Kuomintang are obstinately persisting in their policy of containing, restricting and combatting the Communist Party in preparation for capitulation to Japan, we must stress struggle and not unity; to do otherwise would be a gross error. . . .

Our policy in the Kuomintang areas is different from that in the war zones and the areas behind the enemy lines. In the Kuomintang areas our policy is to have well-selected cadres working underground for a long period, to accumulate strength and bide our time, and to avoid rashness and exposure. . . .

If a member of our Party is forced to join the Kuomintang, let him do so; our members should penetrate the *pao chia*[1] and the educational, economic and military organizations everywhere. . . . Our Party organizations in the Kuomintang areas must be kept strictly

---

1. On August 1, 1932, Chiang Kai-shek promulgated the *pao* and *chia* population census, on the basis of household. It provided that there was to be a head of each household; of each *chia* made up of ten households; and of each *pao* made up of ten *chia*.

secret. . . . Great care must be taken to protect our cadres, and whoever is in danger of being arrested and killed by the Kuomintang while working in an open or semiopen capacity should either be sent to some other locality and go underground or be transferred to the army.

This directive was written by Mao Tse-tung on behalf of the Central Committee of the Chinese Communist Party.

Unity to the Very End

July 1940

All Communists must realize that only through resistance to the very end can there be unity to the very end, and vice versa. Therefore, Communists must set an example in both resistance and unity. Our opposition is directed solely against the enemy and against the determined capitulators and anti-Communists; with all others we must unite in earnest. . . .

Thus, as far as political power is concerned, we stand for united front organs of political power; we do not favor one-Party dictatorship either by the Communist Party or by any other Party, but we stand for the joint dictatorship of all political parties and groups, people in all walks of life and all armed forces, that is, for united front political power. . . .

As for our policies on other matters, whether financial, economic, cultural or educational or anti-espionage, for the sake of resistance we must follow the united front policy by adjusting the interests of the different classes and must oppose both Right and "Left" opportunism. . . .

We are confident that, through the united efforts of all members of our Party, of the friendly parties and armies and the whole people, we shall succeed in preventing capitulation, in conquering the difficulties, in driving out the Japanese aggressors and in recovering our lost territories. The prospects for our War of Resistance are indeed bright.

On Policy

December 25, 1940

In the present high tide of anti-Communist attacks, the policy we adopt is of decisive importance. . . .

In the enemy-occupied and Kuomintang areas our policy is, on the one hand, to develop the united front to the greatest possible extent and, on the other, to have well-selected cadres working underground. With regard to the forms of organization and struggle, our policy is to have well-selected cadres working underground for a long period, to accumulate strength and bide our time. . . .

With respect to the anti-Communist diehards, ours is a revolutionary dual policy of uniting with them, insofar as they are still in favor of resisting Japan, and of isolating them, insofar as they are determined to oppose the Communist Party. . . .

The pro-Japanese big landlords and big bourgeoisie who are against resistance must be distinguished from the pro-British and pro-American big landlords and big bourgeoisie who are for resistance. . . . We build our policy on these distinctions. . . .

We deal with imperialism in the same way. The Communist Party opposes all imperialism, but we make a distinction between Japanese imperialism, which is now committing aggression against China, and the imperialist powers, which are not doing so now. . . .

The organs of political power. The "three-thirds system" under which Communists have only one-third of the places in the organs of political power and many non-Communists are drawn into participation, must be carried out resolutely. . . .

Labor policy. The livelihood of the workers must be improved if their enthusiasm in the fight against Japan is to be fully aroused. . . . Under present conditions, the eight-hour working day cannot be universally introduced in China and a ten-hour working day should still be permitted in certain branches of production. . . .

Land policy. It must be explained to Party members and to the peasants that this is not the time for a thorough agrarian revolution.

. . . Our present policy should stipulate that the landlords shall reduce rent and interest, for this serves to arouse the enthusiasm of the basic peasant masses for resistance to Japan, but the reductions should not be too great. In general, land rent should be reduced by 25 per cent. . . .

Tax policy. Taxes must be levied according to income. Except for the very poor, who should be exempt, all people with an income shall pay taxes to the state. . . .

Anti-espionage policy. We must firmly suppress the confirmed traitors and anti-Communists, or otherwise we shall not be able to protect the anti-Japanese revolutionary forces. . . . Corporal punishment must be abolished in trying criminals. . . .

The rights of the people. It must be laid down that all landlords and capitalists not opposed to the War of Resistance shall enjoy the same rights of person and property, the same right to vote and the same freedom of speech, assembly, association, political conviction and religious belief as the workers and peasants. . . .

Economic policy. We must actively develop industry and agriculture and promote the circulation of commodities. Capitalists should be encouraged to come into our anti-Japanese base areas and start enterprises here if they so desire. Private enterprise should be encouraged and state enterprise regarded as only one sector of the economy. . . .

Cultural and educational policy. This should center on promoting and spreading the knowledge and skills needed for the war and a sense of national pride among the masses of the people. . . . Every base area must establish printing shops, publish books and newspapers and organize distribution and delivery agencies. Every base area must also, as far as possible, set up big schools for training cadres, and the more and bigger, the better.

Military policy. There must be maximum expansion of the Eighth Route and New Fourth Armies, because they are the most reliable armed forces of the Chinese people in pressing on with the national War of Resistance. . . .

All these tactical principles for the united front and the concrete policies formulated in accordance with them must be firmly applied by the whole Party. . . .

This inner-Party directive was written by Mao Tse-tung on behalf of the Central Committee of the Chinese Communist Party.

Order and Statement
on the Southern Anhwei Incident

January 1941
Yenan, January 20, 1941

ORDER OF THE REVOLUTIONARY MILITARY COMMISSION OF THE CENTRAL COMMITTEE OF THE COMMUNIST PARTY OF CHINA

The New Fourth Army of the National Revolutionary Army has won fame both at home and abroad by its distinguished service in the War of Resistance. Commander Yeh Ting has an outstanding record in leading the army against the enemy. Recently, however, while it was moving northward in accordance with instructions, this army was treacherously attacked by the pro-Japanese clique, and Commander Yeh, wounded and exhausted in the fighting, was thrown into jail. . . . Acting Commander Chen Yi and his associates are hereby instructed to devote their efforts to strengthening the army, reinforcing unity within its ranks, ensuring good relations with the people, carrying out the Three People's Principles, adhering to the Testament of Dr. Sun Yat Sen, and consolidating and expanding the Anti-Japanese National United Front in the struggle to defend our people and our country, to carry the War of Resistance forward to the end and to guard against attacks by the pro-Japanese clique.

STATEMENT BY THE SPOKESMAN OF THE REVOLUTIONARY MILITARY COMMISSION OF THE CENTRAL COMMITTEE OF THE COMMUNIST PARTY OF CHINA TO A CORRESPONDENT OF THE HSINHUA NEWS AGENCY

The recent anti-Communist Southern Anhwei Incident had been brewing for a long time. Present developments are but the opening phase of a national emergency. Since the formation of their triple alliance with Germany and Italy,[1] the Japanese aggressors have redoubled their efforts to engineer changes within China so as to find a quick solution to the Sino-Japanese War. Their purpose is to use the Chinese themselves to suppress the anti-Japanese movement and consolidate the rear for Japan's southward drive, so that she will be free to drive south in co-ordination with Hitler's offensive against Britain. A considerable number of ringleaders from the pro-Japanese clique have long entrenched themselves in the Party, government and army organizations of the Kuomintang and have been carrying on agitation day and night. The preparations for their plot were completed by the end of last year. The attack on the New Fourth Army units in southern Anhwei and the reactionary order of January 17[2] are only the first open signs of this plot. Incidents of the gravest nature will now be staged one after another. . . . After all, that is what loyal servants of Japanese imperialism would do. Hence their plan to mass seven divisions in an annihilation campaign, hence their order of January 17, and hence their trial of Yeh Ting. However, I still say that the Chungking spokesman is an idiot, for without being pressed he has let the cat out of the bag and revealed the plans of Japanese imperialism to the whole people.

---

1. The reference is to the tripartite pact between Germany, Italy and Japan signed in Berlin on September 27, 1940.

2. This was an order by Chiang Kai-shek in the name of the Military Council of the National Government, requiring the Communist New Fourth Army to be incorporated into the national, and presumably unified, command. It was denounced by the Chinese Communist Party as a "counterrevolutionary order."

The Situation After the Repulse of the Second Anti-Communist Onslaught

March 18, 1941

The second anti-Communist onslaught, which was touched off by the telegram of Ho Ying-chin and Pai Chung-hsi (dated October 19 last year), reached its climax in the Southern Anhwei Incident and Chiang Kai-shek's order of January 17. . . .

With the world's two major imperialist blocs on the eve of a decisive struggle, that section of China's big bourgeoisie which is pro-British and pro-American and which is still opposed to the Japanese aggressors finds it necessary to seek a slight temporary relaxation in the present strained relations between the Kuomintang and the Communist Party. . . .

At the moment, therefore, Chiang Kai-shek needs a slight temporary easing of the tension.

The recent struggle points to a decline in the standing of the Kuomintang and a rise in that of the Communist Party, and this is the key factor in certain changes that have occurred in the relative strength of the two parties. . . .

The Kuomintang will never relax its policy of oppression of our Party and other progressives or its anti-Communist propaganda in the areas under its rule; therefore our Party must heighten its vigilance. . . . Throughout the country, including, of course, all the base areas, we must reject the erroneous estimate that a final split between the Kuomintang and the Communist Party has either already occurred or is about to occur, together with the many incorrect views arising therefrom.

Conclusions on the Repulse of the
Second Anti-Communist Onslaught

May 8, 1941

As the Central Committee's directive of March 18, 1941, has stated, the second anti-Communist onslaught has come to an end. What has followed since is the continuance of the War of Resistance Against Japan in new circumstances, international as well as domestic. The additional factors in these new circumstances are the spread of the imperialist war, the upsurge of the international revolutionary movement, the neutrality pact between the Soviet Union and Japan. . . .[1]

In the circumstances, the pro-British and pro-American big landlords and big bourgeoisie, who direct all Kuomintang government policy, remain classes with a dual character. On the one hand they are opposed to Japan, and on the other they are opposed to the Communist Party and the broad masses of the people represented by the Party. . . .

Since the pro-British and pro-American big landlords and big bourgeoisie are still resisting Japan and are still using the stick and carrot in dealing with our Party, the policy of our Party is to "do unto them as they do unto us," stick for stick and carrot for carrot. Such is the revolutionary dual policy. So long as the big landlords and big bourgeoisie do not completely turn traitor, this policy of ours will not change.

A whole range of tactics is needed to combat the Kuomintang's anti-Communist policy, and there must be absolutely no carelessness or negligence. . . . If a people's revolutionary force is to avoid extermination by Chiang Kai-shek and to compel him to acknowl-

1. The neutrality pact between the Soviet Union and Japan was concluded on April 13, 1941. At this time, when China, in her War of Resistance Against Japan, looked hopefully for aid from the Soviet Union, the Chinese Communist leadership, in a spirit of ideological brotherhood, hailed the Soviet-Japanese pact as "a major victory for the Soviet Union's peaceful foreign policy."

edge its existence, it has no alternative but to wage a tit-for-tat struggle against his counterrevolutionary policies. . . .

In the struggle against the Kuomintang diehards, the big comprador bourgeoisie must be distinguished from the national bourgeoisie, which has little or no comprador character, and the most reactionary big landlords must be distinguished from the enlightened gentry and the general run of landlords. . . . Many of our comrades, however, still lump the different landlord and bourgeois groups together, as though the entire landlord class and bourgeoisie had turned traitor after the Southern Anhwei Incident; this is an oversimplification of China's complex politics. Were we to adopt this view and identify all the landlords with the Kuomintang diehards, we would isolate ourselves. . . .

There are even more comrades who fail to understand the unity of the national struggle and the class struggle, and who fail to understand united front policy and class policy, and consequently the unity of united front education and class education. . . . Even now they do not understand that for the whole period of the anti-Japanese war the Party has a single integral policy—the national united front policy (a dual policy) which integrates the two aspects, unity and struggle—toward all those in the upper and middle strata who are still resisting Japan, whether they belong to the big landlord class and big bourgeoisie or the intermediate classes. . . .

Other comrades do not understand that the social character of the Shensi-Kansu-Ningsia Border Region and the anti-Japanese base areas in northern and central China is already new-democratic. The main criterion in judging whether an area is new-democratic in character is whether representatives of the broad masses of the people participate in the political power there and whether this political power is led by the Communist Party. . . .

When the example of the anti-Japanese base areas is extended throughout the country, then the whole of China will become a new-democratic republic.

This inner-Party directive was written by Mao Tse-tung for the Central Committee of the Chinese Communist Party.

Volume III

The Period of the War
of Resistance Against Japan, II

Volume III   Contents

Volume III Contents   231

Preface and Postscript to *Rural Surveys*

March and April 1941

PREFACE. MARCH 17, 1941

The present rural policy of the Party is not one of agrarian revolution as during the ten years' civil war, but is a rural policy for the National United Front Against Japan. . . . Many of our comrades still have a crude and careless style of work, do not seek to understand things thoroughly and may even be completely ignorant of conditions at the lower levels, and yet they are responsible for directing work. . . .

The only way to know conditions is to make social investigations, to investigate the conditions of each social class in real life. . . . Only thus can we acquire even the most rudimentary knowledge of China's social problem.

To do this, first direct your eyes downward, do not hold your head high and gaze at the sky. Unless a person is . . . determined to do so, he will never in his whole life really understand things in China.

Second, hold fact-finding meetings. Certainly, no all-around knowledge can be acquired merely by glancing this way and that and listening to hearsay. . . . Holding fact-finding meetings is the simplest, most practicable and most reliable method, from which I have derived much benefit. . . . I approached responsible cadres of middle rank; . . . I approached cadres of the middle and lower ranks, a poor *hsiutsai*,[1] a bankrupt ex-president of the chamber of commerce and a party official in charge of county revenue who had lost his job. All of these people gave me a great deal of information I had never even heard of. . . . Therefore, everyone engaged in practical work must investigate conditions at the lower levels. . . .

Stalin rightly says that "theory becomes purposeless if it is not connected with revolutionary practice." And he rightly adds that "practice gropes in the dark if its path is not illumined by revolutionary theory."[2]

Postscript. April 19, 1941

The experience of the period of the ten years' civil war is the best and most pertinent for the present period, the War of Resistance Against Japan. . . .

The present policy is a dual policy which synthesizes "alliance" and "struggle." In labor policy, it is the dual policy of suitably improving the workers' livelihood and of not hampering the proper development of the capitalist economy. In agrarian policy, it is the dual policy of requiring the landlords to reduce rent and interest and of stipulating that the peasants should pay this reduced rent and interest. In the sphere of political rights, it is the dual policy of allowing all the anti-Japanese landlords and capitalists the same rights of person and the same political and property rights as the workers and peasants and yet of guarding against possible counterrevolutionary activity on their part. . . .

The Communist Party of China is working in a complicated environment, and every Party member, and especially every cadre, must temper himself to become a fighter who understands Marxist tactics. A one-sided and oversimplified approach to problems can never lead the revolution to victory.

1. A *hsiutsai* was a holder of the lowest degree in the imperial examination.
2. J. V. Stalin, "The Foundations of Leninism," *Problems of Leninism* (Engl. ed., Moscow, 1954), p. 31.

Reform Our Study

May 1941

I propose that we should reform the method and the system of study throughout the Party. The reasons are as follows:

I

The twenty years of the Communist Party of China have been twenty years in which the universal truth of Marxism-Leninism has become more and more integrated with the concrete practice of the Chinese revolution. . . . As soon as it was linked with the concrete practice of the Chinese revolution, the universal truth of Marxism-Leninism gave an entirely new complexion to the Chinese revolution. . . .

II

However, we still have shortcomings, and very big ones too. . . .

First, take the study of current conditions . . . the material we have collected is fragmentary and our research work unsystematic . . . and we are lacking in a climate of investigation and study of objective reality. To behave like "a blindfolded man catching sparrows" or "a blind man groping for fish" . . . is the extremely bad style of work that still exists among many comrades in our Party, a style utterly opposed to the fundamental spirit of Marxism-Leninism. . . .

Second, take the study of history. . . . There are many Marxist-Leninist scholars who cannot open their mouths without citing Ancient Greece; but as for their own ancestors—sorry, they have forgotten. . . .

Third . . . many comrades seem to study Marxism-Leninism not to meet the needs of revolutionary practice, but purely for the sake of study. . . . They can only cite odd quotations from Marx, Engels,

Lenin and Stalin in a one-sided manner, but are unable to apply the stand, viewpoint and method of Marx, Engels, Lenin and Stalin. . . .

There are some who are proud, instead of ashamed of knowing nothing or very little of our own history. . . .

For several decades, many of the returned students from abroad have suffered from this malady. Coming home from Europe, America or Japan, they can only parrot things foreign. They become gramophones and forget their duty to understand and create new things. This malady has also infected the Communist Party. . . .

III

In order to explain this idea further, I should like to contrast two opposite attitudes.

First, there is the subjectivist attitude.

With this attitude, a person does not make a systematic and thorough study of the environment, but works by sheer subjective enthusiasm and has a blurred picture of the face of China today. With this attitude, he chops up history, knows only Ancient Greece but not China and is in a fog about the China of yesterday and the day before yesterday. . . .

There is a couplet which portrays this type of person. It runs:

> The reed growing on the wall—top-heavy,
>   thin-stemmed and shallow of root;
> The bamboo shoot in the hills—sharp-tongued,
>   thick-skinned and hollow inside.

Secondly, there is the Marxist-Leninist attitude.

With this attitude, a person applies the theory and method of Marxism-Leninism to the systematic and thorough investigation and study of the environment. He does not work by enthusiasm alone but, as Stalin says, combines revolutionary sweep with practical-ness. . . .[1] Such an attitude is one of shooting the "arrow" at the target. The "target" is the Chinese revolution, the "arrow" is Marx-ism-Leninism. . . . He who adopts this attitude will be neither "top-heavy, thin-stemmed and shallow of root" nor "sharp-tongued, thick-skinned and hollow inside."

Mao Tse-tung made this report to a cadres' meeting in Yenan.

1. J. V. Stalin, "The Foundations of Leninism," *Problems of Leninism* (Russ. ed., Moscow, 1952), p. 80.

Expose the Plot
for a Far Eastern Munich
May 25, 1941

A compromise between Japan and the United States at the expense of China and the creation of an Eastern Munich against communism and against the Soviet Union—such is the new plot which is now being hatched by Japan, the United States and Chiang Kai-shek. We must expose this plot and fight it. . . .

Simultaneously with her military attacks, Japan has launched a rumor-mongering campaign . . . that "the Eighth Route Army is seizing every opportunity to expand its territory" . . . that it "is setting up another Central Government," etc. . . . This is a cunning Japanese scheme to ferment discord between the Kuomintang and the Communist Party. . . .

The armed forces and the people led by the Communist Party have already become the mainstay in the War of Resistance Against Japan. All the calumnies against the Communist Party are aimed at sabotaging the War of Resistance and paving the way for capitulation. We should extend the military successes of the Eighth Route and New Fourth Armies and oppose all the defeatists and capitulationists.

This inner-Party directive was written by Mao Tse-tung for the Central Committee of the Communist Party of China.

On the International
United Front Against Fascism
June 23, 1941

On June 22 the fascist rulers of Germany attacked the Soviet Union. This is a perfidious crime of aggression. . . .

For Communists throughout the world the task now is to mobilize the people of all countries and organize an international united front to fight fascism. . . .

In foreign relations, unite against the common foe with everybody in Britain, the United States and other countries who is opposed to the fascist rulers of Germany, Italy and Japan.

This inner-Party directive was written by Mao Tse-tung for the Central Committee of the Chinese Communist Party.

Speech at the Assembly of Representatives of the Shensi-Kansu-Ningsia Border Region

November 21, 1941

Members of the Assembly! Comrades! Today's inauguration of the Border Region Assembly of Representatives is of great significance. The Assembly has but one objective, the overthrow of Japanese imperialism and the building of a China of New Democracy or, in other words, a China of the revolutionary Three People's Principles. . . .

Why must we put the revolutionary Three People's Principles into effect? Because up to the present time Dr. Sun Yat Sen's revolutionary Three People's Principles have not been translated into reality in all parts of China. Why don't we demand that socialism be put into effect now? Of course socialism is a superior system and has long been in operation in the Soviet Union, but in China today the conditions for it are still lacking. . . .

We have pursued this policy with success and have won the approval of the people all over China. . . . Some Communists still do not know how to co-operate with non-Party people in a democratic way. . . .

We are not a small opinionated sect and we must learn how to open our doors and co-operate democratically with non-Party people, and how to consult with others. Perhaps even now there are Communists who may say, "If it is necessary to co-operate with others, then leave me out." But I am sure there are very few. . . .

Rectify the Party's Style of Work

February 1, 1942

The Party School opens today and I wish it every success.

I would like to say something about the problem of our Party's style of work.

Why must there be a revolutionary Party? There must be a revolutionary Party because the world contains enemies who oppress the people and the people want to throw off enemy oppression. What is the problem now facing our Party? . . . It is the fact that there is something in the minds of a number of our comrades which strikes one as not quite right, not quite proper . . . something wrong with our style of study, with our style in the Party's internal and external relations and with our style of writing. . . . We mean the malady of subjectivism. . . . We mean the malady of stereotyped Party writing.[1] . . .

To accomplish the task of overthrowing the enemy, we must accomplish the task of rectifying these styles within the Party. . . .

Subjectivism is an improper style of study; it is opposed to Marxism-Leninism and is incompatible with the Communist Party. What we want is the Marxist-Leninist style of study. . . .

Our comrades in the Party School should not regard Marxist theory as lifeless dogma. It is necessary to master Marxist theory and apply it, master it for the sole purpose of applying it. . . . Our Party School should also lay down the rule to grade students good or poor according to how they look at China's problems after they have studied Marxism-Leninism, according to whether or not they see the problems clearly and whether or not they see them at all.

Next, let us talk about the question of the "intellectuals." Since China is a semicolonial, semifeudal country and her culture is not well developed, intellectuals are particularly treasured. . . . But we all know there are many intellectuals who fancy themselves very

1. Mao deplores what he considers to be a relapse to the style of writing prescribed in the imperial examinations known as the "eight-legged essay"—trite and stereotyped.

learned and assume airs of erudition without realizing that such airs are bad and harmful. . . . They ought to be aware that . . . workers and peasants sometimes know more than they do. Here some will say, "Ha! You are turning things upside down and talking nonsense." (*Laughter*) But, comrades, don't get excited; there is some sense in what I am saying.

What is knowledge? Ever since class society came into being the world has had only two kinds of knowledge, knowledge of the struggle for production and knowledge of the class struggle. . . . What sort of knowledge is the students' book learning? . . . Such knowledge is in a sense still one-sided. . . . What is most important is to be good at applying this knowledge in life and practice. . . .

What I have said will probably make some people angry. They will say, "According to your explanation, even Marx would not be regarded as an intellectual." I say they are wrong. Marx took part in the practice of the revolutionary movement and also created revolutionary theory. . . . He studied nature, history and proletarian revolution and created dialectical materialism and the theory of proletarian revolution. Thus Marx became a most completely developed intellectual, representing the acme of human wisdom. He was fundamentally different from those who have only book learning.

In order to study theory, however, our cadres of working-class and peasant origin must first acquire an elementary education. Without it they cannot learn Marxist-Leninist theory. . . . In my childhood I . . . was taught only such things as, "The Master said:[2] 'How pleasant it is to learn and constantly review what one has learned.'" Though this teaching material was antiquated, it did me some good because from it I learned to read. . . . The Central Committee of our Party now emphatically requires that our cadres of working-class and peasant origin should obtain an elementary education because they can then take up any branch of study—politics, military science or economics. Otherwise, for all their rich experience they will never be able to study theory. . . .

It follows that to combat subjectivism . . . those with book learning must develop in the direction of practice. . . . Those experienced in work must take up the study of theory and must read seriously. . . . Dogmatism and empiricism alike are subjectivism,

2. This is the opening sentence of the *Confucian Analects*, the record of the dialogues of Confucius and his disciples.

each originating from an opposite pole. . . . However, of the two kinds of subjectivism, dogmatism is still the greater danger in our Party. For dogmatists can easily . . . bluff, capture and make servitors of cadres of working-class and peasant origin who cannot easily see through them; they can also bluff and ensnare the naïve youth. . . .

Let me now speak about the question of sectarianism.

Having been steeled for twenty years, our Party is no longer dominated by sectarianism. Remnants of sectarianism, however, are still found both in the Party's internal relations and in its external relations. . . .

What are the remnants of inner-Party sectarianism? . . . They are . . . first, the assertion of "independence." Some comrades see only the interests of the part and not the whole; they always put undue stress on that part of the work for which they themselves are responsible. . . . They forget the system of democratic centralism in which the minority is subordinate to the majority, the lower level to the higher level, the part to the whole and the entire membership to the Central Committee. . . . Those who assert this kind of "independence" are usually wedded to the doctrine of "me first." . . . Comrade Liu Shao-chi once said of certain people that they have unusually long arms and are very clever in looking after their own interests. "What's mine is mine, and what's yours is mine too." (*Loud laughter*) . . .

Another problem is the relationship between old and new cadres. . . . In his report to the Eighteenth Congress of the Communist Party of the Soviet Union (B.), Comrade Stalin said, ". . . There are never enough old cadres, there are far less than required, and they are already partly going out of commission owing to the operation of the laws of nature." . . . All old cadres, therefore, should welcome the new ones with the utmost enthusiasm and show them the warmest solicitude. . . . The strong point of the new cadres, as Stalin has said, is that they are acutely sensitive to what is new and they are therefore enthusiastic and active to a high degree—the very qualities which some of the old cadres lack. . . .

The remnants of sectarianism must be eliminated from the Party's external as well as its internal relations. . . . Our comrades must realize the truth that Communist Party members are at all times a minority as compared with non-Party people. . . . What reason can we then have for not co-operating with non-Party people? . . .

All sectarian ideas are subjectivist and are incompatible with the real needs of the revolution; hence the struggle against sectarianism and the struggle against subjectivism should go on simultaneously. . . .

Finally, in opposing subjectivism, sectarianism and stereotyped Party writing we must have in mind two purposes: first, "Learn from past mistakes to avoid future ones," and second, "Cure the sickness to save the patient." . . .

I have taken this occasion of the opening of the Party School to speak at length, and I hope comrades will think over what I have said. (*Enthusiastic applause*)

This speech was delivered by Mao Tse-tung at the opening of the Party School of the Central Committee of the Chinese Communist Party.

Oppose Stereotyped Party Writing

February 8, 1942

. . . It does not matter if a person produces stereotyped Party writings only for himself to read. If he passes them on to someone else, the number of readers is doubled, and already no small harm is done. . . . And those who produce stereotyped Party writing always seek large audiences. Thus it has become imperative to expose and destroy it. . . .

During the May Fourth Movement, modern-minded people opposed the use of the classical Chinese language and advocated vernacular Chinese, opposed the traditional dogmas and advocated science and democracy, all of which was quite right. . . . The May Fourth Movement, however, had its own weaknesses. . . . One section inherited its scientific and democratic spirit and transformed it on the basis of Marxism; this is what the Communists and some non-Party Marxists did. Another section took the road of the bourgeoisie; this was the development of formalism toward the Right. But within the Communist Party too . . . some members deviated toward the "Left." . . . So it can be seen that stereotyped Party writing is no accident, but is, on the one hand, a reaction to the positive elements of the May Fourth Movement and, on the other, a legacy, a continuation . . . of its negative elements. . . . If we do not get rid of the poison of stereotyped Party writing and the error of dogmatism found among a section (only a section, of course) of Party comrades, then it will be impossible to arouse a vigorous and lively revolutionary spirit, to eradicate the bad habit of taking a wrong attitude toward Marxism and to disseminate and develop true Marxism. . . .

The first indictment against stereotyped Party writing is that it fills endless pages with empty verbiage. Some of our comrades love to write long articles with no substance, very much like the "footbindings of a slattern, long as well as smelly." . . . On June 22 last year the Soviet Union began waging a gigantic war against aggression, and yet Stalin's speech on July 3 was only the length of an editorial in our *Liberation Daily*. Had any of our gentlemen written that speech . . . it would have run to tens of thousands of words at a minimum. . . .

The second indictment against stereotyped Party writing is that it strikes a pose in order to intimidate people. . . . Writing long-winded and empty articles may be set down to immaturity, but striking a pose to overawe people is not merely immature but downright knavish. Lu Hsun once said in criticism of such people, "Hurling insults and threats is certainly not fighting." . . .[1]

The third indictment against stereotyped Party writing is that it shoots at random, without considering the audience. . . . Communists who really want to do propaganda must consider their audience and bear in mind those who will read their articles and slogans . . . otherwise they are in effect resolving not to be read or listened to by anyone. . . .

1. Lu Hsun, a leading Chinese novelist of the present century and a dedicated reformer who waged a lifelong battle against the many prejudices and ignorances perpetuated in Chinese science, culture, and the social life of the Chinese people, fought against the foreign stereotype as found in their ranks and condemned it in these terms: "A clean sweep should be made of all stereotyped writings, whether old or new. . . . For instance, it is also a kind of stereotype if all one can do is to 'hurl insults,' 'threaten,' or even 'pass sentence' and merely copy old formulas, instead of using formulas derived from science to interpret new facts and phenomena which emerge every day."

The fourth indictment against stereotyped Party writing is its drab language that reminds one of a *piehsan*.[2] Like our stereotyped Party writing, the creatures known in Shanghai as "little *piehsan*" are wizened and ugly. . . . At present many of our comrades doing propaganda work make no study of language. Their propaganda is very dull, and very few people care to read their articles or listen to their talk. . . .

The fifth indictment against stereotyped Party writing is that it arranges items under a complicated set of headings, as if starting a Chinese pharmacy. Go and take a look at any Chinese pharmacy, and you will see cabinets with numerous drawers, each bearing the name of a drug—toncal, foxglove, rhubarb, saltpeter . . . indeed, everything that should be there. . . . The method borrowed from the Chinese pharmacy, which many of our comrades are very fond of, is really the most crude, infantile and philistine of all. It is a formalist method, classifying things according to their external features instead of their internal relations. Since infantile, crude, philistine and lazy-minded formalist methods are prevalent in our Party, we must expose them. . . .

The sixth indictment against stereotyped Party writing is that it is irresponsible and harms people wherever it appears. . . . Often the result is "A thousand words from the pen in a stream, but ten thousand *li* away from the theme." Talented though these writers may appear, they actually harm people. This bad habit, this weak sense of responsibility, must be corrected.

The seventh indictment against stereotyped Party writing is that it poisons the whole Party and jeopardizes the revolution. The eighth indictment is that its spread would wreck the country and ruin the people. These two indictments are self-evident and require no elaboration. . . .

The aforesaid eight counts are our call to arms against stereotyped Party writing. . . .

With the collaboration of the worker Babushkin, Lenin at the end of 1894 wrote the first agitational leaflet of this kind and an appeal to the workers of the Semyannikov Works in St. Petersburg who were on strike.

To write a leaflet, you must consult with comrades who are well posted on the state of affairs. It was on the basis of such investigation

2. A *piehsan* is a beggar who lives in the gutters.

and study that Lenin wrote and worked. "Every leaflet greatly helped to stiffen the spirit of the workers. They saw that the Socialists were helping and defending them. . . ."[3]

The second . . . from Dimitrov's statements[4] at the Seventh World Congress of the Communist International:

Every one of us must make this a law, a Bolshevik law, an elementary rule:

When writing or speaking always have in mind the rank-and-file worker who must understand you, must believe in your appeal and be ready to follow you! You must have in mind those for whom you write, to whom you speak.

Confucius advised, "Think twice," and Han Yu[5] said, "A deed is accomplished through taking thought." That was in ancient times. . . . Lu Hsun said, "Read it over twice at least." . . . In my opinion it does no harm to go over an important article more than ten times . . . before it is published. Articles are the reflection of objective reality, which is intricate and complex and must be studied over and over again before it can be properly reflected. . . .

The Central Committee has now made the decision that we must discard stereotyped Party writing, dogmatism and the like once and for all, and that is why I have come and talked at some length. . . . Everyone should carefully examine himself, talk over with his close friends and the comrades around him whatever he has clarified and really get rid of his own defects.

This speech was delivered by Mao Tse-tung at a cadres' meeting in Yenan.

3. *History of the Communist Party of the Soviet Union* (Moscow, 1951), pp. 36–37.

4. Georgi Dimitrov, "Unity of the Working Class Against Fascism," *Selected Articles and Speeches* (Engl. ed., London, 1951), pp. 116–117.

5. Han Yu (786–824) was a famous Chinese writer of the Tang Dynasty.

Talks at the Yenan Forum on Literature and Art

May 1942

INTRODUCTION. MAY 2, 1942

Comrades! You have been invited to this forum today to exchange ideas and examine the relationship between work in the literary and artistic fields and revolutionary work in general. Our aim is to ensure that revolutionary literature and art follow the correct path of development and provide better help to other revolutionary work in facilitating the overthrow of our national enemy and the accomplishment of the task of national liberation.

In our struggle for the liberation of the Chinese people there are various fronts, among which there are the fronts of the pen and of the gun, the cultural and the military fronts. To defeat the enemy we must rely primarily on the army with guns. But this army alone is not enough; we must also have a cultural army, which is absolutely indispensable for uniting our own ranks and defeating the enemy. . . .

Among the proletariat many retain petty-bourgeois ideas, while both the peasants and the urban petty bourgeoisie have backward ideas; these are burdens hampering them in their struggle. We should be patient and spend a long time in educating them and helping them to get these loads off their backs and combat their own shortcomings and errors, so that they can advance with great strides. . . . Our writings should help them to unite, to make progress, to press ahead with one heart and one mind, to discard what is backward and develop what is revolutionary, and should certainly not do the opposite. . . .

Since the audience for our literature and art consists of workers, peasants and soldiers and of their cadres, the problem arises of understanding them and knowing them well. . . . In this regard, how have matters stood with our writers and artists? I would say they have been lacking in knowledge and understanding; they have been like "a hero with no place to display his prowess." . . . By a "hero with no place to display his prowess," we mean that your collection of great truths is not appreciated by the masses. . . . Here I might mention the experience of how my own feelings changed. I began life as a student and at school acquired the ways of a student; I then used to feel it undignified to do even a little manual labor, such as carrying my own luggage in the presence of my fellow students, who were incapable of carrying anything, either on their shoulders or in their hands. At that time I felt that intellectuals were the only clean people in the world, while in comparison workers and peasants were dirty. . . . But after I became a revolutionary and lived with workers and peasants and with soldiers of the revolutionary army, I gradually came to know them well, and they gradually came to know me well too. . . . I came to feel that compared with the workers and peasants the unremolded intellectuals were not clean, and that, in the last analysis, the workers and peasants were the cleanest people and, even though their hands were soiled and their feet smeared with cowdung, they were really cleaner than the bourgeois and petty-bourgeois intellectuals. . . .

Conclusion. May 23, 1942

Comrades! Our forum has had three meetings this month. In the pursuit of truth we have carried on spirited debates in which scores of Party and non-Party comrades have spoken, laying bare the issues and making them more concrete. This, I believe, will very much benefit the whole literary and artistic movement. . . .

We are Marxists, and Marxism teaches that in our approach to a problem we should start from objective facts, not from abstract definitions, and that we should derive our guiding principles, policies and measures from an analysis of these facts. . . .

What then is the crux of the matter? In my opinion, it consists fundamentally of the problems of working for the masses and how to work for the masses. Unless these two problems are solved . . . properly, our writers and artists will be ill-adapted to their environment and their tasks. . . .

I

The first problem is: literature and art for whom?
This problem was solved long ago by Marxists, especially by Lenin.

As far back as 1905 Lenin pointed out emphatically that our literature and art should "serve . . . the millions and tens of millions of working people." . . .[1]

Indeed, literature and art exist which are for the exploiters and oppressors. Literature and art for the landlord class are feudal literature and art. Such were the literature and art of the ruling class in China's feudal era. . . . Whatever is under the leadership of the bourgeoisie cannot possibly be of the masses. . . .

This question of "for whom?" is fundamental; it is a question of principle. . . . Unless this fundamental problem is solved, many other problems will not be easy to solve. . . . Otherwise the problem of sectarianism can never be solved. Lu Hsun once said:

A common aim is the prerequisite for a united front. . . . The fact that our front is not united shows that we have not been able to unify our aims, and that some people are working only for small groups or indeed only for themselves. If we all aim at serving the masses of workers and peasants, our front will of course be united.[2]

II

Having settled the problem of whom to serve, we come to the next problem, how to serve. To put it in the words of some comrades: Should we devote ourselves to raising standards, or should we devote ourselves to popularization?

In the past, some comrades, to a certain or even a serious extent, belittled and neglected popularization and laid undue stress on raising standards. Stress should be laid on raising standards, but to do so one-sidedly and exclusively, to do so excessively, is a mistake. . . . Since our literature and art are basically for the workers, peasants and soldiers, "popularization" means to popularize among the workers, peasants and soldiers, and "raising standards" means to advance from their present level. . . . Shall we popularize what is needed and . . . accepted by the feudal landlord class . . . the bourgeoisie . . . the petty-bourgeois intellectuals? No, none of these will do. We must popularize only what is needed and can be readily

1. V. I. Lenin, "Party Organization and Party Literature," *Collected Works*, Eng. ed., Moscow 1962, Vol., pp. 48–49.
2. Lu Hsun, "My View on the League of Left-Wing Writers," in *Two Hearts, Complete Works* (Chin. ed.), Vol. IV.

accepted by the workers, peasants and soldiers themselves. . . . Only by starting from the workers, peasants and soldiers can we have a correct understanding of popularization and of the raising of standards and find the proper relationship between the two. . . .

A thing is good only when it brings real benefit to the masses of the people. Your work may be as good as "The Spring Snow," but if for the time being it caters only to the few and the masses are still singing the "Song of the Rustic Poor,"[3] you will get nowhere by simply scolding them instead of trying to raise their level. The question now is to bring about a unity between "The Spring Snow" and the "Song of the Rustic Poor," between higher standards and popularization. Without such a unity, the highest art of any expert cannot help being utilitarian in the narrowest sense; you may call this art "pure and lofty" but that is merely your own name for it which the masses will not endorse. . . .

III

Since our literature and art are for the masses of the people, we can proceed to discuss a problem of inner-Party relations. . . .

Let us consider the first problem. In the world today all culture, all literature and art belong to definite classes and are geared to definite political lines. There is in fact no such thing as art for art's sake, art that stands above classes or art that is detached from or independent of politics. Proletarian literature and art are part of the whole proletarian revolutionary cause; they are, as Lenin said, cogs and wheels in the whole revolutionary machine. . . .[4]

Furthermore, when we say that literature and art are subordinate to politics, we mean class politics, the politics of the masses, not the politics of a few so-called "statesmen." . . .

Let us consider next the question of the united front in the world of literature and art. Since literature and art are subordinate to

3. "The Spring Snow" and the "Song of the Rustic Poor" were songs of the Kingdom of Chu in the third century B.C.; the music of the first was considered to be of a higher level than that of the second. As the story is told in "Sung Yu's Reply to the King of Chu" in Prince Chao Ming's *Anthology of Prose and Poetry*, when someone sang "The Spring Snow" in the Chu capital, only a few dozen people joined in, but when the "Song of the Rustic Poor" was sung, thousands did so.

4. V. I. Lenin, "Party Organization and Party Literature," *Collected Works* (Engl. ed., Moscow, 1962), Vol. X, p. 45.

politics and since the fundamental problem in China's politics today is resistance to Japan, our Party writers and artists must in the first place unite on this issue of resistance to Japan with all non-Party writers and artists. . . .

The petty-bourgeois writers and artists constitute an important force among the forces of the united front in literary and art circles in China. There are many shortcomings in both their thinking and their works, but, comparatively speaking, they are inclined toward the revolution and are close to the working people. Therefore, it is an especially important task to help them overcome their shortcomings and to win them over to the front which serves the working people.

IV

Literary and art criticism is one of the principal methods of struggle in the world of literature and art. . . .

In literary and art criticism there are two criteria, the political and the artistic. According to the political criterion, everything is good that is helpful to unity and resistance to Japan. . . . According to the artistic criterion, all works of a higher artistic quality are good or comparatively good, while those of a lower artistic quality are bad or comparatively bad. . . . But it is also entirely necessary to subject these works to correct criticism according to the criteria of the science of aesthetics, so that art of a lower level can be gradually raised to a higher and art which does not meet the demands of the struggle of the broad masses can be transformed into art that does. . . .

Some comrades lack elementary political knowledge and consequently have all sorts of muddled ideas. Let me cite a few examples from Yenan.

"The fundamental point of departure for literature and art is love, love of humanity." . . . There will be genuine love of humanity—after classes are eliminated all over the world. Classes have split society into many antagonistic groupings; there will be genuine love of all humanity when classes are eliminated, but not now. We cannot love enemies, we cannot love social evils, our aim is to destroy them. This is common sense; can it be that some of our writers and artists still do not understand this?

"Literary and artistic works have always laid equal stress on the bright and the dark, half and half." This statement contains many muddled ideas. It is not true that literature and art have always done this. . . . Soviet literature in the period of socialist construction portrays mainly the bright. It, too, describes shortcomings in work and portrays negative characters, but this only serves as a contrast to bring out the brightness of the whole picture and is not on a so-called "half-and-half basis." . . . If you are a bourgeois writer or artist, you will eulogize not the proletariat but the bourgeoisie, and if you are a proletarian writer or artist, you will eulogize not the bourgeoisie but the proletariat and working people; it must be one or the other. . . .

. . . Then does not Marxism destroy the creative mood? Yes, it does. It definitely destroys creative moods that are feudal, bourgeois, petty-bourgeois, liberalistic, individualist, nihilist, art-for-art's sake, aristocratic, decadent or pessimistic, and every other creative mood that is alien to the masses of the people and to the proletariat. So far as proletarian writers and artists are concerned, should not these kinds of creative moods be destroyed? I think they should; they should be utterly destroyed. And while they are being destroyed, something new can be constructed. . . .

V

Since integration into the new epoch of the masses is essential, it is necessary thoroughly to solve the problem of the relationship between the individual and the masses. This couplet from a poem by Lu Hsun should be our motto:[5]

> Fierce-browed, I coolly defy a thousand pointing fingers,
> Head-bowed, like a willing ox I serve the children.

The "thousand pointing fingers" are our enemies, and we will never yield to them, no matter how ferocious. The "children" here symbolize the proletariat and the masses. All Communists, all revolutionaries, all revolutionary literary and art workers should learn from the example of Lu Hsun and be "oxen" for the proletariat and the masses, bending their backs to the task until their dying day. . . .

Today I have discussed only some of the problems of fundamental orientation for our literature and art movement; many specific problems remain which will require further study. I am confident that comrades here are determined to move in the direction indicated. . . .

5. From Lu Hsun's "In Mockery of Myself" in *The Collection Outside the Collection, Complete Works* (Chin. ed.), Vol. VII.

A Most Important Policy

September 7, 1942

Ever since the Central Committee of the Party put forward the policy of "Better troops and simpler administration," the Party organizations in many anti-Japanese base areas have been applying it, or making plans to apply it. . . . This matter has been discussed several times before in the *Liberation Daily* and we now wish to explain it further. . . .

Why is the policy of better troops and simpler administration important for overcoming the material difficulties? It is clear that the present, and still more the future, war situation in the base areas will not permit us to cling to our past views. Our enormous war apparatus is suited to past conditions. It was then permissible and necessary. But things are different now, the base areas have shrunk. . . .

The enemy is bearing down upon us with his enormous war apparatus, and how dare we reduce ours? . . . Such misgivings are precisely the result of being fettered by circumstance and habit. When the weather changes it is necessary to change one's clothing. . . . People fail to do this at the proper turn and they fall ill. Present conditions in the base areas already require us to shed our winter garments and put on summer clothing so that we can move about nimbly. . . . As for the question of how to deal with the enemy's enormous apparatus, we can learn from the example of how the Monkey King dealt with Princess Iron Fan.[1] The Princess was a formidable demon, but by changing himself into a tiny insect the Monkey King made his way into her stomach and overpowered her. . . . Now it is imperative for us to do a little changing and make ourselves smaller but sturdier, and then we shall be invincible.

This editorial was written by Mao Tse-tung for the *Liberation Daily*, Yenan.

1. The story of how Sun Wu-kung, the monkey god, changed himself into a tiny insect and defeated Princess Iron Fan appears in *Hsi Yu Chi* (*Pilgrimage to the West*), Chapter 19.

The Turning Point
in World War II

October 12, 1942

The Battle of Stalingrad has been compared by the British and American press to the Battle of Verdun, and the "Red Verdun" is now famous all over the world. . . .

Until his victory on the western front, Hitler seems to have been cautious. . . . After his victory on the western front, he became dizzy with success and attempted to defeat the Soviet Union in three months. . . . Hitler vainly hoped to weaken the Soviet Union to such an extent that he would be able to release the main forces of the German Army from the Soviet theater of war for dealing with an Anglo-American attack on the western front. . . . The Soviet Union adopted the policy of first luring the enemy in deep and then putting up a stubborn resistance . . . so that Hitler has been forced to halt his troops before high mountains . . . unable to advance and unable to retreat. . . . Comparing Hitler's position in the first and third stages of the war, we can see that he is on the threshold of final defeat. . . .

The Red Army's defense of Stalingrad in these forty-eight days has a certain similarity to the defense of Moscow last year. That is to say, Hitler's plan for this year has been foiled just as was his plan for last year. But now . . . the Soviet Union will launch a second winter counteroffensive on a vast scale, Britain and the United States will no longer be able to delay the opening of the second front . . . and the people of Europe will be ready to rise up in response. . . . The Battle of Stalingrad will stop the offensive of fascism and is therefore a decisive battle. It is decisive for the whole world war. . . .

Napoleon's political life ended at Waterloo, but the decisive turning point was his defeat at Moscow. Hitler today is treading Napoleon's road, and it is the Battle of Stalingrad that has sealed his doom.

These developments will have a direct impact on the Far East. The coming year will not be propitious for Japanese fascism either. As

time goes on its headaches will grow, until it descends into its
grave. . . .

This editorial was written by Mao Tse-tung for the *Liberation Daily*,
Yenan.

In Celebration of the
Twenty-Fifth Anniversary
of the October Revolution

November 6, 1942

It is with the greatest optimism that we celebrate the anniversary
of the October Revolution this year. I firmly believe that this anniversary marks the turning point not only of the Soviet-German war,
but also of the victory of the world anti-fascist front over the fascist
front. . . .

In celebrating the victory of the Red Army, we the Chinese people
are also celebrating our own victory. . . . It is the task of the
Chinese people to concentrate every effort on beating the Japanese
fascists.

Economic and Financial Problems
in the Anti-Japanese War

December 1942

The general policy guiding our economic and financial work is to
develop the economy and endure supplies. But many of our comrades
place one-sided stress on public finance and do not understand the
importance of the economy as a whole. . . .

In the last five years we have passed through several stages. Our
worst difficulties occurred in 1940 and 1941, when the Kuomintang
created friction by its two anti-Communist drives. . . . But we

pulled through. Not only did the people of the Border Region provide us with grain but, in particular, we resolutely built up the public sector of our economy with our own hands. . . . While we still face many difficulties, the foundation of the public sector of our economy has already been laid. In another year, by the end of 1943, this foundation will be even firmer. . . .

Disregarding the needs of the war, some comrades insist that the government should adopt a policy of "benevolence." This is a mistake. For unless we win the war against Japan, such "benevolence" will mean nothing to the people and will benefit only the Japanese imperialists. . . .

Another mistake is "draining the pond to catch the fish," that is, making endless demands on the people, disregarding their hardships and considering only the needs of the government and the army. . . . The Kuomintang diehards regard construction in the Border Region as a hopeless undertaking . . . and are expecting the Border Region to collapse any day.

After the present conference of senior cadres of the Shensi-Kansu-Ningsia Border Region, we shall put into effect the policy of "Better troops and simpler administration." . . . In carrying it out, we must attain the five objectives of simplification, unification, efficiency, economy and opposition to bureaucracy. . . . If we fully attain these five objectives in the Party, the government and the army, our policy of "Better troops and simpler administration" will achieve its purpose, our difficulties will surely be overcome, and we shall silence the gibes about our approaching "collapse."

This article, originally entitled "A Basic Summing Up of Our Past Work," was the first chapter of *Economic and Financial Problems*, a report delivered by Mao Tse-tung at a conference of senior cadres of the Shensi-Kansu-Ningsia Border Region.

Some Questions Concerning
Methods of Leadership

June 1, 1943

1. There are two methods which we Communists must employ in whatever work we do. One is to combine the general with the particular; the other is to combine the leadership with the masses.

2. In any task, if no general and widespread call is issued, the broad masses cannot be mobilized for action.

3. Experience in the 1942 rectification movement also proves it is essential for the success of the rectification that a leading group should be formed in each unit in the course of the movement, made up of a small number of activists and with the heads of the given unit as its nucleus. . . .

4. In all the practical work of our Party, all correct leadership is necessarily "from the masses, to the masses." . . . And so on, over and over again in an endless spiral, with the ideas becoming more correct, more vital and richer each time. Such is the Marxist theory of knowledge.

5. The concept of a correct relationship between the leading group and the masses in an organization or in a struggle, the concept that correct ideas on the part of the leadership can only be "from the masses, to the masses" . . . must be propagated everywhere during the present rectification movement in order to correct the mistaken viewpoints among our cadres on these questions. . . .

6. Take the ideas of the masses and concentrate on them, then go to the masses, persevere in the ideas and carry them through, so as to form correct ideas of leadership—such is the basic method of leadership. . . . Better leadership comes with greater skill in doing this.

7. In relaying to subordinate units any task . . . a higher organization and its departments should in all cases go through the leader of the lower organization concerned so that he may assume responsibility; in this way both division of labor and unified centralized leadership are achieved. . . .

8. In any given place, there cannot be a number of central tasks at

the same time. At any one time there can be only one central task, supplemented by other tasks of a second or third order of importance. . . .

9. . . . The harder the struggle, the greater the need for Communists to link their leadership closely with the demands of the vast masses, and to combine general calls closely with particular guidance, so as to smash the subjectivist and bureaucratic methods of leadership completely. . . . To combat subjectivist and bureaucratic methods of leadership, we must promote scientific, Marxist methods of leadership both extensively and intensively.

This decision on methods of leadership was written by Mao Tse-tung for the Central Committee of the Chinese Communist Party.

Some Pointed Questions
for the Kuomintang
July 12, 1945

The last few months have witnessed a most unusual and shocking event inside China's anti-Japanese camp, namely, the campaign launched by many Kuomintang-led Party, government and army organizations to wreck unity and undermine the War of Resistance. It assumes the form of an attack on the Communist Party, but is in fact directed against the whole Chinese nation and people. . . .

Day in day out many Kuomintang people have been brazenly spreading propaganda that the Communist Party is "sabotaging the War of Resistance" and "wrecking unity."

We should like to ask the Kuomintang people who are doing all this. . . . According to you, in China, it is the Communists who are "sabotaging the War of Resistance," while you yourselves are most devoted to "the nation above all." Well now, what are you placing "above all" when you turn your backs on the enemy? . . . You are very keen not on "unity" but on "unification." How is it then you are not afraid that the Japanese will "unify" the Chinese nation, including you, out of existence? . . .

To combat the Communist Party the Kuomintang has organized

several hundred detachments of secret agents, into which it has recruited all kinds of scoundrels. For example, on July 6, 1943 . . . the Kuomintang Central News Agency released a news item stating that certain "cultural associations" . . . had held a meeting and resolved to cable Mao Tse-tung calling on him to use the opportunity of the dissolution of the Third International to "dissolve" the Communist Party of China and, in addition, to "abolish the separatist Border Region regime." . . .

There are now many political parties in China—there are even two Kuomintangs. One is the Wang Ching-wei brand. . . . In addition, everywhere in the occupied areas there are the fascist parties created by the Japanese. . . .

Is it possible that you think there is one Communist Party too many? In the whole of China there is only one Communist Party, while there are two Kuomintangs. After all, of which Party is there one too many? . . .

We want to ask you Kuomintang people yet another question. Is it true that the only "discredited" ism in China and indeed in the whole world is Marxism-Leninism and that all the others are great stuff? Apart from Wang Ching-wei's brand of the Three People's Principles . . . what about the fascism of Hitler, Mussolini and Hideki Tojo? . . . What about the Trotskyism of various brands of counterrevolutionary secret services in China? . . .

To be blunt, we strongly suspect that you are working in collusion with the Japanese-sponsored and traitorous parties, and that is why you and they "breathe through the same nostrils." . . . As you and the enemy and the traitors are exactly alike, identical and indistinguishable in so many words and deeds, how can people help suspecting that you are working hand in glove with them or have come to some secret understanding with them? . . .

We hereby appeal to all true patriots among the Kuomintang members who do not approve of the withdrawal of the river defense force for the purpose of attacking the Border Region and do not approve of the demand for the dissolution of the Communist Party: please act now to avert the crisis of civil war. We are willing to cooperate with you to the very end to save the nation.

We believe that these are absolutely just demands.

Mao Tse-tung wrote this editorial for the *Liberation Daily*, Yenan.

Spread the Campaigns to Reduce Rent, Increase Production and "Support the Government and Cherish the People" in the Base Areas

October 1, 1943

1. As the time for autumn harvest is come, the leading bodies in the base areas must ask Party and government organizations at all levels to check up on the application of our policy of rent reduction. Wherever it has not been carried out in earnest, rents must be reduced this year without any exception. . . . As rent reduction is a mass struggle by the peasants, Party directives and government decrees should guide and help it instead of trying to bestow favors on the masses. . . . The government's position should be one of enforcing the decree on rent reduction and adjusting the relative interests of the landlords and the tenants. . . .

2. . . . In the financial and economic field, the Party and government personnel at the county and district levels should devote nine-tenths of their energy to helping the peasants increase production, and only one-tenth to collecting taxes from them. . . . Seven- to ten-day training courses should be given on vegetable growing and pig farming, and on the preparation of better food by the cooks. . . . It is wrong to consider it dishonorable and selfish either for Communists in the countryside to engage in household production in order to support their families or for Communists in government organizations and schools to engage in private spare-time production in order to improve their own living conditions, for all such activity is in the interests of the revolutionary cause. . . .

3. . . . Under the leadership of the local Party, government and mass organizations, the masses on their side should publicly renew their pledge to support the army and give preferential treatment to the families of the soldiers fighting the Japanese, and should set going an ardent campaign for greetings and gifts to the army units. . . . And there should be repeated self-criticism before the masses of any

high-handed behavior by the troops in the base areas toward the Party or government personnel or toward civilians, or any lack of concern for the troops shown by the Party or government personnel or the civilians (each side criticizing itself and not the other) in order that these shortcomings and mistakes may be thoroughly corrected.

This inner-Party directive was written by Mao Tse-tung on behalf of the Central Committee of the Chinese Communist Party.

A Comment on the Sessions of the Kuomintang Central Executive Committee and of the People's Political Council

October 5, 1943

The Kuomintang held the Eleventh Plenary Session of its Central Executive Committee from September 6 to 13, and the Kuomintang Government held the Second Session of the Third People's Political Council from September 18 to 27. Now that all the documents of both these meetings are at hand, we can make a general comment.

The international situation is on the threshold of a great change, whose imminence is sensed on all sides. The European Axis Powers have sensed it, and Hitler is adopting a desperate last-ditch policy. In the main, it is the Soviet Union that is bringing this change about . . . the Red Army has already fought its way to the Dnieper, sweeping all before it. . . . Britain and the United States, too, are taking advantage of the change; Roosevelt and Churchill are waiting for the first sign of Hitler's downfall to thrust into France. . . .

The Kuomintang has also sensed the change. Faced with this situation it feels both joy and fear. Joy, because it imagines that with the war in Europe over, Britain and the United States will be left free to fight Japan on its behalf. Fear, because with the downfall of all three fascist powers the world will enter a great and unprece-dented age of liberation, and the Kuomintang's comprador-feudal fascist dictatorship will become a small island in a vast ocean of freedom and democracy. . . .

What can the Kuomintang be planning to do now, following the Eleventh Plenary Session? There are only three possibilities: (1) Capitulation to Japanese imperialism; (2) dragging along on the old road; and (3) a change in its political line.

Serving the Japanese imperialists' purpose of "hitting the Communists and courting the Kuomintang," the defeatists and capitulationists within the Kuomintang have all along advocated surrender. . . . Some of them may think, "We shall still resist the Japanese while fighting the Communists." This is probably what many officers of the Whampoa clique[1] are thinking. To these gentlemen we Communists would like to put the following questions. Have you forgotten the lessons of the ten years of civil war? . . . Are you really so strong that you can fight a civil war and a war against the foreign foe at the same time? . . . Once you start civil war, you will have to give it your undivided attention and inevitably abandon all thought of "simultaneous resistance"; in the end you will inevitably find yourselves signing a treaty of unconditional surrender to Japanese imperialism. . . .

In March this year, Mr. Chiang Kai-shek published his book *China's Destiny* in which he emphasizes his opposition to communism and liberal ideas, shifts the blame for the ten years of civil war on the Communist Party, slanders the Communist Party, the Eighth Route Army and the New Fourth Army as "warlords of a new type" and "separatists of a new type," and implies that he will finish off the Communists within two years. . . .

The Japanese say, "There is nothing wrong with the line of argument in Chiang Kai-shek's *China's Destiny.*" Has Mr. Chiang or any member of his party ever rebutted this? No, they have not and dare not. . . .

Is there a third direction in which the current situation may develop? Yes, there is. . . . A just and reasonable political settlement . . . between the Kuomintang and the Communist Party, a genuinely democratic and free constitutional government, the aboli-

1. The Whampoa Military Academy was an officers' training school founded by Dr. Sun Yat Sen, who appointed Chiang Kai-shek as its commandant. Many of the Chinese leaders, both civilian and military, had been trained there. Mao Tse-tung's designation of those who were loyal to the Kuomintang as the "Whampoa clique" distinguishes them from those who went over to the Communist side; the latter, in Mao's opinion, being the "patriots."

tion of the fascist dictatorship with its "one party, one doctrine, one leader." . . .

Mr. Chiang Kai-shek announced at the Eleventh Plenary Session:

It should be stated clearly that the central authorities make no demands upon the Communist Party other than it should give up its separatist regime and cease its surprise attacks on the National Army, which sabotage the War of Resistance; it is to be hoped that the Communist Party will carry out its declaration made in the twenty-sixth year of the Republic (1937) calling for united efforts to save the nation and will put into effect the four pledges given in that declaration.

Mr. Chiang's talk of "surprise attacks on the National Army" . . . ought to be applied to the Kuomintang itself, and it is a pity that he is so prejudiced and malicious as to slander the Communist Party. . . .

On September 22 of the twenty-sixth year of the republic (1937), the Central Committee of the Communist Party of China issued a declaration calling for united efforts to save the nation. In it we said:

To strip the enemy of any pretext for his intrigues and to remove any misunderstanding among all well-intentioned doubters, the Central Committee of the Communist Party of China finds it necessary to proclaim its heartfelt devotion to the cause of national liberation. Therefore, it once again solemnly declares to the whole nation: (1) That Dr. Sun Yat Sen's Three People's Principles being what China needs today, our Party is ready to fight for their complete realization; (2) that we shall discontinue the policies of insurrection to overthrow the Kuomintang regime and of forcible confiscation of the land of the landlords; (3) that we shall organize the present Red government as the democratic government of a special region in the hope that state power will be unified throughout the country; and (4) that the Red Army will change its name and designation, will be reorganized as part of the National Revolutionary Army and placed under the Military Council of the National Government, and will be ready for orders to march to the anti-Japanese front and do its duty.

We have completely fulfilled these four pledges; neither Mr. Chiang Kai-shek nor anyone else in the Kuomintang can charge us with having defaulted on a single one of them. . . .

What reason do you have for accusing us of "separatism" while you go back on your own words, refuse the recognition you pledged to the Border Region and refuse to acknowledge its democratic government? Day in day out we ask for recognition and you refuse—who is then responsible? What reason does Mr. Chiang have for railing against "separatism" in his *China's Destiny* without showing the slightest sense of his own responsibility in the matter, though he himself is Director-General of the Kuomintang and head of its government? . . .

An unparalleled change is imminent in the world. We hope that Mr. Chiang Kai-shek and the members of the Kuomintang will conduct themselves well at this great turning point of our era. We hope that all patriotic parties and patriotic people will conduct themselves well at this great turning point of our era.

This editorial was written by Mao Tse-tung for the *Liberation Daily*, Yenan.

Get Organized!

November 29, 1943

On behalf of the Central Committee of the Communist Party I would like to say a few words at this reception it is giving for the labor heroes and heroines and other model workers in production elected from the villages, the factories, the armed forces, the government and other organizations and the schools in the Shensi-Kansu-Ningsia Border Region. What I want to say can be summed up in the words, "Get organized!" . . .

In all the armed units of the Border Region that have been allotted land this year, the soldiers have on the average cultivated 18 *mou* per person; and they can produce or make practically everything. . . . Every soldier needs to spend only three months of the year in production and can devote the remaining nine months to training and fighting. . . .

Among the peasant masses a system of individual economy has

prevailed for thousands of years, with each family or household forming a productive unit. This scattered, individual form of production is the economic foundation of feudal rule and keeps the peasants in perpetual poverty. The only way to change it is gradual collectivization, and the only way to bring about collectivization, according to Lenin, is through co-operatives. . . . We do not expect to organize into co-operatives in one year all the hundreds of thousands of people in the Border Region . . . but this objective can be realized within a few years. . . .

Besides the collective mutual-aid co-operative for agricultural production, there are three other varieties: the multipurpose co-operative . . . which combines . . . transport and credit; the transport co-operative (transport team); and the handicraft co-operative.

With these four kinds of co-operatives . . . we can organize all the forces of the people into a great army of labor. This is the only road to liberation of the people, the only road from poverty to prosperity, and the only road to victory in the War of Resistance. . . .

The Kuomintang only demands things from the people and gives them nothing in return. If a member of our Party acts in this way, his style of work is that of the Kuomintang, and his face, caked with the dust of bureaucracy, needs a good wash in a basin of hot water. . . . We must firmly do away with this style of work before we can have close ties with the masses. . . .

We should check our complacency and constantly criticize our shortcomings, just as we should wash our faces or sweep the floor every day to remove the dirt and keep them clean.

Labor heroes and model workers in production! I hope . . . when you get back to your organizations . . . you will first of all get the masses organized on a voluntary basis into co-operatives, get them even better organized and in even greater numbers. I hope that, when you go back, you will do this work and propagate it, so that by next year's conference of labor heroes we shall have achieved still greater results.

Mao Tse-tung made this speech at a reception in honor of the labor heroes of the Shensi-Kansu-Ningsia Border Region.

Our Study and the Current Situation

April 12, 1944

I

Since last winter, the senior cadres of our Party have been study-ing the question of the two lines that existed in the history of the Party. . . . In the course of the study, comrades have brought up many questions, and the Political Bureau of the Central Committee has reached conclusions on some of the important ones. They are as follows:

1. On the question of what attitude to adopt in studying historical experience. The Central Committee holds that we should enable the cadres to become perfectly clear ideologically on the questions which arose in the history of the Party and that at the same time we should adopt a lenient policy in arriving at decisions about comrades who formerly committed errors. . . .

2. Treat all questions analytically; do not negate everything. The question concerning the line of the central leadership during the period from the Fourth Plenary Session[1] to the Tsunyi Meeting,[2] for example . . . the political tactics, the military tactics and the cadres policy . . . were wrong in their main aspects. . . . On the land question, for instance, their error consisted in the ultra-left policy of allotting no land to the landlords and poor land to the rich peasants, but these comrades were at one with us on confiscating land of the landlords for distribution among peasants who had little or no land. . . .

3. . . . The line of the Sixth National Congress of the Party was basically correct, since that congress defined the character of the present revolution as bourgeois-democratic . . . as an interval be-tween two revolutionary high tides. . . .

1. The Fourth Plenary Session of the Sixth Central Committee of the Communist Party of China was held in January 1931.
2. The Tsunyi Meeting was the enlarged meeting of the Political Bureau called by the Central Committee of the Communist Party of China at Tsunyi, Kweichow Province, in January 1935.

4. On the question of whether the provisional central leadership that was formed in Shanghai in 1931 and the Fifth Plenary Session[3] which it subsequently convened were legal or not. The Central Committee holds that both were legal. . . .

5. On the question of factions in the history of the Party. It should be stated that as a result of the series of changes since the Tsunyi Meeting the factions which formerly existed and played an unwholesome role in the history of our Party no longer exist. . . . What is left is only the remnants of dogmatist and empiricist ideology, which can be overcome by continuing and intensifying our rectification movement. . . .

II

The present situation has two characteristics: one is that the anti-fascist front is growing stronger and the fascist front is declining, and the second is that within the anti-fascist front the people's forces are growing stronger and the anti-popular forces are declining. . . .

The growth of our Party during the War of Resistance Against Japan can be divided into three stages. The first stage was from 1937 to 1940. In 1937 and 1938, the first two years of this stage, the Japanese militarists took the Kuomintang seriously and the Communist Party lightly. . . .

The years 1941 and 1942 formed the second stage. In order to prepare and prosecute the war against Britain and the United States, the Japanese imperialists more actively pursued the policy to which they had switched after the fall at Wuhan, the policy of concentrating on the Communist Party and not on the Kuomintang. . . .

The third stage extends from 1943 to the present. Our various policies have become more effective and, in particular, the rectification movement and the development of production have yielded results of a fundamental nature, thereby making our Party invincible both ideologically and materially. . . . In our base areas . . . the population has risen to over 80 million, including those paying the grain tax only to us and those paying it both to us and to the Japanese and puppets. . . . Our army has grown to 470,000 and our people's militia to 2,270,000, and our Party membership has reached 900,000 and more.

3. The Fifth Plenary Session of the Sixth Central Committee of the Communist Party of China was held in January 1934.

III

In order to win new victories we must call on our Party cadres to get rid of the baggage and start up the machinery. "To get rid of the baggage" means to free our minds of many encumbrances . . . pessimism and depression . . . pride and arrogance. . . .

"To start up the machinery" means to make good use of the organ of thought. Although some people carry no baggage and have the virtue of close contact with the masses, they fail to accomplish anything because they do not know how to think searchingly or are unwilling to use their brains to think much and think hard. . . . Lenin and Stalin often advised people to use their brains, and we should give the same advice. . . . Mencius said, "The office of the mind is to think." He defined the function of the brain correctly. . . . A common saying goes, "Knit the brows and you will hit upon a stratagem." In other words, much thinking yields wisdom. . . . If we get rid of our baggage and start up the machinery, if we march with light packs and know how to think hard, then we are sure to triumph.

From 1942 to 1944 the central organ and senior cadres of the Chinese Communist Party held discussions on the history of the Party, especially of the period from the beginning of 1931 to the end of 1934. The meeting of the Political Bureau of the Central Committee at Tsunyi, Kweichow, in January 1935, established the leadership headed by Mao Tse-tung and set the Party line on the Marxist-Leninist track.

APPENDIX: RESOLUTION ON CERTAIN QUESTIONS
IN THE HISTORY OF OUR PARTY

Adopted on April 20, 1945 by the Enlarged Plenary Session of the Sixth Central Committee of the Communist Party of China

I

Ever since its birth in 1921, the Communist Party of China has made the integration of the universal truth of Marxism-Leninism with the concrete practice of the Chinese revolution the guiding principle in all its work, and Comrade Mao Tse-tung's theory and practice of the Chinese revolution represent this integration. . . .

In the course of its struggle the Party has produced its own leader, Comrade Mao Tse-tung. Representing the proletariat and the Chinese people, Comrade Mao Tse-tung has creatively applied the scientific theory of Marxism-Leninism, the acme of human wisdom to China . . . and he has brilliantly developed the theories of Lenin and Stalin on the colonial and semicolonial question as well as Stalin's theory concerning the Chinese revolution. . . .

II

In the first period of China's new-democratic revolution, from 1921 to 1927, and especially from 1924 to 1927, the great anti-imperialist and anti-feudal revolution of the Chinese people, correctly guided by the Communist International and influenced, impelled forward and organized by the correct leadership of the Chinese Communist Party, advanced rapidly and won great victories. . . . Nevertheless, this revolution ended in defeat because in 1927 the clique of reactionaries in the Kuomintang, which was then our ally, betrayed the revolution. . . .

In the ten years from the defeat of the revolution in 1927 to the outbreak of the War of Resistance Against Japan in 1937, it was the Communist Party of China . . . alone which continued in unity to hold aloft the great banner of anti-imperialism and anti-feudalism under the counterrevolutionary reign of extreme terror. . . . During these struggles the Communist Party of China created the Red Army, established the government of Councils of Workers, Peasants and Soldiers, set up revolutionary bases, distributed land to impoverished peasants and resisted both the attacks of the reactionary Kuomintang Government and, after September 18, 1931, the aggression of Japanese imperialism. . . .

We rejoice especially in the fact that in those ten years our Party, with Comrade Mao Tse-tung as its representative, made very great advances in creatively applying to Chinese conditions the revolutionary theories of Marx, Engels, Lenin and Stalin. At last, toward the end of the Agrarian Revolutionary War, our Party definitely established the leadership of Comrade Mao Tse-tung in the central leading body and throughout the Party. This was the greatest achievement of the Communist Party of China in that period, and it is the surest guarantee of the liberation of the Chinese people. . . .

III

After the defeat of the revolution in 1927, both "Left" and Right deviations occurred in our Party.

The handful of capitulationists of the period of the First Great Revolution, with Chen Tu-hsiu as their representative, became pessimistic about the future of the revolution and gradually turned into liquidationists. They took the reactionary Trotskyite stand,[1] holding that after the 1927 revolution the Chinese bourgeoisie was already victorious over imperialism and the feudal forces, that its rule over the people was being stabilized, and that Chinese society was already one in which capitalism was dominant and would develop peacefully. Therefore . . . the Chinese proletariat must wait until the future to make the "socialist revolution." . . .

On the other hand, petty-bourgeois revolutionary impetuosity, which was aggravated by hatred of the Kuomintang's policy of massacre and by indignation at Chen Tu-hsiu's capitulationism . . . first appeared at the emergency meeting of the Party's Central Committee on August 7, 1927. . . . After the August 7 meeting this "Left" sentiment continued to grow until, at the enlarged meeting of the central leading body in November 1927, it took shape in a "Left" line of putschism (i.e., adventurism) and for the first time brought the "Left" line into a dominant position in the central leading body of the Party. . . .

Cloaking themselves in "Marxist-Leninist theory" and relying on the political and organizational prestige and influence built up by the Fourth Plenary Session, those comrades who were guilty of dogmatism errors were responsible for the domination of the third "Left" line in the Party for four long years, gave it the fullest and most systematic expression ideologically, politically, militarily and organizationally, and enabled it to exercise the most profound influence in the Party and consequently to do the greatest damage. . . .

The comrades who advocated the correct line, with Comrade Mao

1. All Chinese who failed to follow the Chinese Communist Party line in the split between the Kuomintang and the Communists in 1927 were automatically labelled by the Communists "dirty imperialist Kuomintang instruments" or "Trotskyites."

Tse-tung as their representative . . . disagreed with the "Left" line and demanded that it should be corrected. . . . Accordingly, large numbers of cadres and Party members who were opposed to the "Left" line rallied under the leadership of Mao Tse-tung. It was therefore possible for the enlarged meeting of the Political Bureau of the Central Committee, held under the leadership of Comrade Mao Tse-tung in January 1935 at the city of Tsunyi in Kweichow Province, triumphantly to put an end to the domination of the "Left" line in the central leading body and to save the Party at that most critical juncture.

. . . The meeting inaugurated a new central leadership, headed by Comrade Mao Tse-tung—a historic change of paramount importance in the Chinese Communist Party. Precisely because of this change, our Party was able to conclude the Long March victoriously, to preserve and steel a hard core of cadres in the Party and the Red Army. . . . Since the Tsunyi Meeting the political line of the central leading body of the Party, led by Comrade Mao Tse-tung, has been entirely correct. . . .

IV

In order that comrades may have a better understanding of the errors of the various "Left" lines . . . we set forth the main content of these lines where they were contrary to the correct line politically, militarily, organizationally and ideologically.

Politically. As Comrade Stalin[2] pointed out and as Comrade Mao Tse-tung has analyzed in detail . . . China at the present stage is a large semicolonial and semifeudal country, dominated by a number of powerful yet conflicting imperialist countries and by the feudal forces of China; her economic and political development is extremely uneven and lacking in uniformity. . . . This renders it possible in the struggle to make extensive use of the enemy's contradictions and to set up and maintain armed revolutionary base areas. . . . These basic characteristics and basic laws of the Chinese revolution . . . were not comprehended but were contravened both by the various Right lines and by the various "Left" lines. . . . Therefore, the "Left" lines were wrong politically in three main respects.

2. J. V. Stalin, "Questions of the Chinese Revolution," and "The Revolution in China and the Tasks of the Comintern," *Works* (Engl. ed., Moscow, 1954), Vol. VIII, pp. 373–391.

First. The various "Left" lines were in error, above all, on the question of the task of the revolution and the question of class relations. . . . Comrade Mao Tse-tung, like Comrade Stalin, pointed out . . . that the Chinese bourgeois-democratic revolution is in essence a peasant revolution and that the basic task of the Chinese proletariat . . . is therefore to lead the peasants' struggle . . . and that China "must go through such a democratic revolution" before one could speak of the prospect of socialism. . . . The exponents of the "Left" lines were invariably confused about the definite distinction between the democratic revolution and the socialist revolution and . . . they invariably advocated a struggle against the bourgeoisie as a whole, including even the upper petty bourgeoisie. . . . Thus the immediate tasks of the revolution were distorted, the revolutionary forces were isolated and the Red Army movement suffered setbacks. . . .

Second. The various "Left" lines were in error on the question of revolutionary war and revolutionary base areas. Comrade Stalin[3] said, "In China the armed revolution is fighting the armed counter-revolution. That is one of the specific features and one of the advantages of the Chinese revolution." Like Comrade Stalin, Comrade Mao Tse-tung had correctly pointed out as far back as the early period of the Agrarian Revolutionary War that . . . the vast rural areas inhabited by the broad masses of the peasantry are the indispensable, vital positions of the Chinese revolution . . . and that China can and must establish armed revolutionary base areas as the starting point for countrywide victory (democratic unification of the whole country). . . . But the exponents of the various "Left" lines did not understand the specific features of semicolonial and semifeudal Chinese society. . . . They were forever dreaming that the struggles of the workers and the other masses in the cities would suddenly break through the enemy's severe repression and surge forward, erupt into armed insurrections in key cities, achieve "victory first in one or more provinces," and bring about a . . . nationwide victory; and they made this dream the basis on which all their work was planned and organized. . . .

Third. The various "Left" lines were also in error on the directing of tactics for attack and defense. Correct direction of tactics, as Comrade Stalin points out, requires a correct analysis of the situa-

3. J. V. Stalin, "The Prospects of the Revolution in China," *Works* (Eng. ed., FLPH, Moscow, 1954), Vol. VIII, p. 379.

tion . . . "taking advantage of every rift in the camp of its enemies, and the ability to find allies"; and one of the best models is Comrade Mao Tse-tung's direction of the Chinese revolutionary movement. . . . Comrade Mao Tse-tung has always advocated that we "utilize every conflict within the counterrevolution and take active measures to widen the cleavages within it," and "oppose the policy of isolation, and affirm the policy of winning over all possible allies." . . .[4] Comrade Liu Shao-chi's ideas on tactics for work in the White areas are likewise a model. Comrade Liu Shao-chi also advocated that the Party's open organizations of the period of the 1924–27 revolution be transformed systematically and strictly into underground organizations, while "utilizing open legal means as far as possible" in mass work to enable the Party's underground organizations to conceal their strength for a long time. . . .

Militarily. At the present stage of the Chinese revolution, military struggle is the main form of political struggle. . . . Only a people's war, in which the main forces are integrated with regional forces, the regular army with guerrilla units and people's militia, and the armed masses with the unarmed masses, can bring victory over an enemy many times stronger than ourselves. Hence, in strategy, the Red Army must oppose a war of quick decision and, in tactics, must oppose protracted fighting; in strategy, it must adhere firmly to protracted warfare and, in tactics, to quick decisions; in campaigns and battles it must oppose the use of the few to defeat the many and must adhere firmly to the use of the many to defeat the few. The Red Army must therefore carry out the following strategic and tactical principles:

Divide our forces to arouse the masses, concentrate our forces to deal with the enemy.

The enemy advances, we retreat; the enemy camps, we harass; the enemy tires, we attack; the enemy retreats, we pursue.

To extend stable base areas, employ the policy of advancing in waves; when pursued by a powerful enemy, employ the policy of circling around.

Lure the enemy in deep.

Concentrate superior forces, pick out the enemy's weak spots, and fight when you are sure of wiping out part, or the greater part, of the enemy in mobile warfare, so as to crush the enemy forces one by one.

4. J. V. Stalin, "The Foundations of Leninism," *Works* (Engl. ed., Moscow, 1954), Vol. IX, p. 346.

Organizationally. As Mao Tse-tung says, the correct political line should be "from the masses, to the masses." . . . Therefore, just as in each period of the Party's history Comrade Mao Tse-tung has laid down an organizational line serving the political line and maintaining ties with the masses both inside and outside the Party. . . . Proceeding from the interests of the unity of the whole Party, Comrade Mao Tse-tung insisted that the part should obey the whole and, in accordance with the concrete characteristics of the Chinese revolution, he defined the proper relationships between new and old cadres, between outside and local cadres, between army cadres and other cadres working in the locality and between cadres of different departments or localities. . . . The various "Left" lines of the period of the Agrarian Revolutionary War were opposed to Comrade Mao Tse-tung's organizational line. . . . The factionalists did not regard veteran cadres as valuable assets of the Party . . . they punished and dismissed . . . large numbers of veteran cadres. . . . Moreover, in many places where an incorrect policy for suppressing counterrevolutionaries became entangled with the factionalist policy toward cadres, large numbers of fine comrades were unjustly dealt with under false charges. . . .

This Enlarged Seventh Plenary Session hereby declares: Any penalty, or any part of a penalty, that was wrongly inflicted upon a comrade by the exponents of the erroneous line shall be rescinded in accordance with circumstances. Every comrade who upon investigation is proved to have fallen victim to false charges shall be exonerated and reinstated as a Party member, and his memory shall be held in honor by all comrades.

Ideologically. The correctness or incorrectness of any political, military or organizational line has ideological roots—it depends on whether or not the line starts from Marxist-Leninist dialectical materialism and historical materialism and whether or not the line starts from the objective realities of the Chinese revolution and the objective needs of the Chinese people. . . . For Chinese Communists living and fighting in China, the purpose of studying dialectical materialism and historical materialism should be to apply them to the study and solution of the practical problems of the Chinese revolution, as Comrade Mao Tse-tung has done. But, of course, none of the comrades who committed "Left" errors was then able to understand or accept his method, and the exponents of the third "Left" line even slandered him as being a "narrow empiricist." . . .

Empiricism differs from dogmatism in that it starts not from books but from narrow experience. . . . All the useful experience gained by vast numbers of comrades in practical work is a most precious asset. It is definitely not empiricism . . . just as it is definitely not dogmatism, but Marxism-Leninism, to take the theories and principles of Marxism-Leninism as a guide to revolutionary action and not as dogma. But if there are some comrades . . . who do not understand and moreover do not want to acknowledge the truth that "without revolutionary theory there can be no revolutionary movement"[5] and that "in order to lead, one must foresee,"[6] and who consequently belittle the study of Marxism-Leninism which is the summation of world revolutionary experience, and are infatuated . . . with a brainless routinism that leads nowhere; and if they nevertheless sit and give orders from on high, if in their purblindness they style themselves heroes . . . and refuse to heed the criticism of comrades or to practice self-criticism—then indeed these comrades have become empiricists.

V

The errors of the "Left" line in the four aspects discussed above were not accidental; they had very deep social roots.

Just as the correct line represented by Comrade Mao Tse-tung reflected the ideology of the advanced elements of the Chinese proletariat, so the "Left" line reflected the ideology of the Chinese petty-bourgeois democrats. . . . Not only does this class have various weaknesses which distinguish it from the proletariat, but when deprived of proletarian leadership it often veers and falls under the influence of the liberal bourgeoisie, or even of the big bourgeoisie and becomes their prisoner. . . .

But the case is entirely different with those people of petty-bourgeois origin who have voluntarily abandoned their original class

5. V. I. Lenin, "What Is To Be Done?", *Collected Works* (Engl. ed., Moscow, 1961), Vol. V, p. 369.

6. J. V. Stalin, "The Work of the April Joint Plenum of the Central Committee and Central Control Commission," *Works* (Engl. ed., Moscow, 1954), Vol. XI, p. 39.

stand and joined the party of the proletariat. . . . Since such people were close to the proletariat to begin with and joined its party voluntarily, they can gradually become proletarian in their ideology through Marxist-Leninist education in the Party . . . and be of great service to the proletarian forces. . . .

. . . This Enlarged Seventh Plenary Session points out that the policy Comrade Mao Tse-tung has adopted for the present rectification movement throughout the Party and for the study of Party history, namely, "Learn from past mistakes to avoid future ones and cure the sickness to save the patient," and achieve "clarity in ideology and unity among comrades," is a model of the correct attitude for Marxist-Leninists in overcoming errors within the Party. Therefore it has led to great achievements in uniting and raising the level of the whole Party ideologically, politically and organizationally. . . .

VII

This Enlarged Seventh Plenary Session emphatically declares that the practice of the Chinese revolution during the last twenty-four years has proved, and continues to prove, that the line represented by Comrade Mao Tse-tung, the line of struggle in our Party and of the people of the whole country, is entirely correct. . . . Today, with unprecedented unanimity the whole Party recognizes the correctness of Comrade Mao Tse-tung's line and with unprecedented political consciousness rallies under his banner. As Marxist-Leninist ideology, which Comrade Mao Tse-tung represents, more and more profoundly grips more and more of the cadres, the Party members and the masses of the people, the result will surely be tremendous progress and invincible strength for the Party and the Chinese revolution. . . .

Serve the People
September 8, 1944

Our Communist Party and the Eighth Route and New Fourth Armies led by our Party are battalions of the revolution. These battalions of ours are wholly dedicated to the liberation of the people and work entirely in the people's interests. Comrade Chang Szu-teh[1] was in the ranks of these battalions.

All men must die, but death can vary in its significance. The ancient Chinese writer Szuma Chien[2] said, "Though death befalls all men alike, it may be heavier than Mount Tai or lighter than a feather." To die for the people is heavier than Mount Tai, but to work for the fascists and die for the exploiters and oppressors is lighter than a feather. Comrade Chang Szu-teh died for the people, and his death is indeed heavier than Mount Tai. . . .

From now on, when anyone in our ranks who has done some useful work dies, be he soldier or cook, we should have a funeral ceremony and a memorial meeting in his honor. This should become the rule. And it should be introduced among the people as well. When someone dies in a village, let a memorial meeting be held. In this way we express our mourning for the dead and unite all the people.

This speech was delivered by Mao Tse-tung at a memorial meeting for Chang Szu-teh, held by the departments directly under the Central Committee of the Chinese Communist Party.

On Chiang Kai-shek's Speech On the Double Tenth Festival
October 11, 1944

One of the distinguishing features of Chiang Kai-shek's Double Tenth speech[3] is its utter lack of content and his failure to answer any of the questions about which the people are deeply concerned.

1. Chang Szu-teh was a soldier in the Guards Regiment of the Central Committee of the Chinese Communist Party. While making charcoal in the mountains of Ansai County, northern Shensi, after having been wounded during the Long March, he was killed by the collapse of a kiln.
2. Szuma Chien was the famous Chinese historian of the second century B.C., author of the *Historical Records*. The quotation comes from his "Reply to Jen Shao-ching's Letter."
3. The Double Tenth, October 10, is the anniversary of the armed uprising in Wuhan which set off the Revolution of 1911. It is a national holiday in Nationalist China territory, but is ignored by the Chinese Communists.

Chiang Kai-shek declares that the enemy is not to be feared because there are still vast territories in the Great Rear Area. . . . But it is plain to all that without a correct policy and without human effort this capital is not enough, for Japanese imperialism is daily threatening the remaining territories. . . . He also keeps repeating, "We must not lose our self-confidence," which actually indicates loss of confidence among many people within the ranks of the Kuomintang. . . . Chiang Kai-shek has been casting about for some means to restore that confidence. But instead of . . . examining his policy and work in the political, military, economic and cultural fields, he . . . resorts to whitewashing of his mistakes.

. . . Chiang Kai-shek's speech has nothing to show on the positive side, and he has in no way met the Chinese people's eager desire to strengthen the anti-Japanese front. On the negative side, the speech is fraught with dangerous possibilities . . . witness . . . his bitter hatred of the Chinese Communist Party . . . and the anti-Communist civil war he is preparing. However, he will succeed in none of his schemes. Unless he is willing to mend his ways, he will be lifting a rock only to drop it on his own toes. . . . Since he has proclaimed that "the Communist problem should be solved politically," he should not again seek a pretext for preparing civil war.

Mao Tse-tung wrote this commentary for the Hsinhua News Agency.

The United Front in Cultural Work

October 30, 1944

The purpose of all our work is the overthrow of Japanese imperialism. . . . In our work the war comes first, then production, then cultural work. An army without culture is a dull-witted army, and a dull-witted army cannot defeat the enemy. . . .

Among the 1.5 million people of the Shensi-Kansu-Ningsia Border Region there are more than 1 million illiterates . . . and the broad masses are still under the influence of superstition. These are enemies inside the minds of the people. . . . We must call on the masses to arise in struggle against their own illiteracy, superstitions and unhygienic habits. . . . In our education we must have not only regular primary and secondary schools but also scattered, irregular village schools, newspaper-reading groups and literacy classes. . . . Our task is to unite with all intellectuals, artists and doctors of the old type who can be useful, to help them, convert them and transform them. . . . There are two principles here: one is the actual needs of the masses rather than what we fancy they need; and the other is the wishes of the masses, who must make up their own minds instead of our making up their minds for them.

This speech was delivered by Mao Tse-tung at a conference of cultural and educational workers of the Shensi-Kansu-Ningsia Border Region.

We Must Learn to Do Economic Work

January 10, 1945

Heroes of Labor and Model Workers!

. . . You are a bridge between the leadership and the broad masses; through you the opinions of the masses are transmitted to the leadership and vice versa. If you become conceited . . . and if you do not respect others, do not respect the cadres and the masses, then you will cease to be heroes and models. . . .

Since we are in the countryside, where manpower and material resources are scattered, we have adopted the policy of "unified leadership and decentralized management" for production and supply. . . . We have adopted the policies of reducing rent and interest and of organizing mutual aid in labor to heighten the peasants' enthusiasm for production and to increase the productivity of agricultural labor. . . . I have obtained data from various places in northern and central China, all of which show that after rent reduction . . . the productivity of three persons equals that of four in the past. That being the case, 90 million people can do as much as 120 million.

. . . The annual requirements of the army units and the government and other organizations total 260,000 *tan*[1] . . . of husked grain (millet), of which they get 160,000 from the people and produce the rest themselves; if they did not engage in production themselves, either they or the people would go hungry. . . .

In short, apart from those in exceptional circumstances, all army units and government and other organizations must engage in production in the intervals between fighting, training or work. . . . In our present circumstances, every organization or army unit should establish its own "domestic economy" to tide over the difficulties. Unwillingness to do so is a characteristic of loafers and is disgraceful. . . .

Some people say that if the army units go in for production, they will be unable to train or fight and that if the government and other organizations do so, they will be unable to do their own work. This is a false argument. In recent years our army units in the Border Region have undertaken production on a big scale . . . and there is greater unity than ever within the army and between the army and the people. . . .

As regards manufactured goods, the Shensi-Kansu-Ningsia Border Region has decided to become completely self-supporting in cotton, cotton yarn, cotton cloth, iron, paper, and many other things within two years. We . . . must not depend on the outside at all. . . .

In our Border Region and the other Liberated Areas, it will take another two or three years for us to learn every branch of economic work. . . . We must exert ourselves and learn, because China depends on us for her reconstruction.

Mao Tse-tung delivered this speech at a conference of labor heroes and model workers of the Shensi-Kansu-Ningsia Border Region.

1. A *tan* (or *picul*) is 133 pounds avoirdupois weight.

Production Is Also Possible in the Guerrilla Zones

January 31, 1945

It is already admitted . . . that production campaigns can and must be conducted . . . in the Liberated Areas, behind the enemy lines. But whether they can be conducted in the guerrilla zones . . . has not yet been settled in many people's minds. . . .

But now we have proof. In 1944 production was undertaken on a considerable scale in many guerrilla zones with excellent results, according to Comrade Chang Ping-kai's report in the *Liberation Daily* of January 28. The districts and units listed in his report are: central Hopei, the Hsushui-Tinghsien detachment, the Paoting-Mancheng detachment, and the Yunpiao detachment; and in Shansi, the troops in the counties of Taihsien and Kuohsien. Conditions in those areas are most unfavorable:

The place bristles with enemy and puppet strongpoints, and blockhouses and is criss-crossed with ditches, walls and roads, and taking advantage of his military superiority and communication facilities, the enemy often launches surprise attacks and encirclement and "mopping-up" campaigns against us. Under such conditions the guerrilla units often have to shift their positions several times a day.

Nevertheless, the guerrilla units have managed to carry on production in the intervals between fighting. The results are:

Everybody is now better fed—each person has 0.5 *liang*[1] of cooking oil and salt and 1 *chin*[2] of vegetables per day, and 1.5 *chin* of meat per month. Furthermore, toothbrushes, tooth powder and reading primers, which for years were unavailable, are now all provided.

Just look! Who says that production is not possible in guerrilla zones? . . .

1. A *liang* (or *tael*) is a little over 1 ounce avoirdupois weight.
2. A *chin* (or *catty*) is equivalent to 1.33 pounds avoirdupois weight.

All doubts have thus been answered as to whether the army and the people in the guerrilla zones can and must conduct large-scale production campaigns. . . .

War is not only a military and political contest, but also an economic contest. In order to defeat the Japanese aggressors . . . we must apply ourselves to economic work . . . we must achieve greater results than ever before. This is what the Central Committee of the Chinese Communist Party eagerly expects of all our cadres and all the people throughout the Liberated Areas, and we hope this objective will be attained.

Mao Tse-tung wrote this editorial for the *Liberation Daily,* Yenan.

China's Two Possible Destinies
April 23, 1945

Comrades! The Seventh National Congress of the Communist Party of China opens today. . . .

What is the significance of our congress? It is a congress, it should be said, that affects the destiny of China's 450 million people. China can have two destinies. Someone has written a book about one of them;[1] our congress represents China's other destiny and we, too, shall write a book about it.[2] . . .

Two roads lie before the Chinese people, the road of light and the road of darkness. Two possible destinies await China, a destiny of light and a destiny of darkness. . . . The new China or the old China—these are the two prospects facing the Chinese people, the Communist Party of China and our present congress. . . .

Is it possible for our hopes to be realized? We believe it is. The possibility exists, because we already enjoy the following conditions:

1. This refers to Chiang Kai-shek's *China's Destiny,* published in 1943.
2. This refers to Mao Tse-tung's report *On Coalition Government* at the same congress.

(1) A powerful Communist Party with rich experience and a membership of 1,210,000; (2) powerful Liberated Areas with a population of 95,500,000, an army of 910,000 and a militia of 2,200,000; (3) the support of the masses throughout the country; (4) the support of the people of all countries, and especially of the Soviet Union. . . .

We must have a correct policy. The fundamental point of our policy is boldly to mobilize the masses and expand the people's forces so that, under the leadership of our Party, they will defeat the aggressors and build a new China. . . .

This was the opening speech at the Seventh National Congress of the Chinese Communist Party.

On Coalition Government
April 24, 1945

THE FUNDAMENTAL DEMANDS OF THE CHINESE PEOPLE

. . . Decisive victory has been gained in the just and sacred war against the fascist aggressors and the moment is near when the Japanese aggressors will be defeated by the Chinese people in co-ordination with the allied countries. . . . Beyond all doubt, the urgent need is to unite representatives of all political parties and groups and of people without any party affiliation and establish a provisional democratic coalition government . . . to fight in effective co-ordination with the allied countries for the defeat of the Japanese aggressors . . . thus enabling the Chinese people to liberate themselves from the latter's clutches.

THE INTERNATIONAL AND THE DOMESTIC SITUATION

. . . The present military situation is that the Soviet Army is attacking Berlin, and the allied forces of Britain, the United States and France are attacking the Hitlerite remnants in co-ordination with this offensive . . . the defeat of the Japanese aggressors will not be far distant. . . . The Soviet people have built up great strength and become the main force in the defeat of fascism. . . . This new situation is very different from that in World War I. The Soviet Union was not yet in existence then and the people were not politically awakened as they are in many countries today. . . .

This does not mean that there will be no more struggles after the defeat of the fascist aggressor countries, the end of World War II and the establishment of international peace. The remnant forces of fascism which are still widespread will certainly continue to make trouble . . . but . . . victory in the anti-fascist World War II will pave the way for the victory of the people in their postwar struggles. A stable and lasting peace will be ensured only when victory is won in these struggles.

Two Lines in the Anti-Japanese War

The Key to China's Problems

China is one of the five biggest countries taking part in the war against fascism and it is the principal country fighting the Japanese aggressors on the continent of Asia. . . . The Chinese people have heroically fought the Japanese aggressors for eight long years. But for a number of years the Chinese reactionaries have been spreading rumors and misleading public opinion in order to prevent the world from knowing the truth about the role played by the Chinese people in the war. . . . Therefore, this congress should make a proper summing up of all this experience in order to educate the people and provide our Party with a basis for the formulation of policy. . . .

The Kuomintang Government's policy of passive resistance to Japan and its reactionary domestic policy of active repression of the people have resulted in military setbacks, enormous territorial losses, financial and economic crisis, oppression and hardship for the people and the disruption of national unity. . . .

Clearly, there have been two lines in China for a long time, the Kuomintang Government's line of oppression of the people . . . and of passive resistance, and the Chinese people's line of . . . unity for the waging of a people's war. Herein lies the key to all China's problems.

History Follows a Tortuous Course

To help people understand why this question of the two lines is the key to all of China's problems, it is necessary to trace the history of our War of Resistance Against Japan. . . .

Why did the Kuomintang Government of that day adopt a policy of nonresistance? The main reason was that it had wrecked Kuomintang-Communist co-operation and the unity of the Chinese people in 1927. . . . The Northern Expedition was carried out during 1926–27 . . . the northern warlord government was defeated. . . . But at a critical moment in the late spring and early summer of 1927, the treacherous reactionary policies . . . and massacre adopted by the Kuomintang authorities wrecked this national united front. . . . Thereupon unity was replaced by civil war, democracy by dictatorship, and a China full of brightness by a China covered in darkness. But the Chinese Communist Party and the Chinese people were neither cowed nor conquered nor exterminated. . . .

After the invasion of the three northeastern provinces by the Japanese aggressors, the Chinese Communist Party in 1933 proposed that . . . an armistice agreement be concluded to facilitate united resistance to Japan. . . . But the Kuomintang authorities rejected it. . . .

From the Lukouchiao Incident of July 7, 1937, to the fall of Wuhan in October 1938, the Kuomintang Government was relatively active in the war against Japan. . . . All the people, including the Communists and other democrats, earnestly hoped that the Kuomintang Government would seize the opportunity, at a time when the nation was in peril and the people were filled with enthusiasm, to institute democratic reforms and put Dr. Sun Yat Sen's revolutionary Three People's Principles into practice. But their hopes came to naught.

The People's War

During the same period the main forces of the Communist-led Red Army . . . were redesignated as the Eighth Route Army . . .

while the guerrilla units . . . were redesignated as the New Fourth Army. . . .

This army is powerful because all its members have a discipline based on political consciousness; they have come together and they fight not for the private interests of a few individuals or a narrow clique, but for the interests of the broad masses and of the whole nation. The sole purpose of this army is to stand firmly with the Chinese people and to serve them wholeheartedly. . . .

Guided by this purpose, the army has built up a system of strategy and tactics which is essential for the people's war. It is skilled in flexible guerrilla warfare conducted in accordance with the changing concrete conditions and is also skilled in mobile warfare. . . .

Once it is equipped with modern weapons, the army of China's Liberated Areas will become still more powerful and will be able to accomplish the final defeat of the Japanese aggressors.

Two Battle Fronts

From the very beginning there have been two fronts in China's War of Resistance, the Kuomintang front and the front of the Liberated Areas.

After the fall of Wuhan in October 1938, the Japanese aggressors stopped their strategic offensive against the Kuomintang front and gradually shifted their main forces to the front of the Liberated Areas. . . . Adopting a policy designed to deceive the Chinese nation, they induced the traitor Wang Ching-wei to leave Chungking and establish a puppet government in Nanking. . . .

By 1943, the army and the people of the Liberated Areas were pinning down 64 per cent of the Japanese forces invading China and 95 per cent of the puppet troops, while the Kuomintang front faced only 36 per cent of the former and 5 per cent of the latter. . . .

It should also be pointed out that the puppet troops, numbering more than 800,000 men (in both the regular and the local forces), are chiefly composed either of units that surrendered under their Kuomintang commanders or of units organized by the Kuomintang officers after their surrender. . . . This grave situation is being kept from the knowledge of many Chinese and foreigners by the Kuomintang Government's policy of suppressing news.

China's Liberated Areas

China's Liberated Areas, led by the Communist Party, now have a population of 95,500,000. They exist from Inner Mongolia in the north to Hainan Island in the south. . . . This vast liberated territory consists of nineteen major Liberated Areas, covering greater or lesser parts of the provinces of Liaoning, Jehol, Chahar, Suiyuan, Shensi, Kansu, Ningsia, Shansi, Hopei, Honan, Shantung, Kiangsu, Chikiang, Anhwei, Kiangsi, Hupeh, Hunan, Kwangtung and Fukien. Yenan is the center from which guidance is given to all these Liberated Areas. . . . The declaration issued by the Central Committee of the Communist Party of China on September 22, 1937, affirming that "Dr. Sun Yat Sen's Three People's Principles being what China needs today, our Party is ready to fight for their complete realization," has been completely carried into effect in China's Liberated Areas.

The Kuomintang Area

Persisting in its dictatorial rule, the chief ruling clique of the Kuomintang has followed a policy of passive resistance to Japan and a domestic policy directed against the people. In consequence, its armed forces have shrunk to less than half their original size and most of them have virtually lost their combat effectiveness. . . .

Why has such a grave situation arisen under the leadership of the Kuomintang's chief ruling clique? It has arisen because that clique represents the interests of China's big landlords, big bankers and big compradors. . . .

They say that "the Communist problem is a political one and should be solved politically," yet they ruthlessly suppress the Chinese Communist Party militarily, politically and economically, regarding it as "enemy No. 1" and the Japanese aggressors as only "enemy No. 2." . . .

Nevertheless, the Kuomintang is not a homogeneous political party. Many of its cadres and rank and file . . . are dissatisfied with the leadership of this clique . . . the Kuomintang armies, government organs and economic and cultural institutions. . . . Moreover, the reactionary clique itself, divided as it is into several contending factions, is not a close-knit body. Undoubtedly it is wrong to regard the Kuomintang as a homogenous body of reactionaries.

A Contrast

The Chinese people have come to see the sharp contrast between the Liberated Areas and the Kuomintang areas. . . .

The Kuomintang Government attributes its failures to lack of arms. . . . Yet . . . of all China's forces, those of the Liberated Areas lack arms most acutely. . . .

Although the Kuomintang controls vast areas abounding in grain and the people supply it with 70–100 million *tan* annually, its army is always short of food. . . . But although most of China's Liberated Areas . . . have been devastated . . . we have successfully solved the grain problem through our own efforts. . . .

In the Kuomintang areas, the workers, peasants, shop assistants, government employees, intellectuals and cultural workers live in extreme misery. In the Liberated Areas all the people have food, clothing and work. . . .

In the Kuomintang areas the people have no freedom at all. In China's Liberated Areas the people have full freedom.

Who is to blame for all the anomalies which confront the Kuomintang rulers? . . . Are foreign countries to blame for not giving them enough aid, or are the Kuomintang Government's dictatorial rule, corruption and incompetence to blame? Isn't the answer obvious?

Who Is "Sabotaging the War of Resistance and Endangering the State"?

In the light of the indisputable evidence, is it not the Kuomintang Government itself that has been sabotaging the Chinese people's War of Resistance and endangering our country? . . .

Here are two questions.

First, what exactly has made the Kuomintang Government abandon so vast and so well populated a territory, stretching from Heilungkiang Province to Lukouchiso and from Lukouchiao to Kweichow? Can it be anything other than its policy of nonresistance? . . .

Second, what exactly has enabled China's Liberated Areas to

smash the ruthless and prolonged attacks of the Japanese and puppet forces? . . . Can it be anything other than our correct line, the line of a people's war?

"Disobedience to Governmental and Military Orders"

The Kuomintang Government also constantly accuses the Chinese Communist Party of "disobedience to governmental and military orders." All we need say is that fortunately the Chinese Communists, sharing the common sense of the Chinese people, have not obeyed such "governmental and military orders" as in fact would have meant handing over to the Japanese aggressors the Liberated Areas which the Chinese people had recaptured from them amid great difficulties and hardships. . . .

Without the Liberated Areas and the people's army, could the anti-Japanese cause of the Chinese people be what it is today? And can one possibly conceive what the future of the Chinese nation would be?

The Danger of Civil War

To this day the chief ruling clique in the Kuomintang is persisting in its reactionary policy of dictatorship and civil war. There are many signs that it has long been making, and is now stepping up, preparations to unleash civil war as soon as the forces of a certain allied country have cleared a considerable part of the Chinese mainland of the Japanese aggressors. . . . If our fellow countrymen fail to take note, fail to expose its schemes and put a stop to these preparations, then one fine morning they will hear the cannonade of civil war.

Negotiations

After obtaining the consent of other democratic parties, the Communist Party of China put forward the demand at the People's Political Council in September 1944 that the Kuomintang one-Party dictatorship be abolished immediately and a democratic coalition government be formed. . . .

Not only is the Kuomintang unwilling to abolish the one-Party dictatorship and form a coalition government, it is unwilling to introduce a single one of the urgently needed democratic reforms, such as the abolition of the secret police . . . release of political prisoners . . . recognition of the Liberated Areas. . . .

Two Prospects

In the light of the situation as a whole and of the above analysis of the actual international and domestic state of affairs, I would ask everyone here to be on the alert and not to expect that our cause will proceed smoothly. . . . There are two prospects, one good and one bad. One is . . . that the fascist dictatorship will continue and democratic reforms will not be allowed. But there is another aspect . . . that of overcoming all difficulties, uniting the whole people, abolishing the Kuomintang's fascist dictatorship, carrying out democratic reforms . . . and building an independent, free, democratic, united, prosperous and powerful new China. . . .

The great task for us and for the whole people is to avert the first possibility or prospect and work for the second with every ounce of our energy. . . .

The Policy of the Chinese Communist Party

I have analyzed the two lines in China's War of Resistance. Such an analysis is absolutely necessary. For up to this very moment many Chinese people still do not know what is really going on in this war. Many people in the Kuomintang areas and in foreign countries are being kept in the dark by the Kuomintang Government's policy of blockade. . . .

In China's present grave situation, the people, the democrats and democratic parties at home and the people in other countries . . . want to know what the policy of the Chinese Communist Party is for solving the many vital problems of today. . . . Here I shall explain a number of the definite conclusions arrived at by our Party concerning the major policies for solving China's problems.

Our General Program

An agreed common program is urgently needed by the Chinese people . . . for the purpose of . . . completely wiping out the Japanese aggressors and building a new China that is independent, free, democratic, united, prosperous and powerful. . . .

. . . We Communists and the overwhelming majority of the population are agreed on the following fundamental propositions at the present stage of China's development. First, China should not have a feudal, fascist and anti-popular state system under the dictatorship of the big landlords and big bourgeoisie, because eighteen years of government by the chief ruling clique of the Kuomintang have already proved its complete bankruptcy. Second, China cannot possibly establish the old type of democratic dictatorship—a purely national-bourgeois state—and therefore should not attempt to do so, because on the one hand the Chinese national bourgeoisie has proved itself very flabby economically and politically, and on the other . . . a new factor has been present . . . the awakened Chinese proletariat with its leader, the Chinese Communist Party, which has demonstrated its great capacity. . . . Third, it is likewise impossible for the Chinese people to institute a socialist state system at the present stage when . . . social and economic conditions for a socialist state are still lacking.

What then do we propose? We propose the establishment, after the thorough defeat of the Japanese aggressors, of a state system which we call New Democracy, a united front democratic alliance based on the overwhelming majority of the people, under the leadership of the working class. . . .

. . . These views of ours are completely in accord with the revolutionary views of Dr. Sun Yat Sen. In the Manifesto of the First National Congress of the Kuomintang, Dr. Sun wrote:

The so-called "democratic system" in modern states is usually monopolized by the bourgeoisie and has become simply an instrument for oppressing the common people. On the other hand, the Kuomintang's Principle of Democracy means a democratic system shared by all the common people and not privately owned by the few.

. . . The economy of New Democracy which we advocate is likewise in accord with Dr. Sun's principles. On the land question, Dr. Sun championed "land to the tiller." On the question of industry and commerce, Dr. Sun stated in the Manifesto, quoted above:

Enterprises, such as banks, railways and airlines, whether Chinese-owned or foreign-owned, which are either monopolistic in character or too big for private management, shall be operated and administered by the state, so that private capital cannot dominate the livelihood of the people; this is the main principle of the regulation of capital.

In the present stage, we fully agree with these views of Dr. Sun's on economic questions. . . . In accordance with Dr. Sun's principles and the experience of the Chinese revolution, China's national economy at the present stage should be composed of the state sector, the private sector and the co-operative sector. . . .

. . . We Communists do not conceal our political views. Definitely and beyond all doubt, our future or maximum program is to carry China forward to socialism and communism. Both the name of our Party and our Marxist world outlook unequivocally point to this supreme ideal of the future, a future of incomparable brightness and splendor. . . .

Some people are suspicious and think that once in power, the Communist Party will follow Russia's example and establish the dictatorship of the proletariat and a one-Party system. Our answer is that a new-democratic state based on an alliance of the democratic classes is different in principle from a socialist state under the dictatorship of the proletariat. . . . The Chinese system for the present stage . . . is distinguished from the Russian system but is perfectly necessary and reasonable for us, namely, the new-democratic form of state and political power based on the alliance of the democratic classes.

Our Specific Program

Our Party must also have a specific program for each period based on this general program. Our general program of New Democracy will remain unchanged throughout the stage of the bourgeois-democratic revolution, that is, for several decades. . . . What are the immediate demands of the people? We consider the following to be appropriate and minimum demands:

Mobilize all available forces . . . in co-operation with the allies;

Abolish the Kuomintang one-Party dictatorship and establish a democratic coalition government and a joint supreme command;

Punish the pro-Japanese elements, fascists and defeatists. . . . ;

Punish the reactionaries who are creating . . . civil war;

Punish the traitors . . . and agents of the Japanese;

Liquidate the reactionary secret service . . . and abolish the concentration camps;

Revoke all reactionary laws . . . aimed at suppressing the people's freedom. . . . ;

Recognize the legal status of all democratic parties and groups;

Release all patriotic political prisoners;

Withdraw all troops encircling . . . China's Liberated Areas. . . . ;

Recognize the anti-Japanese . . . governments of China's Liberated Areas.

Consolidate and expand the Liberated Areas. . . . ;

Allow the Chinese people to arm themselves and defend . . . their country;

. . . Punish the commanders who are responsible for disastrous defeats;

Improve the recruiting system and living conditions. . . . ;

Give preferential treatment to the families of the soldiers fighting . . . at the front. . . . ;

Provide preferential treatment for disabled soldiers. . . .;

Develop war industries . . . . ;

Distribute the military and financial aid received from the allies impartially to all the armies. . . . ;

Punish corrupt officials. . . . ;

Improve the pay of the middle and lower grade government employees;

Give the Chinese people democratic rights;

Abolish the oppressive *pao-chia*[1] system;

Provide the war refugees . . . with relief;

Appropriate substantial funds . . . for . . . people who have suffered under enemy occupation;

Abolish exorbitant taxes. . . . ;

Introduce rural reforms, reduce rent and interest. . . . ;

Outlaw bureaucrat capital;

Abolish . . . economic controls;

Check the unbridled inflation. . . . ;

Assist private industry. . . . ;

Improve the livelihood of the workers. . . . ;

Abolish Kuomintang indoctrination in education. . . . ;

1. See Note 1, p. 217.

Guarantee the livelihood of the teachers. . . . ;
Protect the interests of the youth, women and children. . . . ;
Give the minority nationalities in China better treatment. . . . ;
Protect the interests of the overseas Chinese. . . . ;
Protect foreign nationals who have fled to China. . . . ;
Improve Sino-Soviet relations.

. . . These demands voice the desires of the Chinese masses and also of broad sections of democratic public opinion in the allied countries. . . .

The immediate demands or specific program of the Chinese people outlined above involve many vital wartime problems and require further elucidation. . . .

Destroy the Japanese aggressors completely, allow no compromise halfway. The Cairo Conference[2] rightly decided that the Japanese aggressors must be made to surrender unconditionally. But the Japanese aggressors are now working behind the scenes for a compromise peace. . . . All intrigues for a compromise must immediately be stopped. . . .

Abolish the Kuomintang one-Party dictatorship, establish a democratic coalition government. To wipe out the Japanese aggressors it is necessary to effect democratic reforms throughout the country. Yet this will be impossible unless the one-Party dictatorship of the Kuomintang is abolished and a democratic coalition government is established. . . .

We Communists propose two steps for the termination of the Kuomintang one-Party dictatorship. First, at the present stage, to establish a provisional coalition government through common agreement among representatives of all parties and people with no Party affiliation. Second, in the next stage, to convene a national assembly after free and unrestricted elections and form a regular coalition government. . . .

This is the only course China can take, whatever the intentions of the Kuomintang or other parties, groups or individuals, whether they like it or not, and whether or not they are conscious of it. This is a historical law, an inexorable trend which no force can reverse. . . .

2. The Cairo Conference held by China, the United States and Britain in November 1943.

Freedom for the people. At present the Chinese people's struggle for freedom is primarily directed against the Japanese aggressors. But the Kuomintang Government is preventing them from fighting the Japanese aggressors by depriving them of their freedom and binding them hand and foot. . . . Freedom is won by the people through struggle, it is not bestowed by anyone as a favor. The people in China's liberated areas have already won their freedom. . . . Unless the people have freedom, there can be no national assembly or government genuinely elected by the people. Is this not clear enough? . . .

In 1925 Dr. Sun Yat Sen declared in his deathbed Testament:

For forty years I have devoted myself to the cause of the national revolution with the aim of winning freedom and equality for China. My experience during these forty years has firmly convinced me that to achieve this aim we must arouse the masses of the people and unite in a common fight with those nations of the world who treat us as equals.

The unworthy successors of Dr. Sun, who have betrayed him, oppress the masses of the people instead of arousing them, and deprive them of all their freedom of speech, press, assembly, association, political conviction and religious belief and freedom of the person. . . . If it lasts much longer, the Chinese people will lose all patience.

Unity of the people. It is imperative to turn a divided China into a united China in order to destroy the Japanese aggressors, prevent civil war and build a new China; such is the historical task of the Chinese people.

But how is China to be united? Through autocratic unification by a dictator or democratic unification by the people? . . . Can there be unity if the people have no freedom or democracy? There will be unity as soon as they have both. . . . It is plain common sense that unless the dictatorship of the anti-popular Kuomintang clique is abolished and a democratic coalition government is formed, not only will it be impossible to carry out any democratic reform in the Kuomintang areas . . . but the calamity of civil war will ensue.

The people's army. . . . In 1944 the Kuomintang Government presented a so-called "memorandum" demanding that the Communist

Party should "disband, within a definite time limit," four-fifths of the armed forces of the Liberated Areas. In 1945 . . . it has further demanded the handing over of all the armed forces of the Liberated Areas by the Communist Party, after which it would grant the Communist Party "legal status." . . .

"The army belongs to the state"—that is perfectly true . . . but what kind of state? . . . The moment a new-democratic coalition government comes into being in China, the Liberated Areas of China will hand their armed forces over to it. . . .

In 1924 Dr. Sun Yat Sen said, "Today should mark the beginning of a new epoch in the national revolution. . . . The first step is to unite the armed forces with the people, and the next step is to turn them into the armed forces of the people."[3] . . . Every patriotic officer in the Kuomintang Army who has any conscience should set about reviving the Sun Yat Sen spirit and transforming his troops. . . .

The land problem. To wipe out the Japanese aggressors and build a new China, it is imperative to reform the land system and emancipate the peasants. Dr. Sun Yat Sen's thesis of "land to the tiller" is correct for the present period of our revolution, which is bourgeois-democratic in nature. . . .

From 1927 to 1936, the Chinese Communist Party adopted various measures for the thorough reform of the land system and put Dr. Sun's "land to the tiller" into effect. It was precisely the reactionary clique of the Kuomintang, that gang of unworthy followers of Dr. Sun Yat Sen, who bared their teeth, showed their claws and fought against "land to the tiller" in ten years of war against the people. . . .

It is the peasants who are the main political force for democracy in China at the present stage. Chinese democrats will achieve nothing unless they rely on the support of the 360 million peasants. . . .

China's numerous revolutionary intellectuals must awaken to the necessity of becoming one with the peasants. The peasants need them and await their help. . . .

The problem of industry. In order to defeat the Japanese aggressors and build a new China, it is necessary to develop industry. But under the Kuomintang Government . . . all the productive forces are

3. From Dr. Sun Yat Sen's "Statement on My Departure for the North," November 10, 1924.

being ruined, and this is true both of agriculture and of industry. . . .

When the political system of New Democracy is won, the Chinese people and their government will have to adopt practical measures in order to build heavy and light industry step by step over a number of years and transform China from an agricultural into an industrial country. . . .

The policy of adjusting the interests of labor and capital will be adopted under the new-democratic state system. On the one hand, it will protect the interests of the workers, institute an eight- to ten-hour working day according to circumstances, provide suitable unemployment relief and social insurance and safeguard trade union rights; on the other hand, it will guarantee legitimate profits to properly managed state, private and co-operative enterprises. . . .

The problem of culture, education and the intellectuals. The calamities brought upon the Chinese people by foreign and feudal oppression also affect our national culture. . . . We need large numbers of educators and teachers for the people, and also people's scientists, engineers, technicians, doctors, journalists, writers, men of letters, artists and rank-and-file cultural workers. . . . Therefore, the task of a people's government is systematically to develop all kinds of intellectually equipped cadres from among the ranks of the people and at the same time take care to unite with and reeducate all the useful intellectuals already available.

The problem of the minority nationalities. The anti-popular clique of the Kuomintang denies that many nationalities exist in China, and labels all excepting the Han nationality as "tribes." . . .

In 1924 Dr. Sun Yat Sen wrote in the Manifesto of the First National Congress of the Kuomintang that "the Kuomintang Principle of Nationalism has a twofold meaning, first, the liberation of the Chinese nation, and second, the equality of all the nationalities in China" and that "the Kuomintang solemnly declares that it recognizes the right to self-determination of all the nationalities in China." . . .

The Communist Party of China is in full agreement with Dr. Sun's policy on nationalities as stated here. . . . Their spoken and written languages, their manners and customs and their religious beliefs must be respected. . . .

The problem of foreign policy. The Communist Party of China agrees with the Atlantic Charter and with the decisions of the international conferences of Moscow, Teheran and the Crimea,[4] because these decisions all contribute to the defeat of the fascist aggressors and the maintenance of world peace. . . .

The Chinese Communist Party fully agrees with the proposals of the Dumbarton Oaks Conference. . . . It welcomes the United Nations Conference on International Organization in San Francisco. It has appointed its own representative on China's delegation to this conference[5] in order to express the will of the Chinese people. . . .

We ask the governments of all the allied countries, and of the United States and Britain in the first place, to pay serious attention to the voice of the Chinese people. . . . If any foreign government helps the Chinese reactionaries and opposes the Chinese people's democratic cause, it will be committing a gross mistake. . . .

The Chinese Communist Party is the most faithful spokesman of the Chinese people, and whoever fails to respect it in fact fails to respect the Chinese masses and is doomed to defeat.

The Tasks in the Kuomintang Areas

. . . In the Kuomintang areas, the people are not free to engage in patriotic activity, and democratic movements are considered illegal, and yet various social strata, democratic parties and individuals are becoming increasingly active. . . .

All the oppressed strata, political parties and social groups in the Kuomintang areas must extend their democratic movement on a broad scale and gradually weld their scattered forces together in order to fight for national unity, the establishment of a coalition government. . . . The Communist Party of China and the people of the Liberated Areas should give them every possible help. . . .

4. The Atlantic Charter was issued jointly by the United States and Britain at the conclusion of their Atlantic Conference in August 1941. The Moscow Conference was held in October 1943 by the foreign ministers of the Soviet Union, the United States and Britain. The Teheran Conference of the Soviet Union, the United States and Britain was held in the capital of Iran in November and December 1943. The Crimea Conference of the Soviet Union, the United States and Britain took place in February 1945 at Yalta.

5. Tung Pi-wu, as the representative of China's Liberated Areas attended the United Nations Conference on International Organization held in San Francisco from April to June 1945.

The Tasks in the Japanese-Occupied Areas

In the occupied areas, Communists should call on all who oppose Japan to follow the French and Italian examples and form organizations and underground forces to prepare armed uprisings, so that when the time comes they can act from the inside in co-ordination with the armies attacking from the outside and so wipe out the Japanese aggressors. . . .

Communists should pursue the broadest united front policy in all the occupied areas. For the overthrow of the common enemy they must unite with anyone who is opposed to the Japanese aggressors and their servile lackeys. . . .

Those Kuomintang reactionaries who have betrayed the nation by organizing open collaborators to fight the Chinese people, the Communist Party, the Eighth Route Army, the New Fourth Army and other armed forces of the people must be warned to repent in time. Otherwise, when the lost territories are recovered, they will certainly be punished for their crimes along with the collaborators with Japan and will be shown no mercy.

The Tasks in the Liberated Areas

Our Party has put its whole new-democratic program into practice in the Liberated Areas with striking results, and so built up tremendous anti-Japanese strength, and from now on this strength should be developed and consolidated in every way. . . .

All religions are permitted in China's Liberated Areas, in accordance with the principle of freedom of religious belief. All believers in Protestantism, Catholicism, Islamism, Buddhism and other faiths enjoy the protection of the people's government so long as they are abiding by its laws. Everyone is free to believe; neither compulsion nor discrimination is permitted. . . .

LET THE WHOLE PARTY UNITE AND FIGHT TO ACCOMPLISH ITS TASKS!

Comrades! Now that we understand our tasks and the policies for accomplishing them, what should be our attitude in carrying out these policies and performing these tasks? . . .

In the twenty-four years since its birth in 1921, the Communist Party of China has gone through three great struggles—the Northern Expedition, the Agrarian Revolutionary War and the War of Resistance Against Japan which is still going on. From its very beginning our Party has based itself on the theory of Marxism-Leninism. . . .

The universal truth of Marxism-Leninism, which reflects the practice of proletarian struggle throughout the world, becomes an invincible weapon for the Chinese people when it is integrated with the concrete practice of the revolutionary struggle of the Chinese proletariat and people. . . .

Conscientious practice of self-criticism is still another hallmark distinguishing our Party from all other political parties. As we say, dust will accumulate if a room is not cleaned regularly, our faces will get dirty if they are not washed regularly. Our comrades' minds and our Party's work may also collect dust, and also need sweeping and washing. The proverb, "Running water is never stale and a door hinge is never worm-eaten," means that constant motion prevents the inroads of germs and other organisms. . . .

. . . Without the Chinese Communists as the mainstay of the Chinese people, China can never achieve independence or liberation, or industrialization and the modernization of her agriculture.

Comrades! I firmly believe that with the Communist Party of China armed with the experience of the three revolutions, we can accomplish our great political task.

Thousands upon thousands of martyrs have heroically laid down their lives for the people; let us hold their banner high and march ahead along the path crimson with their blood!

A new-democratic China will soon be born. Let us hail that great day!

This was the political report made by Mao Tse-tung to the Seventh National Congress of the Chinese Communist Party.

The Foolish Old Man
Who Removed the Mountains

June 11, 1945

We have had a very successful congress. We have done three things. First, we have decided on the line of our Party, which is boldly to mobilize the masses and expand the people's forces so that . . . they will defeat the Japanese aggressors. . . . Second, we have adopted the new Party constitution. Third, we have elected the leading body of the Party—the Central Committee. . . .

When the congress closes, many comrades will be leaving for their posts and the various war fronts. Comrades, wherever you go, you should propagate the line of the congress and, through the members of the Party, explain it to the broad masses.

. . . We should fire the whole people with the conviction that China belongs not to the reactionaries but to the Chinese people. There is an ancient Chinese fable called "The Foolish Old Man Who Removed the Mountains." . . . His house faced south and beyond his doorway stood the two great peaks, Taihang and Wangwu, obstructing the way. He called his sons and, hoe in hand, they began to dig up these mountains. . . . Another graybeard, known as the Wise Old Man, saw them and said derisively, "How silly of you to do this! It is quite impossible for you few to dig up these two huge mountains." The Foolish Old Man replied, "When I die, my sons will carry on; when they die, there will be my grandsons, and then their sons and grandsons, and so on to infinity. High as they are, the mountains cannot grow any higher and with every bit we dig, they will be that much lower. Why can't we clear them away?" . . . God was moved by this, and he sent down two angels, who carried the mountains away on their backs. Today, two big mountains lie like a dead weight on the Chinese people. One is imperialism, the other is feudalism. . . . Our God is none other than the masses of the Chinese people. If they stand up and dig together with us, why can't these two mountains be cleared away?

Yesterday, in a talk with two Americans who were leaving for the

United States, I said that the U.S. Government was trying to undermine us and this would not be permitted. . . . I said to these two Americans, "Tell the policymakers in your government that we forbid you Americans to enter the Liberated Areas because your policy is to support Chiang Kai-shek against the Communists, and we have to be on our guard. . . . We will not permit you to nose around everywhere. Since Patrick J. Hurley[1] has publicly declared against co-operation with the Chinese Communist Party, why do you still want to come and prowl around in our Liberated Areas?" . . .

We firmly believe that, led by the Chinese Communist Party and guided by the line of its Seventh Congress, the Chinese people will achieve complete victory, while the Kuomintang's counterrevolutionary line will inevitably fail.

This was Mao Tse-tung's concluding speech at the Seventh National Congress of the Chinese Communist Party.

On Production by the Army for Its Own Support and on the Importance of the Great Movements for Rectification and for Production

April 27, 1945

In the existing circumstances in which our army is facing extreme material difficulties and is engaged in dispersed operations, it is absolutely inadmissible for the leading bodies to assume full responsibility for provisioning the army, for to do so would both hamper the initiative of the large numbers of officers and men at the lower levels and fail to satisfy their needs. . . . If only the leadership at the higher levels sets the tasks well and gives the lower levels a free hand to overcome difficulties by their own efforts, the problem will be solved. . . .

1. Patrick J. Hurley, a Texan, was appointed United States Ambassador to China toward the end of 1944. He occupied that post for about one year.

In our circumstances, production by the army for its own support, though backward or retrogressive in form, is progressive in substance and of great historic significance. . . . Let us ask two army units . . . to choose between . . . the higher levels supplying them with all their means of livelihood and the higher levels supplying little or nothing but letting them produce for themselves all that they need, or . . . even less than half of what they need. . . . Which will they prefer? After a year's serious experiment in production for self-support, they will surely answer that the second method yields better results and be willing to adopt it. . . .

Production by the army for its own support has not only improved the army's living conditions and lightened the burden on the people, thereby making it possible further to expand the army. In addition, it has had many immediate effects. They are . . . . Improved relations between officers and men. . . . Better attitude to labor. . . . Strengthened discipline. . . . Improved relations between the army and the people. . . .

This was an editorial written by Mao Tse-tung for the *Liberation Daily*, Yenan.

The Hurley-Chiang Duet Is a Flop

July 10, 1945

Convened to camouflage Chiang Kai-shek's dictatorial regime, the Fourth People's Political Council opened in Chungking on July 7. It was the smallest opening session on record. Not only was nobody present from the Chinese Communist Party, but many members of the Council from other groups were absent too. Out of a total membership of 290, only 180 turned up. . . .

This will probably be the end of the whole business about convoking the National Assembly on November 12 this year. The imperialist Patrick J. Hurley has had something to do with this business . . . that put some stiffening into Chiang Kai-shek's New Year's Day speech . . . in which he announced his determination to "hand state power back to the people" on November 12. . . . He had the audacity to say that the Chinese Communist Party must hand over its troops before he would bestow "legal status" upon it. In all this, the backing of His Worship Patrick J. Hurley was decisive. In a statement in Washington on April 2, Hurley did his best to boost Chiang Kai-shek's "National Assembly" and other such nasty schemes in addition to denying the role of the Chinese Communist Party. . . . At the moment Hurley seems to be lying low, busying himself with no one knows what, with the result that Chiang Kai-shek has to talk twaddle before the People's Political Council. . . .

One thing, however, is certain: ever since the Chinese people began raising their voices in protest against this National Assembly, even the enthusiasts for "constitutional monarchy" have been worried about our "monarch." . . .

Whether or not there is a national assembly is one thing and whether or not there is a minimum of democratic reforms is quite another. The former can be dispensed with for the time being, but the latter must be introduced immediately. . . .

The question you must answer is: How is it that you are willing to "hand state power back to the people" but not willing to institute democratic reforms?

Mao Tse-tung wrote this comment for the Hsinhua News Agency.

On the Danger of the Hurley Policy

July 12, 1945

It has become increasingly obvious that the policy of the United States toward China as represented by its Ambassador Patrick J. Hurley is creating a civil war crisis in China. . . .

When Hurley visited Yenan as Roosevelt's personal representative in November 1944, he expressed agreement with the Chinese Communist Party's plan for the abolition of the Kuomintang one-Party dictatorship and the establishment of a democratic coalition government. But later he changed his tune and went back on what he had said in Yenan. This change was crudely revealed in his statement in Washington on April 2. In the interim, according to the selfsame Hurley, the Kuomintang Government represented by Chiang Kai-shek seems to have turned into Beauty and the Chinese Communist Party into the Beast. . . . If the Hurley policy continues, the U.S. Government will fall irretrievably into the deep stinking cesspool of Chinese reaction. . . . If the Hurley policy of aiding and abetting the reactionary forces in China and antagonizing the Chinese people with their immense numbers continues unchanged, it will place a crushing burden on the government and people of the United States and plunge them into endless trouble. This point must be brought home to the people of the United States.

This comment was written for the Hsinhua News Agency.

Telegram to Comrade William Z. Foster

July 29, 1945

Comrade William Z. Foster and the National Committee of the Communist Party of the United States of America:

We are glad to learn that the special convention of the Communist Political Association of the United States has resolved to repudiate Browder's revisionist, that is, capitulationist line,[1] has re-established Marxist leadership and revived the Communist Party of the United States. We hereby extend to you our warm congratulations on this great victory of the working class and the Marxist movement in the United States. . . .

1. Earl Browder was the General Secretary of the Communist Party of the United States from 1930 to 1944.

The Last Round with the Japanese Invaders

August 9, 1945

The Chinese people heartily welcome the Soviet Government's declaration of war on Japan on August 8. The Soviet Union's action will very much shorten the war against Japan. . . . In these circumstances, all the anti-Japanese forces of the Chinese people should launch a nationwide counteroffensive in close and effective co-ordination with the operations of the Soviet Union and the other allied countries. . . .

A new stage in China's war of national liberation has arrived, and the people of the whole country must strengthen their unity and struggle for final victory.

Volume IV

The Third
Revolutionary Civil War
Period

Volume IV   Contents

Volume IV Contents 311

The Situation and Our Policy
After the Victory in the War
of Resistance Against Japan

August 13, 1945

These are days of tremendous change in the situation in the Far East. The surrender of Japanese imperialism is now a foregone conclusion. The decisive factor for Japan's surrender is the entry of the Soviet Union in the war. . . .

In these circumstances, what are the relations among the different classes in China and what are the relations between the Kuomintang and the Communist Party at present? . . . As everyone knows, Chiang Kai-shek, the political representative of China's big landlords and big bourgeoisie, is a most brutal and treacherous fellow. His policy has been . . . to conserve his forces and prepare for civil war. . . . The victory he has been waiting for has arrived, and now this "Generalissimo" is about to "come down from the mountain." . . .

With regard to Chiang Kai-shek's plot to launch a civil war, our Party's policy has been clear and consistent, that is, resolutely to oppose civil war and prevent civil war. . . . The opponents of civil war consist only of the Chinese Communist Party and the Chinese people—it is a pity that the do not include Chiang Kai-shek and the Kuomintang. . . .

Last year an American correspondent asked me, "Who has given you the power to act?" I replied, "The people." . . . The ruling

315

Kuomintang hasn't given us any power. . . . On March 1 this year Chiang Kai-shek stated that the Communist Party would have to turn over its army before it could acquire legal status. . . . We have not turned over our army, and so we have no legal status and are "defying laws human and divine." Our duty is to hold ourselves responsible to the people. . . .

To whom should the fruits of victory in the War of Resistance belong? It is very obvious. Take a peach tree for example. When the tree yields peaches they are the fruits of victory. Who is entitled to pick the peaches? Ask who planted and watered the tree. Chiang Kai-shek squatting on the mountain did not carry a single bucket of water, and yet he is now stretching out his arm from afar to pick the peaches. "I, Chiang Kai-shek, own these peaches," he says, "I am the landlord, and you are my serfs and I won't allow you to pick any." . . .

Chiang Kai-shek talks about "building the country." From now on the struggle will be, build what sort of country? To build a new-democratic country of the broad masses of the people under the leadership of the proletariat? Or to build a semicolonial and semifeudal country under the dictatorship of the big landlords and the big bourgeoisie? . . .

Chiang Kai-shek will face many difficulties if he tries to let loose a civil war. . . . The situation today is vastly different from that in 1937. . . . Today the level of political consciousness in our Party is very much higher. . . . Nevertheless, among the people, and chiefly among those living in the Japanese-occupied and Kuomintang areas, there are still a good many who believe in Chiang Kai-shek and have illusions about the Kuomintang and the United States of America. . . .

It is up to us to organize the people. As for the reactionaries in China, it is up to us to organize the people to overthrow them. . . .

. . . We stress regeneration through our own efforts. . . . Chiang Kai-shek, on the contrary, relies entirely on the aid of U.S. imperialism, which he looks upon as his mainstay. . . . But U.S. imperialism while outwardly strong is inwardly weak. . . . An American once said to me, "You should listen to Hurley and send a few men to be officials in the Kuomintang government."[1] I replied

1. According to the annotator of the English-language edition of *Selected Works* published in Peking, the American referred to was Colonel David D. Barrett, head of the U.S. Army Observer Group in Yenan.

. . . "If we become officials . . . a coalition government must be set up on a democratic basis." He said, "If you don't . . . the Americans will curse you . . . and will back Chiang Kai-shek." I replied . . . "The day will surely come when you will find it impossible to back him any longer." . . .

The Soviet Union has sent its troops, the Red Army has come to help the Chinese people drive out the aggressor. . . . The propaganda organs of the United States and Chiang Kai-shek hoped to sweep away the Red Army's political influence with two atom bombs. . . . Can atom bombs decide wars? No, they can't. Atom bombs could not make Japan surrender. . . . If atom bombs could decide the war, then why was it necessary to ask the Soviet Union to send its troops? Some of our comrades, too, believe that the atom bomb is all-powerful; that is a big mistake. . . .

The entry of the Soviet Union into the war has decided Japan's surrender and the situation in China is entering a new period. Between the War of Resistance and the new period there is a transitional stage. The struggle during this transitional stage is to oppose Chiang Kai-shek's usurpation of the fruits of victory. . . . Being prepared, we shall be able to deal properly with all kinds of complicated situations.

This speech was delivered by Mao Tse-tung at a meeting of cadres in Yenan.

Chiang Kai-shek Is Provoking Civil War
August 13, 1945

A spokesman for the Propaganda Department of the Kuomintang Central Executive Committee has made a statement describing as "a presumptuous and illegal act" the order[1] setting a time limit for the

1. The first paragraph of Chu Teh's order reads:

"In accordance with the provisions of the Potsdam Declaration, any anti-Japanese armed forces in the Liberated Areas may serve notice on enemy troops and headquarters in cities and towns or along communication lines in the vicinity, requiring them to hand over their arms to our fighting forces within a given time; when they have handed over their arms, our forces will protect

surrender of the enemy and the puppets, which was issued by Chu Teh, Commander-in-Chief of the Eighteenth Group Army, on August 10 from the General Headquarters in Yenan. The comment is absolutely preposterous. Its logical implication is that it was wrong of Commander-in-Chief Chu Teh to act in accordance with the Potsdam Declaration. . . . No wonder that even before the enemy's actual surrender, Chiang Kai-shek, China's fascist ringleader, autocrat and traitor to the people, had the audacity to "order" the anti-Japanese armed forces in the Liberated Areas to "stay where they are, pending further orders," that is, to tie their own hands and let the enemy attack them. . . .

---

their lives in accordance with our regulations on the lenient treatment of prisoners of war."

The Potsdam Declaration with respect to Japan said only (July 26, 1945):

"Article 8. The terms of the Cairo Declaration shall be carried out. . . .
Article 13. We call upon the government of Japan to proclaim now the unconditional surrender of all Japanese armed forces, and to provide proper and adequate assurances of their good faith in such actions. The alternative for Japan is prompt and utter destruction."

The Cairo Conference (ended December 1, 1943) required Japan:

"Paragraph 3. To restore to China the lost lands of Manchuria, Formosa and the Pescadores."

The articles of surrender signed by the representatives of Japan on September 2, 1945, on board the U.S.S. *Missouri* in Tokyo Bay required:

"Article 1, Paragraph a—The senior Japanese commanders and all ground, sea, air and auxiliary forces (excluding Manchuria), Formosa and French Indochina north of 10 degrees North Latitude shall surrender to Generalissimo Chiang Kai-shek.
Paragraph b—Forces in Manchuria and Korea north of 38 degrees North Latitude to surrender to the Commander-in-Chief of Soviet forces in the Far East."

The document of surrender by Japan was signed by the representatives of Japan, United States, United Kingdom, Union of Socialist Soviet Republics, Australia, Canada, France, The Netherlands, and New Zealand.

Nowhere in the Potsdam Declaration, the Cairo Declaration, or in the Tokyo surrender agreement was there any permission for recognition of any authority in China to be exercised by the Chinese Communists. The contrary was expressed in the surrender agreement of September 2, 1945, which was signed by the Soviet Union, and which explicitly called for Japanese surrender to Generalissimo Chiang Kai-shek.

The surrender of Japanese forces north of 38 degrees North Latitude to the armed forces of the Soviet Union led, in 1950, to the armed invasion of south Korea by north Korean, and later Chinese, Communists.

Both the comment by the spokesman for the Propaganda Department of the Kuomintang Central Executive Committee and Chiang Kai-shek's "orders" are from beginning to end provocations to civil war . . . the Kuomintang reactionaries are pitifully stupid. . . .

After all, who has the right to accept the surrender of the Japanese and puppets? . . . To speak plainly, in China only the anti-Japanese armed forces of the Liberated Areas have the right to accept the surrender of the enemy and puppet troops. . . .

If this is not done, the Chinese people will deem it most improper.

This was a commentary written by Mao Tse-tung for the Hsinhua News Agency.

Two Telegrams from the Commander-in-Chief of the Eighteenth Group Army to Chiang Kai-shek

August 1945

TELEGRAM OF AUGUST 13

We have received through the Chungking radio two Central News Agency dispatches, one carrying the order you sent us and the other your order to the officers and men in various war zones. Your order to us reads, "All units of the Eighteenth Group Army should stay where they are, pending further orders." . . . Your order to the officers and men in various war zones was reported as follows: "The Supreme Command today sent telegrams to the officers and men in various war zones, ordering them to step up the war effort and in accordance with existing military plans and orders actively to push forward without the slightest relaxation"—that's more like it! But what a pity you have given this order only to your own troops, and not to us, and that you have given us something quite different. . . . We hold that you have given a wrong order, an order so wrong that we have to inform you we firmly reject it. For your order to us is not only unjust but also runs counter to China's national interest and benefits only the Japanese aggressors and the traitors to the motherland.

Telegram of August 16

At a time when our common enemy, the Japanese Government, has accepted the terms of the Potsdam Declaration, I hereby address to you the following statement and demands of all the anti-Japanese armed forces and all the 260 million people in China's Liberated Areas and Japanese-occupied areas.

The people of China's Liberated Areas and the Communist Party of China have proposed many times to you that a democratic coalition government of the whole country be formed in order to stop internal strife, mobilize and unite the people's anti-Japanese forces throughout China. . . . But our proposals have invariably been rejected by you and your government. We are extremely dissatisfied with all this. . . .

I demand that you consult with us, so that we may reach common views before you, your government and your Supreme Command accept the surrender of the Japanese and puppets and conclude any post-surrender agreements or treaties. . . .

I ask you to prevent civil war. The way to do this is for the armed forces of the Liberated Areas to accept the surrender of the enemy and puppet troops they have encircled, while your armed forces accept the surrender of the enemy and puppet troops you have encircled. . . . If you act otherwise, it will lead to adverse consequences. . . .

I ask you immediately to abolish the one-Party dictatorship, call a conference of all parties to set up a democratic coalition government. . . .

. . . You alone, of all the high commanders of the allied forces, have given an absolutely wrong order. . . . Therefore, taking my stand on the common interest of China and the allies, I shall firmly and completely oppose your order so long as you do not openly admit your error and countermand this wrong order. . . . I declare to you, I am a patriotic soldier, I cannot act otherwise. . . . I request your early reply.

These telegrams were written by Mao Tse-tung for Chu Teh, Commander-in-Chief of the Chinese Communist Eighteenth Group Army.

On a Statement by Chiang Kai-shek's Spokesman

August 16, 1945

A spokesman for Chiang Kai-shek, commenting on the alleged violation by the Communist Party of Generalissimo Chiang Kai-shek's order to Commander-in-Chief Chu Teh, said at a press conference in Chungking on the afternoon of August 15, "The orders of the Generalissimo must be obeyed," and "Those who violate them are enemies of the people." A Hsinhua News Agency correspondent states: This is an open signal by Chiang Kai-shek for all-out civil war. . . . For the purpose of unleashing civil war, Chiang Kai-shek had already invented many terms, such as "alien party," "traitor party," "traitor army," "rebel army," "traitor areas," "bandit areas." . . . The slight difference this time is the addition of a new term, "enemy of the people." . . . Whenever the term, "enemy of the people," is used in China, everyone knows who is meant. There is a person in China who betrayed Sun Yat Sen's Three People's Principles and the Great Revolution of 1927. . . . After all he has done, can there be any dispute as to whether Chiang Kai-shek is an enemy of the people? . . . The Communist Party of China is firmly opposed to civil war. The Soviet Union, the United States and Britain declared in the Crimea, "establish conditions of internal peace" and "form interim governmental authorities broadly representative of all democratic elements in the population and pledged to the earliest establishment through free elections of governments responsive to the will of the people."[1] That is exactly what the Communist Party of China has persistently advocated—the formation of a "coalition government." The carrying out of this proposal can prevent civil war. But there is one precondition—strength. If all the people unite and increase their strength, civil war can be prevented.

This commentary was written by Mao Tse-tung for the Hsinhua News Agency.

1. From the communiqué of the Yalta Conference of the United States, the United Kingdom, and the Soviet Union, February 11, 1945.

On Peace Negotiations with the Kuomintang
—Circular of the Central Committee of the Communist Party of China

August 26, 1945

The speedy surrender of the Japanese invaders has changed the whole situation. Chiang Kai-shek has monopolized the right to accept the surrender, and for the time being (for a stage) the big cities and important lines of communication will not be in our hands. Nevertheless, in northern China we should still fight hard, fight with all our might to take what we can. . . . We should gain control of whatever we can, even though temporarily. . . .

At present the Soviet Union, the United States and Britain all disapprove of civil war in China; at the same time our Party has put forward the three great slogans of Peace, Democracy and Unity, and is sending Comrades Mao Tse-tung, Chou En-lai and Wang Jo-fei[1] to Chungking to discuss with Chiang Kai-shek the great issues of unity and national reconstruction; thus it is possible that the civil war plot of the Chinese reactionaries may be frustrated. . . . We on our side are prepared to make such concessions as are necessary and as do not damage the fundamental interests of the people. . . . But we must at all times firmly adhere to, and never forget, these principles: unity, struggle, unity through struggle; to wage struggles with good reason, with advantage and restraint; and to make use of contradictions, win over the many, oppose the few and crush our enemies one by one. . . .

To sum up, our Party is confronted with many difficulties which must not be ignored, and all Party comrades must be well prepared mentally. But the general trend of the international and internal situation is favorable to our Party and to the people. So long as the

---

1. Wang Jo-fei was one of the earliest members of the Communist Party of China, and a member of its Fifth and Seventh Central Committees. During 1944–46 he took part on three occasions in negotiations between the Communist Party and the Kuomintang. In April 1946, he was killed in an air crash while returning to Yenan.

whole Party is united as one, we shall be able to overcome all difficulties step by step.

This inner-Party circular was drafted by Mao Tse-tung for the Central
Committee of the Chinese Communist Party two days before Mao
went to Chungking for the meeting with Chiang Kai-shek.

On the Chungking Negotiations

October 17, 1945

Let us talk about the present situation. That is what our comrades are interested in. This time the negotiations between the Kuomintang and the Communist Party at Chungking have lasted for
forty-three days. The results have already been published in the newspapers. The representatives of the two parties are continuing to
negotiate. The negotiations have borne fruit. The Kuomintang has
accepted the principles of peace and unity, recognized certain democratic rights of the people and agreed that civil war should be averted
and that the two parties should co-operate in peace to build a new
China. On these points agreement has been reached. There are other
points on which there is no agreement. The question of the Liberated
Areas has not been solved, and that of the armed forces has not really
been solved either. . . .

The Kuomintang is negotiating with us on the one hand, and is
vigorously attacking the Liberated Areas on the other. . . . Why does
the Kuomintang mobilize so many troops to attack us? Because long
ago it made up its mind to wipe out the people's forces, to wipe us
out. . . . In Chungking, some people think that Chiang Kai-shek is
unreliable and deceitful and that negotiations with him can lead
nowhere. . . . I told them that . . . we were firmly convinced
. . . that this would be the case. . . . I also met many foreigners,
including Americans, who sympathize with us. The broad masses of
the people in foreign countries are dissatisfied with the reactionary
forces in China and sympathize with the Chinese people's forces.
They also disapprove of Chiang Kai-shek's policies. We have many
friends in all parts of the country and of the world. . . .

All the means of propaganda in China, except the Hsinhua News Agency, are now controlled by the Kuomintang. They are all rumor factories. Concerning the current negotiations, they have spread the rumor that the Communist Party just wants territory and will make no concessions. . . . But we have said we are ready to make concessions. First, we proposed cutting our present armed strength to 48 divisions. As the Kuomintang has 263 divisions, this means our strength would be about one-sixth of the total. Later, we proposed a further reduction to 43 divisions. . . . Does this mean that we are going to hand over our guns to the Kuomintang? Not that either. If we hand over our guns, won't the Kuomintang have too many? The arms of the people, every gun and every bullet, must all be kept, must not be handed over. . . .

Now a few more words about our work. . . .

Many local cadres will be leaving their native places for the front. . . . We comrades are like seeds and the people are like the soil. Wherever we go, we must unite with the people, take root and blossom among them. . . . We must all go out to mobilize the masses, expand the people's forces and under the leadership of our Party, defeat the aggressor and build up a new China. . . .

This report was made by Mao Tse-tung to a meeting of cadres after his return from Chungking.

The Truth About the Kuomintang Attacks

November 5, 1945

In a dispatch from Chungking, dated November 3, the United Press reported that Wu Kuo-chen, Director of the Propaganda Department of the Kuomintang Central Executive Committee, had declared that "the government is entirely on the defensive in this war" and had proposed measures for "restoring communications." A Hsinhua News Agency reporter asked the spokesman for the Communist Party of China about this.

The spokesman for the Communist Party of China replied to the reporter as follows: "What Wu Kuo-chen said about being 'on the defensive' is a complete lie." . . .

The Hsinhua News Agency reporter went on to ask the spokesman for the Communist Party of China his views on the measures proposed by Wu Kuo-chen for restoring communications. The spokesman replied: These are nothing but stalling tactics. The Kuomintang authorities are mustering large forces and are trying to swamp all the Liberated Areas as in a great flood. . . . Why are the troops of the Liberated Areas, which fought strenuously and bitterly against Japan for eight years, not qualified to accept the Japanese surrender? . . . Local self-government is explicitly stipulated in the October 10 Agreement, and Dr. Sun Yat Sen long ago advocated the popular election of provincial governors; why does the Kuomintang Government still insist on dispatching local officials? . . .

In order quickly to stop the anti-popular and anti-democratic civil war which has now spread all over the country, we advocate the following:

1. All the Kuomintang Government forces that have entered the Liberated Areas . . . should be withdrawn immediately to their original positions. . . .

2. All puppet troops should be immediately disarmed and disbanded. . . .

3. The people's democratic self-government in all the Liberated Areas should be recognized. . . .

The spokesman said: "Only in this way can civil war be averted; otherwise there is absolutely no safeguard against it." . . .

This statement prepared by Mao Tse-tung was issued in the name of the spokesman for the Chinese Communist Party.

Rent Reduction and Production Are Two Important Matters for the Defense of the Liberated Areas

November 7, 1945

The Kuomintang, aided by the United States, is mobilizing all its forces to attack our Liberated Areas. Countrywide civil war is already a fact. Our Party's present task is to mobilize all forces, take the stand of self-defense, smash the attacks of the Kuomintang, defend the Liberated Areas and strive for the realization of peace. To achieve this aim the following have become very urgent tasks. See to it that in the Liberated Areas the peasants generally get the benefits of rent reduction, and that the workers and other laboring people benefit by appropriate wage increases and improved conditions; at the same time, see to it that the landlords can still make a living and that the industrial and commercial capitalists can still make profits. Unfold a large-scale production drive next year, increase the output of food and daily necessities, improve the people's livelihood, provide relief for victims of famine and for refugees and meet the needs of the army. Only when the two important matters of rent reduction and production are well handled can we overcome our difficulties, support the war and win victory. . . .

This inner-Party directive was drafted by Mao Tse-tung for the Central Committee of the Chinese Communist Party.

Policy for Work in the Liberated Areas for 1946

December 15, 1945

. . . The year 1945 will soon be over, and in 1946 we must pay attention to the following points in the work in all the Liberated Areas: .

1. . . . If no new development makes the Kuomintang stop its civil war . . . the central task of all the Liberated Areas is still to take a stand of self-defense and do their utmost to smash the Kuomintang attacks.

2. Spread the Kao Shu-hsun movement.[1]

3. . . . For the time being, we should stop expanding the number of troops and should make use of the intervals between battles to stress the training of troops. . . .

4. Reduce rent. . . . As for the workers, their wages should be appropriately raised. . . .

5. Production . . . should surpass any previous year in scale and achievements.

6. Finance . . . Decentralize management, give consideration to both army and people and to both public and private interests, and stress both production and economy. . . .

7. Support the government and cherish the people; support the army and give preferential treatment to the families of the armymen who fought in the War of Resistance. . . .

8. Relief . . . should depend mainly on mutual aid by the masses themselves, in addition to government measures. . . .

9. . . . There are large numbers of cadres from other areas doing the leading work at all levels. . . . The leading bodies of each area must tirelessly counsel these cadres to take good care of the local cadres and treat them with great warmth and goodwill. . . .

10. Calculate everything on a long-term basis. No matter how the situation develops, our Party must always calculate on a long-term basis, if our position is to be invincible. . . .

These ten points should receive special attention in our work in 1946. . . .

This inner-Party directive was drafted by Mao Tse-tung for the Central Committee of the Chinese Communist Party.

---

1. On October 30, 1945, Kao Shu-hsun, Deputy Commander of the Kuomintang's 11th War Zone, defected from the front in Hantan, Hopei Province, with one corps and one column.

Build Stable Base Areas in the Northeast

December 28, 1945

1. Our Party's present task in the Northeast is to build base areas, stable military and political base areas in eastern, northern and western Manchuria. . . .[1]

2. It should now be made clear that these base areas are not to be built in the big cities or along the main communication lines that are or will be occupied by the Kuomintang; under present conditions this is not practicable. . . .

3. After we have decided on the location of our stable base areas and disposed our forces and after our army's numerical strength has greatly increased, mass work will be the center of gravity of our Party's work in the Northeast. . . .

4. . . . Large numbers of our cadres and armed forces in the Northeast are newcomers, unfamiliar with the place and the people. Cadres are dissatisfied because we cannot occupy large cities and they are impatient with the arduous work of arousing the masses and building base areas. . . . Again and again we must teach all cadres from other areas to pay attention to investigation and study, to acquaint themselves with the place and the people and to resolve to become one with the people of the Northeast. . . .

5. Promptly delimit military areas and subareas in western, eastern and northern Manchuria and divide our forces into field armies and regional troops. . . .

6. This time over 100,000 of our troops have entered the Northeast and Jehol; the army there has recently expanded by more than 200,000, and the trend is to keep on expanding. . . .

7. . . . The Party organizations in the Northeast should now do everything possible to draw workers and intellectuals into our army

1. The eastern Manchuria base area included Kirin, Hsi-an, Antu, Yenchi, Tunhua and other places east of the Shenyang-Changchun section of the Chinese Changchun Railway. The northern Manchuria base included Harbin, Mutankiang, Pei-an and Kiamusze, among others. The western Manchuria base area included Tsitsihar, Tao-an, Kailu, Fuhsin, Chengchiatun, Fuyu and other places west of the Shenyang-Changchun section of the Chinese Changchun Railway.

and into the various construction tasks in the base areas, besides paying attention to underground work in the Kuomintang areas.

This directive, drafted by Mao Tse-tung for the Central Committee of the Chinese Communist Party, was addressed to its Northeast Bureau. Upon declaration of war by the Soviet Union against Japan, Soviet troops launched a massive attack upon the Japanese forces in Manchuria. Chinese Communist troops simultaneously entered the area, under command of Lin Piao, who was named by Mao Tse-tung as his heir apparent in 1969. Weapons captured from the Japanese by the Soviet Army were turned over to the Chinese Communists.

Some Points in Appraisal of the Present International Situation

April 1946

1. The forces of world reaction are definitely preparing a third world war, and the danger of war exists. . . . The question in the relations between the United States, Britain and France and the Soviet Union . . . is a question of compromise earlier or compromise later. . . .

2. The kind of compromise mentioned above does not mean compromise on all international issues. That is impossible so long as the United States, Britain and France continue to be ruled by reactionaries. . . .

3. Such compromise between the United States, Britain and France and the Soviet Union can be the outcome only of resolute, effective struggles by all the democratic forces of the world against the reactionary forces of the United States, Britain and France. . . .

This document was written by Mao Tse-tung to counteract the Chinese Communist pessimistic appraisal of world affairs at the time. It was not made public then and was circulated only among some leading members of the Central Committee.

Smash Chiang Kai-shek's Offensive by a War of Self-defense

July 20, 1946

1. Chiang Kai-shek, after violating the truce agreement . . . is now launching another large-scale offensive against us in eastern and northern China. . . .

2. . . . Although Chiang Kai-shek has U.S. aid, the feelings of the people are against him, the morale of his troops is low, and his economy is in difficulty. . . .

3. For defeating Chiang Kai-shek . . . the temporary abandonment of certain places or cities is . . . unavoidable . . . in order to win final victory.

4. In order to smash Chiang Kai-shek's offensive we must co-operate closely with the masses of the people and win over all who can be won over. . . .

5. In order to smash Chiang Kai-shek's offensive we must plan on a long-term basis. . . . We live plainly and work hard, we take care of the needs of both the army and the people; this is the very opposite of the situation in Chiang Kai-shek's areas, where those at the top are corrupt and degenerate, while the people under them are destitute. Under these circumstances, we shall surely be victorious. . . .

This inner-Party directive was drafted by Mao Tse-tung for the Central Committee of the Chinese Communist Party.

Talk with the American Correspondent Anna Louise Strong[1]

August 1946

STRONG: Do you think there is hope for a political, a peaceful settlement of China's problems in the near future?

MAO: That depends on the attitude of the U.S. Government. If the American people stay the hands of the American reactionaries who are helping Chiang Kai-shek fight the civil war, there is hope for peace. . . .

STRONG: What if the United States makes it clear that it will give Chiang Kai-shek no more help from now on?

MAO: There is no sign yet that the U.S. Government and Chiang Kai-shek have any desire to stop the war within a short time. . . .

STRONG: What do you think of the possibility of the United States starting a war against the Soviet Union?

MAO: There are two aspects to the propaganda about an anti-Soviet war. On the one hand, U.S. imperialism is indeed preparing a war against the Soviet Union; the current propaganda about an anti-Soviet war, as well as other anti-Soviet propaganda, is political preparation for such a war. On the other hand, the propaganda is a smoke screen put up by U.S. reactionaries to cover many actual contradictions immediately confronting U.S. imperialism. . . .

To start a war, the U.S. reactionaries must first attack th American people. They are already attacking the American people—oppressing the workers and democratic circles in the United States

1. Anna Louise Strong was born in Nebraska in 1885. She became a Quaker, social worker, child welfare exhibit expert, reporter, editor, lecturer, writer—first at her home in Seattle, then for thirty years in Moscow, and later on in Peking where at the age of eighty-four (1969) she is now living.

Anna Louise Strong earned her Ph.D. at the University of Chicago in 1908, and visited Hankow in 1925, where this writer first met her and obtained an interview for her with Marshal Wu Pei-fu which appeared in the Sunday magazine of *The New York Times*. She returned to Hankow in 1927, and ever since has been a militant Chinese Communist advocate.

Miss Strong, who spent the last twelve years of her life in China, died on March 29, 1970, in Peking, at the age of 84.

politically and economically and preparing to impose fascism there. The people of the United States should stand up and resist the attacks of the U.S. reactionaries. I believe they will. . . .

Using various pretexts, the United States is making large-scale military arrangements and setting up military bases in many countries. . . . I believe it won't be long before these countries come to realize who is really oppressing them, the Soviet Union or the United States. The day will come when the U.S. reactionaries find themselves opposed by the people of the whole world. . . . I think the American people and the peoples of all countries menaced by U.S. aggression should unite and struggle against the attacks of the U.S. reactionaries and their running dogs in these countries. Only by victory in this struggle can a third world war be avoided; otherwise it is unavoidable.

STRONG: That is very clear. But suppose the United States uses the atom bomb? Suppose the United States bombs the Soviet Union from its bases in Iceland, Okinawa and China?

MAO: The atom bomb is a paper tiger which the U.S. reactionaries use to scare people. It looks terrible, but in fact it isn't. Of course, the atom bomb is a weapon of mass slaughter, but the outcome of a war is decided by the people, not by one or two new types of weapon.

All reactionaries are paper tigers. . . . The czar was just a paper tiger. Wasn't Hitler once considered very strong? But history proved that he was a paper tiger. So was Mussolini, so was Japanese imperialism. . . .

Chiang Kai-shek and his supporters, the U.S. reactionaries, are paper tigers too. . . .

. . . Although the Chinese people still face many difficulties and will long suffer hardships from the joint attacks of U.S. imperialism and the Chinese reactionaries, the day will come when these reactionaries are defeated and we are victorious. The reason is simply this: the reactionaries represent reaction, we represent progress.

This was considered by Mao Tse-tung to be a very important statement. In it he put forward his thesis, "All reactionaries are paper tigers."

Concentrate a Superior Force to Destroy the Enemy Forces One by One

September 16, 1946

The method of fighting by concentrating a superior force to destroy the enemy forces one by one must be employed not only in the disposition of troops for a campaign but also in the disposition of troops for a battle. . . .

In the disposition for a battle . . . we should concentrate an absolutely superior force . . . select one (not two) of the weak spots in the enemy's positions, attack it fiercely and be sure to win. This accomplished, swiftly exploit the victory and destroy the enemy forces one by one. . . .

The principle of concentrating our forces to wipe out the enemy forces one by one has been a fine tradition of our army ever since its founding more than a decade ago; this is not the first time it has been put forward. . . . Now that Chiang Kai-shek's army has acquired more powerful weapons, it is necessary for our army to lay special stress on the method of concentrating a superior force to wipe out the enemy forces one by one. . . .

The principle of concentrating our forces to wipe out the enemy forces one by one is aimed chiefly at annihilating the enemy's effective strength, not at holding or seizing a place. . . .

However, we must hold or seize territory wherever the relative strength of the enemy and our own forces makes this possible or wherever such territory is significant for our campaigns or battles; to do otherwise would be a mistake. Therefore, those who succeed in holding or seizing such territory should also be commended.

This inner-Party directive was drafted by Mao Tse-tung for the Revolutionary Military Commission of the Central Committee of the Chinese Communist Party.

The Truth About U.S. "Mediation" and the Future of the Civil War in China

Talk with the American Correspondent A. T. Steele,[1] September 29, 1946

STEELE: Sir, do you consider that the U.S. effort to mediate in the Chinese civil war has failed? If the policy of the United States continues as at present, what will it lead to?

MAO: I doubt very much that the policy of the U.S. Government is one of "mediation." Judging by the large amount of aid the United States is giving Chiang Kai-shek to enable him to wage a civil war on an unprecedented scale, the policy of the U.S. Government is to use the so-called mediation as a smoke screen for strengthening Chiang Kai-shek's policy of slaughter so as to reduce China virtually to a U.S. colony. . . .

STEELE: How long will the Chinese civil war go on? What will be its outcome?

MAO: If the U.S. Government abandons its present policy of aiding Chiang Kai-shek . . . the Chinese civil war is sure to end at an early date. . . .

STEELE: Sir, do you consider Chiang Kai-shek the "natural leader" of the Chinese people? . . . If the Kuomintang tries to convene a National Assembly without participation of the Communist Party, what action will the Communist Party take?

MAO: There is no such thing in the world as a "natural leader." . . . The National Assembly must be convened jointly by various political parties, in line with the resolutions adopted by the Political Consultative Conference; otherwise we will firmly oppose it.

---

1. Archibald Trojan Steele was Far East correspondent for the New York *Herald Tribune* from 1931 to 1941; in Russia 1941–42; again in the Far East 1943–46, and for the Chicago *Daily News* in the Far East from 1946 to 1950. He is author of a survey published by the Council on Foreign Relations in 1966, *The American People and China*.

A Three Months' Summary

October 1, 1946

The Central Commitee directive of July 20 on the current situation stated: "We can defeat Chiang Kai-shek. The whole Party should be fully confident of this." . . .

The total of Chiang Kai-shek's regular troops attacking the Liberated Areas, not counting the puppet troops, the peace preservation corps and communications police corps, is more than 190 brigades. . . . Of the 190 odd brigades, 25 have been wiped out by our army in the past three months. . . .

In the coming period our task is to wipe out some 25 more enemy brigades. The completion of this task will make it possible to halt Chiang Kai-shek's offensive and recover part of our lost territory. . . .

In the past three months of war we have pinned down south of the Great Wall several of Chiang Kai-shek's crack forces, which he had originally planned to send to the Northeast, and have thus gained time for resting and consolidating our troops and for arousing the masses in the Northeast. . . .

The experience of the past three months has proved that in order to wipe out 10,000 enemy troops we have to pay a price of 2,000 to 3,000 casualties of our own. This unavoidable. . . .

The experience of these three months has proved that the peasants stood with our Party and our army against the attacks of Chiang Kai-shek's troops wherever the Central Committee's directive of May 4[1] was carried out firmly and speedily and the land problem was solved radically and thoroughly. . . .

The Kuomintang reactionaries, under the direction of the United States, have violated the truce agreement and the resolutions of the Political Consultative Conference of January this year and are determined to wage the civil war in their attempt to destroy the

1. This refers to the "Directive on the Land Question" issued by the Central Committee of the Communist Party of China on May 4, 1946. The Central Committee decided, in view of the peasants' demand for land, to change the land policy they had instituted of reduction of rent and interest to confiscation of the land of the landlords and its distribution among the peasants.

people's democratic forces. . . . More and more people now realize
the truth that Marshall's[2] mediation is a fraud and that the Kuomintang is the archcriminal of the civil war.

This inner-Party directive was drafted by Mao Tse-tung for the Central
Committee of the Chinese Communist Party.

Greet the New High Tide
of the Chinese Revolution

February 1, 1947

All circumstances now show that the situation in China is about to
enter a new stage of development. This new stage . . . will develop
into a great new people's revolution. . . .

. . . In seven months of fighting, from last July to this January,
we wiped out 56 brigades of Chiang Kai-shek's regular forces which
invaded the Liberated Areas. . . . If our armies can wipe out
another 40 to 50 brigades in the next few months and bring the
grand total up to about 100, there will be an important change in the
military situation.

Meanwhile, a great people's movement is unfolding in the Kuomintang areas. The riots of the people in Shanghai, which began on
November 30 of last year as a result of the Kuomintang's persecution
of the street vendors, and the student movement in Peiping, which
began last December 30 as a result of the rape of a Chinese girl
student by U.S. soldiers, both mark a new upsurge in the struggle of
the people in the Chiang Kai-shek areas. . . .

The circumstances in which this situation has arisen are that U.S.

2. In December 1945 the United States Government sent General
George C. Marshall to China as the President's special representative to
attempt mediation between the Nationalist Government of China and the
Communists. He failed utterly, for the simple reason that the only solution
acceptable to the Communists was one which would give them control of the
government of China. The mission was one which he indirectly admitted, in
a telephone conversation with this writer at his home in Leesburg, Virginia,
was quite futile.

imperialism and its running dog Chiang Kai-shek have replaced Japanese imperialism and its running dog Wang Ching-wei and adopted the policies of turning China into a U.S. colony, launching a civil war and strengthening the fascist dictatorship. . . .

These reactionary policies of U.S. imperialism and Chiang Kai-shek have forced all strata of the Chinese people to unite for their own salvation. . . .

The illegal and divisive "National Assembly," which was convened by Chiang Kai-shek in order to isolate our Party and other democratic forces, and the bogus constitution fabricated by that body enjoy no prestige at all among the people. . . . Our Party and other democratic forces adopted the policy of refusing to participate in the bogus National Assembly; this was perfectly correct. . . .

In order to gain a respite in which to replenish his troops and launch a fresh offensive, to obtain new loans and munitions from the United States and to allay the indignation of the people, Chiang Kai-shek is perpetrating a new hoax by demanding the resumption of so-called peace negotiations with our Party. Our Party's policy is not to refuse negotiations and in this way expose his deception. . . .

The military problem. In the past seven months of bitter fighting our army has proved that it can certainly smash Chiang Kai-shek's offensive and win final victory. . . .

The land problem. In about two-thirds of the territory in each Liberated Area, the Central Committee's directive of May 4, 1946, has been put into effect, the land problem has been solved and the policy of land to the tillers has been carried out. . . .

The reactionary forces and we both have difficulties. But the difficulties of the reactionary forces are insurmountable because they are forces on the verge of death and have no future. Our difficulties can be overcome because we are new and rising forces and have a bright future.

This inner-Party directive was drafted by Mao Tse-tung for the Central Committee of the Chinese Communist Party.

On the Temporary Abandonment of Yenan and the Defense of the Shensi-Kansu-Ningsia Border Region—Two Documents Issued by the Central Committee of the Communist Party of China

November 1946 and April 1947

DIRECTIVE OF NOVEMBER 18, 1946

Chiang Kai-shek is at the end of his rope. He wants to strike at our Party and strengthen himself by two methods, by convening the "National Assembly" and by attacking Yenan. Actually, he will accomplish the very opposite. . . . In short, Chiang Kai-shek has taken the road to ruin; as soon as he makes these two moves of convening the "National Assembly" and attacking Yenan, all his trickery will be exposed; this will help the progress of the People's War of Liberation. . . .

CIRCULAR OF APRIL 9, 1947

In order to save its moribund regime, the Kuomintang, besides taking such steps as convening the bogus National Assembly, drawing up the bogus constitution, driving out the representative agencies of our Party from Nanking, Shanghai and Chungking and proclaiming a break between the Kuomintang and the Communist Party, has taken the further step of attacking Yenan, the seat of our Party's Central Committee and the General Headquarters of the People's Liberation Army. . . .

In these circumstances, the Central Committee has decided as follows:

1. We must defend and expand the Shensi-Kansu-Ningsia Border Region. . . .
2. The Central Committee . . . and the General Headquarters of the People's Liberation Army must remain in the Shensi-Kansu-Ningsia Border Region. . . .

3. . . . We have set up a Working Committee of the Central Committee, with Comrade Liu Shao-chi as secretary . . . to carry out the tasks entrusted to it by the Central Committee.

These three decisions were made last month and have already been put into effect. You are hereby notified.

The Concept of Operations
for the Northwest War Theater

April 15, 1947

1. The enemy is now quite tired, but not yet tired out. He is in considerable difficulties with his food supply, but not yet in extreme difficulties. . . .

2. At present, despite the enemy's fatigue and shortage of food, his policy is to drive our main force east across the Yellow River, then seal off Suiteh and Michih and "exterminate" our troops there separately. . . .

3. Our policy is to continue our former method, that is, to keep the enemy on the run in this area for a time (about another month); the purpose is to tire him out completely, reduce his food supplies drastically and then look for an opportunity to destroy him. . . . This may be called the tactics of "wear and tear," that is, of wearing the enemy down to complete exhaustion and then wiping him out.

4. As you are now in localities east and north of Wayaopao, it would be best to induce the enemy to move to the north . . . then induce the enemy to move east . . . and induce the enemy to move west again.

5. But within a few days you must order the entire 359th Brigade . . . southward to make a surprise attack on the area south of the Yenchang-Yenan line and north of the Yinchuan-Lochuan line and cut the enemy's food transport line.

6. Please reply whether you consider the above views sound.

This telegram was sent by Mao Tse-tung to the Northwest Field Army commanded by Peng Teh-huai, Ho Lung, Hsi Chung-hsun, and others.

The Chiang Kai-shek Government Is Besieged by the Whole People

May 30, 1947

The Chiang Kai-shek Government, hostile to the whole people, now finds itself besieged by the whole people. . . .

The traitorous Chiang Kai-shek clique and its master, U.S. imperialism, have wrongly appraised the situation. They overestimated their own strength and underestimated the strength of the people. . . .

There are now two battle fronts in China. The war between Chiang Kai-shek's invading troops and the People's Liberation Army constitutes the first front. Now a second front has emerged, that is, the sharp struggle between the great and righteous student movement and the reactionary Chiang Kai-shek Government. . . . Public sympathy is all on the side of the students, Chiang Kai-shek and his running dogs are completely isolated, and his ferocious features have been completely unmasked. . . .

The extremely reactionary financial and economic policies long pursued by the Chiang Kai-shek Government have now been aggravated by the Sino-U.S. Treaty of Commerce, the most treasonable treaty ever known. On the basis of this treaty, U.S. monopoly capital and Chiang Kai-shek's bureaucrat-comprador capital have become tightly intertwined and control the economic life of the whole country. The results are unbridled inflation . . . soaring prices . . . bankruptcy of industry and commerce. . . .

On every battlefield Chiang Kai-shek's army has met with defeat. . . . As more and more news of the defeats of Chiang Kai-shek's troops at the front reaches his rear areas, the broad masses of the people there, suffocating under the oppression of his reactionary government, see more and more hope of ending their sufferings and winning their emancipation. . . .

This commentary was written by Mao Tse-tung for the Hsinhua News Agency.

Strategy for the Second Year of the War of Liberation

September 1, 1947

In the first year's fighting (from July last year to June this year), we wiped out 97½ regular brigades, or 780,000 men, and puppet troops, peace preservation corps and others totaling 340,000—altogether 1,120,000 of the enemy. . . .

In the second year of fighting, our army's basic task is to launch a countrywide counteroffensive, that is, to use our main forces to fight our way to exterior lines, carry the war into the Kuomintang areas . . . and completely wreck the Kuomintang's counterrevolutionary strategy. . . .

The keys to victory in fighting in the Kuomintang areas are, first, to be good at seizing the opportunities for fighting, to be brave and determined and win as many battles as possible; and, second, to carry out resolutely the policy of winning the masses and enable the broad masses to benefit so that they side with our army. . . .

The operational principles of our army are still the same as those laid down before:

Attack dispersed, isolated enemy forces first. . . .

Take medium and small cities and extensive rural areas first; take big cities later.

Make wiping out the enemy's effective strength our main objective. . . .

In every battle, concentrate an absolutely superior force, encircle the enemy forces completely, strive to wipe them out thoroughly and do not let any escape from the net. . . .

On the one hand, be sure to fight no battle unprepared . . . on the other hand, give full play to our fine style of fighting. . . .

Strive to draw the enemy into mobile warfare. . . .

Resolutely attack and seize all fortified points and cities which are weakly defended. . . .

Replenish our strength with all the arms and most of the soldiers captured from the enemy. . . .

The above sums up the year's fighting and sets forth the principles for future fighting. . . .

This inner-Party directive was drafted by Mao Tse-tung for the Central Committee of the Chinese Communist Party when he and the Central Committee were at Chukuanchai, northern Shensi. It formulated the basic policy of carrying the war into the Kuomintang areas—passing from the stage of strategic defensive to strategic offensive.

Manifesto of the Chinese People's Liberation Army
October 1947

The Chinese People's Liberation Army, having smashed Chiang Kai-shek's offensive, has now launched a large-scale counteroffensive. . . . Wherever our troops go, the enemy flees pell-mell before us and the people give thunderous cheers. The whole situation between the enemy and ourselves has fundamentally changed as compared with a year ago. . . .

Chiang Kai-shek's present policy of civil war is no accident but is the inevitable outcome of the anti-popular policy which he and his reactionary clique have consistently followed. As far back as 1927, Chiang Kai-shek, devoid of all gratitude, betrayed the revolutionary alliance between the Kuomintang and the Communist Party and betrayed the revolutionary Three People's Principles and the Three Great Policies of Sun Yat Sen; then he set up a dictatorship, capitulated to imperialism, fought ten years of civil war and brought on the aggression of the Japanese bandits. . . . Wherever Chiang Kai-shek's troops go, they murder and burn, rape and loot, carry out the policy of three atrocities and behave exactly like the Japanese bandits. . . . Funds for the civil war are borrowed from the United States on a large scale. In return for its favors, Chiang Kai-shek has presented U.S. imperialism with military bases and the rights of air flight and navigation and concluded with it a commercial treaty of enslavement[1]—acts of treason many times worse than those of Yuan Shi-kai. . . .[2]

. . . Today, the overwhelming majority of the people throughout the country . . . hope that our army will quickly . . . overthrow Chiang Kai-shek and liberate all China.

We are the army of the Chinese people and in all things we take the will of the Chinese people as our will. The policies of our army represent the urgent demands of the Chinese people and chief among them are the following:

1. Unite workers, peasants, soldiers, intellectuals and business-men. . . .

2. Arrest, try and punish the civil war criminals headed by Chiang Kai-shek.

3. Abolish the Chiang Kai-shek dictatorship. . . .

4. Abolish the rotten institutions of the Chiang Kai-shek regime. . . .

5. Confiscate the property of the four big families of Chiang Kai-shek, T. V. Soong, H. H. Kung, and the Chen Li-fu brothers. . . .

6. Abolish the system of feudal exploitation and put into effect the system of land to the tillers.

7. Recognize the right to equality and autonomy of the minority nationalities. . . .

8. Demand that the U.S. Government withdraw its troops stationed in China. . . . Unite in a common struggle with all nations which treat us as equals. . . .

Down with Chiang Kai-shek!
Long live New China!

This political manifesto was drafted by Mao Tse-tung for the General Headquarters of the Chinese People's Liberation Army. It was issued on October 10, 1947, and was known as the "October 10 Manifesto."

1. This refers to the "Sino-U.S. Treaty of Friendship, Commerce and Navigation" concluded between Nationalist China and the United States on November 4, 1946.

2. Yuan Shi-kai was the most powerful of the several warlords of north China in the last years of the Ching Dynasty. After the Ching Dynasty was overthrown by the revolt of the military in Wuchang in 1911, he became the first President of the Republic of China. He failed in an attempt to make himself Emperor, and died in June 1916.

On the Reissue of the Three Main Rules of Discipline and the Eight Points for Attention—Instruction of the General Headquarters of the Chinese People's Liberation Army

October 10, 1947

A. Our army's Three Main Rules of Discipline and Eight Points for Attention have been practiced for many years, but their contents vary slightly in army units in different areas. They have now been unified and are hereby reissued. . . .

B. The Three Main Rules of Discipline are as follows:

1. Obey orders in all your actions.
2. Don't take a single needle or piece of thread from the masses.
3. Turn in everything captured.

C. The Eight Points for Attention are as follows:

1. Speak politely.
2. Pay fairly for what you buy.
3. Return everything you borrow.
4. Pay for anything you damage.
5. Don't hit or swear at people.
6. Don't damage crops.
7. Don't take liberties with women.
8. Don't ill-treat captives.

The Present Situation and Our Tasks

December 25, 1947

The Chinese people's revolutionary war has now reached a turning point. That is, the Chinese People's Liberation Army has beaten back the offensive of several million reactionary troops of Chiang Kai-shek, the running dog of the United States of America, and gone over to the offensive. . . . In this land of China, the People's Liberation Army has turned back the wheel of counterrevolution—of U.S. imperialism and its lackey, the Chiang Kai-shek bandit gang—and sent it down the road to destruction and has pushed the wheel of revolution forward along the road to victory. This is a turning point in history. . . .

The rear areas of the People's Liberation Army are much more consolidated now than eighteen months ago. The reason is that our Party, standing resolutely on the side of the peasants, has carried out the land reform. During the War of Resistance Against Japan, our Party . . . changed its prewar policy of confiscating the land of the landlords and distributing it among the peasants to the policy of reducing rent and interest. . . . After the Japanese surrender, the peasants urgently demanded land, and we made a timely decision to change our land policy from reducing rent and interest to confiscating the land of the landlord class for distribution among the peasants. . . . But there should be no more repetition of the wrong ultra-Left policy, which was carried out in 1931–34, of "allotting no land to the landlords, and poor land to the rich peasants." . . . Here two fundamental principles must be observed. First, the demands of the poor peasants and farm laborers must be satisfied; this is the most fundamental task in the land reform. Second, there must be firm unity with the middle peasants, and their interests must not be damaged. As long as we grasp these two basic principles, we can certainly carry out our tasks in the land reform successfully. . . . Furthermore, as the rich peasants have more and better land, the demands of the poor peasants and farm laborers cannot be satisfied unless this land is distributed. . . . In determining class status, care must be taken to avoid the mistake of classifying middle peasants as rich peasants. . . . The whole Party must understand that thoroughgoing reform of the land system[1] is a basic task of the Chinese revolution in its present stage. If we can solve the land problem universally and completely, we shall have obtained the most fundamental condition for the defeat of all our enemies. . . .

The new-democratic revolution aims at wiping out only feudalism and monopoly capitalism, only the landlord class and the bureaucrat-capitalist class (the big bourgeoisie), and not at wiping out capitalism in general, the upper petty bourgeoisie or the middle bourgeoisie. In view of China's economic backwardness . . . it will still be necessary to permit the existence for a long time of the . . . upper petty bourgeoisie and middle bourgeoisie. . . . This capitalist sector will still be an indispensable part of the whole national economy. The upper petty bourgeoisie referred to here are small industrialists and merchants employing workers or assistants. In addition, there are also great numbers of small independent craftsmen and traders who employ no workers or assistants and, needless to say, they should be firmly protected. After the victory of the revolution all over the country, the new-democratic state will possess huge state enterprises taken over from the bureaucrat-capitalist class and . . . in these

---

1. The National Land Conference of the Communist Party of China was held in September 1947 in Hsipaipo Village, Hopei Province. The Outline Land Law of China, adopted by the conference on September 13, was published by the Central Committee of the Communist Party of China on October 10, 1947. It stipulated the following:

Abolish the land system of feudal and semifeudal exploitation and put into effect the system of land to the tillers.

All the land of the landlords and the public land in the villages is to be taken over by the local peasant associations and, together with all other land there, is to be equally distributed among the entire rural population, regardless of sex or age.

The peasant associations of the villages shall take over the draft animals, farm tools, houses, grain and other property of the rich peasants, distribute all this property among the peasants and other poor people who are in need of it and allot the same share to the landlords.

Thus the Outline Land Law not only confirmed the principle of "confiscation of the land of the landlords and its distribution among the peasants" laid down in the May 4 directive, but, in the view of the Central Committee, it also "made up for the lack of thoroughness in the directive, which had shown too much consideration for certain landlords."

circumstances the existence and development of these small and middle capitalist sectors will present no danger. . . .

To sum up, the economic structure of New China will consist of: (1) the state-owned economy, which is the leading sector; (2) the agricultural economy, developing step by step from individual to collective; and (3) the economy of small independent craftsmen and traders and the economy of small and middle private capital. . . . Any principle, policy or measure that deviates from this general objective is wrong. . . .

When the reactionary Chiang Kai-shek clique launched the countrywide civil war against the people in 1946, the reason they dared take this risk was that they relied not merely on their own superior military strength but mainly on the U.S. imperialists with their atom bombs, whom they regarded as "exceptionally powerful" and "matchless in the world." On the one hand, they thought U.S. imperialism could meet their military and financial needs with a stream of supplies. On the other, they wildly speculated that "war between the United States and the Soviet Union is inevitable," and that the "outbreak of a third world war is inevitable." . . .

But, in fact, is U.S. imperialism after World War II as powerful as Chiang Kai-shek and the reactionaries of other countries imagine? Can it really pour out a stream of supplies for them? No, that is not so. The economic power of U.S. imperialism, which grew during World War II, is confronted with unstable and daily shrinking domestic and foreign markets. The further shrinking of these markets will cause economic crises to break out. The war boom in the United States of America was only temporary. The strength of the United States of America is only superficial and transient. Irreconcilable domestic and international contradictions, like a volcano, menace U.S. imperialism every day; U.S. imperialism is sitting on this volcano. This situation has driven the U.S. imperialists to draw up a plan for enslaving the world. . . .

Within the United States, there are people's democratic forces which are getting stronger every day. . . . The Communist and Workers parties of nine European countries have established their Information Bureau and issued a call to the people of the world to rise against the imperialist plan of enslavement. . . .

We are soberly aware that on our way forward there will still be all kinds of obstacles and difficulties and that we should be prepared to deal with the maximum resistance and desperate struggle by all our enemies, domestic and foreign. But so long as we can grasp the science of Marxism-Leninism, have confidence in the masses, stand closely together with the masses and lead them forward, we shall be fully able to surmount any obstacle and overcome any difficulty. Our strength will be invincible. This is the historic epoch in which world capitalism and imperialism are going down to their doom and world socialism and people's democracy are marching to victory. The dawn is ahead, we must exert ourselves.

This report was made by Mao Tse-tung to a meeting of the Central Committee of the Chinese Communist Party held on December 25–28, 1947, at Yangchiakou, northern Shensi.

On Setting Up a System of Reports

January 7, 1948

In order to provide the Central Committee with timely information so that it can help all areas, either before or after the event, to avoid mistakes or commit fewer mistakes and win even greater victories in the revolutionary war, the following system of reports is instituted, beginning with this year.

1. For each bureau or sub-bureau of the Central Committee, the secretary is responsible for submitting to the Central Committee and its chairman a comprehensive bi-monthly report (written by himself, not by his assistants). The report should cover military, political, land reform, Party consolidation, economic, propaganda and cultural activities. . . . It should be written and telegraphed early in every odd month. . . .

2. Leaders of field armies and military areas . . . must also submit comprehensive policy reports and requests for instructions every two months, beginning this year. These should cover the discipline of the troops, their living conditions, the morale of commanders and

fighters, any deviations that have arisen . . . and the methods for overcoming them. . . .

This inner-Party directive was drafted by Mao Tse-tung for the Central Committee of the Chinese Communist Party.

On Some Important Problems of the Party's Present Policy

January 18, 1948

THE PROBLEM OF COMBATTING ERRONEOUS TENDENCIES WITHIN THE PARTY

Oppose overestimation of the enemy's strength. For example: fear of U.S. imperialism; fear of carrying the battle into the Kuomintang areas; fear of wiping out the comprador-feudal system, of distributing the land of the landlords and of confiscating bureaucrat capital; fear of a long-drawn-out war; and so on. . . . While we correctly point out that, strategically, with regard to the whole, we should take the enemy lightly, we must never take the enemy lightly in any part, in any specific struggle. If, with regard to the whole, we overestimate the strength of our enemy and hence do not dare to overthrow him . . . we shall be committing a right opportunist error. If, with regard to each part . . . we are not prudent . . . we shall be committing a "left" opportunist error. . . .

SOME CONCRETE PROBLEMS OF POLICY IN THE LAND REFORM AND MASS MOVEMENTS

The interests of the poor peasants and farm laborers and the forward role of the poor peasant leagues must be our first concern. . . . The slogan, "The poor peasants and farm laborers conquer the country and should rule the country," is wrong. In the villages, it is the farm laborers, poor peasants, middle peasants and other working people, united together under the leadership of the Chinese Communist Party . . . and not the poor peasants and farm laborers alone . . . who should rule the country. In the country as a whole, it is the workers, peasants (including the new rich peasants), small independent craftsmen and traders, middle and small capitalists oppressed and injured by the reactionary forces, the students, teachers, professors and ordinary intellectuals, professionals, enlightened gentry, ordinary government employees, oppressed minority nationalities and overseas Chinese, all united together under the leadership of the working class (through the Communist Party), who conquer the country and should rule the country, and it is not merely some of the people who conquer the country and should rule the country.

We must avoid adopting any adventurist policies toward the middle peasants. . . . We must avoid adopting any adventurist policies toward middle and small industrialists and merchants. . . . We must avoid adopting any adventurist policies toward students, teachers, professors, scientific workers, art workers and ordinary intellectuals. . . . Those enlightened gentry who went through hardships and tribulations together with our Party and actually made some contribution should be given consideration according to the merits of each case, provided that this does not interfere with land reform. . . . We must distinguish between new rich peasants and the old rich peasants. . . .

After the people's courts have given the handful of archcriminals who are really guilty of the most heinous crimes a serious trial and sentenced them . . . it is entirely necessary for the sake of revolutionary order to shoot them and announce their execution. That is one side of the matter. The other side is that we must insist on killing less and must strictly forbid killing without discrimination. To advocate killing more or killing without discrimination is entirely wrong; this would only cause our Party to forfeit sympathy, become alienated from the masses and fall into isolation. . . .

On the Problem of State Power

The new-democratic state power is the anti-imperialist and antifeudal state power of the masses of the people led by the working class. . . . The working class through its vanguard, the Communist

Party of China, exercises the leadership in this state belonging to the masses of the people and in its government. . . .

The organs of state power of the People's Republic of China are the people's congresses at different levels and the governments at different levels which these congresses elect. . . .

In the future after the revolution triumphs throughout the whole country, the central government and the local governments at all levels should be elected by the people's congresses at corresponding levels.

The Problem of the Relationship Between Those Who Lead and Those Who Are Led in the Revolutionary United Front

The leading class and the leading party must fulfill two conditions in order to exercise their leadership of the classes, strata, political parties and people's organizations which are being led:

(a) Lead those who are led (allies) to wage resolute struggle against the common enemy and achieve victories;

(b) bring material benefits to those who are led or at least not damage their interests and at the same time give them political education.

Without both these conditions, or with only one, leadership cannot be realized. . . .

This inner-Party directive was drafted by Mao Tse-tung for the Central Committee of the Chinese Communist Party.

The Democratic Movement in the Army

January 30, 1948

The policy for political work in our army units is fully to arouse the masses of soldiers, the commanders and all working personnel in order to achieve, through a democratic movement under centralized leadership, three major objectives, namely, a high degree of political unity, an improvement in living conditions and a higher level of military technique and tactics. The Three Check-ups and Three Improvements[1] now being enthusiastically carried out in our army units are intended to attain the first two of these objectives through the methods of political and economic democracy. . . .

The masses of soldiers should have the right to expose the errors and misdeeds of bad elements among the cadres. . . . Moreover, the soldiers should have the right, when necessary, to nominate those whom they trust from their own ranks for lower level cadre posts, subject to appointment by the higher level. . . . This is not to be the rule, however, but is to be done only when necessary.

This inner-Party directive was drafted by Mao Tse-tung for the Revolutionary Military Commission of the Central Committee of the Chinese Communist Party.

Different Tactics for Carrying Out the Land Law in Different Areas

February 3, 1948

In carrying out the Land Law, it is necessary to distinguish three kinds of areas and to adopt different tactics for each.

1. Old Liberated Areas established before the Japanese surrender. In general, land in these areas has long been distributed, and only a part of the distribution needs to be readjusted. . . .

2. Areas liberated between the Japanese surrender and the time of the general counteroffensive, that is, in the two years between September 1945 and August 1947. These now form the largest part

---

1. The "Three Check-ups" here mean checking on class origin, ideology and style of work; in the armed units, the check-ups were on class origin, performance of duty and will to fight. The "Three Improvements" mean organizational consolidation, ideological education and rectification of style of work.

of the Liberated Areas and can be called the semi-old Liberated Areas. . . . In these areas the Land Law is entirely applicable, the distribution of land should be universal and thorough. . . .

3. Areas newly liberated since the general counteroffensive. In these areas the masses have not yet been aroused, the Kuomintang, the landlords and rich peasants still have great influence, and all our work has not yet taken root. Therefore, we should not try to enforce the Land Law all at once but should do it in two stages. The first stage is to neutralize the rich peasants and strike blows exclusively at the landlords. . . . The second stage is to distribute the land rented out by the rich peasants, their surplus land and part of their other property, and to distribute that portion of the land of the landlords which was not thoroughly distributed in the first stage. The first stage should take about two years and the second a year. . . .

This was a telegram sent by Mao Tse-tung to Liu Shao-chi.

Correct the "Left" Errors in Land Reform Propaganda

February 11, 1948

In the past few months our news agency[1] and newspapers in many places have publicized without discrimination or analysis many unsound reports and articles containing "Left" deviationist errors. Here are some examples:

They did not propagate the line of relying on the poor peasants and farm laborers and firmly uniting with the middle peasants . . . but one-sidedly propagated a poor peasant-farm laborer line. They did not propagate the view that the proletariat should unite with all working people and . . . national bourgeoisie, the intellectuals and other patriots . . . who do not oppose land reform. . . .

Serious "Left" deviations existing in certain Liberated Areas have been either praised or ignored. . . . A few run completely counter

1. The Hsinhua News Agency is the official propaganda organ of the People's Republic of China, and is controlled by the Central Committee of the Communist Party of China.

to the principles and standpoint of Marxism-Leninism and depart completely from the line of the Central Committee. It is expected that the bureaus and the sub-bureaus of the Central Committee . . . will check up on the propaganda work of the last few months on the basis of Marxist-Leninist principles . . . correct their errors and see to it that their work helps to ensure victory in these great struggles—the war, the land reform, Party consolidation, the working-class movement—and to ensure victory in the whole anti-imperialist and anti-feudal revolution. . . .

This inner-Party directive was drafted by Mao Tse-tung for the Central Committee of the Chinese Communist Party.

Essential Points in Land Reform in the New Liberated Areas

February 15, 1948

Do not be impetuous. The speed of land reform should be determined according to the circumstances, the level of political consciousness of the masses and the strength of leading cadres. . . .

Land reform in a new Liberated Area should be divided into two stages. In the first stage, strike blows at the landlords and neutralize the rich peasants. . . . The second stage is the equal distribution of land, including the land rented out by the rich peasants and their surplus land. . . .

Do not start the work in all places at the same time, but choose strong cadres to carry it out first in certain places to gain experience, then spread the experience step by step and expand the work in waves. . . .

Pay strict attention to the protection of industry and commerce. Take a long-term view in the planning and management of economic and financial affairs. The armed forces and district and township governments should all guard against waste.

This inner-Party directive was drafted by Mao Tse-tung for the Central Committee of the Chinese Communist Party.

On the Policy Concerning
Industry and Commerce

February 27, 1948

Party organizations in certain places have violated the policy of the Central Committee of the Party concerning industry and commerce and seriously damaged both. These mistakes must be speedily corrected. . . .

Precautions should be taken against the mistake of applying in the cities the measures used in rural areas for struggling against landlords and rich peasants and for destroying the feudal forces. . . . A sharp distinction should also be made between the correct policy of developing production, promoting economic prosperity . . . and narrow-minded policy of "relief," which purports to uphold the workers' welfare but in fact damages industry and commerce and impairs the cause of the people's revolution. . . .

A revolutionary Party is carrying out a policy whenever it takes any action. . . . Therefore, before any action is taken, we must explain the policy, which we have formulated in the light of the given circumstances, to Party members and to the masses. Otherwise, Party members and the masses will depart from the guidance of our policy, act blindly and carry out a wrong policy.

This inner-Party directive was drafted by Mao Tse-tung for the Central Committee of the Chinese Communist Party.

On the Question of the National Bourgeoisie
and the Enlightened Gentry

March 1, 1948

The Chinese revolution at the present stage is in its character a revolution against imperialism, feudalism and bureaucrat capitalism waged by the broad masses of the people under the leadership of the proletariat. . . . The aim of the Chinese revolution at the present stage is to overthrow the rule of imperialism, feudalism and bureaucrat capitalism and to establish a new-democratic republic of the broad masses of the people with the working people as the main force; its aim is not to abolish capitalism in general.

We should not abandon the enlightened gentry who co-operated with us in the past and continue to co-operate with us at present, who approve of the struggle against the United States and Chiang Kai-shek and who approve of the land reform. . . .

The national bourgeoisie is a class which is politically very weak and vacillating. . . . However, because they are important economically and may either join in the struggle against the United States and Chiang Kai-shek or remain neutral in that struggle, it is possible and necessary for us to unite with them. Before the birth of the Communist Party of China, the Kuomintang headed by Sun Yat Sen represented the national bourgeoisie and acted as the leader of the Chinese revolution of that time (a nonthorough democratic revolution of the old type). But after the Communist Party of China was born and demonstrated its ability, the Kuomintang could no longer be the leader of the Chinese revolution (a new-democratic revolution). . . .

At the present stage the majority of the national bourgeoisie has a growing hatred of the United States and Chiang Kai-shek; its left-wingers attach themselves to the Communist Party and its right-wingers to the Kuomintang, while its middle elements take a hesitant, wait-and-see attitude between the two parties. These circumstances make it necessary to . . . be prudent in dealing with the economic position of this class and in principle we should adopt a blanket policy of protection. Otherwise we shall commit political errors. . . . At the present stage, what we require of them is that they favor the struggle against the United States and Chiang Kai-shek, favor democracy (not be anti-Communist) and favor the land reform. If they can meet these requirements, we should unite with them without exception and while uniting with them educate them.

This inner-Party directive was drafted by Mao Tse-tung for the Central Committee of the Chinese Communist Party.

On the Great Victory in the Northwest and on the New Type of Ideological Education Movement in the Liberation Army

March 7, 1948

Commenting on the recent great victory of the Northwest People's Liberation Army, a spokesman for the General Headquarters of the People's Liberation Army said: This victory has changed the situation in the Northwest and will effect the situation in the Central Plains. It has proved that through the new type of ideological education movement in the army by the methods of "pouring out grievances" and of the "Three Check-ups" the People's Liberation Army will make itself invincible.

The spokesman said: On this occasion, the Northwest People's Liberation Army suddenly encircled an enemy brigade at Yichuan, and Hu Tsung-nan ordered Liu Kan, Commander of his 29th Corps, to rush four brigades of two reorganized divisions from the Lochuan-Yichun line to the relief of Yichuan. They were the 31st and 47th Brigades of the Reorganized 27th Division and the 53rd and 61st Brigades of the Reorganized 90th Division, totaling more than 24,000 men; they reached the area southwest of Yichuan on February 28. The Northwest People's Liberation Army started a battle of annihilation and in thirty hours of fighting on February 29 and March 1 completely wiped out these reinforcements, letting none escape from the net. More than 18,000 men were captured, and more than 5,000 were killed and wounded; Liu Kan himself, Yen Ming, Commander of the 90th Division, and other officers were killed. Then on March 3 we captured Yichuan and here again wiped out over 5,000 men of the 24th Brigade of the enemy's Reorganized 76th Division which was defending the city. In this campaign we wiped out, all told, one corps headquarters, two division headquarters and five brigades of the enemy, a total of 30,000 men. This is our first great victory in the Northwest theater." . . .

The spokesman emphatically pointed out: The combat effectiveness of our Northwest Field Army is far higher than at any time last year. . . . What is most noteworthy, however, is the new type of ideological education movement in the army, which was carried out for more than two months last winter by the methods of pouring out grievances and the Three Check-ups. The correct unfolding of the movement for pouring out grievances (the wrongs done to the laboring people by the old society and by the reactionaries) and the Three Check-ups (on class origin, performance of duty and will to fight) greatly heightened the political consciousness of commanders and fighters throughout the army in the fight for the emancipation of the exploited working masses, for nationwide land reform and for the destruction of the common enemy of the people, the Chiang Kai-shek bandit gang. . . .

The spokesman said: It is not only in the Northwest that this new type of ideological education movement in the army has been carried out . . . it is being carried on in the People's Liberation Army throughout the country. . . . This ideological education movement is bound to make the People's Liberation Army invincible. However desperate the exertions of the Chiang Kai-shek bandit gang and its master, U.S. imperialism, against the great struggle of the Chinese people's democratic revolution, victory will certainly be ours.

This commentary was drafted by Mao Tse-tung for the spokesman of the General Headquarters of the Chinese People's Liberation Army.

A Circular on the Situation

March 20, 1948

In recent months the Central Committee has concentrated on solving, in the new conditions, problems concerning specific policies and tactics for land reform, industry and commerce, the united front, Party consolidation and the work in the new Liberated Areas; it has also combatted Right and "Left" deviations within the Party, mainly "Left" deviations. The history of our Party shows that Right deviations are likely to occur in periods when our Party has formed a united front with the Kuomintang and that "Left" deviations are likely to occur in periods when our Party has broken with the Kuomintang. . . .

Certain democratic personages, who had believed that a so-called "third road" was still possible and had placed themselves midway between the Kuomintang and the Communist Party because of certain illusions about the United States and Chiang Kai-shek and because of their skepticism as to whether our Party and the people had the strength to defeat all enemies at home and abroad, found themselves in a passive position in the face of the sudden Kuomintang offensive; eventually in January 1948, they accepted our Party's slogans and declared themselves against Chiang Kai-shek and the United States and for unity with the Communist Party and the Soviet Union. . . .

We do not contemplate setting up the Central People's Government this year, because the time is not yet ripe. After the bogus National Assembly[1] elects Chiang Kai-shek President later in the year and he is even more thoroughly discredited, after we score bigger victories and expand our territories, preferably after the capture of one or two of the country's largest cities, and after northeastern China, northern China, Shantung, northern Kiangsu, Honan, Hupeh and Anhwei are all linked together in one contiguous area, it will be entirely necessary to establish the Central People's Government. The time will probably be in 1949. . . .

This inner-Party circular was written by Mao Tse-tung for the Central Committee of the Chinese Communist Party.

Speech at a Conference of Cadres in the Shansi-Suiyuan Liberated Area

April 1, 1948

Comrades! Today I wish to speak chiefly on some problms relating to our work in the Shansi-Suiyuan Liberated Area and also on some problems relating to our work in the country as a whole.

1. The National Assembly of the Republic of China, held from March 29 to May 1, 1948, elected Chiang Kai-shek as President and Li Tsung-jen as Vice President.

I

In my opinion, the work of land reform and of Party consolidation carried out during the past year in the area led by the Shansi-Suiyuan Sub-Bureau of the Central Committee of the Communist Party of China has been successful. . . .

"From now on" the people of the Shansi-Suiyuan Liberated Area are saying, "no one will ever again dare to be feudalist, to bully others or indulge in corruption." . . .

The most fundamental method of work which all Communists must firmly bear in mind is to determine our working policies according to actual conditions. When we study the causes of the mistakes we have made, we find that they all arose because we departed from the actual situation at a given time and place and were subjective in our working policies. This should be a lesson for all comrades. . . .

Those Party members and cadres who have made mistakes but can still be educated and are different from the incorrigibles should all be educated and not abandoned, whatever their class origin. It is likewise correct that you have carried out, or are carrying out, this policy. . . .

The great mass struggles for land reform and Party consolidation have taught and brought to the fore tens of thousands of activists and cadres. They are linked with the masses and will be a most precious asset of the People's Republic of China. Henceforth, we should strengthen their education so that they will make constant progress in their work. Meanwhile they should be warned not to let success and commendation make them conceited and self-satisfied. . . .

The task before the Shansi-Suiyuan Party organization is to make the greatest effort to complete the land reform and Party consolidation, to continue and support the People's War of Liberation, to refrain from any further increase in the people's burden but appropriately to lighten it, and to restore and develop production. . . . You have a widespread agriculture and handicraft industry as well as some light and heavy industries using machinery. I hope you will do a good job in leading these productive enterprises, otherwise you cannot be called good Marxists. . . .

You can see clearly that neither the Party consolidation, nor the ideological education in the army, nor the land reform, all of which

we have accomplished and all of which have great historic significance, could be undertaken by our enemy, the Kuomintang. . . .
They are so corrupt, so torn by ever-increasing and irreconcilable
internal quarrels, so spurned by the people and utterly isolated and so
frequently defeated in battle that their doom is inevitable. This is the
whole situation of revolution versus counterrevolution in China. . . .

Feudalism is the ally of imperialism and bureaucrat capitalism and
the foundation of their rule. Therefore, the reform of the land system
is the main content of China's new-democratic revolution. . . . We
support the peasants' demand for equal distribution of land in order
to help arouse the broad masses of peasants speedily to abolish the
system of landownership by the feudal landlord class, but we do not
advocate absolute equalitarianism. Whoever advocates absolute
equalitarianism is wrong. There is a kind of thinking now current in
the countryside which undermines industry and commerce and
advocates absolute equalitarianism in land distribution. Such thinking is reactionary, backward and retrogressive in nature. . . . Except
for the most heinous counterrevolutionaries and local tyrants, who
have incurred the bitter hatred of the broad masses, who have been
proved guilty and who therefore may (and ought to) be punished, a
policy of leniency must be applied to all, and any beating or killing
without discrimination must be forbidden. . . .

You comrades know that our Party has laid down the general line
and general policy of the Chinese revolution. . . . If we actually
forget the Party's general line and general policy, then we shall be
blind, half-baked, muddleheaded revolutionaries . . . and the work
will suffer. . . .

Let me repeat . . . . To rely on the poor peasants, unite with the
middle peasants, abolish the system of feudal exploitation step by step
and in a discriminating way, and develop agricultural production—
this is the general line and general policy of the Communist Party of
China in the work of land reform during the period of the new-
democratic revolution.

A Talk to the Editorial Staff
of the *Shansi-Suiyuan Daily*

April 2, 1948

Our policy must be made known not only to the leaders and to the cadres but also to the broad masses. Questions concerning policy should as a rule be given publicity in the Party papers or periodicals. We are now carrying out the reform of the land system. The policies of land reform should be published in the papers and broadcast on the radio so that the broad masses all know them. Once the masses know the truth and have a common aim, they will work together with one heart. This is like fighting a battle; to win a battle the fighters as well as the officers must be of one heart. . . .

A basic principle of Marxism-Leninism is to enable the masses to know their own interests and unite to fight for their own interests. The role and power of the newspapers consists in their ability to bring the Party program, the Party line, the Party's general and specific policies, its tasks and methods of work before the masses in the quickest and most extensive way. . . .

You comrades are newspapermen. Your job is to educate the masses, to enable the masses to know their own interests, their own tasks and the Party's general and specific policies. . . .

To be good at translating the Party's policy into action of the masses, to be good at getting not only the leading cadres but also the broad masses to understand and master every movement and every struggle we launch—this is an art of Marxist-Leninist leadership. . . .

To teach the masses, newspaper workers should first of all learn from the masses. You comrades are all intellectuals. Intellectuals are often ignorant and often have little or no experience in practical matters. . . . To change from lack of understanding to understanding, one must do things and see things; that is learning. Comrades working on the newspapers should go out by turns to take part in mass work, in land reform work for a time; that is very necessary. . . . Only thus will you be able to do your work well, will you be able to shoulder your task of educating the masses.

The *Shansi-Suiyean Daily* made very great progress following the conference of secretaries of prefectural Party committees last June. . . . But since January this year, when we began to correct "Left" deviations, your paper seems to have lost some of its spirit. . . . When you have summed up your experience in combatting Right and "Left" deviations and become more clearheaded, your work will improve. . . .

Your shortcomings lay chiefly in drawing the bowstring much too tight. If a bowstring is too taut, it will snap. The ancients said, "The principle of Kings Wen and Wu was to alternate tension with relaxation."[1] Now "relax" a bit and the comrades will become more clearheaded. . . .

Newspapers run by our Party and all the propaganda work of our Party should be vivid, clear-cut and sharp and should never mutter and mumble. That is the militant style proper to us, the revolutionary proletariat. Since we want to teach the people to know the truth and arouse them to fight for their own emancipation, we need this militant style. A blunt knife draws no blood.

Telegram to the Headquarters of the Loyang Front After the Recapture of the City

April 8, 1948

Loyang is now recaptured[2] and can probably be securely held. In our urban policy, pay attention to the following points:

Be prudent in the liquidation of the organs of Kuomintang rule,

1. From the *Book of Rites,* Miscellaneous Records, Part II. "Kings Wen and Wu could not keep a bow in permanent tension without relaxation. Nor would they leave it in a permanent state of relaxation without tension. The principle of Kings Wen and Wu was to alternate tension with relaxation." Wen and Wu were the first two Kings of the Chou Dynasty (twelfth to third century B.C.).

2. Loyang (Honanfu) was an important city in a highly developed agricultural area of western Honan Province. It was taken by the People's Liberation Army on March 14, 1948, but subsequently evacuated. It was recaptured from Nationalist Government forces on April 5, 1948.

arrest only the chief reactionaries and do not involve too many persons.

Set a clear line of demarcation in defining bureaucrat capital; do not designate as bureaucrat-capital and do not confiscate all the industrial and commercial enterprises run by Kuomintang members. . . . The workers and technicians in these industrial and commercial enterprises should be organized to participate in management, and their competence should be trusted. . . .

Forbid peasant organizations to enter the city to seize landlords and settle scores with them. . . . Those who have committed the most heinous crimes may be sent back to the villages to be dealt with. . . .

Do not be in a hurry to organize the people of the city to struggle for democratic reforms and improvements in livelihood. These matters can be properly handled in the light of local conditions only when the municipal administration is in good working order, public feeling has become calm, careful surveys have been made. . . .

Do not raise the slogan, "Open up the granaries to relieve the poor." Do not foster among them the psychology of depending on the government for relief. . . .

Plan everything on a long-term basis. It is strictly forbidden to destroy any means of production, whether publicly or privately owned, and to waste consumer goods. Extravagant eating and drinking are forbidden, and attention should be paid to thrift and economy. . . .

This telegram was drafted by Mao Tse-tung for the Central Committee of the Chinese Communist Party.

Tactical Problems of Rural Work in the New Liberated Areas

May 24, 1948

It is necessary to give overall consideration to the tactical problems of rural work in the new Liberated Areas. . . . Premature distribution of land would prematurely place the entire burden of military requirements on the peasants instead of on the landlords and rich peasants. In the sphere of social reform, it is better not to distribute movable property[1] and land, but instead to reduce rent and interest universally so that the peasants will receive tangible benefits. . . . In this way, social wealth will not be dispersed and public order will be comparatively stable, and this will help us concentrate all our forces on destroying the Kuomintang reactionaries.

This was a telegram from Mao Tse-tung to Teng Hsiao-ping.

The Work of Land Reform and of Party Consolidation in 1948

May 25, 1948

It is necessary to pay attention to the seasons. In areas designated by the bureaus or sub-bureaus of the Central Committee, the whole of next autumn and winter, that is, the seven months from this September to next March, must be devoted to carrying out the following tasks in the proper order:

1. Make an investigation of rural conditions.
2. Carry out the initial work for Party consolidation in accordance with correct policy. A working corps or working team sent by a higher organ to a rural district must first of all unite with all the activists and better members in the local Party branch and together with them lead the work of land reform.
3. Organize or reorganize or strengthen the poor peasant leagues and the peasant associations and launch the land reform struggle.
4. Identify class status according to correct criteria.
5. Distribute feudal land and property in accordance with correct policy. The final result of the distribution must be such that it is considered fair and reasonable by all the main strata and that the landlords too feel that there is a way for them to make a living and that this is assured.

1. "Movable property" refers to grain, clothing, money, jewelry, and other valuables.

6. Form people's representative conferences and elect government councils at the township (or village), district and county levels.

7. Issue land certificates fixing the ownership of land.

8. Adjust or revise the rates of the agricultural tax (i.e., public grain). These rates must conform to the principle of giving consideration to both public and private interests; in other words, they must on the one hand help support the war and on the other get the peasants interested in restoring and developing production, which will help improve their livelihood.

9. Complete the work of the organizational consolidation of the Party branches in accordance with correct policy.

10. Shift our work from land reform to rallying all the rural working people and to organizing the labor power of the landlords and rich peasants in a general struggle to restore and develop agricultural production. Start organizing small-scale work-exchange groups and other co-operative units according to the principles of voluntary participation and exchange of equal values; prepare seed, fertilizer and fuel; work out production plans; issue agricultural credits (chiefly loans for means of production, to be definitely repaid and to be strictly distinguished from relief grants) when necessary and possible; draw up plans, where possible, for building water conservancy works.

This whole process of work from land reform to production, a process which all comrades directly engaged in land reform must be brought to understand so that they can avoid one-sidedness in their work and, without missing the seasons, accomplish all the above tasks in the coming autumn and winter.

This inner-Party directive was drafted by Mao Tse-tung for the Central Committee of the Chinese Communist Party.

The Concept of Operations
for the Liaohsi-Shenyang Campaign[1]

September and October 1948

THE TELEGRAM OF SEPTEMBER 7

We are prepared to bring about the fundamental overthrow of the Kuomintang in about five years, counting from July 1946. This is possible. Our objective can be attained provided we destroy about 100 brigades of Kuomintang regular troops every year, or some 500 brigades over the five years. In the past two years our army has annihilated a total of 191 brigades of enemy regulars, an average of 95½ brigades a year, or nearly 8 brigades a month. In the next three years it is required that our army should wipe out 300 or more brigades of enemy regulars. . . .

If in the two months of September and October, or a little longer, you can wipe out the enemy along the line from Chinchow to Tangshan and take Chinchow, Shanhaikuan and Tangshan, you will have achieved the task of wiping out some 18 enemy brigades. . . . Because the enemy forces in and near Chinchow, Shanhaikuan and Tangshan are isolated from each other, success in attacking and wiping them out is pretty certain, and there is also a fair hope of success in capturing Chinchow and in attacking enemy reinforcements. . . .

THE TELEGRAM OF OCTOBER 10

1. From the day you start attacking Chinchow, there will be a period when the tactical situation will be very tense. . . .

2. If the enemy's reinforcements from Shenyang advance to the area north of the Taling River just after you have taken Chinchow

1. The Liaohsi-Shenyang campaign was a hard-fought battle in the western part of Liaoning Province and in the Shenyang-Changchun area (both in Manchuria), between September 12 and November 2, 1948.

and when you are thus able to shift your forces to encircle them, then it will be possible to wipe out these reinforcements as well. The key to all this lies in striving to capture Chinchow in about a week.

3. Decide on the disposition of your troops for checking the enemy reinforcements according to your progress in attacking Chinchow and their progress in advancing both from the east and from the west. . . . If most of the Chinchow enemy forces have been wiped out and the capture of the city is imminent, then you should let the enemy forces from Shenyang advance deep into the area north of the Taling River, so that you can make a timely shift of your forces to encircle them and wipe them out at your convenience.

4. You must center your attention on the operations in Chinchow and strive to capture this city as quickly as possible. Even if none of the other objectives is attained and Chinchow alone is captured, you will have won the initiative, which in itself will be a great victory. . . .

These telegrams addressed to Lin Piao, Lo Jung-huan and other commanders were drawn up by Mao Tse-tung for the Revolutionary Military Commission of the Central Committee of the Chinese Communist Party. The success of this campaign laid the groundwork for Communist victory throughout northeast China.

On Strengthening the Party Committee System

September 20, 1948

The Party committee system is an important Party institution for ensuring collective leadership and preventing any individual from monopolizing the conduct of affairs. It has recently been found that in some (of course not all) leading bodies it is the habitual practice for one individual to monopolize the conduct of affairs and decide important problems. . . . This situation must be changed. From now on, a sound system of Party committee meetings must be instituted in all leading bodies. . . .

Party committee meetings must be divided into two categories, standing committee meetings and plenary sessions, and the two should not be confused. . . . In the army, the person in command has the right to make emergency decisions during battle and when circumstances require.

This decision was drafted by Mao Tse-tung for the Central Committee of the Chinese Communist Party.

On the September Meeting—Circular of the Central Committee of the Communist Party of China

October 10, 1948

In September 1948 the Central Committee convened a meeting of the Political Bureau, attended by seven members of the Political Bureau, fourteen members and alternate members of the Central Committee and ten important functionaries, including principal leading comrades in the Party and army in northern China, eastern China, the Central Plains and northwestern China. This meeting convened by the Central Committee had the largest attendance of any since the Japanese surrender. The meeting examined the work of the past period and set the tasks for the period ahead. . . .

In the last two years of fighting, from July 1946 to June 1948, the People's Liberation Army has wiped out 2,640,000 enemy troops, including 1,630,000 captured. The main war booty of the two years amounts to nearly 900,000 rifles, over 64,000 heavy and light machine guns, 8,000 pieces of light artillery, 5,000 pieces of infantry artillery and 1,100 heavy mountain and field guns. In these two years the People's Liberation Army has grown from 1,200,000 men to 2,800,000. Our regular troops have increased from 118 brigades to 176, that is, from 610,000 men to 1,490,000. The Liberated Areas now cover 2,350,000 square kilometers, or 24.5 per cent of China's total area of 9,597,000 square kilometers; their population is 168 million, or 35.3 per cent of China's total of 475 million; and they have 586 large, medium and small cities, from county towns up, or 29 per cent of China's total of 2,009 such cities. . . .

Our Party membership has increased from 1,210,000 in May 1945 to 3,000,000 at present. In 1927, before the Kuomintang betrayal of the revolution, it was 50,000; after the Kuomintang betrayal of that year it dropped to about 10,000; in 1934, as a result of the successful development of the agrarian revolution, it rose to 300,000; in 1945, because of the successful development of the War of Resistance Against Japan, it rose to 1,210,000; and now . . . it has reached 3,000,000. . . .

The military strength of the Kuomintang was 4,300,000 men in July 1946. In the past two years, 3,090,000 of its men have either been wiped out or have deserted, and 2,440,000 have been recruited. Its present strength is 3,650,000. It is estimated that in the coming three years the Kuomintang may still be able to recruit 3,000,000 men and that some 4,500,000 will probably be wiped out or desert. Thus, as a result of five years' fighting, the remaining military strength of the Kuomintang will probably be only some 2,000,000. Our army now has 2,800,000 men. In the coming three years we plan to admit into our forces 1,700,000 captured soldiers (estimated at 60 per cent of the total we shall capture) and to mobilize 2,000,000 peasants to join the army. Allowing for depletion, our army, as a result of five years' fighting, will probably approach 5,000,000 men. If five years' fighting brings these results, then it may be said that we have overthrown the reactionary rule of the Kuomintang completely. . . .

The task of seizing political power throughout the country demands that our Party should quickly and systematically train large numbers of cadres to administer military, political, economic, Party, cultural and educational affairs. . . . We should make use of large numbers of working personnel from the Kuomintang's economic, financial, cultural and educational institutions, excluding the reactionary elements. . . .

. . . We are arranging . . . to convene a conference in 1949 of the representatives of all China's democratic parties, people's organizations and democrats without Party affiliation, in order to establish the provisional central government of the People's Republic of China. . . .

The Sixth National Labor Congress[1] has been successfully held

1. The Sixth National Labor Congress was held in Harbin in August 1948. The All-China Federation of Trade Unions was re-established at the congress. The previous five National Labor Congresses were held in 1922, 1925, 1926, 1927, and 1929, respectively.

and the All-China Federation of Trade Unions has been founded. In the first half of next year a National Women's Congress will be convened to form the All-China Federation of Democratic Women,[2] a National Youth Congress will be convened to form the All-China Youth Federation,[3] and the New Democratic Youth League[4] will be established.

This inner-Party circular was drafted by Mao Tse-tung for the Central Committee of the Chinese Communist Party. The September 1948 meeting was held in Hsipaipo Village, Hopei Province.

The Concept of Operations
for the Huai-Hai Campaign[5]

October 11, 1948

Here are a few points for your consideration concerning the dispositions for the Huai-Hai campaign.

1. In the first stage of this campaign, the central task is to concentrate forces to wipe out Huang Po-tao's army, effect a breakthrough

2. The First National Women's Congress was held in March 1949 in Peiping. The All-China Federation of Democratic Women was founded at this congress, and later renamed the National Women's Federation of the People's Republic of China.

3. The first session of the National Youth Congress was held in May 1949 in Peiping. The All-China Federation of Democratic Youth was founded at this session, and later renamed the All-China Youth Federation.

4. The New Democratic Youth League was founded in January 1949 in accordance with a decision of the Central Committee of the Communist Party of China. Its First National Congress was held in Peiping in April 1949. It was renamed the Communist Youth League at its Third National Congress in May 1957.

5. The Huai-Hai campaign was decisive in the war between the People's Liberation Army and the forces of the Republic of China. It was fought over a wide territory in central China—in Kiangsu, Shantung, Anhwei, and Honan Provinces, centering on Hsuchow, and extending as far as Haichow in the east, Shangchiu in the west, Lincheng (later renamed Hsuehcheng) in the north, and the Huai River in the south.

in the center and capture Hsinanchen, the Grand Canal Railway Station, Tsaopachi, Yihsien, Tsaochuang, Lincheng, Hanchuang, Shuyang, Pihsien, Tancheng, Taierchuang and Linyi. To achieve these objectives, you should use two columns to wipe out each enemy division. . . .

2. In the second stage, use about five columns to attack and wipe out the enemy in Haichow, Hsinpu, Lienyunkang and Kuanyun and capture these towns.

3. In the third stage, it may be assumed that the battle will be fought around Huaiyin and Huai-an. By that time . . . we must be prepared again to use about five columns as the attacking force, while using the rest of our main force to strike at and hold down the enemy's reinforcements. This stage will also take about two to three weeks. . . .

4. You are to complete the Huai-Hai campaign in two months, November and December. . . . By autumn your main force will probably be fighting to cross the Yangtze.

This telegram, addressed to the Eastern China and Central Plains Field Armies and the Bureaus of the Central Committee of the Communist Party of China in those two areas, was drafted by Mao Tse-tung. Chinese Communist sources claim that in this campaign over 555,000 Nationalist troops were "wiped out," and that on its conclusion, on January 10, 1949, the Nationalist Government at Nanking "fell apart."

Revolutionary Forces of the World Unite, Fight Against Imperialist Aggression!
November 1948

At this time, when the awakened working class and all genuine revolutionaries of the world are jubilantly celebrating the thirty-first anniversary of the Great October Socialist Revolution of the Soviet

Union, I recall a well-known article by Stalin, written in 1918 on the first anniversary of that revolution. In that article Stalin said:[1]

The great world-wide significance of the October Revolution chiefly consists in the fact that:

1. It has widened the scope of the national question and converted it from the particular question of combatting national oppression in Europe into the general question of emancipating the oppressed peoples, colonies and semi-colonies from imperialism;

2. It has opened up wide possibilities for their emancipation and the right paths towards it, has thereby greatly facilitated the cause of emancipation of the oppressed peoples of the West and the East, and has drawn them into the common current of the victorious struggle against imperialism;

3. *It has thereby erected a bridge between the socialist West and the enslaved East,* having created a new front of revolutions *against* world imperialism, extending from the proletarians of the West, through the Russian revolution, to the oppressed peoples of the East.

History has developed in the direction pointed out by Stalin. The October Revolution . . . has created a new front of revolutions against world imperialism. . . . This front of revolutions has been created and developed under the brilliant guidance of Lenin, and after Lenin's death, of Stalin. . . .

The radiance of the October Revolution shines upon us. . . . We enjoy the support of the Communist parties and the working class of the world. . . . Before long, people will witness the complete destruction of the whole reactionary regime of the Kuomintang by the Chinese people. The Chinese people are brave, so is the Communist Party of China, and they are determined to liberate all China.

This article was written by Mao Tse-tung in commemoration of the thirty-first anniversary of the October Revolution for the organ of the Information Bureau of the Communist and Workers Parties of Europe, *For a Lasting Peace, For a People's Democracy.* It appeared in the twenty-first issue in 1948.

1. In "The October Revolution and the National Question," Section III, "The World-wide Significance of the October Revolution," J. V. Stalin, *Works* (Engl. ed., Moscow, 1953), Vol. IV, pp. 169–170.

The Momentous Change in China's Military Situation

November 14, 1948

The military situation in China has reached a new turning point and the balance of forces between the two sides in the war has undergone a fundamental change. The People's Liberation Army, long superior in quality, has now become the superior in numbers as well. This is a sign that the victory of the Chinese revolution and the realization of peace in China are at hand. . . .

Accordingly, the war will be much shorter than we originally estimated. . . .

The enemy is collapsing rapidly, but the Communists, the People's Liberation Army and people of all walks of life throughout the country must continue to unite as one man and redouble their efforts; only thus can we finally and completely wipe out the reactionary forces and build a united, democratic people's republic in the whole country.

This commentary was written by Mao Tse-tung for the Hsinhua News Agency.

The Concept of Operations for the Peiping-Tientsin Campaign

December 11, 1948

The enemy forces in Changchiakou, Hsinpao-an and Huailai and in the entire area of Peiping, Tientsin, Tangku and Tangshan—except a few units, such as certain divisions of the 35th, 62nd and 94th Corps, which still have a fairly high combat effectiveness for the defense of fortified positions—have little offensive spirit; they are like birds startled by the mere twang of a bowstring. This is especially the case since you advanced south of the Great Wall. . . .

Our real aim is not to encircle Peiping first but rather to encircle Tientsin, Tangku, Lutai and Tangshan first. . . .

In the two weeks beginning from today . . . cut the links between the enemy forces . . . and then wipe out the enemy forces one by one. . . .

The sequence of attacks will be roughly the following: first, the Tangku-Lutai sector; second, Hsinpao-an; third, the Tangshan sector; fourth, the Tientsin and Changchiakou sectors; and, lastly, the Peiping sector.

What are your views on this plan? What are its shortcomings? Are there any difficulties in its execution? Please consider all this and reply by telegraph.

This was a telegram drafted by Mao Tse-tung for the Revolutionary Military Commission of the Central Committee of the Communist Party of China and addressed to Lin Piao, Lo Jung-huan and other military commanders. This was the decisive campaign in the Communist take-over of mainland China from the Nationalist Government.

Message Urging Tu Yu-ming and Others to Surrender

December 17, 1948

General Tu Yu-ming, General Chiu Ching-chuan, General Li Mi and all corps, division and regiment commanders of the two armies under Generals Chiu Ching-chuan and Li Mi:

You are now at the end of your rope. Huang Wei's army was completely wiped out on the night of the fifteenth, Li Yen-nien's army has taken to its heels and fled south, and it is hopeless for you to think of joining them. Are you hoping to break through? How can you break through when the People's Liberation Army is all around? . . . Your soldiers and many of your officers have no stomach for any more fighting. You . . . should understand and sympathize with the feelings of your subordinates and families, hold their lives dear, find a way out for them as early as possible and stop sending them to a senseless death. . . . Immediately order all your troops to lay down their arms and cease resistance.

Our army will guarantee life and safety to you, high-ranking officers, and to all officers and men. This is your only way out. Think it over! If you feel this is right, then do it. If you still want to fight another round, you can have it, but you will be finished off anyway.[1]

Headquarters of the Central Plains
People's Liberation Army
Headquarters of the Eastern China
People's Liberation Army

This broadcast was written by Mao Tse-tung for the Headquarters of the Central Plains and the Eastern China People's Liberation Armies.

Carry the Revolution Through to the End

December 30, 1948

The Chinese people will win final victory in the great War of Liberation. Even our enemy no longer doubts the outcome. . . .

The enemy will not perish of himself. Neither the Chinese reactionaries nor the aggressive forces of U.S. imperialism in China will step down from the stage of history of their own accord. Precisely because they realize that the countrywide victory of the Chinese People's War of Liberation can no longer be prevented by purely military struggle, they are placing more and more importance each day on political struggle. . . .

The U.S. Government has changed its policy of simply backing the Kuomintang's counterrevolutionary war to a policy of embracing two forms of struggle:

1. After receiving this message, the commanders to whom it was addressed continued their resistance to the Communist attack and were defeated. Tu Yu-ming was captured and Chiu Ching-chuan killed; only Li Mi escaped.

1. Organizing the remnants of the Kuomintang's armed forces and the so-called local forces to continue to resist the People's Liberation Army south of the Yangtze River and in the remote border provinces, and

2. Organizing an opposition faction within the revolutionary camp to strive with might and main to halt the revolution where it is, or, if it must advance, to moderate it and prevent it from encroaching too far on the interests of the imperialists and their running dogs. The British and French imperialists support this U.S. policy. . . .

The question now facing the Chinese people, all democratic parties and all people's organizations is whether to carry the revolution through to the end or to abandon it halfway. . . .

In the long period of more than twenty years from the counter-revolutionary *coup d'état* of April 12, 1927, to this day, have the Chinese reactionaries headed by Chiang Kai-shek and his ilk not given proof enough that they are a gang of bloodstained executioners, who slaughter people without blinking? Have they not given proof enough that they are a band of professional traitors and the running dogs of imperialism? Think it over, everybody! . . . Relying on U.S. imperialism, they have plunged 475 million of our compatriots into a huge civil war of unprecedented brutality and slaughtered millions upon millions of men and women. . . . Only by completely destroying the Chinese reactionaries and expelling the aggressive forces of U.S. imperialism can China gain independence, democracy and peace. Isn't this truth clear enough by now? . . .

In 1949 the Political Consultative Conference, with no reactionaries participating and having as its aim the fulfillment of the tasks of the people's revolution, will be convened, the People's Republic of China will be proclaimed, and the Central Government of the Republic will be established. This government will be a democratic coalition government under the leadership of the Communist Party of China, with the participation of appropriate persons representing the democratic parties and people's organizations. . . .

The year 1949 will be a year of tremendous importance. We should redouble our efforts.

This New Year message for 1949 was written by Mao Tse-tung for the Hsinhua News Agency.

On the War Criminal's Suing for Peace

January 5, 1949

In order to preserve the forces of Chinese reaction and U.S. aggression in China, Chiang Kai-shek, China's No. 1 war criminal and chieftain of the Kuomintang bandit gang, issued a statement on New Year's Day suing for peace. The war criminal Chiang Kai-shek says:

I have no desire of my own other than that the peace negotiations should not impair the country's independence and integrity but instead should help the rehabilitation of the people; that the sacred constitution should not be violated by my action and that democratic constitutionalism should not be thereby undermined; that the form of government of the Republic of China should be guaranteed and the legally constituted authority of the Republic of China should not be interrupted; that the armed forces should be definitely preserved and that the people should be allowed to continue their free way of life and maintain their present minimum standard of living.

. . . If only peace can be realized, I certainly do not care whether I remain in office or retire, but will abide by the common will of the people.

People should not think that there is something ridiculous about a war criminal suing for peace, nor should they think that such a bid for peace is really disgusting. . . . For the Chinese people can tell from this that the "peace" about which there has lately been so much clamor is exactly what this Chiang Kai-shek gang of murderers and their U.S. master urgently need.

Chiang Kai-shek has confessed the gang's whole plot. The main points of this plot are as follows:

"The peace negotiations should not impair the country's independence and integrity." . . . "Peace" is absolutely all wrong if it impairs such treaties as the Sino-U.S. Treaty of Friendship, Commerce and Navigation, the Sino-U.S. Air Transport Agreement . . . if it interferes with China's becoming a U.S. colony. . . .

"The sacred constitution should not be violated by my action" . . .

it would be very dangerous—it would mean the finish of the whole of the comprador and landlord classes, the end of the Kuomintang gang of bandits and the arrest and punishment of all the war criminals. . . .

"The armed forces should be definitely preserved"— . . . just as the life of Chia Pao-yu of the Grand View Garden depended upon a piece of jade in his necklace,[1] the life of the Kuomintang depends upon its army, so how can one say that its army should not be "preserved," or should only be "preserved" but not "definitely" so?

"The people should be allowed to continue their free way of life and maintain their present minimum standard of living"—this means the Chinese comprador and landlord classes must preserve their freedom to oppress and exploit the people of the whole country, and their freedom to maintain their present standard of lordly, luxurious, loose and idle living, while the . . . exploited maintain . . . a life of cold and hunger. . . .

But is everything going well, without any hitch? There is a hitch, it is said. What is the hitch? President Chiang says:

It is regrettable that there are people in our government who have come under the influence of malicious Communist propaganda and are consequently in a wavering state of mind, having almost lost their self-confidence. Spiritually menaced by the Communists, they see only the enemy's strength but not our own huge strength, which is tens of times greater than the enemy's. . . .

One may ask, "Is there a market for such news?" . . . As we said long ago, Chiang Kai-shek has lost his soul, is merely a corpse, and no one believes him any more.

This commentary was the first of a series written by Mao Tse-tung for the Hsinhua News Agency.

1. Chia Pao-yu was a character in *The Dream of the Red Chamber*, an eighteenth-century Chinese novel, and the Grand View Garden was his family garden. It was said that Chia Pao-yu was born with a piece of jade in his mouth. This jade was "the root of his life" and had to be worn constantly around his neck; he was not to part with it. If he lost it, he would lose his wits.

Statement on the Present Situation
by Mao Tse-tung, Chairman of the Central
Committee of the Communist Party of China

January 14, 1949

Two and a half years have gone by since July 1946, when the reactionary Nanking Kuomintang Government, with the aid of the U.S. imperialists, violated the will of the people, tore up the truce agreement and the resolutions of the Political Consultative Conference and launched the countrywide counterrevolutionary civil war. . . .

The People's Liberation Army has overcome unparalleled difficulties, grown in strength and equipped itself with huge quantities of arms given to the Kuomintang Government by the U.S. Government. In two and a half years, it has wiped out the main military forces of the reactionary Kuomintang Government and all its crack divisions. Today the People's Liberation Army is superior to the remnant military forces of the reactionary Kuomintang Government in numbers, morale and equipment. . . .

In these circumstances, in order to preserve the remnant forces of the Kuomintang Government and in order to gain a breathing space before making new onslaughts to destroy the revolutionary forces, Chiang Kai-shek, China's No. 1 war criminal, chieftain of the Kuomintang bandit gang and bogus President of the Nanking Government, advanced the proposal on January 1 of this year that he was willing to hold peace negotiations with the Communist Party of China. The Communist Party of China considers this proposal hypocritical. . . . The Communist Party of China is willing to hold peace negotiations with the reactionary Nanking Kuomintang Government or with any local governments or military groups of the Kuomintang on the basis of the following terms:

1. Punish the war criminals;
2. Abolish the bogus constitution;

3. Abolish the bogus "constituted authority";

4. Reorganize all reactionary troops on democratic principles;

5. Confiscate bureaucrat capital;

6. Reform the land system;

7. Abrogate treasonable treaties;

8. Convene a Political Consultative Conference without the participation of reactionary elements, and form a democratic coalition government to take over all the powers of the reactionary Nanking Kuomintang Government and of its subordinate governments at all levels.

The Communist Party of China holds that the above terms express the common will of the people throughout the country and that only a peace based on these terms can be called a genuine democratic peace. . . .

Comment by the Spokesman
for the Communist Party of China
on the Resolution of the
Nanking Executive Yuan

January 21, 1949

The Central News Agency, the official news agency of the reactionary Nanking Kuomintang Government, said in a dispatch of January 19 that the Executive Yuan, at a meeting at 9 A.M. on the same day, had extensively discussed the current situation and passed the following resolution:

In deference to the desire of the people of the whole country to realize an early peace, the Government hereby expresses its considered wish, first, together with the Communist Party of China, to effect an immediate and unconditional cessation of hostilities, and then, to appoint delegates to enter into peace negotiations.

The spokesman for the Communist Party of China states: "This resolution of the Nanking Executive Yuan makes no mention of the statement proposing peace negotiations issued on January 1 by Chiang Kai-shek, the bogus Nanking President, or of the statement proposing peace negotiations issued on January 14 by Chairman Mao Tse-tung of the Communist Party of China; nor does it indicate which of the two statements it supports and which it opposes, but instead puts forward a proposal of its own, as if neither the Kuomintang nor the Communist Party had made any proposals on January 1 and January 14; all this is utterly incomprehensible." . . .

Hasn't the conclusion been conformed that Nanking's peace proposal is hypocritical? The spokesman for the Communist Party says: "Nanking has now fallen into a state of anarchy, the bogus President has one proposal and the bogus Executive Yuan has another. With whom is one to deal?"

On Ordering the Reactionary Kuomintang Government to Re-arrest Yasuji Okamura, Former Commander-in-Chief of the Japanese Forces of Aggression in China, and to Arrest the Kuomintang Civil War Criminals—Statement by the Spokesman for the Communist Party of China

January 28, 1949

The Central News Agency of the reactionary Nanking Kuomintang Government reported in a dispatch dated January 26:

A Government spokesman made the following statement. In the past month the Government has taken various measures and steps for an early conclusion of the war in order to alleviate the sufferings of the people. Furthermore, on the twenty-second of this month, the Government formally appointed a delegation to the peace negotiations. . . .[1] But in a broadcast from northern Shensi by the Hsinhua News Agency on the twenty-fifth,[2] a spokesman for the Communist Party of China, while

1. The delegation appointed by the Nationalist Government consisted of Shao Li-tse, Chang Chih-chung, Huang Shao-hung, Peng Chao-hsien, and Chung Tien-hsin.
2. On January 25, 1949, the spokesman for the Chinese Communist Party declared: "We have permitted the reactionary Nanking Government to send

indicating willingness to negotiate a peaceful settlement with the Government, resorted to unbridled insults and vilification and used absurd and offensive language. He also said that the place for the negotiations could not be fixed until Peiping was completely liberated. . . . Is it not stalling for time and prolonging the disaster of war? . . .

In another dispatch dated January 26, Nanking's Central News Agency reported from Shanghai:

Following a review of his case on the twenty-sixth by the Nationalist Defense Ministry's Military Court for the Trial of War Criminals, the Japanese war criminal General Yasuji Okamura, former commander-in-chief of the Japanese Expeditionary Forces in China, was declared Not Guilty. . . .

In view of the above, the spokesman for the Communist Party of China makes the following statement:

1. The Communist Party of China and the General Headquarters of the Chinese People's Liberation Army declare that . . . you must re-arrest Yasuji Okamura immediately and return him to prison without fail. . . . This matter is closely related to your request for negotiations with us. . . . We have the right to order you to re-arrest Yasuji Okamura and be responsible for turning him over to the People's Liberation Army at a time and place to be specified by us. . . .

2. . . . We tell you gentlemen of Nanking frankly: you are war criminals, you will be brought to trial. We have no faith in your mouthings about "peace" or "the will of the people." You relied on the power of the United States, violated the will of the people . . . and launched this most ruthless, anti-popular, anti-democratic, counterrevolutionary civil war. . . . Besides arresting the Japanese war criminal Yasuji Okamura, you must at once set about arresting a batch of civil war criminals and, first of all, the forty-three war criminals in Nanking, Shanghai, Fenghua and Taiwan who were listed in the statement by an authoritative person in the Communist Party of China on December 25, 1948. The most important among

---

a delegation for peace negotiations to us not because we recognize that government as still qualified to represent the Chinese people, but because it still has some remnants of the reactionary armed forces. . . ."

them are Chiang Kai-shek, T. V. Soong, Chen Cheng, Ho Ying-chin, Ku Chu-tung, Chen Li-fu, Chen Kuo-fu, Chu Chia-hua, Wang Shih-chieh, Wu Kuo-chen, Tai Chuan-hsien, Tang En-po, Chou Chih-jou, Wang Shu-ming and Kuei Yung-ching.[3] Of particular importance is Chiang Kai-shek, who has now fled to Fenghua[4] and will very likely flee abroad and seek the protection of U.S. or British imperialism; therefore you must quickly arrest this criminal and not let him escape. . . .

3. We demand that the reactionary Nanking Government reply to the above two points.

4. Nanking will be notified at another time concerning the preparations both sides should make in connection with the remainder of the eight terms.

Peace Terms Must Include the Punishment of Japanese War Criminals and Kuomintang War Criminals —Statement by the Spokesman for the Communist Party of China

February 5, 1949

The statement on the question of peace negotiations made on January 28 by the spokesman for the Communist Party of China was answered on January 31 by a spokesman of the reactionary traitorous Kuomintang Government. In his reply, the spokesman of the reac-

3. T. V. Soong had served as Minister of Finance, president of the Executive Yuan, and special envoy to the United States. Chen Cheng was Vice President of the Republic of China and Chief of the General Staff. Ho Ying-chin was Minister of National Defense. Ku Chu-tung was then Chief of Staff of the Nationalist Army. Chen Li-fu, Chen Kuo-fu, and Chu Chia-hua were Kuomintang politicians. Wang Shih-chieh had been Minister of Foreign Affairs. Wu Kuo-chen (known as "K.C.") was the Mayor of Shanghai. Tai Chuan-hsien was a close member of Chiang Kai-shek's "brains trust." Tang En-po was commander of the Nationalist forces in the Nanking-Shanghai-Hangchow area. Chou Chih-jou commanded the Nationalist Air Force. Wang Shu-ming was deputy commander of the air force. Kuei Yung-ching was commander of the Nationalist Navy.

4. A county in Chekiang Province, the birthplace of Chiang Kai-shek.

tionary traitorous Kuomintang Government quibbled about the points raised by the spokesman for the Communist Party of China. . . . "The Communist Party of China," he added, "does not seem to be serious enough in its attitude." . . . Our attitude was indeed not serious enough insofar as we still spoke of the reactionary traitorous Kuomintang government as a government. . . . We have now deliberately added the word "traitorous" to your title, and you ought to accept it. Your government has long been traitorous, and it was only for the sake of brevity that we sometimes omitted the word; now we can omit it no longer. In addition to all the crimes of treason you committed in the past, you have now committed another, and a very serious one, which must be discussed at the meeting for peace negotiations. . . . Whether or not you call it causing complication, the matter must be discussed; and since it happened after January 14 and was not included in the eight terms we originally presented, we therefore deem it necessary to add to the first term a new item, the punishment of Japanese war criminals . . . and the punishment of Chiang Kai-shek and other civil war criminals. . . . These war criminals have to be arrested; even if they flee to the remotest corners of the globe, they must be arrested. . . . But since you state that you find it rather difficult to arrest them immediately—all right, then, prevent them from escaping; under no circumstances must you let these creatures run away. . . . Gentlemen of the hypothetical, token, reactionary, traitorous Kuomintang "Government" (mind you, the word "Government" is in quotes) at Nanking or Canton or Fenghua or Shanghai! If you think that our attitude in this statement is again not serious enough, please excuse us, for it is the only attitude we can take toward you.

Turn the Army into a Working Force

February 8, 1949

Your telegram of the fourth has been received. It is very good that you are speeding training and consolidation and preparing to start moving one month ahead of schedule. . . . From now on, the formula followed in the past twenty years, "First the rural areas, then the cities," will be reversed and changed to the formula, "First the cities, then the rural areas." The army is not only a fighting force, it is mainly a working force. All army cadres should learn how to take over and administer cities. . . . In short, all urban problems, with which in the past our army cadres and fighters were unfamiliar, should from now on be shouldered by them. . . . The army is still a fighting force, and in this respect there must be absolutely no relaxing; to relax would be a mistake. Nevertheless, the time has come for us to set ourselves the task of turning the army into a working force. . . . The army is a school. Our field armies of 2,100,000 are equivalent to several thousand universities and secondary schools. We have to rely chiefly on the army to supply our working cadres. You must understand this point clearly. Since severe fighting is basically over, replenishment of the army's manpower and equipment should be kept within suitable limits, and too much must not be demanded as regards quantity, quality and completeness, lest this should cause financial crisis. . . .

This telegram was written by Mao Tse-tung for the Revolutionary Military Commission of the Central Committee of the Chinese Communist Party in reply to one from the Second and Third Field Armies. It was sent also to other field armies.

Why Do the Badly Split Reactionaries Still Idly Clamor for "Total Peace"?

February 15, 1949

The reactionary Kuomintang rule is collapsing more rapidly than was expected. . . . On January 1 of this year, the Kuomintang reactionaries began to lift a rock called the "peace offensive"; they intended to hurl it at the Chinese people, but now it has dropped on their own feet. . . . In fact, this magic weapon, the peace offensive, was made in U.S. factories and was delivered to the Kuomintang more than half a year ago. It was Leighton Stuart[1] himself who let out the secret. After Chiang Kai-shek issued his so-called New Year's Day message, Stuart told a correspondent of the Central News Agency that this was "what I myself have consistently worked for." According to U.S. news agencies, that correspondent lost his rice bowl for publishing this "off the record" remark. . . . Although Chiang Kai-shek and Li Tsung-jen[2] and the Americans had made all kinds of arrangements for this plot and hoped to put on a fairly good puppet show, the result was contrary to their expectations; not only did the audience dwindle, but even the actors themselves vanished from the stage one after another. In Fenghua, Chiang Kai-shek continues to direct his remnant forces in his "status of retirement," but he has lost his legal status and those people who believe in him are getting fewer and fewer. . . .

Thus, all that is left for Li Tsung-jen to see from the ramparts of the "Stone City"[3] is,

> The sky brooding low over the land of Wu and Chu,
> With nothing between to meet the eye.[4]

. . . The farce of the badly split and disintegrating Kuomintang's demand for a "total peace" reached its climax in the statement issued on February 9 in Shanghai by the war criminal Teng Wen-yi, head of the Bureau for Political Work of the bogus Ministry of National

1. John Leighton Stuart was United States Ambassador in China from 1947 to 1949.
2. In a ceremonial, rather than factual, withdrawal from the office of President, Chiang Kai-shek turned over the reins of government to Acting President Li Tsung-jen.
3. The "Stone City" was an ancient name for Nanking.
4. Lines from an ode by the fourteenth-century Chinese poet, Sadul, of the Yuan Dynasty. The first half of the ode reads:

> From the ramparts of the Stone City
> One sees the sky brooding low over the land of Wu and Chu,
> With nothing between to meet the eye.
> Pointing to strategic points famous in the Six Dynasties,
> Only the green hills stand like walls.
> Where army flags blotted the sun
> And masts of war vessels touched the clouds
> Snow-white skeletons lie scattered
> North and south of the River
> How many warriors died!

Defense. . . . According to a Central News Agency dispatch from Shanghai on February 9:

Teng Wen-yi was asked by a reporter, "Has Acting President Li approved the four points in your public statement?"[5] Teng Wen-yi answered, "I am speaking from the stand of the Ministry of National Defense, and the four points made today were not submitted beforehand to Acting President Li." . . .

A Bureau for Political Work of the Ministry of National Defense can contradict the Ministry of National Defense as well as the Acting President. . . . Total power is in the hands of the Chinese people, the Chinese People's Liberation Army, the Communist Party of China . . . not in the hands of the badly split and disintegrating Kuomintang. One side wields total power, while the other is hopelessly split and disintegrated, and this is the result of the prolonged struggle of the Chinese people and the prolonged evil-doing of the Kuomintang. No serious person can ignore this basic fact of the political situation in China today.

The Kuomintang Reactionaries Turn from an "Appeal for Peace" to an Appeal for War

February 16, 1949

From the time the bandit Chiang Kai-shek launched his peace offensive on January 1, the heroes of the reactionary Kuomintang clique kept on repeating at great length their willingness to "shorten the duration of the war," "alleviate the sufferings of the people." . . . But early in February they suddenly began to play down their peace tune and strike up the old tune of "fighting the Communists to the bitter end." . . . On February 13 the Propaganda Department

5. In his written statement on the "Development of Peace and War," Teng Wen-yi set forth the following four points: (1) The government wants peace; (2) the Chinese Communist Party wants war; (3) the local peace at Peiping has become a hoax; (4) we will stop at no sacrifices in order to fight the Communists to the bitter end.

of the Kuomintang Central Executive Committee issued a "Special Directive for Propaganda" to "all Party headquarters and Party papers" which stated: . . .

Rather than surrender unconditionally, the Government should fight to the bitter end.

The eight terms Mao Tse-tung put forward in his January 14 statement would ruin the nation, and the Government should not have accepted them.

The Communist Party of China should bear the responsibility for wrecking peace. Instead, it has now drawn up a list of so-called war criminals which includes all the Government leaders and has even demanded that the Government first arrest them; this clearly shows how truculent and unreasonable the Communist Party is. Unless the Communist Party of China changes this behavior, it will indeed be difficult to find a way to peace negotiations.

There is no more of the pathetic anxiety for peace negotiations of two weeks ago. There is no further mention of those famous phrases, "shorten the duration of the war," "alleviate the sufferings of the people." . . . All you broad masses of the people of the Yangtze Valley and the south—workers, peasants, intellectuals, urban petty bourgeoisie, national bourgeoisie, enlightened gentry and Kuomintang members with a conscience—your attention please! . . . You and we are on the same side. The handful of diehards will soon topple from their pinnacle, and a people's China will soon emerge.

On the Kuomintang's Different Answers to the Question of Responsibility for the War

February 18, 1949

After the conclusion of the War of Resistance, the Government, following a policy of peace and national reconstruction, endeavored to solve peacefully the problem of the Communist Party of China. For a period of a year and a half the Communist Party of China broke every agreement and therefore it should bear the responsibility for wrecking peace. Instead, it has drawn up a list of so-called war criminals which includes all the Government leaders and has even demanded that the Government first arrest them; this clearly shows how truculent and unreasonable the Communist Party is. Unless the Communist Party of China changes this behavior, it will indeed be difficult to find a way to peace negotiations.

The above is the entire argument on the question of the responsibility for the war which the Propaganda Department of the Central Executive Committee of the Kuomintang advanced in a "Special Directive for Propaganda" issued on February 15, 1949. It is the argument of none other than War Criminal No. 1, Chiang Kai-shek. In his New Year's Day statement he said:

> . . . As soon as the War of Resistance came to an end, our Government proclaimed its policy of peace and national reconstruction and moreover sought to solve the Communist problem by means of political consultations and military mediation. But contrary to our expectations, the Communist Party for a period of a year and a half wilfully obstructed all agreements and proposals and made it impossible to carry them out. . . . This Government was thus driven to the painful necessity of mobilization to put down the rebellion.

Sun Fo,[1] feeling that something was amiss, put forward a different argument about the responsibility for the war in a speech broadcast on the evening of the same day Chiang Kai-shek issued his New Year's Day statement. Sun Fo said:

> . . . Three years ago . . . we called together representatives from various quarters and public personages for a Political Consultative Conference. . . . Thanks especially to the kind mediation of Mr. Marshall, President Truman's special envoy, we agreed upon specific measures for settling various disputes. . . . Unfortunately . . . none of the various

1. Sun Fo, son of Dr. Sun Yat Sen, was President of the Executive Yuan at this time. When Communist military victories compelled him to move the Nationalist Government headquarters from Nanking to Canton, he made a speech on February 7, 1949, in which he deplored the failure of his government to put into effect his father's Three People's Principles, a failure which resulted, he said, in "the spread of Communist influence." When the break occurred in 1927 between the Communists and the Nationalist Government, Sun Fo remained loyal to the Republic of China, but his stepmother, Mme Sun Yat Sen, the former Ching-ling Soong (one of the three Soong sisters, of whom May-ling Soong married Chiang Kai-shek), fled overland with the Chinese Communists and their Russian advisers from Hankow to Moscow.

parties concerned would entirely forego its selfish interests . . . and so the disaster of war again occurred. . . .

Sun Fo is a little bit more "fair" than Chiang Kai-shek. You see, unlike Chiang Kai-shek, he does not shift the responsibility for the war entirely onto the Communist Party, but divides the blame equally among "the various parties concerned." . . . Here you see two Kuomintangites at loggerheads, Sun Fo and Chiang Kai-shek.

A third Kuomintangite has come forward, saying, "No, in my opinion, the responsibility should be borne entirely by the Kuomintang." His name is Li Tsung-jen. On January 22, 1949, Li Tsung-jen issued a statement in his capacity as "Acting President." Regarding the responsibility for the war, he said:

The three years' civil war that followed the eight Years' War of Resistance has not only completely destroyed the country's last hope of recovery . . . but has also spread ruin everywhere north and south of the Yellow River. . . .

Here Li Tsung-jen makes a statement but names no names; he fixes the responsibility neither on the Kuomintang, nor on the Communist Party, nor on any other quarter; yet he has stated one fact, that this . . . has occurred . . . "north and south of the Yellow River." . . . Could it have been caused by the people and the people's army there, fighting among themselves? Since Li Tsung-jen was once chief of Chiang Kai-shek's Peiping Headquarters . . . he has reliable information about where and how this . . . took place. . . .

On January 19 Sun Fo's Executive Yuan passed a resolution . . . saying: "First, effect an immediate and unconditional cessation of hostilities, and then appoint delegates to enter into peace negotiations." . . . Even such a war criminal as Chiang Kai-shek knows that without negotiations it is impossible to cease hostilities and restore peace; on this point Sun Fo is far behind Chiang Kai-shek.

As is generally known, Sun Fo is listed as a war criminal because he has all along supported Chiang Kai-shek in launching and continuing the war. As late as June 22, 1947, he was still saying that a "settlement will finally come, provided militarily we fight to the end" and that "at present peace negotiations are out of the question, and the Government must crush the Communist Party of China or be overthrown by it." . . . But now he is making irresponsible and carping comments from the sidelines. . . . Whether tried according to the law of the state or judged according to the Party discipline of the Kuomintang, Sun Fo cannot escape the caning he deserves.

Report to the Second Plenary Session of the Seventh Central Committee of the Communist Party of China

March 5, 1949

I

With the conclusion of the Liaohsi-Shenyang, Huai-Hai and Peiping-Tientsin campaigns, the main force of the Kuomintang Army has been destroyed. Only a million odd of its combat troops are left, dispersed over vast areas from Sinkiang to Taiwan and over extremely long fronts. . . . It must never be assumed that, once they yield to us, the counterrevolutionaries turn into revolutionaries, that their counterrevolutionary ideas and designs cease to exist. Definitely not. Many of the counterrevolutionaries will be remolded, some will be sifted out, and certain die-hard counterrevolutionaries will be suppressed.

II

The People's Liberation Army is always a fighting force. Even after countrywide victory, our army will remain a fighting force during the historical period in which classes have not been abolished in our country and the imperialist system still exists in the world. . . .

III

. . . The center of gravity of the Party's work has shifted from the village to the city. In the south the People's Liberation Army will occupy first the cities and then the villages. Attention must be given both to city and village and it is necessary to link closely urban and rural work, workers and peasants, industry and agriculture. . . .

IV

On whom shall we rely in our struggles in the cities? Some muddleheaded comrades think we should rely not on the working class but on the masses of the poor. Some comrades who are even more muddleheaded think we should rely on the bourgeoisie. . . . We must criticize these muddled views. We must wholeheartedly rely on the working class, unite with the rest of the laboring masses, win over the intellectuals and win over to our side as many as possible of the national bourgeois elements . . . or neutralize them. . . . Meanwhile we shall set about our task of construction and learn, step by step, how to administer cities and restore and develop their production. . . .

V

Conditions in the south are different from those in the north, and the Party's tasks must also be different. The south is still under Kuomintang rule. There, the tasks of the Party and the People's Liberation Army are to wipe out the Kuomintang's reactionary armed forces in city and countryside, set up Party organizations . . . mop up the remnant Kuomintang forces and restore and develop production. . . .

VI

We have already carried out extensive economic construction, and the Party's economic policy has been implemented in practice and has achieved marked success. However, there are still many muddled views within the Party on the question of why we should adopt this kind of economic policy and not another, that is, on a question of theory and principle. How should this question be answered? . . .

1. The proletariat and its Party, because they have been oppressed by manifold enemies, have become steeled and are qualified to lead

the Chinese people's revolution. Whoever overlooks or belittles this point will commit Right opportunist mistakes. . . .

2. We have abolished, or will soon abolish, the age-old feudal ownership of land. . . . We will soon have the possibility of modernizing our agriculture and handicrafts step by step. In their basic form, however, our agriculture and handicrafts . . . are somewhat as they were in ancient times, and will remain so for a fairly long time to come. Whoever overlooks or belittles this point will commit "Left" opportunist mistakes. . . .

3. The confiscation of bureaucrat capital and its transfer to the people's republic led by the proletariat will enable the people's republic to control the economic lifelines of the country and will enable the state-owned economy to become the leading sector of the entire national economy. . . .

4. China's private capitalist industry, which occupies second place in her modern industry, is a force which must not be ignored. . . . In this period, all capitalist elements in the cities and countryside which are not harmful but beneficial to the national economy should be allowed to exist and expand. . . . We shall adopt well-measured and flexible policies for restricting capitalism from several directions according to the specific conditions in each place, each industry and each period. . . . We must not restrict the private capitalist economy too much or too rigidly, but must leave room for it to exist and develop within the framework of the economic policy and planning of the people's republic. . . .

5. Scattered, individual agriculture and handicrafts, which make up 90 per cent of the total value of output of the national economy, can and must be led prudently, step by step, and yet actively to develop toward modernization and collectivization; the view that they may be left to take their own course is wrong. . . .

6. The restoration and development of the national economy of the people's republic would be impossible without a policy of controlling foreign trade. . . . The two basic policies of the state in the economic struggle will be regulation of capital at home and control of foreign trade. Whoever overlooks or belittles this point will commit extremely serious mistakes.

7. . . . With the leadership of the Communist Party of China, plus the support of the working class of the countries of the world and chiefly the support of the Soviet Union, the speed of China's

economic construction will not be very slow, but may be fairly fast. . . .

VII

Old China was a semicolonial country under imperialist domination. Thoroughly anti-imperialist in character, the Chinese people's democratic revolution has incurred the bitter hatred of the imperialists who have done their utmost to help the Kuomintang. We must . . . refuse to recognize the legal status of any foreign diplomatic establishments and personnel of the Kuomintang period, refuse to recognize all the treasonable treaties of the Kuomintang period. . . . As for ordinary foreign nationals, their legitimate interests will be protected and not encroached upon. As for the question of the recognition of our country by the imperialist countries, we should not be in a hurry to solve it now and need not be in a hurry to solve it even for a fairly long period after countrywide victory. . . .

VIII

All the conditions are ripe for convening the Political Consultative Conference and forming a democratic coalition government. All the democratic parties, people's organizations and democrats without Party affiliation are on our side. . . . The disintegrating Kuomintang has alienated itself from all the masses. We are preparing to have negotiations with the reactionary Nanking Government. . . . Our policy is not to refuse negotiations, but to demand that the other side accept the eight terms in their entirety and to allow no bargaining. . . . The negotiations on an overall basis are tentatively fixed for late March. We hope to occupy Nanking by April or May, then convene the Political Consultative Conference in Peiping, form a coalition government and make Peiping the capital. . . .

IX

The people's democratic dictatorship, led by the proletariat and based on the worker-peasant alliance, requires that our Party conscientiously unite the entire working class, the entire peasantry and the broad masses of revolutionary intellectuals; these are the leading and basic forces of the dictatorship. Without this unity, the dictatorship cannot be consolidated. It is also required that our Party unite with as many as possible of the representatives of the urban petty bourgeoisie and national bourgeoisie who can co-operate with us . . . give them work, entrust them with the responsibility and authority that should go with their posts and help them do their work well. . . .

X

Very soon we shall be victorious throughout the country. This victory will breach the western front of imperialism and will have great international significance. . . . With victory the people will be grateful to us and the bourgeoisie will come forward to flatter us. It has been proved that the enemy cannot conquer us by force of arms. However, the flattery of the bourgeoisie may conquer the weak-willed in our ranks. . . . We must guard against such a situation. . . . The comrades must be taught to remain modest, prudent and free from arrogance and rashness in their style of work. . . . Not only can the Chinese people live without begging alms from the imperialists, they will live a better life than that in the imperialist countries.

The Seventh Central Committee of the Chinese Communist Party held its Second Plenary Session in Hsipaipo Village, Hopei Province, from March 5 to 13, 1949. Thirty-four members and nineteen alternate members of the Central Committee were present. After the session, the Central Committee moved its headquarters from Hsipaipo to Peiping.

Methods of Work of Party Committees

March 13, 1949

1. The secretary of a Party committee must be good at being a "squad leader." . . . To be a good "squad leader," the secretary should study hard and investigate thoroughly. . . . If the "squad members" do not march in step, they can never expect to lead tens of millions of people in fighting and construction. . . .

2. Place problems on the table. This should be done not only by the "squad leader" but by the committee members too. Do not talk behind people's backs. . . .

3. "Exchange information." This means that members of a Party committee should keep each other informed and exchange views on matters that have come to their attention. . . .

4. Ask your subordinates about matters you don't understand or don't know, and do not lightly express your approval or disapproval. . . . We should "not feel ashamed to ask and learn from people below."[1]

5. Learn to "play the piano." In playing the piano all ten fingers are in motion; it won't do to move some fingers only and not others. . . . Wherever there is a problem we must put our finger on it, and this is a method we must master. Some play the piano well and some badly, and there is a great difference in the melodies they produce. Members of Party committees must learn to "play the piano" well.

6. "Grasp firmly." That is to say, the Party committee must not merely "grasp," but must "grasp firmly," its main tasks. One can get a grip on something only when it is grasped firmly, without the slightest slackening. Not to grasp firmly is not to grasp at all. . . .

7. "Have a head for figures." That is to say, we must attend to the quantitative aspect of a situation or problem and make a basic quantitative analysis. . . . To this day many of our comrades . . . have no "figures" in their heads and as a result cannot help making mistakes.

8. "Notice to Reassure the Public." Notice of meetings should be given beforehand; this is like issuing a "Notice to Reassure the Public," so that everybody will know what is going to be discussed and what problems are to be solved and can make timely preparations. . . .

9. Talks, speeches, articles, and resolutions should all be concise and to the point. Meetings also should not go on too long.

10. Pay attention to uniting and working with comrades who differ with you.

11. Guard against arrogance. Celebration of birthdays . . . and naming places after Party leaders is . . . forbidden. . . .

1. The quotation is from the *Confucian Analects,* Book V, "Kungyeh Chang."

The members of the Political Bureau and I personally feel that only by using the above methods can Party committees do their work well. . . .

This was part of Mao Tse-tung's concluding speech at the Second Plenary Session of the Seventh Central Committee of the Chinese Communist Party.

Whither the Nanking Government?
April 4, 1949

Two roads are open to the Nanking Kuomintang Government and its military and administrative personnel. Either they cling to the Chiang Kai-shek clique of war criminals and its master, U.S. imperialism, that is, continue to be the enemy of the people and so perish together with the Chiang Kai-shek clique of war criminals in the People's War of Liberation. Or they come over to the people, that is, break with the Chiang Kai-shek clique of war criminals and U.S. imperialism, perform meritorious service in the People's War of Liberation to atone for their crimes and so obtain clemency and understanding from the people. There is no third road. . . .

The Nanking Government of Li Tsung-jen and Ho Ying-chin is . . . a tool of Chiang Kai-shek and the U.S. Government. . . . We should like to speak plainly to the Nanking Government. . . . This is your last chance. Don't lose it. The People's Liberation Army will soon advance south of the Yangtze River. We are not bluffing. . . .

We are not forcing you to make up your minds. The Nanking Government and its delegation are free to make up their minds or not to. That is to say, you may either listen to Chiang Kai-shek and Leighton Stuart and side with them irrevocably, or listen to us and side with us; you are free to choose. But there is not much time for you to make your choice. The People's Liberation Army will soon start its march, and there is no opportunity left for hesitation.

Order to the Army
for the Countrywide Advance

April 21, 1949

Comrade commanders and fighters of all field armies, comrades of the People's Liberation Army in the guerrilla areas of the south!

The Agreement on Internal Peace, drafted after long negotiations between the delegation of the Communist Party of China and the delegation of the Nanking Kuomintang Government, has been rejected by that government. . . .[1] The rejection of this agreement

1. On April 1, 1949, the Kuomintang Government delegation headed by Chang Chih-chung arrived in Peiping to negotiate peace with the delegation of the Communist Party of China. An Agreement on Internal Peace was drafted after a half month of negotiations. The agreement (final amended version) was handed to the Nanking Government delegation by the delegation of the Communist Party of China on April 15 and was rejected by the Nanking Government on April 20. The full text of the agreement (final amended version) is as follows:

In the 35th year of the Republic of China, the National Government at Nanking, with the aid of the Government of the United States of America, defied the will of the people, wrecked the truce agreement and the resolutions of the Political Consultative Conference and, on the pretext of opposing the Communist Party of China, launched a country-wide civil war against the Chinese people and the Chinese People's Liberation Army. This war has lasted two years and nine and a half months. It has brought untold disaster to the people throughout the country. The country has suffered tremendous losses of financial and material resources, and its sovereignty has been further infringed. The people of the whole country have always expressed dissatisfaction with the National Government at Nanking for its violation of Dr. Sun Yat-sen's revolutionary Three People's Principles and of his correct policies of alliance with Russia, co-operation with the Communist Party and assistance to the peasants and workers, and for its violation of his revolutionary testament. In particular, the whole people have voiced their opposition to the launching of the present unprecedented large-scale civil war by the National Government at Nanking and to the erroneous political, military, financial, economic, cultural and foreign policies and measures which that government has adopted in its pursuit of the civil war. The National Government at Nanking has completely forfeited the confidence of the entire people. In the present civil war its troops have already been defeated by the People's Liberation Army led by the Communist Party of China and commanded by the Chinese People's Revolutionary Military Commission. Finding itself in this situation, the National Government at Nanking proposed to the Communist Party of China on January 1 of the

shows that the Kuomintang reactionaries are determined to fight to the finish the counterrevolutionary war which they started. . . . The rejection of this agreement shows that the Li Tsung-jen Government at Nanking was utterly hypocritical in professing to accept the Chinese Communist Party's eight terms for peace as the basis for negotiations. . . . In these circumstances we order you as follows:

1. Advance bravely and annihilate resolutely, thoroughly, wholly and completely all the Kuomintang reactionaries within China's

---

38th year of the Republic of China that negotiations should be held for the cessation of the civil war and the restoration of peace. On January 14 of the same year, the Communist Party of China issued a statement agreeing to this proposal of the Kuomintang government at Nanking and putting forward eight terms as the basis for the peace negotiations between the two sides. These terms are as follows: punish the war criminals; abolish the bogus constitution; abolish the bogus "constituted authority"; reorganize all reactionary troops on democratic principles; confiscate bureaucrat-capital; reform the land system; abrogate treasonable treaties; convene a New Political Consultative Conference without the participation of reactionary elements and form a democratic coalition government to take over all the power and authority of the reactionary Nanking Kuomintang government and of its subordinate governments at all levels. These eight basic terms were agreed to by the National Government at Nanking. Thereupon, the Communist Party of China and the National Government at Nanking appointed their respective delegations, fully empowered to conduct negotiations and to sign an agreement. The delegates of both parties met in Peiping, have affirmed first of all that the National Government at Nanking should bear the full responsibility for the present civil war and for all its erroneous policies and have agreed to conclude this agreement.

SECTION ONE

Article 1. In order to distinguish between right and wrong and to establish responsibility, the delegation of the Communist Party of China and the delegation of the National Government at Nanking (hereinafter referred to as both sides) affirm that, as a matter of principle, punishment shall be meted out to the war criminals of the National Government at Nanking who are held responsible for launching and prosecuting the present civil war, but that they will be dealt with on the merits of each case in accordance with the following conditions:

Item 1. All war criminals, no matter who they are, may be cleared of the charge of being war criminals and treated with leniency, provided they show by actual deeds that they are really sincere in distinguishing right from wrong and are determined to make a clean break with their past, thus facilitating the progress of the cause of the Chinese people's liberation and the peaceful settlement of the internal problem.

Item 2. All incorrigible war criminals, no matter who they are, shall be severely punished if they obstruct the progress of the cause of the people's

borders who dare to resist. Liberate the people of the whole country. Safeguard the independence and integrity of China's territory and sovereignty.

---

liberation, hinder the peaceful settlement of the internal problem, or go so far as to instigate rebellion. The Chinese People's Revolutionary Military Commission will be responsible for suppressing the ringleaders of rebellion.

Article 2. Both sides affirm that the National Government at Nanking was wrong in pronouncing General Yasuji Okamura, war criminal in the Japanese aggression against China, not guilty and releasing him on January 26 of the 38th year of the Republic of China and in granting permission on January 31 of the same year for the repatriation to Japan of 260 other Japanese war criminals. The cases of all these Japanese war criminals shall be reopened as soon as the Democratic Coalition Government of China, the new central government representing the people throughout China, is formed.

SECTION TWO

Article 3. Both sides affirm that the "Constitution of the Republic of China," adopted by the "National Assembly" convened by the National Government at Nanking in November of the 35th year of the Republic of China, shall be abolished.

Article 4. After the abolition of the "Constitution of the Republic of China," the fundamental law to be observed by the state and the people shall be determined in accordance with the resolutions of the New Political Consultative Conference and the Democratic Coalition Government.

SECTION THREE

Article 5. Both sides affirm that the entire legally constituted authority of the National Government at Nanking shall be abolished.

Article 6. After the Democratic Coalition Government is formed, the people's democratic constituted authority shall be established, and all reactionary laws and decrees shall be annulled in all places entered and taken over by the People's Liberation Army.

SECTION FOUR

Article 7. Both sides affirm that all armed forces under the Nanking National Government (all the ground, naval and air forces, gendarmerie, communications police corps, local troops, all military institutions, academies, factories, rear-service establishments, etc.) shall be reorganized into the People's Liberation Army on democratic principles. After the signing of the Agreement on Internal Peace, a national reorganization committee shall be established at once to take charge of this work of reorganization. The reorganization committee is to consist of seven to nine members, four to five of whom shall be appointed by the People's Revolutionary Military Commission, and three to four by the National Government at Nanking, with one of the members appointed by the People's Revolutionary Military Commission serving as chairman and one of the members appointed by the National Government at Nanking serving as vice-chairman. In places entered and taken over by the People's Liberation Army, regional sub-committees of the reorganization com-

2. Advance bravely and arrest all the incorrigible war criminals. No matter where they may flee, they must be brought to justice and punished according to law. Pay special attention to arresting the bandit chieftain Chiang Kai-shek.

---

mittee may be established as required. The proportion of the members of both sides in the sub-committees and the allocation of the posts of chairmen and vice-chairmen shall be the same as in the national reorganization committee. A reorganization committee shall be established for the navy and another for the air force. All matters relating to the People's Liberation Army's entry into, and taking over of, the areas at present administered by the National Government at Nanking shall be decided by orders issued by the Chinese People's Revolutionary Military Commission. The armed forces of the National Government at Nanking must not resist the entry of the People's Liberation Army.

Article 8. Both sides agree that the reorganization plan in each region shall be carried out in two stages:

Item 1. The first stage—assembling and regrouping.

Point 1. All the armed forces under the Nanking National Government (ground, naval and air forces, gendarmerie, communications police corps, local troops, etc.) shall be assembled and regrouped. The principle of regrouping shall be as follows: the reorganization committee shall, on the basis of the actual local conditions, order such armed forces in the areas entered and taken over by the People's Liberation Army to move, area by area and stage by stage, to the designated places for assembling and regrouping, according to their original designations, formations and numerical strength.

Point 2. Before the People's Liberation Army enters and takes over all the armed forces under the Nanking National Government shall be held responsible for maintaining local order and preventing any acts of sabotage where they are stationed: in all large and small cities, along important lines of communication and rivers, at seaports and in the villages.

Point 3. In the above-mentioned places, when the People's Liberation Army enters and takes over, the armed forces under the Nanking National Government shall, in accordance with the orders of the reorganization committee and its sub-committees, hand over peacefully and move to the designated places. While moving to the designated places and after arriving there, the armed forces under the Nanking National Government shall observe strict discipline and shall not disturb local order.

Point 4. When, in compliance with the orders of the reorganization committee and its sub-committees, the armed forces under the Nanking National Government leave their original stations, the local police or peace preservation corps stationed in those places shall not withdraw, but shall be responsible for maintaining local peace and order and shall obey the directions and orders of the People's Liberation Army.

Point 5. The reorganization committee, its subcommittees and the local governments shall be responsible for providing all the armed forces of the Nanking National Government which are being moved or assembled with necessary supplies, such as grain, fodder, bedding and clothing.

3. Proclaim to all Kuomintang local governments and local military groups the final amended version of the Agreement on Internal Peace. In accordance with its general ideas, you may conclude local

---

Point 6. The reorganization committee and its sub-committees shall, according to the actual conditions in various areas, order the authorities of the Nanking National Government to hand over, area by area and stage by stage, all its military establishments (institutions, schools, factories, storehouses and the like, belonging to all its organizations ranging from the Ministry of National Defence to the Combined Rear-Service Headquarters), all its military installations (naval ports, forts, air bases and the like) and all its military supplies to the People's Liberation Army and the latter's Military Control Commissions in various places.

Item 2. The second stage—reorganization area by area.
Point 1. After the ground forces under the Nanking National Government (infantry, cavalry, special arms, gendarmerie, communications police corps and local troops) have moved to the designated places and have been assembled and regrouped, area by area and stage by stage, the reorganization committee shall, according to the actual conditions in different areas, draw up plans for their reorganization area by area and carry out these plans at specified times. The principle of reorganization shall be that all the above-mentioned ground forces, after being assembled and regrouped, shall be reorganized into regular units of the People's Liberation Army in conformity with its democratic system and regular structure. The reorganization committee and its sub-committees shall be responsible for handling the cases of those soldiers who have been found eligible for retirement because of age or disability and who wish to retire, as well as the cases of those officers and non-commissioned officers who wish to retire or take up other occupations; the committees shall provide them with facilities to return home and with means of livelihood, so that everyone will be properly placed and no one will commit misdeeds because he lacks means of support.
Point 2. After the naval and air forces under the Nanking National Government have moved to the designated places and been assembled and regrouped, area by area and stage by stage, they shall be reorganized according to their original designations, formations and numerical strength by the navy and air force reorganization committees, in conformity with the democratic system of the People's Liberation Army.
Point 3. All the armed forces under the Nanking National Government, after being reorganized into the People's Liberation Army, must strictly observe the Three Main Rules of Discipline and the Eight Points for Attention of the People's Liberation Army and loyally abide by the military and political systems of the People's Liberation Army, without any violation.
Point 4. The officers and men who have retired after reorganization must respect the local people's governments and obey the laws and decrees of the People's Government. The people's governments and the people of various localities shall be considerate of these retired officers and men and shall not discriminate against them.

agreements with those who are willing to cease hostilities and to settle matters by peaceful means.

4. After the People's Liberation Army has encircled Nanking, we are willing to give the Li Tsung-jen Government at Nanking another

---

Article 9. After the signing of the Agreement on Internal Peace, all the armed forces under the Nanking National Government must cease conscripting or recruiting soldiers or other personnel. They must be responsible for protecting all their arms and ammunition, equipment, military institutions and installations and military matériel, and must not destroy, conceal, transfer or sell any of them.

Article 10. After the signing of the Agreement on Internal Peace, the National Government at Nanking must, in case any of its armed forces refuses to carry out the reorganization plan, assist the People's Liberation Army to enforce the reorganization plan and ensure its thorough execution.

SECTION FIVE

Article 11. Both sides agree that all bureaucrat-capitalist enterprises and property (including banks, factories, mines, vessels, companies and shops) acquired or seized during the rule of the National Government at Nanking through the use of political prerogatives and the influence of wealth and position shall be confiscated and become the property of the state.

Article 12. In areas not yet entered and taken over by the People's Liberation Army, the National Government at Nanking shall be held responsible for supervising the bureaucrat-capitalist enterprises and property mentioned in Article 11 so that no theft or concealment, damage, transfer or secret sale shall occur. Assets which have already been moved shall be frozen wherever found, and their being subsequently removed, transported abroad or damaged shall not be permitted. Bureaucrat-capitalist enterprises and property located abroad shall be declared the property of the state.

Article 13. In areas already entered and taken over by the People's Liberation Army, the bureaucrat-capitalist enterprises and property mentioned in Article 11 shall be confiscated by the local Military Control Commissions or institutions authorized by the Democratic Coalition Government. Private shares in them, if any, shall be investigated; after they have been verified as being in fact private and not secretly transferred bureaucrat-capital, they shall be recognized, and their owners shall be permitted to remain shareholders or to withdraw their shares.

Article 14. Bureaucrat-capitalist enterprises dating from the period prior to the rule of the National Government at Nanking, as well as those dating from the period of the rule of the National Government at Nanking, which are neither large nor harmful to the national economy and the people's livelihood, shall not be confiscated. But among these, the enterprises and property of certain persons who have committed criminal offences, such as reactionaries guilty of heinous crimes which have been reported by the people and confirmed, shall be confiscated.

Article 15. In cities not yet entered and taken over by the People's Liberation Army, the provincial, municipal and county governments under the National Government at Nanking shall be responsible for protecting the people's opportunity to sign the Agreement on Internal Peace, if that government has not yet fled and dispersed and desires to sign it.

MAO TSE-TUNG
Chairman of the Chinese People's
Revolutionary Military Commission

CHU TEH
Commander-in-Chief of the Chinese
People's Liberation Army

This order was drafted by Mao Tse-tung, and upon the refusal of the Republic of China's government leaders at Nanking to accept it, the Communist forces began their southward attack. On April 23 they took

---

democratic forces and their activities in the locality and must not suppress or injure them.

SECTION SIX

Article 16. Both sides affirm that the feudal system of landownership in the rural areas of China shall be reformed step by step. After the entry of the People's Liberation Army, reduction of rent and interest shall generally be carried out first and distribution of land later.

Article 17. In areas not yet entered and taken over by the People's Liberation Army, the local governments under the National Government at Nanking shall be responsible for protecting the organizations of the peasant masses and their activities and must not suppress or damage them.

SECTION SEVEN

Article 18. Both sides agree that all treaties and agreements concluded with foreign states during the rule of the National Government at Nanking and other diplomatic documents and archives, open or secret, shall be handed over by the National Government at Nanking to the Democratic Coalition Government and examined by the Democratic Coalition Government. All treaties or agreements which are detrimental to the Chinese people and their state, especially those which are in the nature of selling out the rights of the state, shall be either abrogated, or revised, or new treaties and agreements shall be concluded instead, as the case may be.

SECTION EIGHT

Article 19. Both sides agree that after the signing of the Agreement on Internal Peace and before the formation of the Democratic Coalition Government, the National Government at Nanking and its *yuan*, ministries, com-

Nanking; and Shanghai on May 27; and in central China, on the Yangtze River, they took the strategic Yangtze Valley center of Wuhan —Wuchang, Hankow, and Hanyang—on May 17. By the end of Decem-

---

missions and other organs shall temporarily continue to function but must consult the Chinese People's Revolutionary Military Commission in the conduct of affairs and assist the People's Liberation Army in matters relating to the taking over and handing over of the various areas. After the formation of the Democratic Coalition Government, the National Government at Nanking shall immediately hand over to the Democratic Coalition Government and proclaim its own termination.

Article 20. Upon the handing over of the National Government at Nanking and its local governments at various levels and all their subordinate organs, the People's Liberation Army, the local people's governments and the Democratic Coalition Government of China shall take care to enlist all the patriotic and useful persons among the former's personnel, give them democratic education and assign them to suitable posts so that they will not become destitute and homeless.

Article 21. Before the People's Liberation Army enters and takes over, the National Government at Nanking and its subordinate local governments in the provinces, cities and counties shall be responsible for maintaining peace and order in their respective areas, looking after and protecting all government organizations and state-owned enterprises (including banks, factories, mines, railways, postal and telegraph offices, aircraft, vessels, companies, warehouses and all communications facilities) and other movable and immovable properties belonging to the state; and no destruction, loss, removal, concealment, or sale is permitted. Books, archives, antiques, valuables, bullion, foreign currencies and all properties and assets which have been removed or concealed shall be frozen at once wherever they are found, pending their take-over. As for those properties which have been sent abroad or were originally abroad, the National Government at Nanking shall be responsible for their recovery and safekeeping and be prepared to hand them over.

Article 22. All the powers as well as the properties and assets of the state in areas already entered and taken over by the People's Liberation Army shall be taken over by the local Military Control Commissions, the local people's governments or institutions authorized by the Coalition Government.

Article 23. After the Agreement on Internal Peace has been signed by the delegation of the National Government at Nanking and carried out by that government, the delegation of the Communist Party of China will take the responsibility of proposing to the preparatory committee of the New Political Consultative Conference that the National Government at Nanking should be permitted to send a number of patriotic persons as representatives to the Conference; after securing the approval of its preparatory committee, the representatives of the National Government at Nanking may attend the New Political Consultative Conference.

Article 24. After the National Government at Nanking has sent its representatives to the New Political Consultative Conference, the Communist Party of China will take the responsibility of proposing to the Conference that in the interests of co-operation there should be included in the Democratic Coalition

ber 1949, the Communist forces had taken all the mainland of China, with the exception of Tibet—which they invaded and took by force in May 1951.

Proclamation of the
Chinese People's Liberation Army

April 25, 1949

The Kuomintang reactionaries have rejected the terms for peace and persist in their stand of waging a criminal war against the nation and the people. The people all over the country hope that the People's Liberation Army will speedily wipe out the Kuomintang reactionaries. . . . We hereby proclaim the following eight-point covenant by which we, together with the whole people, shall abide.

1. Protect the lives and property of all the people. . . .

2. Protect the industrial, commercial, agricultural and livestock enterprises of the national bourgeoisie. All privately owned factories, shops, banks, warehouses, vessels, wharves, farms, livestock farms and other enterprises will without exception be protected against any encroachment. . . .

3. Confiscate bureaucrat capital. All . . . enterprises operated by the reactionary Kuomintang Government and the big bureaucrats shall be taken over by the people's government. . . .

4. Protect all public and private schools, hospitals, cultural and educational institutions, athletic fields and other public welfare establishments. . . .

Government a number of patriotic persons from the National Government at Nanking.

The delegations of both sides declare: We hereby assume the responsibility of signing this agreement for the sake of the liberation of the Chinese people and the independence and freedom of the Chinese nation and for the sake of an early conclusion of the war and the restoration of peace so that the commencement of the great task of production and construction on a nation-wide scale will be facilitated and so that our country and people will steadily attain prosperity, strength and well-being. It is hoped that the people of the entire country will unite as one to struggle for the complete fulfilment of this agreement. This agreement shall enter into force immediately upon signature.

5. Except for the incorrigible war criminals and counterrevolutionaries who have committed the most heinous crimes, the People's Liberation Army and the people's government will not hold captive, arrest or subject to indignity any officials . . . in the Kuomintang's . . . Government.

6. In order to ensure peace and security in both cities and rural areas and to maintain public order, all stragglers and disbanded soldiers are required to report and surrender to the People's Liberation Army or the people's government in their localities. . . .

7. The feudal system of landownership in the rural areas is irrational and should be abolished. To abolish it, however, preparations must be made and the necessary steps taken. Generally speaking, the reduction of rent and interest should come first and land distribution later. . . .

8. Protect the lives and property of foreign nationals. It is hoped that all foreign nationals will follow their usual pursuits and observe order. . . . Otherwise, they shall be dealt with according to law by the People's Liberation Army and the people's government.

The People's Liberation Army is highly disciplined; it is fair in buying and selling and is not allowed to take even a needle or a piece of thread from the people. It is hoped that the people throughout the country will live and work in peace and will not give credence to rumors or raise false alarms. This proclamation is hereby issued in all sincerity and earnestness.

MAO TSE-TUNG
Chairman of the Chinese People's
Revolutionary Military Commission

CHU TEH
Commander-in-Chief of the Chinese
People's Liberation Army

On the Outrages by British Warships —Statement by the Spokesman of the General Headquarters of the Chinese People's Liberation Army

April 30, 1949

We denounce the preposterous statement of the warmonger Churchill. In the British House of Commons on April 26, Churchill demanded that the British Government should send two aircraft carriers to the Far East for "effective power of retaliation." What are you "retaliating" for, Mr. Churchill? British warships together with Kuomintang warships intruded into the defense area of the Chinese People's Liberation Army and fired on the People's Liberation Army, causing no less than 252 casualties among our loyal and gallant fighters. . . . The Yangtze is an inland waterway of China. What right have you British to send in your warships? . . . Prime Minister Attlee said that the People's Liberation Army "would be prepared to allow the ship (the *Amethyst*) to proceed to Nanking but only on condition that she should assist the People's Liberation Army to cross the Yangtze." Attlee lied. . . . The People's Liberation Army does not want the armed forces of any foreign country to help it cross the Yangtze or to do anything else. On the contrary, the People's Liberation Army demands that Britain, the United States and France quickly withdraw their armed forces—their warships, military aircraft and marines stationed in the Yangtze and Whangpoo Rivers and other parts of China. . . .

This statement was drafted by Mao Tse-tung for the spokesman of the General Headquarters of the Chinese People's Liberation Army.

Address to the Preparatory Committee of the New Political Consultative Conference

June 15, 1949

FELLOW DELEGATES,

Today the Preparatory Committee of our New Political Consultative Conference[1] is holding its inaugural session. The task of this committee is to complete all necessary preparations and speedily convene the New Political Consultative Conference, which will form a democratic coalition government. . . .

The people of the whole country supporting their own People's Liberation Army have won the war. . . . Nanking, the capital of the Kuomintang reactionaries, is now in our hands. Shanghai, Hangchow, Nanchang, Wuhan and Sian have been liberated. At this very moment, the field armies of the People's Liberation Army are conducting a great march unprecedented in Chinese history into the southern and northwestern provinces. . . .

This is a victory for the people of all China, and also a victory for the peoples of the whole world. The whole world, except the imperialists and the reactionaries in various countries, is elated and inspired by this great victory of the Chinese people. . . .

The Chinese people will see that, once China's destiny is in the hands of the people, China, like the sun rising in the East, will illuminate every corner of the land with a brilliant flame, swiftly clean up the mire left by the reactionary government, heal the

1. The committee met at Peiping from June 15 to June 19, 1949. It was composed of 114 members representing twenty-three organizations and groups, including the Communist Party of China, the various other parties described by the Communist Party as "democratic parties," and "democratic" personages. The conference was called the New Political Consultative Conference to distinguish it from the Political Consultative Conference which had opened at Chungking on January 10, 1946. Its name was changed to the Chinese People's Political Consultative Conference at its First Plenary Session on September 21, 1949.

wounds of war and build a new, powerful and prosperous people's republic worthy of the name.

Long live the People's Republic of China!

Long live the democratic coalition government!

Long live the great unity of the people of the whole country!

On the People's Democratic Dictatorship

June 30, 1949

IN COMMEMORATION OF THE TWENTY-EIGHTH ANNIVERSARY OF THE COMMUNIST PARTY OF CHINA

The first of July 1949 marks the fact that the Communist Party of China has already lived through twenty-eight years. Like a man, a political party has its childhood, youth, manhood and old age. The Communist Party of China is no longer a child or a lad in his teens but has become an adult. When a man reaches old age, he will die; the same is true of a Party. When classes disappear, all instruments of class struggle . . . will wither away and end their historical mission; and human society will move to a higher stage. . . .

The Russians made the October Revolution and created the world's first socialist state. Under the leadership of Lenin and Stalin, the revolutionary energy of the great proletariat and laboring people of Russia, hitherto latent and unseen by foreigners, suddenly erupted like a volcano, and the Chinese and all mankind began to see the Russians in a new light. Then, and only then, did the Chinese enter an entirely new era in their thinking and their life. They found Marxism-Leninism, the universally applicable truth, and the face of China began to change.

It was through the Russians that the Chinese found Marxism. Before the October Revolution, the Chinese were not only ignorant of Lenin and Stalin, they did not even know of Marx and Engels. The salvos of the October Revolution brought us Marxism-Leninism. . . .

In 1919, the May Fourth Movement took place in China. In 1921, the Communist Party of China was founded. Sun Yat Sen, in the depths of despair, came across the October Revolution and the Communist Party of China. He welcomed the October Revolution, welcomed Russian help to the Chinese and welcomed co-operation with the Communist Party of China. . . .

Twenty-four years have passed since Sun Yat Sen's death, and the Chinese revolution, led by the Communist Party of China, has made tremendous advances both in theory and practice and has radically changed the face of China. . . .

When we have beaten the internal and external reactionaries by uniting domestic and international forces, we shall be able to do business and establish diplomatic relations with all foreign countries on the basis of equality, mutual benefit and mutual respect for territorial integrity and sovereignty. . . .

"Victory is possible even without international help." This is a mistaken idea. In the epoch in which imperialism exists, it is impossible for a genuine people's revolution to win victory in any country without various forms of help from the international revolutionary forces. . . .

"We need help from the British and U.S. governments." This, too, is a naïve idea in these times. Would the present rulers of Britain and the United States, who are imperialists, help a people's state? . . .

Let readers refer to Dr. Sun Yat Sen's Testament; his earnest advice was not to look for help from the imperialist countries but to "unite with those nations of the world which treat us as equals." Dr. Sun had experience; he had suffered; he had been deceived. We should remember his words and not allow ourselves to be deceived again. Internationally, we belong to the side of the anti-imperialist front headed by the Soviet Union, and so we can turn only to this side for genuine and friendly help, not to the side of the imperialist front. . . .

In 1924 a famous Manifesto was adopted at the Kuomintang's First National Congress, which Sun Yat Sen himself led and in which the Communists participated. The Manifesto stated:

The so-called democratic system in modern states is usually monopolized by the bourgeoisie and has become simply an instrument for oppressing the common people. On the other hand, the Kuomintang's Principle of Democracy means a democratic system shared by all the common people and not privately owned by the few.

Apart from the question of who leads whom, the Principle of Democracy stated above corresponds as a general political program to what we call People's Democracy or New Democracy. A state system which is shared only by the common people and which the bourgeoisie is not allowed to own privately—add to this the leadership of the working class, and we have the state system of the people's democratic dictatorship. . . .

Sun Yat Sen advocated "arousing the masses of the people" or "giving assistance to the peasants and workers." But who is to "arouse" them or "give assistance" to them? Sun Yat Sen had the petty bourgeoisie and the national bourgeoisie in mind. As a matter of fact, they cannot do so. Why did forty years of revolution under Sun Yat Sen end in failure? Because in the epoch of imperialism the petty bourgeoisie and the national bourgeoisie cannot lead any genuine revolution to victory. . . .

To sum up our experience and concentrate it into one point, it is: the people's democratic dictatorship under the leadership of the working class (through the Communist Party) and based upon the alliance of workers and peasants. This dictatorship must unite as one with the international revolutionary forces. This is our formula, our principal experience, our main program. . . .

Cast Away Illusions, Prepare for Struggle

August 14, 1949

It is no accident that the U.S. State Department's White Paper on China–U.S. Relations and Secretary of State Acheson's Letter of Transmittal to President Truman have been released at this time.[1] The publication of these documents reflects the victory of the Chinese people and the defeat of imperialism, it reflects the decline of the entire world system of imperialism. The imperialist system is

1. The United States White Paper, *United States Relations with China*, was published by the U.S. State Department on August 5, 1949. Secretary Acheson's Letter of Transmittal to President Truman was dated July 30, 1949. The main body of the White Paper, divided into eight chapters, deals with Sino–U.S. relations in the period from 1844 to 1949.

riddled with insuperable internal contradictions, and therefore the imperialists are plunged into deep gloom.

Imperialism has prepared the conditions for its own doom. These conditions are the awakening of the great masses of the people in the colonies and semicolonies and in the imperialist countries themselves. Imperialism has pushed the great masses of the people throughout the world into the historical epoch of the great struggle to abolish imperialism. . . .

To serve the needs of its aggression, imperialism ruined the Chinese peasants by exploiting them through the exchange of unequal values and thereby created great masses of poor peasants, numbering hundreds of millions and comprising 70 per cent of China's rural population. . . .

Acheson's White Paper admits that the U.S. imperialists are at a complete loss as to what to do about the present situation in China. The Kuomintang is so impotent that no amount of help can save it from inevitable doom. . . . Acheson says in his Letter of Transmittal:

The unfortunate but inescapable fact is that the ominous result of the civil war in China was beyond the control of the government of the United States. Nothing that this country did or could have done within the reasonable limits of its capabilities could have changed that result; nothing that was left undone by this country has contributed to it. It was the product of internal Chinese forces, forces which this country tried to influence but could not. . . .

. . . He should treat People's China on the basis of equality and mutual benefit and stop making trouble. But no, says Acheson, troublemaking will continue, and definitely so. . . . Says Acheson:

. . . ultimately the profound civilization and the democratic individualism of China will reassert themselves and she will throw off the foreign yoke. I consider that we should encourage all developments in China which now and in the future work toward this end.

How different is the logic of the imperialists from that of the people! Make trouble, fail, make trouble again, fail again . . . till their doom; that is the logic of the imperialists . . . and they will never go against this logic. This is a Marxist law. . . .

Fight, fail, fight again, fail again, fight again . . . till their victory; that is the logic of the people, and they too will never go against this logic. This is another Marxist law. . . .

The slogan, "Prepare for struggle," is addressed to those who still cherish certain illusions about the relations between China and the imperialist countries, especially between China and the United States. . . .

Acheson openly declares that the Chinese democratic individualists will be "encouraged" to throw off the so-called "foreign yoke." That is to say, he calls for the overthrow of Marxism-Leninism and the people's democratic dictatorship led by the Communist Party of China. . . . Acheson and his like are doing this filthy work and, what is more, they have openly published it. What a loss of face! . . .

China is in the midst of a great revolution. . . . The conditions are favorable for winning over and uniting with all those who do not have a bitter and deepseated hatred for the cause of the people's revolution. . . . Progressives should use the White Paper to persuade all these persons.

This article and the four that follow—"Farewell, Leighton Stuart!" "Why It Is Necessary to Discuss the White Paper," " 'Friendship' or Aggression?" and "The Bankruptcy of the Idealist Conception of History" —were commentaries written by Mao Tse-tung for the Hsinhua News Agency.

Farewell, Leighton Stuart![1]

August 18, 1949

It is understandable that the date chosen for the publication of the U.S. White Paper was August 5, a time when Leighton Stuart had departed from Nanking for Washington but had not yet arrived there, since Leighton Stuart is a symbol of the complete defeat of the U.S. policy of aggression. Leighton Stuart is an American born in

1. John Leighton Stuart was born in China in 1876. He began missionary work in China in 1905 and, in 1919, became president of Yenching University, an American-sponsored university in Peking. On July 11, 1946, he was appointed United States Ambassador in China.

China; he has fairly wide social connections and spent many years running missionary schools in China; he once sat in a Japanese jail during the War of Resistance; he used to pretend to love both the United States and China and was able to deceive quite a number of Chinese. Hence, he was picked out by George C. Marshall, was made U.S. Ambassador to China and became a celebrity in the Marshall group. . . .

Let those Chinese who are shortsighted, muddleheaded liberals or democratic individualists listen. Acheson is giving you a lesson; he is a good teacher for you. He has made a clean sweep of your fancied U.S. humanity, justice and virtue. Isn't that so? Can you find a trace of humanity, justice or virtue in the White Paper or in Acheson's Letter of Transmittal? . . .

The United States has plenty of money. But unfortunately it is willing to give money only to the Chiang Kai-shek reactionaries, who are rotten to the core. . . .

We Chinese have backbone. Many who were once liberals or democratic individualists have stood up to the U.S. imperialists and their running dogs, the Kuomintang reactionaries. . . . What matter if we have to face some difficulties? Let them blockade us! Let them blockade us for eight or ten years! By that time all of China's problems will have been solved. Will the Chinese cower before difficulties when they are not afraid even of death? Lao Tzu said, "The people fear not death, why threaten them with it?"[2] U.S. imperialism and its running dogs, the Chiang Kai-shek reactionaries, have not only "threatened" us with death but actually put many of us to death. . . . We have come triumphantly through the ordeal of the last three years, why can't we overcome these few difficulties of today? Why can't we live without the United States?

When the People's Liberation Army crossed the Yangtze River, the U.S. colonial government at Nanking fled helter-skelter. Yet His Excellency Ambassador Stuart sat right, watching wide-eyed, hoping to set up shop under a new signboard and to reap some profit. But what did he see? . . . He was left out in the cold, "standing all alone, body and shadow comforting each other."[3] There was nothing more for him to do, and he had to take to the road, his briefcase under his arm.

2. A quotation from Lao Tzu, Chapter LXXIV.
3. A quotation from Li Mi's "Memorial to the Emperor."

Leighton Stuart has departed and the White Paper has arrived. Very good. Very good. Both events are worth celebrating.

Why It Is Necessary
to Discuss the White Paper

August 28, 1949

We have criticized the U.S. White Paper and Acheson's Letter of Transmittal in three articles. . . . Forums on the White Paper are being held and the entire discussion is still developing. . . . All this is very good and is of great educational value.

The whole world is now discussing the Chinese revolution and the U.S. White Paper. This is no accident, this shows the great significance of the Chinese revolution in world history. . . .

The White Paper is a counterrevolutionary document which openly demonstrates U.S. imperialist intervention in China. . . . The fact that public revelation has replaced concealment is a sign that imperialism has departed from its normal practice. Until a few weeks ago . . . the governments of the imperialist countries . . . never told the truth in their statements or official documents but had filled or at least flavored them with professions of humanity, justice and virtue. . . . Two factions of counterrevolutionaries have been competing with each other. One said, "Ours is the best method." The other said, "Ours is the best." When the dispute was at its hottest, one faction suddenly laid its cards on the table and revealed many of its treasured tricks of the past—and there you have the White Paper.

. . . Acheson begins his Letter of Transmittal to Truman with the story of how he compiled the White Paper. His White Paper, he says, is different from all others, it is very objective and very frank:

This is a frank record of an extremely complicated and most unhappy period in the life of a great country to which the United States has long been attached by ties of closest friendship. . . . The inherent strength of our system is the responsiveness of the Government to an informed and critical public opinion which totalitarian governments, whether Rightist or Communist, cannot endure and do not tolerate.

. . . What does Acheson mean by "informed and critical public opinion"? Nothing but the numerous instruments of propaganda, such as the newspapers, news agencies, periodicals and broadcasting stations which are controlled by the two reactionary parties in the United States, the Republicans and the Democrats, and which specialize in the manufacture of lies and in threats against the people. Of these things Acheson says rightly that the Communists "cannot endure and do not tolerate" them (nor do the people). That is why we have . . . forbidden them the freedom to go on poisoning the souls of the Chinese people on Chinese soil. . . .

The U.S. Government still has a veil of democracy, but it has been cut down to a tiny patch by the U.S. reactionaries and become very faded, and is not what it used to be in the days of Washington, Jefferson and Lincoln. The reason is that the class struggle has become more intense. When the class struggle becomes still more intense the veil of U.S. democracy will inevitably be flung to the four winds. . . .

"Friendship" or Aggression?

August 30, 1949

Seeking to justify aggression, Dean Acheson harps on "friendship" and throws in loss of "principles."

Acheson says:

The interest of the people and the Government of the United States in China goes far back into our history. Despite the distance and broad differences in background which separate China and the United States, our friendship for that country has always been intensified by the religious, philanthropic and cultural ties which have united the two peoples. . . . The record shows that the United States has consistently maintained and still maintains those fundamental principles of our foreign policy toward China which include the doctrine of the Open Door, respect for the administrative and territorial integrity of China, and opposition to any foreign domination of China.

Acheson is telling a barefaced lie when he describes aggression as "friendship."

. . . The United States was one of the first countries to force China to cede extraterritoriality[1]—witness the Treaty of Wanghia of 1844. . . .[2] In this very treaty, the United States compelled China to accept American missionary activity, in addition to imposing such terms as the opening of five ports for trade. . . .

All the "friendship" shown to China by U.S. imperialism over the past 109 years (since 1840 when the United States collaborated with Britain in the Opium War), and especially the great act of "friendship" in helping Chiang Kai-shek slaughter several million Chinese in the last few years—all this had one purpose, namely, it "consistently maintained those fundamental principles of our foreign policy toward China which include the doctrine of the Open Door, respect for the administrative and territorial integrity of China, and opposition to any foreign domination of China." . . .

Whether noninterference in China's domestic affairs also counts as a principle, Acheson didn't say; probably it does not. Such is the logic of the U.S. mandarins. Anyone who reads Acheson's Letter of Transmittal to the end will attest to its superior logic.

The Bankruptcy of the Idealist Conception of History

September 16, 1949

The Chinese should thank Acheson, spokesman of the U.S. bourgeoisie, not merely because he has explicitly confessed to the fact that the United States supplied the money and guns and Chiang Kai-shek the men to fight for the United States and slaughter the Chinese people and because he has thus given Chinese progressives evidence with which to convince the backward elements. . . . The

1. "Extraterritoriality" in China refers to consular jurisdiction. Under extraterritorial privilege, foreign nationals in China were not subject to the jurisdiction of Chinese law, and could be tried in civil or criminal cases only in their countries' consular courts in China.

2. The Treaty of Wanghia was signed in Wanghia Village, near Macao, in July 1844. Its thirty-four articles stipulated that whatever rights and privileges, including consular jurisdiction, were gained by Britain through the Treaty of Nanking (as a result of China's defeat by Britain in the Opium War) would also accrue to the United States.

Chinese should thank Acheson also because he has fabricated wild tales about modern Chinese history; and his conception of history is precisely that shared by a section of the Chinese intellectuals, namely, the bourgeois idealist conception of history. . . .

What are Acheson's wild fabrications about modern Chinese history? . . . Acheson says: "The population of China during the eighteenth and nineteenth centuries doubled, thereby creating an unbearable pressure upon the land." . . .

Do revolutions arise from overpopulation? . . . Was the American Revolution against Britain 174 years ago also due to overpopulation? Acheson's knowledge of history is nil. He has not even read the American Declaration of Independence. Washington, Jefferson and others made the revolution against Britain because of British oppression and exploitation of the Americans, and not because of any overpopulation in America. Each time the Chinese people overthrew a feudal dynasty it was because of the oppression and exploitation of the people by that feudal dynasty, and not because of any overpopulation. . . . In Mongolia, where the land is so vast and the population so sparse, a revolution would be inconceivable according to Acheson's line of reasoning, yet it took place some time ago.

According to Acheson, China has no way out at all. A population of 475 million constitutes an "unbearable pressure" and, revolution or no revolution, the case is hopeless. Acheson pins great hope on this: . . . that China will remain in perpetual chaos and that her only way out is to live on U.S. flour, in other words, to become a U.S. colony. . . .

It is a very good thing that China has a big population. Even if China's population multiplies many times, she is fully capable of finding a solution; the solution is production. The absurd argument of Western bourgeois economists like Malthus[1] that increases in food cannot keep pace with increases in population was not only thoroughly refuted in theory by Marxists long ago, but has also been completely exploded by the realities in the Soviet Union and the Liberated Areas of China after their revolutions. . . .

1. T. R. Malthus (1766–1834), Anglican clergyman and economist. In his *Essay on Population* (1798) he wrote that "population unchecked . . . increases in geometrical ratio . . . [while] the means of subsistence . . . could not possibly be made to increase faster than in an arithmetical ratio."

"The impact of the West" is given by Acheson as the second reason why the Chinese revolution occurred. Acheson says:

> For more than three thousand years the Chinese developed their own high culture and civilization, largely untouched by outside influences. . . . Then in the middle of the nineteenth century the heretofore impervious wall of Chinese isolation was breached by the West. These outsiders brought with them aggressiveness . . . technology . . . a high order of culture . . . which played an important part in stimulating ferment and unrest.

To those Chinese who do not reason clearly, what Acheson says sounds plausible—the influx of new ideas from the West gave rise to the revolution.

Against whom was the revolution directed? . . . The Revolution of 1911 was directed against imperialism. . . .

Being the spokesman of an imperialist government, Acheson naturally does not want to breathe even a word about imperialism. He describes imperialist aggression thus: "These outsiders brought with them aggressiveness . . ." "Aggressiveness"—what a beautiful name! . . .

The Chinese Communist Party "had been organized in the early twenties under the ideological impetus of the Russian revolution." Here Acheson is right. This ideology was none other than Marxism-Leninism. . . . Since they learned Marxism-Leninism, the Chinese people have ceased to be passive in spirit and gained the initiative. . . . In its spiritual aspect, this culture of the Chinese people already stands higher than any in the capitalist world. Take U.S. Secretary of State Acheson and his like, for instance. The level of their understanding of modern China and of the modern world is lower than that of an ordinary soldier of the Chinese People's Liberation Army.

Up to this point, Acheson, like a bourgeois professor lecturing on a tedious text, has pretended to trace the causes and effects of events in China. Revolution occurred in China, first, because of overpopulation, and second, because of the stimulus of Western ideas. You see, he appears to be a champion of the theory of causation. But in what follows, even this bit of tedious and phoney theory of causation disappears, and one finds only a mass of inexplicable events. Quite unaccountably, the Chinese fought among themselves for power and money, suspecting and hating each other. An inexplicable change took place in the relative moral strength of the two contending parties, the Kuomintang and the Communist Party, the morale of one party dropped sharply to below zero, while that of the other rose sharply to white heat. What was the reason? Nobody knows. Such is the logic inherent in the "high order of culture" of the United States as represented by Dean Acheson.

Index

About the Editor

Bruno Shaw has been an Associated Press correspondent in China, a newspaper publisher and editor in Hankow, Hupeh Province, and an associate editor of the *China Weekly Review* (Shanghai). During the Northern Expedition of the joint Kuomintang-Communist revolution, he became the first newspaper correspondent to interview Chiang Kai-shek.

He founded the *Hankow Herald*, an English-language daily newspaper. The *Herald* was printed on a secondhand Japanese flat-bed press, and type was handset by Chinese compositors who could not read English. Eventually the paper progressed to linotype and English-speaking operators, and in several years it achieved the largest circulation of any English-language newspaper in China.

Mr. Shaw was one of the few foreign newspaper men in China sufficiently fluent in the language to be able to move about the country without the need of an interpreter. In his travels elsewhere in the Far East, he became well acquainted with Malaya, Borneo, the Philippines, Japan, and Korea. He counted among his personal friends many hundreds of Asian people, including Syngman Rhee, late President of Korea, Ramon Magsaysay, late President of the Philippines, and President Chiang Kai-shek of the Republic of China.

Immediately after the Japanese attack upon China at Lukouchiao (Marco Polo Bridge), near Peking, Shaw was asked by the Chinese government to set up a public information bureau in the United States; he then founded and directed the Trans-Pacific News Service, which was later renamed the Chinese Information Service, in New York City. He was concurrently appointed National Director of the American Bureau for Medical Aid to China and of the United Council for Civilian Relief in China. When the Japanese bombed Pearl Harbor, he joined the Far Eastern division of the Office of War Information.

Bruno Shaw was the creator and commentator of the WQXR radio program "Mapping the News" sponsored by the New York *Post*. He was also the commentator of "You Decide" on WNEW and of a news program on ABC. He produced and narrated a newsreel feature for the Embassy Newsreel Theatres which was syndicated nationally; and he participated in many "Author Meets the Critics" and "Books on Trial" radio and TV programs. His articles have been published in the *Saturday Evening Post, Colliers, The New Leader, The Elks Magazine,* and other American publications.